THE GIFTS of ECCENTRICS:
Imagination in Reality

David J. Weeks

This book is dedicated to the memory of John Graham-White, a superb guide and generous mentor who really cared, and who taught me to listen for interesting questions.

TABLE OF CONTENTS

Preface

My father was born in a small village in the South Wales valleys in Edwardian times, when Great Britain was the heart of its Empire. He did not have an easy life. His father, my grandfather, brought his family to America, the land of limitless opportunity, several years before the Great Depression took hold. My dad always thought the people of his former homeland, however class-ridden they remained, were also very tolerant, able to accept people very different from themselves. He saw this as a great ideal, but also realized that most Americans also did more than simply aspire to a similar ideal.

It could be said that the longstanding cultural diversity in Britain and America has led to a broadening of hearts and minds. The influences of both countries instilled in me the desire to find out, if I could, how true my father's impressions and understandings were. This was one reason why I first undertook the research presented in this book.

Unknown to me when I first set out to understand those among us who go to extraordinary lengths to maintain their differentness, I would be initiating the world's first scientific study of eccentrics. I was enthused by the continuing excitement of the possibility of recovering the thoughts and accounts of previously unheard, neglected or suppressed sources. I hope the eccentrics' examples will make a strong case for greater tolerance in society.

My research project about eccentrics first started as an idea in 1984. In the same year it received formal approval from the Ethics of Research Committee of the Royal Edinburgh Hospital. I also conducted what turned out to be a rather overlapping study on gifted children and their needs. In 1993, the regional Ethics of Research Committee also approved my research on non-conformists who had been ostracized by their families. This book is drawn from these projects, and is based substantially on comprehensive interviews and personality tests, all of which were conducted on eccentrics living in the community across the British isles. After I completed these studies I continued to meet with a number of the eccentrics I had previously studied, and, over the years, to hear from, and meet, many more eccentrics living in the United Kingdom and abroad.

Because of the nature of these studies, the structured interviews incorporated a clinical mental state examination. None of the interviewees were clinical patients of the author, nor were any in treatment with any other psychiatrist or psychologist at the time of interview. Because of the ambiguous connotations, and the unwarranted social stigma still attaching in some people's minds to the designation "eccentric", aliases have been used to protect the personal privacy of the participants. Due to some eccentrics' insistence, there were however a small number of exceptions to the use of alias names or initials. This was done only with the informed consent and express permission of the subjects concerned, and only after detailed debriefing and discussion.

Chapter 1. Introduction --- "Are You Eccentric?"

Light of lights also is That called, beyond the darkness. It is with them. It is the aim of wisdom, to be gained by wisdom, in the heart of each. It is set firm.

Bhagavadgita

Introduction

What does it mean to be eccentric? An eccentric act does not necessarily make the individual who performs it an eccentric person. One illustrious anthropologist has called eccentricity "an intractable category", and furthermore, that there is a "fundamental ambiguity in the attribution of eccentricity" [1]. True enough: eccentrics comprise one of the most obstinately diverse groupings of individuals in the world and possibly the hardest to define. Eccentricity manifests itself in a great variety of ways. The various forms of eccentricity probably lie along a spectrum, and can be quite complex.

Part of this has to do with other peoples' perceptions. Human societies throughout the world seem to have a need to identify, and sometimes define, what is "normal" and "abnormal". As I was soon to discover, there is no such thing as a typical eccentric. Eccentrics are as delightfully varied as the rest of humankind, if not more so. A mystery to many, trying to find out may be seen to many as too daunting a prospect. Indeed, when I first started my research project on eccentrics, I didn't think I knew any of the answers. Nor did anyone else. So one of the goals of my investigations was to produce a definition, a description, of what a "typical" eccentric was like.

How do eccentrics see and define themselves? Whilst some of them accept that they are different from other people, other eccentrics are not convinced of their eccentricity and will readily deny it, blaming this on the perception of others. One volunteer proclaimed with considerable disdain, "My family tells me that I am eccentric. I think that I am just superior and ahead of my time". Another took this upending degree of denial a step further: "Naturally, I do not think I am eccentric. The eccentricity lies with the rest whose views differ from mine." Single-mindedness is a characteristic these people shared without any misgiving: "I see no merit in conformity, and have little difficulty in standing up alone on points of principle."

One could argue that those who are most oblivious to their inimitable strangeness possess that special quality in the highest degree. However, as I hope to show, eccentrics are unassailably and beyond any doubt very different.

"That so few now dare to be eccentric, marks the chief danger of our time," remarked the nineteenth century English philosopher, John Stuart Mill. He also added, ". . . the amount of eccentricity in a society has generally been proportional to the amount of genius, mental vigour, and moral courage which it contained." The satirist Alan Coren, in his book *The Sunday Inspector*, observed, "She used to eat chops in the small hours of the morning and sleep in a hat. Once, she arrived home at seven a.m. carrying a gate. Who am I to say there is anything wrong with her?"

Although eccentrics have been with us for a very long time, it appears that many people are unable to delineate what is meant by the term "eccentric". There is no accurate or psychologically relevant definition, though many people feel that they can identify an eccentric person when they meet one. The two quotations above, some one hundred years apart, illustrate just how readily people are prepared to label someone as "eccentric". The quote from John Stuart Mill's essay "On Liberty" implied that the development of society and eccentricity are interdependent, that the wayward individual has an integral part to play in the shaping of society. Alan Coren, on the other hand, probably found his German au pair either a source of amusement or a cause for concern.

A few popular adjectives that are readily applied to eccentrics include non-conforming, rebellious and whimsical, though very little is known about their actual personalities. If we look for an archetypal eccentric we find that there is none. Some eccentrics have been described as loners. Many have been inveterately unorthodox, carrying out their eccentricities with great enthusiasm. That their behaviour is often paradoxical, when viewed from the outside, may or may not be of great concern to them. Many of them are doing what they want to do, and they are usually also resistant to outside influence. The eccentricity personality trait or eccentric personality type has been assumed to have a life-long enduring quality. Further, whilst it is popularly believed that eccentrics are not mentally ill, for all that was known about them, some possibly could have deep-seated neurotic conflicts or ways of thinking that verge on the psychotic.

Existing compendiums of eccentric lives tended to describe each individual in isolation, but failed to look for, or correlate, any common psychological factors. There may not, of course, be any shared factors between, for example, the eighteenth century Edinburgh judge who had such an affection for pigs that he slept in bed with his favourite one, and the present day healthy living vegetarian who religiously does a hundred one-armed sit-ups every day and has not visited a doctor for over fifty years, though both have been labelled as eccentric.

The popular definitions of eccentricity encompass a variety of features derived from actual observations and elementary deductions. To say that eccentrics are people who perform eccentric acts may be true, but it does not advance our understanding. Since the label can be used as both deprecatory or something positive to be achieved, as either mildly discreditable or something to be highly prized, may indicate something more than that our labels and notions may be overly flexible.

In textbooks on abnormal psychology, bizarreness, defined as any deviation from accepted standards of behaviour or from consensual reality, has been used as one practical criterion of psychological abnormality. Whereas formal thought disorder has been considered to be crucial in the diagnosis of schizophrenia, the prevalence and significance of minor variants of thought disorder --- for instance, associative dyscontrol, cognitive slippage, or cognitive disinhibition --- in which words, images and thoughts are less well-filtered by an individual's mind, or connected to other words and thoughts too loosely or too haphazardly, are only relatively recently becoming better understood.

Being eccentric implies that the individuals affected are inscrutably complicated. It is necessary for the holistic social scientist to deal with the total personality. A rounded picture must include the eccentricities, divergences, and false starts that are part and parcel of any "normal" person. Everyone has an eccentric or slightly quirky side if you look closely enough, though it may be more deeply buried in some. There is no harm in acknowledging this in a way that is free from value judgements. Though the word "eccentric" has fewer pejorative connotations than, for example, "neurotic", it is noticeable that there are substantial cultural differences in one's willingness to entertain this possibility about oneself or others.

To better understand the thought processes and personalities of people who come to regard themselves, or are regarded by others, as eccentric, it strikes me as interesting to study those who have managed to create or find unusual thinking strategies that have helped them to operate successfully within their environment. Such a study would also be an ideal setting for learning about illogical thought processes, and perhaps to understand a little more about the deeper human mystery that is schizophrenia.

If eccentricity is positively associated with the ability to conceive startlingly original artistic and technological breakthroughs, it behoves psychologists to attempt to understand the factors that stimulate and inhibit not only lateral thinking, but also the conditions in which it may freely flourish. Similar cognitive processes, I hypothesized, may underlie both eccentric thinking and promote creativity.

The fledgling science of psychology takes itself, its image, and its methods, far too seriously. It has turned its back on the excitement of guesswork, on intellectual exploration and search, and the wonderment of speculation that is fundamental to scientific activity and frequently to the thinking of many people. Human evolution needs human eccentricity and although psychologists, in an age of increasing standardisation and homogenisation, may react suspiciously or adversely to overly peculiar ideas and to idiosyncratic people, they should also recognise the rebellious fun in those who march to a different drummer.

How the study began

The unusualness of people is seen every day, and may explain in part some of our less comfortable interpersonal experiences. Many people become ill at ease when confronted with someone of an extreme character, into which group may fall the eccentric. It is also possible to be viewed as an attractive eccentric, for instance, if you are a disarmingly vague and distracted "absentminded professor" type, provided some of your ideas work some of the time, or if you can persuade others that your thoughts have that uncanny ring of truth about them. Alternatively, if you are in a minority group that the majority has doubts and misunderstandings about, you could very easily be dismissed as a crank or a fanatic, indeed exactly what you feel deep down you are not. Indeed, many individuals in minority groups may feel they do not have the luxury of being outspoken or to act differently from the majority.

How does society really treat an eccentric? Derisively, with barely concealed contempt, or with dignity and respect? Uncommon variations in lifestyles are experiments in living, and these are often masterminded or carried forward by eccentric people. When I first started my study, I met a man, a health food restauranteur who became known as being eccentric simply because he taught meditation and yoga to his staff to help them cope sympathetically with their customers.

On the other hand, it is unkind to label every extraordinary person as "crazy" or "unstable". However, explanations of behaviour based upon an underlying mental illness are used by the mass media and others to handily account for the diverse kinds of rule-breaking for which society has no better explanation. Eccentrics, on the other hand, can be treated permissively, given wider allowances, and can generally continue with their activities as long as they do not threaten others. If someone craves the extreme reactions of others, however hostile, to be met with tolerance or indifference is often the greatest affront. However, as the link between personal eccentricity and social non-conformity is poorly understood, this interface was also in need of further investigation.

Another significant link derives from this interest in the extremes of non-conformity. There could be implications in terms of how we think about creativity and social evolution. The one cannot exist without the other. Without diversity, there can be no change and no evolution, either in terms of social learning or biological inheritance. Charles Darwin's observations of development within the plant and animal kingdoms placed some emphasis on the survival of the fittest. Perhaps if evolutionary science had been based upon human psychology and human societies, their thinking would have turned to the survival of the more creative, or maybe the survival of the rule-breakers and the rule-followers. Darwin was aware of the need for the greatest possible diversity; in *The Origin of Species* he wrote, "A high degree of variability is obviously favourable, as freely giving the materials for natural selection to work on."

In a world that is changing in unstable ways, and doing so increasingly rapidly, who can say which individuals will be best able to meet the challenges of the future? Darwin's point was that the best-adapted individuals, as demonstrated by greater variation in a favourable direction, would inevitably increase whenever and wherever the opportunity to do so offered itself. Although this process can take tens of thousands of human lifetimes before any anatomical changes can be produced, the evolution of human creativity in the social sphere can make an impact more rapidly and much more forcibly. It may be that eccentrics are in the vanguard of these creative movements, or perhaps their inclination for thinking the unthinkable lends itself to being incorporated therein, though by other individuals.

It could be that amongst eccentrics there will be a higher proportion of people who are, completely or partially, creative thinkers. They may also contain a number of fuzzy- or woolly-minded thinkers, which in itself may not necessarily be detrimental. Psychological research could then lead into studying how new forms of knowledge are attained. Knowledge can be conceived as serving as the basis for reasoning by information-processing systems and by expert systems, though these systems are not sufficient in themselves to discover and use new lines of reasoning. Piecing together an appropriate line of reasoning that leads to the solution of a problem is the job of the inference process and the problem-solving strategy that employs it. Inference processes can be very much of the "common sense" sort in which relevant knowledge is simply chained; in other words, a syllogism is created, for example, if X implies Y, and Y implies Z, then X implies Z. Such inference processes have been studied for centuries and many different procedures are known. The science of Artificial Intelligence uses only a few of the inference procedures from the logician's kit. Some of these methods allow for reasoning "inexactly" from knowledge that is uncertain. One of these, a favourite of Artificial Intelligence, is Resolution, constructed on a foundation of mathematical logic formulated in the 1960s by the logician Alan Robinson.

Resolution is non-intuitive and especially suited for computer programming. Could it be that the evolution of other related theories, for instance, the theories of Fuzzy Logic, Fuzzy Sets and Fuzzy Distortion, are best suited for studying people who themselves may be fuzzy thinkers? Fuzzy Logic and the others allow for shades of grey, especially where there are numerous possibilities rather than only the two allowed in classical binary logic. They refer to processes where an exact prediction of cognitive distortion is not possible, since errors in them will depend upon the current state of the organism, together with "noise" sources, for example, where "noise" would mean interference in normal patterns of thought. Problems that require innovation often present novel facets, and are complex and ill-defined. The derived techniques seem ideal for dealing with exploratory research in which there would be multiple alternatives and greater uncertainty.

The amount that a social system can bend to accept or encourage individuality can be a measure of its soundness, vision and health. Some influential theorists have undoubtedly exaggerated the significance and steadiness of patterns of living that are expressed as embodiments of the ideal, be it the American concept of rugged individualism or the failed Marxist notion of dialectic materialism. Adherents of these ideologies have sometimes erred. Dissidents in the old Soviet Union were treated as schizophrenics, whereas schizophrenics in the West have been treated like dissidents. Leaders and politicians have repeatedly underestimated the capacity of men and women to resist, transform and innovate within their own environments. Under their surface behaviour and lip service oratory, many have seemed to adhere to a rather bland, passive, overly socialised concept of man, one that weakly reflects the real social pressures acting upon real people. Their concepts are implausible to other observers of social behaviour who did not already subscribe to one or another of the above doctrines. Some social revolutions, such as the Beat Generation or the Hippie counter-culture, took place against a background of ridicule, opposition and eventual backlash. Their actions, and the mainstream society's reactions and interdictions, could be seen as attesting to the sickness of the underlying social structure, or its inability to tolerate defections en masse.

How does one proceed in a study of eccentrics? Where are they, do they still exist, or has present day society changed to such an extent that it neither accommodates nor tolerates them? Indeed, the description and concept of eccentricity has been protean and changeable from one context to another, possibly because eccentricity, like beauty, is in the eye of the beholder. Jean-Bedel Bokassa, a President of the Central African Republic, then, in 1977, its self-proclaimed Emperor (though without an empire), was an excellent illustration of this confusion of clear definition. In David Lamb's book *The Africans*, he remarks that Bokassa's eccentricities had received a great deal of attention. It may of course have been a source of amusement to his fellow dictators that Bokassa celebrated Mother's Day by executing all prisoners accused of matricide, spent over fifteen million pounds on his coronation, and converted his country to either Christianity or Islam (at least twice) depending on who, at the time, was financing his corrupt regime. Someone who was responsible for the massacre of over eighty children because they refused to wear a school uniform bearing his portrait could never correctly be regarded as eccentric.

For the purposes of a study of eccentricity, the first hurdle to be overcome was that of definition. Different dictionaries offered different definitions. Most mention non-specific oddness (of personality), unconventionality (in reference to accepted patterns of social behaviour), and singular behaviour in terms of its component actions or goals. Other associated adjectives included words like anomalous, capricious, irregular, peculiar, devious, and slightly mad. Ultimately, the early working definition included people who may have had bizarre or unusual hobbies, activities or interests, or who displayed irrational thinking and behaviour. Also, these people may often feel that they were the odd ones out when in company, though paradoxically they also could be sociable. They might have felt ahead of their time, or wished to have lived and behaved as in times gone by.

The more often clinical psychologists have looked for irrational thinking among their patients, the more they have found it. For instance, individuals suffering from depression have a particular ultra-pessimistic thinking pattern of viewing themselves, the world and the future. So, I asked, what about non-patients, people managing their lives in the community? Eccentricity itself is not a condition that requires medical attention, although eccentric people cannot be assumed to be immune from the effects of adverse mental processes, ones that could begin insidiously, and that could proceed malignantly without the benefit of full awareness.

It is an open secret that experimental psychologists know a great deal about how second year female undergraduates perform in their narrow and sometimes deliberately deceptive experiments, and psychiatrists know about how people who have broken down think and talk. Unfortunately for the advancement of science, these two groups of experts very rarely communicate with each other. Furthermore, adult non-patients are only very infrequently studied by either group. Seemingly inexplicable events therefore may seem to be such because no one has attempted to explain the thinking of the people who precipitate and participate in them. A study of eccentricity might be a very effective way of bridging this discontinuity in our knowledge.

Psychologists should be prepared to deal with the totality of human perception, motivation and personality. They should try to understand why men and women interact with their environment in the ways that they do, and why they do one thing rather than another. They must also study the enigmatic problem of consciousness and self-awareness, and disorders in both.

In the quest to discover more about the psychological thought processes of eccentrics, several computer searches of primary sources, backed up by a manual examination of all available social science and psychiatric literature, revealed little of any significance. Of the four best known text books of clinical psychiatry, three make no mention of it at all, whilst the fourth comments briefly upon it as a form of "predominantly inadequate or passive psychopathy", observing further with clinical detachment that it is "usually difficult to distinguish the symptoms of eccentricity from schizophrenic manifestations." The concealed fact is that these summary statements were based only on haphazard clinical observations.

Normally, medical research recruits its volunteers from patients with particular disorders, others who are asked or recommended, and people in allied hospital-related occupations, who often act as control subjects. The problem was how to raise the required number of volunteers for a study on eccentricity. Eccentrics often view themselves seriously and may not wish to take part in a study where they feel they might be ridiculed. The two most common methods of exploratory research --- population survey sampling and consecutive clinical referrals from the medical profession --- were out of the question. Both methods would be prohibitively costly and totally ineffective.

As burglars know, there can be many ways to get past a locked door. For my study, the only course that seemed open to me was to advertise. At first, I took this step hesitantly and reluctantly. From previous experience it had been found that in order to recruit the number needed for psychological surveys, advertisements placed in the local newspapers drew sufficient volunteers. Advertising presents other problems, such as the question of self-selection. A volunteer would have to decide if he thought he was eccentric or not. This was overcome in some cases by the study being brought to the attention of the potential volunteer by another person. The use of this "snowball technique" also meant that the volunteers might be derived from a wider area and therefore be a more representative sampling base.

What evolved out of necessity was a new method of survey sampling, which I subsequently designated as "multimedia survey sampling". I began by placing a number of advertisements on file cards in a range of establishments: pubs, wine bars, launderettes, libraries, supermarkets, colleges and universities. Worded simply, they read "Eccentric? If you feel that you might be, contact Dr. David Weeks at the Royal Edinburgh Hospital".

At this point, every effort was made to ensure that the locations of these advertisements were as representative as possible. They could not be placed exclusively in one kind of place, where only one type of person would go, but where they might be seen by as broad a cross-section of the population as possible. As well as being distributed fairly according to social class distribution, it was also necessary to see that the advertisements were disseminated across a wide geographical area. I sampled a diverse range of sites in all of Edinburgh's Electoral Register districts.

Soon after this phase was completed, a local journalist spotted one of the cards that I had placed rather hopefully in the University of Edinburgh Staff Club. This led to an article in the middle of a local evening newspaper, which led in turn to a larger article in a national newspaper.

Having followed that track so far, I soon realised that our sampling throughout all the mass media had to be as comprehensive as the file card advertisement campaign was. This meant that I had to break through to the mass-circulation press in order to receive representative coverage and representative volunteers. I therefore sent out press releases to every national newspaper, though some reporters had already found the story for themselves. Radio and television interviews followed. This further increased the representativeness of the sample. In this respect coverage was excellent, with programmes on all four national BBC Radio channels, as well as on a number of London-based and local radio stations. Stories about the research appeared amidst pop music, at the end of the national news, on chat shows, on phone-ins, and on science and medical programmes. Various times of day were covered, from early morning breakfast television and radio to late night topical spots. The contents of our hospital mailbag assumed an increasingly bizarre and exotic appearance.

Initial exploratory investigation in any field can exclude at the outset no potential subject on any grounds whatever. The more assiduously the study was carried out in terms of recruiting volunteers from as many different sites as possible, the more representative would be the subject pool, and therefore the findings would be substantially more reliable and valid. No stone could be left unturned, no lead not followed up. All the readers, listeners and viewers that the basic appeal reached, based on combined circulation and audience research figures, totalled at least thirty million people in the United Kingdom between 1984 and 1988. Aside from the national census, this was the largest population group ever sampled in the United Kingdom.

The resulting publicity given to the study by the use of the snowball and multimedia survey sampling techniques attracted one hundred and thirty self-styled eccentrics, seventy-four men and fifty-six women. Whilst they ranged across the entire social spectrum --- including a deputy chairman of a large industry, an architect, a puppeteer, a credit company representative, a chiropractor, and several hermits --- they had many things in common. This numerical response supports the international belief that Britain is indeed the heartland of the eccentric.
(See Table 1.)

Table 1. Demographic characteristics of the sample

Social class *	I	II	III		IV		V
	59%	21%	11%		6%		3%
Age	16 -19	20 - 29	30 - 39	40 - 49	50 - 59	60 - 69	70 - 80
	4%	10%	17%	21%	25%	16%	7%
Years of education	6 - 9	10 - 13	14 - 17		18 - 21		22+
	10%	38%	37%		11%		4%

*(By Registrar General occupational category)

As can be seen from Table 1, the research informants tended to be predominantly upper middle class, professionals and managers, and from all age groups (the average age was forty-seven, the median age was fifty), and somewhat better educated than the general population (mean years of education fourteen, median years of education fifteen). The degree of involvement and attentiveness towards their spare time activities and other interests is shown in Table 2. A high interest in sports was significantly gendered. Interest in this area was shown by more male than female eccentrics. Both male and female eccentrics preferred more solitary non-competitive non-team sports.

Table 2. Activities and interests

	None	A little	A lot	Obsessional
Degree of interest in spare time activities	1%	7%	44%	48%
Degree of interest in reading	2%	27%	34%	37%
Degree of interest in politics	20%	25%	38%	17%
Degree of interest in sports	32%	38%	27%	3%
Degree of interest in science	26%	16%	34%	24%

The questions asked were selected in order to discover if there were any symptoms of psychiatric disorder, to ascertain the personality of each volunteer, and to gather much background information. Thus I included questions concerning not only their interests, but also their preoccupations, experiences, and perceptions. Some were very specific, to test current hypotheses; many were general because of the exploratory nature of this study. I also sought to elicit representative samples of each subject's speech. Standard personality questionnaires were also used to gather supplementary information on normal personality traits and the possibility and types of personality disorder. Throughout all this I hoped to capture the way that their minds worked.

The structured interviews were conducted informally in the homes of the volunteers wherever this was possible. The advantage of this was that the volunteers would be more relaxed and confident, thereby placing them under less stress. Consequently, I believe that most of their answers were as spontaneous as possible in such a situation. The conversations recorded with these individuals allowed me to hear their refreshing insights into how their minds worked. They presented interesting self-accounts and were wholeheartedly engaged in this cooperative discourse. In so doing they demonstrated their capability to be fully introspective, putting the lie to the notion that eccentric people exhibit very little in the way of insight, self-consciousness or self-awareness. One of the major psychological fallacies --- as psychologist Gordon Allport put it, "The individual has lost the right to be believed" --- and this has had the result of psychology not taking people's subjective experience seriously.

I was particularly interested in recording fairly long speech samples for further analysis, the duration of each interview being at least ninety minutes. There were several reasons for this. One related to the ideals of descriptive psychology: I wanted this to be as full an acknowledgement of the range of individual psychological qualities and abilities as possible. I explicitly set out to grasp not only the beliefs and outlooks of our subjects, but also their way of believing. This approach is fundamentally reflexive; the research participants were respected as perceptive and active, as being in a privileged position with regard to the workings of their own psyches. Many felt almost compelled to explain themselves, to make sense of themselves. I discussed with them some of their characteristic actions and the grounds on which they based their retrospective appraisals of themselves and others. This method is positively ideographic. It can convincingly demonstrate the uniqueness of each person's points of view.

I set out to elicit the full repertoire of concepts, be they valid or not, and however apparently incongruous, held by each individual. This could help the participants to rethink disparate events in their lives, as well as connecting memories, true or false, that were previously isolated or disconnected. As John Barth wrote in his *Dunyaziad*, "Some fictions, (the Genie) asserted, were so much more valuable than fact, that in rare instances their beauty made them real". This also summed up Sigmund Freud's early approach to looking at the irrationality of the disturbed people he encountered in therapy. His initial theories could have led to a wider, more inclusive revolution in society, but he backtracked; his agenda didn't go very far improving liberty, equality or fraternity in society. Freud's grand scheme was incomplete. There are other kinds of irrationality.

Chapter 2. Generous Misers, the Art of Odd Guise, and Emperors Who Weren't (Eccentrics in History, 1550 - 1950)

The vulgar thus through imitation err
As oft the learn'd by being singular
Alexander Pope

Akenside was a young man warm with every notion connected with the sound of liberty, and by an eccentricity which such dispositions do not easily avoid, a lover of contradiction, and no friend to anything established.
Samuel Johnson

So would I bridle thy eccentric soul
In reason's sober orbit bid it roll
Whitehead on Churchill

The past is littered with people as renowned for their quixotries and quiddities as for any other traits. I reckoned it would be illuminating to have a closer look at some historical eccentrics, to examine their social backgrounds and uncover any patterns of unusual behaviour. From the available material it was possible to do a small but detailed historiometric analysis of one hundred and fifty eccentrics from 1550 to 1950. Distinctive aspects of these eccentrics' behaviour could then be used as broad indicators of what to look for in our main investigation of modern eccentrics. There may well have been eccentrics before 1550, though lay concepts about personality were probably too different or not sufficiently developed before then.

A very early use of the word "eccentric" was demonstrated in reports about a grieving follower of Mary, Queen of Scots, the Lady Margaret Lambourne, who, having attempted to assassinate Queen Elizabeth and spoken forthrightly to her intended victim, was granted a pardon and safe conduct out of England. Another early exemplar was the Honourable Henry Hastings (1551 – 1641), a country squire who delighted in hunting, fishing and chasing "alluring wenches" all his days. A contemporaneous source described him as an "original in the age in which he lived, or rather he was the copy of our ancient nobility in hunting and warlike times."

It is thought that people have generally become somewhat less superstitious and more disposed to explain the curious features of others by using psychological concepts. Not only is the historical record somewhat opaque, but also the further back one goes the less reliable are the records, largely due to cultural developments and upheavals in society. Older standards of behaviour differed from current ones. In addition, it is difficult to trust attributions concerning complicated subjective impressions. There have been shifts in vocabulary and language usage over time to complicate the elucidation and understanding of archival records. Until at least the mid-nineteenth century, the concept of eccentricity was fairly all-encompassing, including people who had physical disabilities, and some who had "miraculously" survived freak accidents.

One needs to explain why there appear to have been so few eccentrics in this four hundred year long period. A breakdown of their distribution in time, era by era, may help our understanding of those contexts most conducive to producing eccentrics. My sample of historical eccentrics includes all those so designated by their contemporaries. It includes all that my research team could find in a variety of archival searches, and cross-verify from at least two independent sources.

Eccentrics went relatively unnoticed or were poorly documented between the reigns of Elizabeth I and George I. The notion of what was meant by eccentricity was either poorly developed, or eccentrics may have actually been fewer in number. Eccentrics began to flower around 1725, with a peak in numbers around the last quarter of the eighteenth century. The Hanoverian kings presided over a century of unparalleled elegance and many newfound concerns about what did or did not amount to "good taste". Great Britain was becoming rich and resourceful, an internationally powerful country. During these years, new intakes among the wealthy landed gentry were seen to act more unusually, not only by their aristocratic "betters" but also by their more established counterparts. It wasn't simply a matter of these men and women wanting to imitate their superiors and failing to do so in ways that were deemed appropriate. They brought with them behaviours that were substantially different and more down to earth. In addition, the middle classes began to hold sway in terms of values, aspirations, well-ordered manners and etiquette, as well as their obvious consumption of goods and services. The pleasure gardens of Vauxhall and Ranelagh in Chelsea became sites where prosperous men and the likes of Beau Brummell would disport themselves in the latest fashionable attire.

It is tempting to speculate about the possible connections between the political philosophies that came to revolutionary fruition in the latter part of the eighteenth century, and the major outbursts of eccentricity taking place then in Britain, France and America. However, not many eccentric people were directly involved in the new free-thinking ideologies. Several eccentrics came under the sway of the romantic idealism of Jean-Jacques Rousseau, a philosopher radically egalitarian for his time. Several other eccentrics could be considered to be early proto-democrats. However, in England the majority of eccentrics were conservative to the point of xenophobia, and many more were politically naïve.

Some of these eccentrics were really not eccentric but had disorders that today would be recognised as psychiatric illness. In days when treatments were barbarous it may have been somewhat better for such unfortunate people to be regarded as indisposed eccentrics. The disclosure of genuine psychiatric disorder amongst several historical eccentrics did sometimes surface during their lifetimes. Lord George Gordon, an eighteenth century politician who had been accused of high treason, was subsequently diagnosed as mentally ill. So too was the Duchess of Queensberry (1703-77), wife of Charles, the third Duke of Queensberry. Before her marriage she had been for a time confined to a straitjacket, and her illness continued into her married life. Both of these people have nevertheless been included in previous works documenting historical eccentrics.

One lively lady, whose eccentricities stayed with her throughout her ninety-one years, was Susanna Kennedy, Countess of Eglintoune. She was six feet tall, strikingly beautiful, extremely elegant and witty, and had many admirers, some of whom were notable in their own right. As one commentator said, "Her appearance in Edinburgh, which took place about the time of the 1707 Union with England, gained her a vast accession of lovers among the nobility and gentry, and set all the fancies of the period agog." Several of her beaux were moved to write poems and songs in lavish praise of her grace and "startling comeliness", comparing her favourably to Helen of Troy and Cleopatra. She always maintained that the secret of her beauty and enduring youth was that she never wore face paint or any other artificial cosmetics, and washed her face daily in sow's milk.

That she married Sir Archibald Eglintoune, a man many years older than she, came as no surprise to her. Apparently, whilst walking in her father's gardens at Culzean Castle, a hawk landed on her shoulder with Sir Archibald's name upon its bells. This was considered by her to be an infallible omen of one's fate. Susanna had seven daughters by Sir Archibald, but he threatened divorce when no son was born. Being a "forthright lady of many virtues", Susanna readily agreed to a separation, provided he returned to her everything she possessed at the time of their marriage. Thinking it was only a matter of money, Sir Archibald consented. The Countess was no fool. "No, no, my Lord!" she exclaimed, "That will not do. Return to me my youth, beauty, and virginity, and then dismiss me as you please." Sir Archibald, realising the abject hopelessness of his situation, never again raised the subject. In the following year Susanna gave birth to the long-awaited male heir.

Lady Eglintoune's children only ever addressed her as "Her Ladyship", and her eldest son, who inherited the title on the death of his father in 1729, also came to be addressed formally by his brothers and sisters as "Lord Eglintoune" at their mother's instigation. In later life, Lady Susanna complained of never having received true gratitude from anyone other than four-footed animals. Her favourites were rats, which she kept in vast numbers, summoning them to the dining room at meal times by tapping on an oak panel. On cue, a dozen or so rats would appear out of the woodwork and join her at the dining table. After dinner, on a quiet command, her rodent friends would retire in an orderly fashion to their usual habitat in the wainscoting to await their next call to their Ladyship's presence.

Throughout the seventeenth and eighteenth centuries, when the mentally ill from the poorer sections of society were incarcerated in mad houses, the mentally ill of the middle and upper classes were often looked after at home on a more private, individual basis. There have also been cases in the past where sane persons have been confined to institutions for the mentally ill. Is it possible that some of them were really guilty of nothing more than simply displaying signs of eccentric behaviour? Was it that their eccentric behaviour was misinterpreted? Pierre Janet (1859-1947), who helped to liberate many victims from French asylums, suggested that a poor patient was committed to a public hospital as mad, though if he was wealthy then he would be isolated somewhere within the confines of his own home as a harmless eccentric. Other eccentrics in the past were mistaken for escaped mental patients. Sir Thomas Barrett-Lennard (1826-1919), who was always shabbily dressed, was continually misidentified as a gardener or servant. On one occasion, whilst returning from a meeting of the local asylum committee that he chaired, he was mistaken for a patient and then briefly detained against his will.

Eccentrics had decreased numerically by about half in the first quarter of the nineteenth century. This however has been regarded as the beginning of the first Golden Age of eccentricity. This was because the rich upper classes could really do things on a much larger and more dramatic scale during that century. Despite their burgeoning activities, their numbers remained stable throughout the Victorian and Edwardian epochs. Meanwhile, the new entrepreneurial classes, trying to appear to act primly proper, instilled in their wives and children more conforming attitudes. During the Jazz Age following the human catastrophe that was World War I there was a small resurgence of free-thinking eccentricity in both men and women that presaged its great modern renaissance.

Biographical research into historical characters reveals that the aristocracy and the landed gentry had considerably more eccentrics amongst their number than those from the working classes. Dukes, countesses, churchmen and wealthy landowners did indeed have their exploits well documented. It was however the upper middle class that was numerically preponderant (see Table 3). Whether this was truly the case, or rather more was known about individuals from these groups because of their social standing and greater social range and mobility, remains unclear. Many upper class individualists possessed much greater scope and opportunity to indulge their fantasies, and some of their activities, such as folly building, did create work during the hard times of impoverishment and mass unemployment [1].

Table 3. Social class distribution of the historical sample

Aristocrats	16%
Landed gentry	21%
Upper middle class	49%
Lower middle class	10%
Working class	4%

Follies are personal in a way that other examples of architecture seldom can be. Their greatness lies in their atmospheres and distinctive personalities. I have been inside a home that was built in the shape of a giant pineapple and have seen a "tree" built from stone in the midst of a dense Scottish Highland forest. Whilst the building of architectural follies was not an exclusive preserve of the eccentric, it was one of several recurring activities that have come to be associated in the public's mind as a typical eccentric endeavour. The obscure reasons behind this activity have been attributed to some nearly forgotten, and quite different, aesthetic theories. It could have been pure self-indulgence, or a desperate attempt for complete isolation. Or perhaps those who initiated the creation of follies saw a need to leave their mark on the countryside by constructing such amazingly striking buildings. It is ironic that some of the folly builders were remembered more for their personal eccentricities than for their buildings, some of which did not endure intact, even in the short term.

William Beckford (1759 - 1844) was the premier folly builder of his age. Haunted by the scandal created by his teenage passion for the sixteen-year old William Courtney of Powderham Castle, and the scurrilous gossip that ensued, he was forced into exile abroad until the Napoleonic Wars began. It is significant that upon his return to his ancestral home in Wiltshire, he surrounded his land with a seven-mile long, twelve-foot high wall surmounted with ugly iron spikes. He was also, in reality, England's wealthiest commoner, a notable aesthete, and the author, at the age of only twenty-one, of the enduring early Romantic literary work, *Vathek*. It was a hybrid combination of novel elements, the new Orientalism with the Gothic style of Horace Walpole's *The Castle of Otranto*. Beckford's Arabian stories influenced a number of the Romantic poets and writers, including Lord Byron, Mary Shelley, John Keats, Robert Southey, and Thomas Moore, as well as twentieth century authors such as H. P. Lovecraft.

The unexpected death of Beckford's wife left him a deeply lonely figure with a romantic preoccupation for solitary wandering. A consummate art collector, he also acquired many other unusual items from far and wide, eventually establishing the largest cabinet of curiosities in the world, comprising strange books, erotica, skeletons, skulls, and natural history specimens [2].

Beckford's first architectural folly was an elaborate convent, built deliberately as a ruined shrine, where he meditated on his theories of sentimentality and perpetual escapism. There was also Beckford's Tower just outside Bath. Standing 120 feet high, Beckford was dissatisfied with its height, admitting ". . . such as it is, it is a famous landmark for drunken farmers on their way home from market."

His most famous building project was most extraordinary. A diarist in 1798 wrote, "(The) New building is to be called Fonthill Abbey --- the Spire to be 17 feet higher than the top of St. Peter's at Rome. The Abbey to be endowed, & Cathedral services to be performed in the most splendid manner that the Protestant religion will admit." The grandiose abbey had a fan-vaulted gallery at one end, a lengthwise interior vista totalling over three hundred feet, and the gargantuan octagonal tower in which Beckford hoped to reside. Not helped by an inadequate architectural overseer, the first attempt at the high tower was fabricated from shoddy materials on weak foundations and collapsed within a few months. This was followed by a second effort constructed in stone and brick masonry, though still on shaky foundations, and was erected with impetuous speed.

Beckford once said, "Some people drink to forget their unhappiness. I do not drink, I build." He was unable to brook a more serene approach to his construction projects for any reason. Once he had an idea, it had to be carried out as rapidly as possible, and multiple setbacks increased this tendency --- he found it difficult to even contemplate the idea of delayed gratification. He once diverted five hundred workmen from Windsor Castle to work on the phantasmagoric Fonthill Abbey. He bribed these men with strong ale fortified with liberal doses of port and brandy, and had them work around the clock. It was said that this resulted in Fonthill Abbey being built by tired men in an advanced state of intoxication. In 1825, three years after he disposed of it and a quarter of a century after its completion, the Abbey's great tower collapsed once more. The building materials again were found to be flimsy, and though there were people inside the Abbey at the time, no one noticed it crumbling until dust poured through the windows. The fall of the tower had been almost silent.

To be eccentric is to make oneself significantly different from everyone else, to be fundamentally at odds with the customs and traditions permitted by the culture of the time. As a description, however, usage of the term presupposes the ability to notice and distinguish the real causes of many forms of differentness. Inversions of gender identifications and corresponding forms of dress have often led to confusion in the assignment of individual non-conformity. For instance, the Native American custom of tolerance toward Two-Spirit people, previously called *berdache* --- an accepted form of transvestism in which certain men and women took on the dress and duties of the opposite gender --- produced a minority of individuals who could openly express ordinarily forbidden personal tendencies. However, the similarities between these individuals' behaviour precludes them from being considered eccentric; they conformed fairly closely to a widespread culturally transmitted template. Male and female Two-Spirits have been documented in over one hundred and thirty native tribes in every region of North America [3, 4]. For much the same reason, most of the participants of alternative group movements or counter-cultures, for example, those following bohemian lifestyles, should no more readily be considered to be eccentric than adherents of conventional versions of society.

Though eccentricity is a phenomenon affecting both men and women, male eccentrics have been more widely recorded than their female counterparts. Historically, for every female eccentric there have been about nine male eccentrics. This says a great deal about the contrasting power relations of this time period. The males, who demonstrated greater variability in their behaviour, came from all walks of life --- earls, artists, high court judges and hermits. Female eccentrics, on the other hand, were drawn almost exclusively from the aristocracy and were primarily extraverts. They were outrageous and splendidly wild in their behaviour, and though very typically living heartily to well-advanced years, chronological age did not diminish their eccentric habits.

Eccentricity was not, however, the exclusive purview of the high and mighty. One historical eccentric, who could not in any way lay claim to any form of noble family pedigree, was an Edinburgh pedlar called Henry Prentice, who is reputed to have been the first man in Scotland to cultivate potatoes on a large scale. A much respected "worthy", Lord Minto, who loaned him a horse and cart to transport the potatoes into town, assisted him in this venture. Arriving in Edinburgh, Prentice sold all his potatoes, as well as the noble lord's horse and cart. To his peers he became a "great curio", and was said never to have shaken the hand of anyone over the age of two. Having given most of his money away to the keepers of the poor houses, he negotiated the purchase of his final resting place in one of the more salubrious cemeteries in Edinburgh. He demanded that the undertaker mount a funeral procession consisting of a hearse and four coaches, and that he personally take responsibility for screwing down the coffin lid free of charge. To ensure his notoriety he erected a monument over his grave with the following inscription:

Be not anxious how I lived,
But rather how you yourself should die.

Many of eccentrics known to historians lived well into old age. It was not unusual for some of them to live for eighty or ninety years, at a time when the average life expectancy for those who survived childhood was somewhere between thirty-five and forty-five years. The mean age for male eccentrics was seventy-two years; for female eccentrics it was eighty-one years. One speculation about this is that their preoccupations gave their lives meaning and provided them with clear and specific goals. Their resulting happiness, indirectly, may have protected them physically via the body's immune response system, which we know to be intimately interrelated with the nervous system and endocrine system.

One common factor many of these men and women shared was their unblinking fascination with death and all things connected with it. One elderly eccentric had a collection of coffins that he invited his houseguests to try out for size. He used one as a liquor cabinet, while another had folding doors and glass windows. The numerous stories concerning humorous and complicated wills also derive from fact rather than legend. One aged eccentric woman had her coffin made and kept at her home for several years before her death. From time to time she would climb into it just to make sure it was comfortable. Her servants were summoned on these occasions and were asked to provide their frank impressions of the overall effect.

Scholarly circles were fertile grounds for the development of the eccentric lifestyle. That great English gentleman, the portly Dr. Johnson, was not only a genius of prodigious wit, scholarship, and courage, but also one who would delight in rolling down steep hills to amuse his friends. However, most academic eccentrics tended to be shy, quiet, and socially unobtrusive. It was said that they adopted eccentric mannerisms and ways of teaching to attract more students to their lectures. Many absentmindedly lost themselves in their reveries, indifferent to their surroundings and the practicalities of everyday life. Some had difficulty in coping with ordinary activities, including ordinary communication. John Barrett (1753 - 1821), a Vice-Provost and Professor of Oriental Languages at Trinity College, Dublin, spoke Latin and Greek fluently, but his English was appalling. The eminent physicist, James Clerk Maxwell, came to be known as "Dafty Maxwell" whilst at the University of Edinburgh.

Their contemporaries regarded eccentrics in many different ways. Those eccentrics who were extravert in character were well-liked, outgoing and popular, and often held in high esteem by their friends. Introverts, on the other hand, had few friends and were treated with suspicion. Others were misunderstood or thought mad, a point of view that still exists today.

It is difficult to assess personality retrospectively from the yellowing, mouldy pages of primary source archive material. There was, in fact, insufficient data on fifteen per cent of the historical sample. Only broad sweeps of the brush have been possible, at best, though one can usually discriminate between introversion and extraversion from the records. This was attempted.

I decided that recluses might first be considered as introverts, unless there was evidence to the contrary, for instance, many friends and acquaintances, or recorded instances of sociability or impulsiveness. Independent descriptions by two or more contemporaneous eyewitnesses also reinforced a personality assessment. Still, the evidence was often contradictory. In the case of Henry Lee Warner (1722-1802), there is ample positive evidence of extraversion: "Well liked by many. He is a truly amiable man. He is too good. He has an extreme tenderness of disposition." Others however might see him as a thinking introvert. He slept all day so as to concentrate on his nocturnal scholarly pursuits without interruption. Because of his hours, he went through his life peacefully but with little company. The fact that his attire --- gold-laced coat, silk neck cloth and curved-toe shoes --- was half a century out of date went politely unremarked. On the other hand, few would contradict the description of William Jennings (1701 - 1797) as an introvert, a wealthy miser who loaned money to gamblers and accumulated vast profits, "so cold and unsocial was his animal constitution".

Or take the case of the Honourable Henry Cavendish (1731 - 1810), a Fellow of the Royal Society. His introversion, reclusiveness and taciturn attitude were extreme. He forbade his bankers to speak to him about his money or his housekeepers to speak to him at all. He was painfully shy, and could not bear to be interrupted about trivial matters. To ensure his privacy, he developed an elaborate ritualised system of letterbox openings and double doors within his house. After meeting a maid on the staircase by accident, he had a second stairway built to spare himself any such further close encounters. His contemporary, Lord Brougham, recalled Cavendish's panic-provoked quirks at scientific meetings, especially "the shrill cry he uttered as he shuffled from room to room".

His biographer, Dr. George Wilson, wrote of him: "He did not love; he did not hate; he did not hope; he did not fear; he did not worship as others do. An intellectual head thinking, a pair of wonderfully acute eyes observing, and a pair of very skilful hands experimenting or recording, are all I realize in reading his memorials." He added that Cavendish "probably uttered fewer words in the course of his life than any man who ever lived to fourscore years, not at all excepting the monks of La Trappe". Yet Cavendish was a brilliant scientist, the first to realise that water was not a single element but composed of hydrogen and oxygen. He also discovered, though neglected to publish, two fundamental principles of electricity --- Coulomb's Law and Ohm's Law --- years before they dawned on Charles Coulomb or George Ohm. He also accurately calculated the weight of the earth and investigated the powerful electric shocks delivered by torpedo fish.

Using various biographical clues, I deduced that roughly three quarters of the historical sample could be seen as mainly extravert, and the remaining quarter introvert. The evidence for some of this particular exercise was admittedly tenuous, sometimes only single word descriptions such as "reticent", "surly", or "piquant".

Some great eccentrics broke all the bounds of propriety; thus much is known about their behaviour, though their underlying motivation remains unknown. One such person was the Shropshire squire "Mad Jack" Mytton, a more reckless version of Evel Knievel in his time, whose life was understandably briefer (1796 - 1834) than the average for this group. "So extraordinary a hell raiser was Mytton," wrote his biographer, "that to apologise properly for his career would be well nigh impossible." Expelled from both Westminster School and Harrow for fighting, he gave away money and spent about a half million pounds on alcohol in only seventeen years. Port was his favourite drink, five bottles a day, though in a pinch eau de cologne or lavender water would do. His wardrobe contained 150 pairs of riding breeches, 700 pairs of boots, over 1,000 hats, and nearly 3,000 shirts.

A daredevil sportsman, what Mytton really enjoyed was risking his life. Fear was not in his vocabulary. He became famous for taking jumps on horseback or in horse-drawn carriages that no sane person would contemplate. A phrase was coined at the time to describe anything too tough to attempt – "it would do for Mytton". He scorned caution and wondered why others did not do likewise. He was shocked to hear from a friend that he had never been in a crash. "What ho!" cried Mytton, "Never you say! What a dammed slow fellow you must have been all your life!" He then deliberately overturned the gig he was already driving at great speed. Luckily --- and Mytton was usually incredibly lucky --- no one was hurt.

Havoc broke loose at one of Mytton's dinner parties when he appeared in full hunting pink, mounted on his fully-grown pet bear Nell. In the ensuing panic, with his friends jumping out of windows or clambering behind and under the furniture, Mytton called out "Tally ho", spurring on his wild-looking mount, who promptly retaliated by sinking her teeth into his leg.

His friends soon found that giving Mytton sage advice fell on deaf ears. He told one such friend, "What the devil is the use of my having a head on my shoulders if I am obliged to make use of yours?" His next act was to set himself on fire in order to cure himself of persistent hiccoughs, saying, "Damn this hiccough! I will frighten it away!" After the conflagration, Mytton exalted, "Well, the hiccough is gone, by God!" He survived this foolish stunt, and on the very next day, swathed in bandages like a latter-day mummy, dined out with a friend. At the end of 1832, he met and married the love of his life, Susan, his third wife, and they set off together to the continent for further adventures.

Elton John may own more sets of glasses than Jack Mytton owned riding breeches, but we accept the former fact because it became part of his stage act. The mark of a true eccentric is that the dividing line between the act and the person becomes lost in the mists of legend and self-mythologizing. True eccentrics are seldom acting. Strong individuals with strange inclinations, they are not afraid to express themselves. They repudiate nothing. They refuse to compromise.

Their degree of free expression could be so excessive that contemporaries often believed the eccentric had not only exceeded the bounds of good taste but also had crossed the fine line between obsession and madness. Their lay diagnoses were, as often as not, incorrect. For example, in late eighteenth century Sicily, the Prince of Palagonia, a shy man afraid of everyone, was thought mad simply because he had devoted his life to the study of monsters and chimeras. The interior of his house was filled with statues, mirrors and surrealistic pyramids of cups, bowls and saucers cemented together. The windows were full of coloured glass and his bedroom was likened to Noah's Ark, full of marble statues of many different kinds of animals. He had surrounded his house with six hundred statues of imaginary creatures, some so hideous that the local authorities wanted to order their destruction. The Prince reacted to the possibility of this unhappy turn of events with infinite pathos. The citizens relented when they realised that their proposed actions would break the Prince's heart.

This is but one example of how the historical eccentrics, like some of their modern counterparts, could attract contrasting responses. (See Table 4 below)

Table 4: Historical eccentrics – how contemporaries responded to them

With endearment	36%
Esteemed	13%
Shocked	12%
Ridiculed	11%
With suspicion	11%
Mildly disconcerted	8%
Taking unfair advantage	7%
Disliked	7%
With curiosity	3%

These responses speak volumes for the greatly varying tolerance levels of the "normal" non-eccentric individuals concerned, some enlightened and accepting, some not.

Not only were people with unusual preoccupations wrongly considered to be mentally ill; some people widely regarded in their own time as eccentric did in fact have a variety of disturbances (see Table 5). One surprising absence from this list is schizophrenia.

Table 5. Retrospective diagnoses of historical eccentrics

Diagnosis	Number	Percentage
Mania / hypomania	7	4.7%
Obsessive-compulsive neurosis	3	2%
Phobia	3	2%
Depression	2	1.3%
Alcoholism	2	1.3%
Compulsive gambling	1	0.7%
Anxiety state	1	0.7%
TOTAL	19	12.7%

Particular positive characteristics of these disturbed "eccentrics" may have influenced their peers to regard them as eccentric rather than mad. This was no doubt so in the touching case of Joshua Abraham Norton (?1819 - 1880). Born in London and raised in South Africa, Norton figured briefly as a prosperous gentleman merchant in Gold Rush California. He was said to have "seen the elephant", contemporary slang for risking everything on an elusive gold strike. However, he managed to build up a considerable fortune in San Francisco as a property speculator. He saw his next main chance when in 1853 he gambled a quarter of a million dollars in an effort to corner the rice market. He bought up and stockpiled all the available rice, artificially inflating the price. Soon afterwards, when several ships laden with rice sailed into the harbour, the market became glutted, prices plummeted, and Norton went bust.

Reduced to working in a Chinese-run factory and living in a seedy rooming house, this sudden reversal of fortunes, along with Norton's consequent loss of self-esteem, would today be reckoned as an "ongoing stressful adverse life event or life situation". Such events could be discerned in sixty per cent of those "eccentrics" judged to be mentally ill. Norton soon confided to his friends that he was really Norton I, Emperor of California. In 1856, in the same year that he filed for bankruptcy, he also issued his first imperial edict. By 1859 he decided that California was not big enough for him, or did not have sufficient authority to name him Emperor of all he surveyed. His solution was delivered in September of that year to the editor of the *San Francisco Bulletin*, who printed it without comment: "At the peremptory request and desire of a large majority of the citizens of the United States, I, Joshua A. Norton, declare and proclaim myself Emperor of these United States; and in virtue of the authority thereby in me vested, do hereby order and direct the representatives of the different States of the Union to assemble in Musical Hall, of this city, on the first day of February next, then and there to make such alterations in the existing laws of the Union as may ameliorate the evils under which the country is labouring and thereby cause confidence to exist, both at home and abroad, both in our stability and in our integrity.
Signed,
    Norton I, Emperor of the United States and Protector of Mexico."

With this letter to the citizens of San Francisco, he became an instant celebrity. He went on to dissolve both main political parties and the Republic, and was undeterred when these moves were disregarded. He began wearing a blue military uniform with gold-plated epaulettes given to him by some local army officers. He also wore a sword, a tall beaver hat bearing a plume, a feather and a rosette. When his uniform of office became a bit frayed around the edges, the city's Board of Supervisors, with much ceremony, appropriated money for a new one. Norton in turn ennobled them. He printed his own money in twenty-five and fifty cent denominations, which was accepted freely in most shops and restaurants. He felt that his due was somewhat higher than this, and would try to negotiate loans of several million dollars from his old banking friends.

Norton was a benevolent despot and believed in fair play. He advocated a wage increase for sailors and the novel idea of building a bridge across San Francisco Bay. He never missed a session of the State Senate, where a special chair was reserved for him. Emperor Norton treated all his responsibilities with great earnestness, going walkabout among his loyal subjects, inspecting building sites, and ensuring that the streetcars ran on time. He attended a different church every week so as to avoid sectarian jealousies. His edicts also showed an erratic nature: "Off with Denis Kearney's head," he ordered during a period of anti-Chinese agitation; and later, "Death to Emperor Maximilian" over the matter of the foreign tyrant usurping Norton's southern lands and prerogatives.

San Franciscans offered nothing less than their warmth and charity to Norton. Robert Louis Stevenson admired them for the spirit of their affection and the dignity they conferred on Norton. As a judge remarked, releasing Norton from an erroneous arrest, "He has shed no blood, robbed no one and despoiled no country, which is more than can be said for most fellows in the king line." When Norton died, the *San Francisco Chronicle* headlined "Le Roi Est Mort". He was given a lavish funeral, with 10,000 mourners lining the route of the procession.

The irony of this tale is that Norton was treated as a harmless eccentric in his own day, and still is so regarded by many. Today he would be recognised as suffering from mania, vigorously battered with physical treatments, tranquillised, stabilised, and if he objected, probably compelled to be made normal against his will. One can only marvel at how people, before the heyday of biological psychiatry, got it so right in humanitarian terms despite being utterly confused about what was really happening before their very eyes.

It would therefore be worthwhile to try to clarify this area of ambiguity, this supposed fine line between eccentricity and psychiatric disorder. One can only wonder how many refuseniks, dissidents and other prickly, uncomfortable people have been persecuted by means of psychiatry, not for their personal beliefs, but as a direct result of immoral, rigid or overhasty mis-diagnosis.

Chapter 3. The Living Sea of Waking Dreams
(Eccentricity and Psychiatric Disorder)

"Blessed are the cracked, for they shall let in the light."

The Eighth Beatitude, as recorded from an eccentric

There was very little reason to suspect that eccentrics possess any special immunity or protection from mental illness. On the other hand, some of their eccentricities could be explicable in terms of known, or presumed, psychiatric conditions, perhaps of lesser severity or of fluctuating degree. Some milder forms of schizophrenia, schizotypal conditions or schizophrenia arrested at an early stage, could be implicated.

Delusions need not necessarily be horrifying or particularly different from the "normal" thoughts of a non-deluded person. Delusions may not always arise out of the blue; they may also percolate quietly below the surface for months or years.

Previous definitions of a delusion may have constricted the types of experiences seen to be admissible for closer investigation. A definition of delusion is "a belief that is not true to fact, cannot be corrected by an appeal to the reason of the person entertaining it, and is out of harmony with the person's education and surroundings" [1]. Schizophrenic delusions are seen to be utterly implausible in reference to the individual's culture. So-called "primary" delusions have been thought to appear suddenly, carrying an immediate and vivid sense of conviction [2]. These delusions do not usually come alone; they are interlinked into a web of other false beliefs. For example, a schizophrenic who believed that he could cause an earthquake by his thoughts alone may also believe that the mind of a famous rock guitarist also possessed the ability to travel through past and future times. Such closed and circular mixtures of thoughts often contain outright fallacies and logical contradictions, and the individual is largely unwilling or unable to conceive that these startling discrepancies are basically wrong. It is from such delusions that the sufferer's more worrying behaviours can be precipitated. In such cases, those so affected live in a kind of private limbo.

The ideal type of study required would be one in which children and adolescents with odd ideas or behaviour, or young people whose parents held odd ideas or exhibited odd behaviour, were located, and systematically interviewed and followed up at intervals. This could be attempted only with families who would be willing not only to allow their lives to be intruded upon with little warning, but also for their innermost thoughts and behaviours to be repeatedly examined. Such people would be extraordinary in allowing others to try to objectify their subjective ideation, fantasies and introspective selves. Not only would such a study be difficult to do over a long expanse of time, but also the information retrieved might be compromised by the nature of the study itself.

Categories or dimensions?

The censorship that the waking mind imposes on itself as a matter of routine, so unremarkable, normal and ordinary as to be the apotheosis of the banal, presents a further barrier to our understanding. As the Spanish writer Pio Baroja has said, "Most of us swim in the ocean of the commonplace." Some psychiatrists would like us to believe that there is an unbridgeable gap between certain people and the rest of us. This is epitomised by the broad Freudian concept of schizophrenia --- that even a touch of schizophrenia is still schizophrenia [3]. There is a tendency for classifiers of mental disorders to discuss the subjects of "borderline" and "schizotypal" disorders in such a way as to suggest that eccentricity bears a close resemblance to those conditions, or that eccentricity *is* a mental disorder, albeit of a mild sort [4]. These potential and perhaps undiscovered candidates for patienthood might be judged as ill or maladjusted by strict psychiatric standards though they might never come to viewed as such by themselves or others.

On the other hand, there is an assumption that eccentricity blends or merges somehow into mental disorder. There is a common folk belief in an overlap, or a "fine line" between normal and obviously abnormal people. People in the community will readily voice the opinion that eccentrics could be a link in this continuum. They are less sure whether there is movement along this dimension, though some psychiatrists have believed that there may be [5, 6, 7]. Other psychiatrists do commonly assert that eccentricity shades into the domains of disorder.

Some theorists take a different stance, based on different underlying premises. For example, the Italian judge and playwright Ugo Betti, sometimes referred to as the Italian Kafka, felt that "All of us are mad. If it were not for the fact every one of us is slightly abnormal, there would not be any point in giving each person a separate name." The existentialist psychiatrist R. D. Laing, by saying that "Schizophrenia is a successful attempt not to adapt to the pseudo-social realities", blurred the distinctions so far as to impute that schizophrenics are not only heroic, but choose by an exercise of rational free will to set out on their voyages of inner discovery [8]. The corollary of this is that not only is reality an illusion or a fiction, but that it also appears to some people as in some way inherently dangerous.

Most experts would claim, if pressed, that these are absurd or otherwise incorrect interpretations, and that instead, one should think of there being two independent and separate categories --- one to do with whether psychiatric disorder is present or absent (and if present, which one) and the other to do with whether the person has a personality disorder or not (and if present, which one). This view was enshrined in the "multi-axial" classification systems devised by the American Psychiatric Association, the series of Diagnostic and Statistical Manuals [9].

Criticisms have been raised in implicit dissent, indirectly, in generalities, or by inference [10, 11, 12]. Peter Tyrer and his colleagues suggested that it may be mistaken wisdom to separate mental illness diagnoses from personality disorder because some clinical presentations, such as chronic anxiety or atypical depression, occur so frequently that they might be better understood by using symptomatic and personality data in combination [13].

Supporters of multi-dimensional diagnostic patterns, probably the majority of psychiatrists, would usually place an eccentric into a personality disorder category rather than a mental illness category. It should be remembered that personality disorder is *not* mental illness. This however is at odds with the average layman's ideas on the subject. The average layman believes that the outrageous eccentric may be mentally ill.

The marginalisation of some eccentric people may point to one of the problems of mental health practice: what to do with people with rare, less decipherable or unusual characteristics. It may also be indicative of ambivalence in the face of ambiguity. There must inevitably be people who do not fit easily into any classification system. Whether the source of this categorical incongruity resides within the person, or in some poorly defined mental illness or the long-term interaction between personality and mental illness, is as yet unclear.

Might folk wisdom be wrong?

When it comes to the eccentric there is undoubted disagreement between expert professional belief and the beliefs of the wider community. As Coulter [14] has convincingly shown, ascriptions about mental illness are integrally rooted in commonsense cultural understandings, though to suggest that these might transcend well-trained psychiatric expertise may be a step too far. Members of the general public, as much as scientists, want to understand inexplicable events, or at least to receive credible explanations for events that are not within the ambit of common knowledge. How much both parties rely on perceived opinion, and tacitly share in its communication, can only begin to be perceived by trying to understand the so-called deviant's perspective. Apparently silly acts and meaningless behaviour may possibly then be apprehended as being integral to meaningful human experience, albeit as symbolic displays of defiance, brave negations of "the system", determined self-romanticising of individual compulsions, though not random, accidental, or weird coincidences. Eccentrics, of all people, might be able to provide evidence from their unique existential perspectives more ably than others.

Most psychiatrists and psychologists have very little direct cumulative experience of eccentrics. A psychiatrist may only meet several in his entire career, and then rather unusually, under inauspicious circumstances. Luckily, eccentrics are pretty deft at avoiding admission to mental hospitals. In one prestigious teaching mental hospital serving a city with a population of approximately 500,000 people, over a ten-year period only two out of 23,350 patients received at their in-patient discharge a primary diagnosis of eccentric personality. One of them was an older woman admitted to hospital briefly to research a sleep problem, and to be withdrawn from her redundant sleeping pills.

The second in-patient was a twenty-one year old university dropout, admitted because a voluntary counsellor did not really know what to make of him, though he put in writing that he suspected schizophrenia. The young man in question had been expelled from a quasi-religious cult after living with them for six weeks. "They found me disruptive," he said. "I was clogging up the works, I could not concentrate on the mental side and was permanently spaced out. I became a nuisance and they asked me to leave." The examining psychiatrist found that he spoke "easily and at length but away from the subject, unable to define clearly the topics of conversation". This patient's answers were described as "often overly intellectualised and detached, introspective and often with a high element of narcissism. On occasions his flow of thought appeared to halt suddenly and for no reason." This young man also seemed acutely aware of the reactions of other people towards him. When his mother was interviewed she said spontaneously, "When I get depressed I wonder what I have done to have such eccentric children, but when I'm well I feel glad that they have such individuality." The patient discharged himself against medical advice after less than seventy-two hours in hospital.

As we shall see, the act of affixing a psychiatric label without sufficient attention to the potential patient's personality, family background, and former beliefs can be a perilous project. The major difference of views that has occurred too often is between a familial-social-behavioural-environmental network description and a medicalized diagnosis with a treatment intervention to follow from it. These potentially opposing perspectives would not be due only to the unreliability of psychiatric diagnosis, about which psychiatrists have been candid [15, 16], but to the perceived need of doctors to be able to communicate clearly and tersely with each other in ways that signal shared professional opinions. These considerations may in turn be derived from hierarchical power relationships and ordinary career motivations.

If a psychiatrist was fairly sure of his ground, there is a strong likelihood that an eccentric individual would still receive some other label, usually consisting of a diagnosis of some mental illness or personality disorder. Disparities between everyday commonsense beliefs and professional belief systems may signal a true and real gap in our knowledge about the nature of human nature. The crucial question is whether or not eccentrics share *any* of the usual, typical core characteristics of the mentally disturbed.

A technique of discovery

It was with the above question in mind that I investigated the possible presence of various forms of so-called first-rank and second-rank symptoms of schizophrenia, and other signs of thought disorder in our eccentric sample [17]. To do this, I utilized the primary interview instrument used by research psychiatrists --- the Present State Examination, or PSE, a specially worked out series of carefully worded questions designed to elicit the symptoms of mental illness [18]. This method is based on a comprehensive assessment of a person's current and recent mental state. It was standardised to achieve comparability between different trained examiners. The basis of its underlying technique is borne out by clinical observations and an emphasis on the importance of listening to the subject's description of unusual experiences. The PSE questions were supplemented by open-ended questioning with the intention of drawing out full and complete answers about each informant's history, background and interests.

The Present State Examination was developed over a decade, and has been used in interviewing millions of people. Versions of it have been tested in a variety of settings, including two large-scale international studies [19, 20]. Its extended use over a long period of time has demonstrated how much of the variability of psychiatric diagnosis, due to subjective elements in defining, recognising, and classifying symptoms, can be reduced to more tolerable levels.

The PSE is a semi-structured interview with suggested probes for each symptom. It covers a subject's symptomatology during the previous four weeks, and abnormalities of speech and behaviour during the interview. Inter-rater reliability, the amount of agreement between independent assessors, is satisfactory. Each symptom is rated on a three- or four-point scale and there is a detailed manual giving definitions of the symptoms to be rated and indicating the levels of severity required for each point on the scale. To assess and prove the PSE's validity, computerised diagnoses were tested against clinical diagnoses during a UK-USA diagnostic comparison research project [19], and by the International Pilot Study of Schizophrenia [20]. In the latter study, only 9% of PSE diagnoses did not match with the patients' clinical diagnoses.

A number of PSE questions concern the central and obvious symptoms of schizophrenia --- visual and auditory hallucinations, and various types of delusions. In this context, these are profoundly distorting anomalies of subjective self-experience suffered by individuals who often find them inexplicable. They can occur intrusively and pervasively. Other questions on the PSE were derived from Kurt Schneider's first-rank symptoms of schizophrenia [17]. These included the following questions:

1. Hearing one's own thoughts spoken aloud.
2. Hallucinatory voices in the form of statement and reply, so that the subject hears voices speaking about him in the third person.
3. Hallucinatory voices in the form of a running commentary.
4. Bodily hallucinations, in which the subject has sensations in his body that he "knows" are produced by external agencies.
5. Thought withdrawal, in which the subject believes that his thoughts seem to be taken out of his head, as though some external person or force were removing them.

6. Thought insertion, in which the subject believes thoughts are being put into his head which he knows are not his own.
7. Thought broadcasting, in which the subject feels that his thoughts are being broadcast, so that other people know with certainty what he is thinking.
8. Thought blocking, in which the stream of conscious thought can itself become disordered. In this, a gap appears in a sequence of thought. The subject is often aware of this difficulty, and will mention or complain of it. If the person has been speaking he pauses abruptly, and when he speaks again he goes off at a tangent, like a recording with a space arbitrarily cut out of it.
9. Delusional perception, in which an abnormal significance, usually of a self-referencing nature, is attributed to a normal perception without any logical reason. For example, a patient seen by the author heard a kindly neighbour bang a door loudly, and knew in that instant that this signified that she was being systematically persecuted, without there being any objective evidence whatever to confirm malevolent intent.
10. Any events in the spheres of feelings, motivations, and free will that are experienced as manufactured or influenced by others.

Although Schneider's first-rank symptoms have proved useful for defining schizophrenia, they may also be of questionable diagnostic value, since they may be symptoms of severe breakdown [21]. However, they refer to specific, primarily verbal expressions that most people would find bizarre and difficult to perceive as "normal". These symptoms also possess enduring face validity. They have stood up well against the test of time, and have helped to differentiate, with good validity and specificity, schizophrenia and paranoid psychosis from other psychiatric disorders [22]. Formal thought disorder might show overly personalized styles of reasoning and overly fluid conceptual boundaries, which in turn may be connected to various delusional ideas. Verbal expressions based on such symptoms also make their bearer appear almost impossible to identify with, at least, it is said, without substantial deliberate efforts to empathise.

The original source of the theory behind these first-rank symptoms of schizophrenia is the work of the enigmatic and tragic Victor Tausk (1879 - 1919), who was the eldest of nine children. More than most of his colleagues at the time, he was able to grasp intuitively the inner turmoil in the minds of the disturbed. Now almost forgotten as an early contributor to Freud's program of psychoanalysis, he was the first member of the Vienna Psychoanalytic Society to study the psychoses clinically. This came at a time when Freud was interested only in treating much less disordered people.

A seriously underestimated thinker and caring clinician repeatedly making original achievements in his field, Tausk was one of the first doctors to study and treat military personnel psychologically traumatized by war. In elucidating a viable concept of personal identity, he was the first psychiatrist to draw attention to the loss of "ego boundaries" as a primary problem in schizophrenia [23]. This refers to a person's belief that everyone knows what one is thinking, that his thoughts are not enclosed within his own mind but are spread throughout the world and occur simultaneously in the minds of others, and that he might become influenced by the thoughts of other individuals, organisations or machines. Or the person may assign some of his feelings to the natural world outside himself. When suffering from these distortions of consciousness, the person in question seems no longer able to realise that he is a separate psychological entity. The individual may feel engulfed by another person or a more powerful agency. In moments of extremity, not only severe mental illness, the seemingly clear-cut distinctions of ego boundaries can be lost. In a creative person with more discrete paranoid tendencies, this could, for instance, be translated into the belief that others are trying to steal and elaborate his best ideas.

It is bitterly ironic that, over a period of six years, Freud and Tausk were acutely aware of each other's originality to the point where they each may have wondered who was deriving seminal ideas from whom. Freud believed in the possibility of "wordless communication" or "thought transference", intimations of thoughts without the mediation of known intellectual processes, what nowadays would be called mental telepathy. They were both presciently concerned about issues of scientific precedence, and eventually felt creatively inhibited in each other's company, lest one of them give away an important clue to the other, who could then progress to develop a particular thought into greater significance. What is doubly ironic, and uncanny, is that in Tausk's case there may well have been some foundation for his suspicions [24].

Special emphasis was placed during my eccentricity project on the discernment of thought disorder, and specifically on the PSE symptoms that point to its likelihood. The main reason for doing this was because eccentricity has been mentioned as a feature in schizophrenia [4], in people predisposed to schizophrenia though not necessarily suffering from it [25], schizoid personality [26, 27], schizoid personality disorder [28], and Asperger's syndrome [29]. Also, in every study since the beginning of the twentieth century, the most commonly occurring trait seen in the well, non-psychotic relatives of schizophrenic patients has been eccentric behaviour and demeanour, though usually in combination with instability, social isolation, coolness and suspiciousness [30]. Furthermore, although individuality is important to the eccentric, in schizophrenia every force impinging from the outside is feared as a threat to, or an attack on, the sufferer's individuality [31].

I simply stood this clinical evidence on its head, and wondered if symptoms that turned up frequently in schizophrenia would turn up amongst the sample of eccentrics. This would show if there was more than a circumstantial relatedness between the two conditions. Because schizophrenics might act eccentrically does not necessarily mean that eccentrics have schizophrenia. The crucial test was to ascertain the frequency of occurrence and the severity of characteristic first-rank symptoms of schizophrenia among eccentrics, using the questions and criteria laid out in the Present State Examination. The results of this were indeed surprising: the answers to my questions were unexpected, and they were the first tangible evidence that the eccentrics' mental lives were unlike anything noted previously by any other psychologist.

Beginning to cut through the Gordian knot

As can be seen in Table 6 and Table 7, symptoms commonly associated with schizophrenia were prevalent in the eccentric sample, albeit in mild form and infrequent occurrence. These mild and infrequent symptoms can best be described as subtle "micro-psychotic episodes" of the type that the noted psychopathologist Paul Meehl [32] described as one of several diagnostic signs of either a pre-schizophrenic state or schizotypal personality. Thought insertion was the sole exception; to a person, each subject believed very much that his or her thoughts were uniquely and originally his or her own. This was a characteristic pattern that ran through each individual's entire self-presentation.

Table 6. PSE first-rank symptoms of schizophrenia among the eccentrics

Symptom	Symptom absent	Symptom mild		Symptom severe
		Infrequent	Sometimes	
Thoughts being read	76 (58%)	47 (37%)	7 (5%)	---
Thought insertion	130 (100%)	---		---
Thought broadcast	120 (92%)	5 (4%)	4 (3%)	1 (1%)
Thought echo/commentary	73 (56%)	55 (42%)		2 (2%)
Thought withdrawal	83 (64%)	39 (30%)	7 (5%)	1 (1%)
Delusions of Alien forces controlling mind	110 (84%)	15 (12%)	4 (3%)	1 (1%)

This was the first time that these symptoms have been picked up to this extent from any sample derived directly from the community. In point of fact, the thought disorder and delusion questions from the PSE previously were very often omitted from random community surveys of mental illness, precisely because they were thought to occur uncommonly. It was believed that if someone had these symptoms, he or she would already have been diagnosed and be under treatment. However, not all of the above symptoms cause reciprocally widening alienation from others, nor do they inevitably immobilize the possibility of positive personal changes. Research in the Netherlands has shown that the incidence of subclinical psychotic experiences in the general population is around a hundred times greater than traditional estimates of the incidence of psychotic disorders such as schizophrenia [33]. It has become increasingly clearer that an unknown number of people undergo remarkable and curious experiences, some of which are transformative and might even be positive, that would unfold less happily had they been prematurely referred to a psychiatrist.

Hearing voices is also prevalent to some degree throughout the population, experienced by many people without any discernible mental disorder, though more frequently in those shaped by, or currently undergoing, a multiplicity of unfavourable circumstances. Between three per cent and ten per cent of people regularly hear voices that are not heard by other people. Far from all such voices become malevolent or distressing to those who can hear them, though some voices may be heard during times of stress. For many, these auditory hallucinations can be sympathetic or heartening, providing the hearer with a friendly source of support and comfort. A good proportion of those who can hear voices consider the experience to be a valuable and positive aspect of their lives. Some find that it can provide positively creative ways of coping with adversity.

Table 7. Other PSE symptoms of schizophrenia among the eccentrics

Symptom	Symptom absent	Mild/doubtful	Moderate	Severe
Auditory Hallucinations	87 (67%)	17 (13%)	15 (12%)	11 (8%)
Visual Hallucinations	84 (64%)	14 (11%)	15 (12%)	17 (13%)
Delusional Misinterpretation	71 (54%)	27 (21%)	25 (19%)	7 (6%)
Persecutory Delusions	52 (40%)	51 (39.5%)	25 (19%)	2 (1.5%)
Religious Delusions	61 (47%)	46 (35%)	16 (12%)	7 (6%)
Paranormal Delusions	96 (73.5%)	15 (12%)	11 (8%)	8 (6.5%)

The second significant finding is that although there was a high proportion (95 out of 130 eccentric informants, or 73%) of the sample with one or more of these symptoms, only *one* individual had a full-blown psychosis at interview. This was a male subject, Simon, who in addition to having many of the cardinal signs and symptoms of paranoid schizophrenia also demonstrated delusions of grandiose ability and grandiose identity. He would have been recognised as being unequivocally ill by any psychiatrist within ten minutes. The following excerpt from this man's interview shows his typical way of talking about himself: "To Monty (Field Marshal Montgomery) I was better known as the Chief Scout of the British Army. Captured Cicero . . . took British invasion plans, then changed them to suit us. History books all lie, saying that Britain was invincible. By becoming German, I literally killed Rommel, outclassed General von Runstadt. Directed the British in the Battle of the Bulge even before it happened. [brief bout of uncontrollable laughter] No one has shot me yet! So keeping out of the limelight line of sight has proved without doubt using one's own initiative and mind. No stupid spy stories' ideas, cannot catch you out with letters, phone tapping, meeting people, reading papers, but they only know the name the grandson of General . . . No one knows where he is. He sends funny postcards to the government telling them openly what's going to happen. News for everybody!"

(Simon, age fifty-eight)

What was more surprising about the above volunteer was that he too had wholly avoided doctors and psychiatrists, and had never been properly diagnosed or treated. In fact, the evidence does suggest that the prevalence of "abnormal" psychiatric symptoms in ostensibly normal populations is quite high. When one studies actual referrals to psychiatrists for out-patient treatment, or actual in-patient admissions to hospital, and compare these to complaints about people living in the community with possible abnormal behaviour, one finds that there are many would-be "cases" that never come to medical or psychiatric attention. States of being that are characteristic of mental illness are widespread in the broader community. The number of untreated cases in the community with "abnormal" psychiatric symptoms may indeed be higher than the cases receiving treatment [34, 35]. Added to this are the increasing numbers of psychiatrically diagnosed patients who are being treated and cared for in the community.

Delusions based on paranormal beliefs

Occurring more commonly in this study were the kinds of minimal delusional belief that some would wish to think of as merely "normal" irrationality rather than partial delusion. At best, some eccentrics seem to have an affinity for the uncanny, and for supernatural explanations. Such is the case in the following excerpt from another eccentric informant, Peter, here expressing his beliefs about the creatures that inhabit his paranormal universe: "It can be dangerous. You can create sort of low entities, low, low people, because I do believe there is another world, and I don't think this is the only one, and I think animates, I call them, sort of low animals . . . would come and could interfere and could play a lot of mischief with you. I felt strange energies. Sometimes I wonder if I've ever been possessed by one. I don't know, hope not . . . I did see half a cat float by in the air when I was in Belfast --- I was telling them about it --- they had never had a cat in their boarding house --- it looked like half a cat. I don't know whether at work I imagined I saw somebody who died in a horrific firebombing --- I was coming up from the shop floor . . . just for a minute . . . and there he was . . . I have seen these sorts of beings on one or two occasions since."

(Peter, age sixty)

There is clearly a hallucinatory quality to this account. The connection between illusory misperception and ingrained beliefs is not lost in such individuals. It is also clearly evident in many of the individuals susceptible to similar symptoms. Take, for another example, this verbatim account by Jon, who embodied many of the key elements of eccentricity: "Possibly a jag (injection), before going into the operating theatre . . . I have seen a Christ-like figure . . . but I have seen them when I have had no jag as well. I see figures . . . not every day of the week . . . but that is just me . . . I have run after figures . . . absolutely bonkers . . . out of my mind . . . then you discover when you look back through history books that Lady so-and-so stayed in that same room in the castle and she had seen a spectre on this hill and so on . . . so I hadn't imagined it after all. I delve in this, and would trace back that spectre or whatever it was, and that lady, the lady did exist.

"Wanting to get to nature, I have gone out to places that maybe I shouldn't have. I felt myself teetering on the edge of an abyss. This becomes sort of murky. There could have been strange changes in me. I have had long walks through nocturnal landscapes. I have gone to cemeteries --- not to prove a point that I was bonkers when I chased a cloaked figure --- I'm no spiritualist anyway, but I have given lectures on it and somebody has come up and they have said something --- if I am talking I don't like to be interrupted, it is bad manners, and I am like thinking, 'What the hell did that person say . . . that was funny.' . . . I will have to go back the next time to the same place, but I wasn't giving a lecture so I have no right to be on the platform . . . but I inveigled my way in so I could get a better view. . . I had the CID (Criminal Investigation Department) and the Psychic College looking for this cloaked figure . . . who I described.

"If you scratch the surface of Life, there's a lot of weirdness underneath! I was talking to this couple and this lady came up and said, 'I believe you are looking for her,' and I thought, 'Oh no!' and again was interrupted . . . 'I have been looking for someone but it certainly wasn't you!' This woman repeated the exact same words that had been repeated in my vision, so I had to take them seriously . . . I said 'You write your name and address down there and I will come and see you tonight' --- I would have got a shock if it had been Aberdeen. It turned out that I had described her spirit guide. 'I hadn't seen you. I had seen your spirit guide.' I can't help it!"

(Jon, age sixty-one)

To this man, each instance of things out of the ordinary is both a revelatory experience and a fragment of evidence for his ideas. Extraordinary occurrences come to be taken with an air of acceptance, and almost predictability. Truth is conceived of as revealed light. When it happens the first time, its illumination is blinding, though eventually such exceptional events come almost to be expected, if not taken for granted. Wreathed in their new understandings of secret connections, the saved, and the savants, are luminous, undaunted, victorious. They carry, and glow with, an inner light. Inspiration becomes revelation, and both seem to be transmitted from an apparent external, barely knowable agency.

Religious delusions

In this occult tendency, the external agency assumes a universal spiritual dimension, and its bearer may contract the sense of shouldering an outwardly unwanted mission. For non-conformists of all shades, resistance against authority or the attractions of social conformity sometimes also can have a spiritual dimension, rationalized believably with a sense of an existential responsibility to a higher cause. For instance, James Joyce in *A Portrait of the Artist as a Young Man* wrote about how he discovered that he felt compelled "to forge the conscience of his race in the smithy of his soul".

This way of thinking, and its content, comes out in the way these affected people talk about their beliefs. However, as the eminent philosopher A. J. Ayer pointed out, ". . . sentences which simply express moral judgements do not say anything . . . They are unverifiable for the same reason as a cry of pain or a word of command is unverifiable --- because they do not express genuine propositions." He also opined that religious experiences could also be based on self-deception, unless the believer "can formulate his 'knowledge' in propositions that are empirically verifiable." [36]

More strictly delusional content seeks to be all-inclusive, and to encompass cosmic verities. These primitive thought-feelings share many similarities with those experienced by mystics of many persuasions and temperaments, Zen Buddhists, artists, and delusional psychiatric patients [37]. Time and space become suspended, and there are dramatic oscillations of mood. In what we think of as our current age of rational thinking and scepticism, their degree of subjective certainty that anything is possible in the spiritual realm might imply a qualitative departure from the encumbrances of ordinary sense. With the latter comes an increase in feelings of personal freedom. There is also an equal and opposite intensification: delusion can fixate a person's beliefs into an unshakable stasis. The paradox is that the sense of a new or revitalised purpose sometimes also brings with it real feelings of transitory shame.

In our sample of one hundred and thirty eccentric people there was a significant association between having a paranormal delusion and having a religious delusion (r = + 0.31, p < 0.001). [The small r refers to the degree of positive correlation, or association, between the two types of delusion. The small p refers to the probability, or the likelihood that such a correlation could be the product of chance. In this case, the correlation is deemed highly statistically significant because it could have arisen by chance in less than one in a thousand instances.] Put another way, more than four-fifths of those with paranormal delusions also had experienced at least one religious delusion. Forms and rituals of normal religion have been interpreted in the past as showing similarities with obsessive acts [38]. Bizarre religious practices based upon superstitious notions have been considered to be less harmful because they are acted on in common with other likeminded believers within a particular culture. Other beliefs have been compared with the religious themes presented by some delusional schizophrenics [39]. In addition, paranormal mythology sometimes interpenetrates normal religious beliefs.

One of the eccentric informants, a faithful Quaker, described the relationships between his beliefs: "I used to think I had one or two familiar dream environments long ago where separate dreams fitted into another life. I sometimes also have a superstitious feeling that if things go well for me it is because I have been trying hard to do what is right, to the benefit of others. Knowledge of the spirit in all of us can most usefully derive from individual experience of ourselves, and, on occasion, from others more attuned to such matters. I feel that there is a little bit of God in everyone. There are other links between people too, such as telepathy. God is entirely within people. All people."

(Grant, age forty)

Certain prophetic or clairvoyant dreams, because they seem unusual and uncanny, are one of the sources originating within an individual's mind that then lead on to, or seem to corroborate, more commonly occurring paranormal and religious beliefs. Such dreams are given as evidence of otherworldly explanations because they contain within them kernels of truth or the communicable expression of more universal existential yearnings. For people who feel sufficiently sensitive to receive and interpret such dreams, the dreams initially make them feel uneasy, are somewhat more memorable, are difficult to dismiss out of hand, and offer significant meaningfulness. The messages they contain, occasionally giving them an essence of some veracity, also hold out the promise of revealing to receptive dreamers where they stand in relation to others in their here-and-now social environment.

Unusual theological theorising can also spring from a preceding interest in scientific matters. Either can interlock with other beliefs that are at least atypical. Take, for instance, the following interview excerpt from another of the eccentric informants, which I include at length to show the interweaving connections, baffling discontinuities between different content areas, and how an ostensibly scientific approach can blend into assertion and speculation: "I got my religious beliefs by scientifical reasoning. I believe that my brainwaves are from the Holy Spirit. I believe that I have an intellectual relation with God and Jesus via the Holy Spirit, which does not mean that I feel physically surrounded by God and Jesus. I believe that God communicates with me in the form of brainwaves via the Holy Spirit. Once, I prayed for an indication or proof of a supposition, and I found that indication written in a book that I had already bought that same day. I meet so many people who do not understand or believe my theories --- scientists --- or who take offence at the scientific solution of the theological problems --- so-called Christians. Even the most advanced dogmatic systems display only the caricature of science, although the orthodox denominations suggest that their dogmatic systems are drafted rectilinearly, ie., not contrary to the Bible.

"My theory of the descent of man is contrary to the evolution theory but also such that most people should call me a racist if they knew of it. According to several calculations, I expect God's millennial kingdom of peace about the year 2000.

"The ten tribes of Israel arrived, after many wanderings, either voluntarily, as Celts, Gaels, Cimmerians, or forced via the Assyrian exile, as Germanics or Nordics, into Western Europe, and established there some Christian kingdoms. One or more of these kingdoms must form a bridgehead for the establishment of God's millennial Messianic kingdom Israel, and as such I consider the kingdom of Great Britain to be it, of which the Davidic throne will be occupied by Jesus.

"It is difficult to obtain an idea of the relation between material and spiritual things, but much of this may be explained mathematically if you assume that spiritual matter with respect to material matter has relative velocities which exceed the velocity of light, but then in a spiritual space. Mathematically, it may be demonstrated that under definite conditions a material particle and a spiritual particle, which hit upon each other and then integrate with each other, disappear, such that the new particle is neither material nor spiritual. The Creation of Heaven and Earth out of God, not out of nothing as many learn, may be considered as a reversed process, so that this may also be explained mathematically. From the foregoing may be a mathematical-metaphysical explanation for the appearance of ghosts, angels, and Unidentified Flying Objects. Physicists cannot, by definition, realise such a metaphysical act, so that we must assume that only God is capable of this."

(Ian, age fifty-two)

Some of Ian's above ideas are not original to him, but would be properly called "received ideas". For example, the notion of the "descent of man" has been taught, until fairly recently, in some primary and secondary faith schools, and not necessarily fundamentalist ones either. Little wonder that Richard Dawkins in his book *The God Delusion* may have felt justified in using such potentially hurtful and stigmatising psychiatric language to describe his atheistic thesis. However, it would be more realistic to confine the terminology of mental illness to genuinely strange beliefs in unusual individuals rather than the blanket condemnation of all "believers". The diagnosis of a psychiatric disorder should not be made solely on the basis of a person's or a group's faith or beliefs, however absurd rational scientifically-minded people might consider them to be.

If one were to ask eccentric individuals how they came by some of their extraordinary ideas, or why they harboured such beliefs, their immediate answer would be in the form of "evidence", although derived from hallucinatory experience (for example, "Because many of the departed ask me for help, without problem."), or from near death experiences (for example, "On no less than five occasions my life has been prolonged or spared. For example, my heart stopped for a full minute after a knee operation. It was then that I grasped my most profound insight."). The following individual's description shows what is known as depersonalisation, a symptom of fear and panic which commonly can occur under such conditions: "I talk to somebody sometimes, I don't know who it is, generally when I am looking for some kind of sign or signal or message. I don't know who that is --- it may be God, it may be me . . . another part of me. The main thing which started me becoming interested in parapsychology was that I was in a very nasty car smash and the police sergeant told me that I was lucky to be alive, and I was sure I was going to die, it was the only time in my life that I have been certain that I was going to die.

"I was on the correct side of the road, not travelling very fast and this furniture van is going very fast down the hill, we were inside a forty mile an hour limit. He couldn't take the corner, and he came right at me. I was in a Mini with the furniture van coming right at me, and I just sat there terrified for less than a second and then when I was terrified --- 'I know this is it, this is it,' I said to myself, 'This is the end of everything.' The next question that came into my mind was, 'I wonder what happens next,' and at that moment it was almost as if I had left the car --- I don't feel I was in the car seat anymore and I was in an absolutely strange sort of ecstasy --- it is terribly difficult to describe but I seemed to be merged --- it was as if I had almost disappeared --- the fact that I can feel this meant that I was there in a sense, it seemed to be merged with everything else in this marvellous ecstasy, and the next thing I was aware of, it was as if two giants were throwing my car, a little toy car, to each other, it might have been up in the air, somersaulting and careering; I seemed to be thrown about the car and I was sitting doing the aircraft emergency drill, I protected my head and everything, and I had this strange experience and I was very surprised I remember. This must have been seconds --- I found myself sitting --- 'Good heavens, I am still sitting' --- I remember saying that to myself, 'I am still sitting here in the front seat, the driving seat of my own car.' My mind was whirling."

(Lorna, age forty-eight)

Of note in this is that it was such a lived experience that there are telling changes in tense; those changes are not there for dramatic effect alone. The significance of such events is that they stay in the eccentric person's memory, and indeed, reverberate down the years, as in the following: "My whole religious outlook has been tempered by an experience I had as a small child listening to music --- the whole thing ties up and I found it a very interesting circle because I had experience of, as it were, touching God, and that changes one's whole ideas. Bible stories seem pretty crass when you have experienced that, so this has, although I was only a toddler, affected my whole outlook. In a sense I am very certain of things, but I don't need anything that the Church offers me. I was lifted above myself, outwith myself and met the angels and came face to face with God and felt I knew everything and could know everything.

"It was very brief but it was quite interesting how being so small I have remembered --- every time I heard the music that aroused it in the first place I recalled the whole experience, until I was in my twenties, so the music prompted my memory, time and time again. It has changed my whole view. Everybody is equally close, it is whether . . . it is a choice whether you choose to look that way or not, but everybody is the same. Yes, I suppose I have a great confidence in myself. Having had that one experience, things are on a different level. One is experiencing it in a different way --- from a point of view of a certainty as opposed to a doubt. My inner work has to do with expanding consciousness."

(Helene, age forty-five)

Helene was one of a number of informants who had both religious and paranormal experiences, and she interpreted these in terms of mysticism and psychic energy, and also from a scientific perspective: "I tend to have flashes when I see things from the past occurring on many occasions; I can't always turn it on, which is a pity, because I sometimes want to. These are things like being aware --- I had a horrible sensation every time I visited a battlefield, so strongly that I then got to the point, whenever I had this sensation, that I knew that I was on a battlefield. I also found it very unpleasant visiting places where other ghastly things had happened, but again it is a different sensation. I have learnt to know it --- there are all sorts of varieties of this thing as well as having time lapses, vaguely seeing or experiencing things that have happened in the past. Never clear enough to put into my research unfortunately. I don't see things as much as perhaps becoming aware of things.

"Probably the most spectacular thing I have seen was a grand new shining dragon over York Cathedral . . . very intriguing. I very rarely become that aware of whatever these forces are. The only thing I have heard that I feel is outside me, a very strange phenomenon, has happened at places that some people call earth power points, in connection with Ley lines, which I am sceptical about but I haven't discarded completely, but at these power points I hear music, which knowing enough about music, I understand what it is, I understand what music itself is . . . I think it is the same as what some people call 'fairy music', but I don't know. I think somewhere in the depths of this there will turn out to be a scientific explanation."

(Helene, age forty-five)

Several of the eccentric informants with religious preoccupations put forward "causes" originating in earlier development with transcendental experiences, carrying much emotion and sustaining their conviction over a lifetime: "About age eight, I climbed a tree and found a part of God there --- a strong feeling of God's love for me and all living things. God is the total universe, I have a twenty-four hour constant awareness of my love for the human species and all life everywhere."

(June, age fifty)

"I touched an absolute rock bottom, I don't think I ever felt so alone, so desperate, so shattered in all my life. I felt alone wherever I was, on my own or not. Nowhere felt like home. I cried aloud, 'God, why am I so bad that even the church rejects me?' and suddenly this happened --- light flooded the April dusk --- I can't describe this because this is the light that never was on land or sea --- a quality of light --- it was soft, yet it was clear and shining and it was in through everything. I was sitting looking out at the rolling hills and they seemed transformed, they were lit from within --- and the daffodils around the lawn, I remember them --- everything had a quality of life which was extra to what the daffodils would have. Even the furniture in the room seemed sort of pulsey with this kind of life.

"Then it moved from there to a feeling that time had stopped and that I was in a stage of timelessness, and I thought, 'This is eternity,' and I did a bit of thinking about eternity. 'Eternity,' I thought, 'is here and now'. It is a dimension, underlying the flux of things, if you like, the passing seconds, it is here and now --- and I seemed to know then that in eternity I was fully known and understood, and then it was as if I mounted a ladder through different stages, from timelessness I moved into something which was --- after timelessness came, what? Anyway, I maybe haven't got it in sequence --- but there was a stage of peace and joy, and then came an ecstatic epiphany, and then I was in the kingdom of love --- the Living Presence --- and I was at one with this powerful spiritual force, and I knew it was within me and without me and that this was the beating heart which sustained creation to the furthest galaxy, if you like.

"Then there was a period of enlightenment, when I seemed to know the whole secret of the universe. I just seemed to know everything, all the causes of strife and wars and misery. Unfortunately, I didn't remember these, but what I did remember was that people were blind. The hour was late by this time, I didn't know how long it lasted --- it got dark and the curious thing was that this light was within the darkness --- I was still in this tremendous state of ecstasy, and underneath me I knew here, now and always, in life and in death, were the everlasting hours. I had nothing whatsoever to fear."

(Kirstin, age forty-eight)

There is a great emphasis placed on the forces of inner and outer harmony, nature, and a cosmic order ineffably beyond the expression of mere words. These forces are doing battle with, and finally vanquishing, what are seen to be society's claims for conventional humdrum sufferance, and are able to overcome people's petty cynicism.

This type of mystical approach has been called Promethean [40]. In those who show it, there is an idealistic ordering of values that shows a strong belief in the necessity for significant change. In regard to the eccentrics' serious ideals, they are more than fantasies put into action, and are far from unimportant. There is a wish to remake the world so that other people will come to follow the new true believer's revitalized example and precepts that they had previously misunderstood or derided. Unlike the opinions of the psychiatrist Leon Salzman, who said that such messianic dedication was "an attempt to deal with extreme feelings of worthlessness" [41], this proved not to be the case with the eccentric informants. In addition to their main salvation-related orientation, they also stressed the goodness of possessing a rich inner life of heightened self-awareness, insight, and a deep sympathy with all living things. The eccentrics did not however repudiate the desire to control other people. Objectively, they were not very receptive or responsive to others, and usually they did not feel the need to be of service to specific groups, or to meet the needs of other people. They were equally able to abstain from, or partake enthusiastically in, what one eccentric called "the earthly delights and pleasures".

Differences between eccentrics with and without schizophrenia-like symptoms

Part of the descriptive task in an exploratory study is not only to find the similarities and common features of the group in question, but also to find distinguishing features or differences between group members. The first such exercise I undertook was to compare and contrast eccentrics with schizophrenic-like symptoms from eccentrics without such symptoms. The initial step was to formulate a measure of their psychoticism or psychosis-proneness relative to each other. This measure was composed of the severity of their schizophrenic-like symptoms multiplied by the number of them. It would then be possible to divide the entire sample into two, forming a sub-group of those on the "normal" side of this continuum (scoring low on this factor), and another sub-group of those on the "abnormal" side of this continuum (scoring high on this factor). This is known as a median split. A more complicated way of grouping the informants would be to divide the original group into three sub-groups --- those with low psychoticism, those with middle-level psychoticism, and those with high total psychoticism.

The data from the resulting sub-groups was then submitted to a complex mathematical technique known as discriminant function analysis. This can help to pick out the crucial differences between the sub-groups. The results derived are in terms of locating which variables, either alone or in combination, best account for, or explain, the sub-group differences. These variables can then better help to define the differences between the two or three sub-groups.

Using this technique I established that the median-split high psychoticism and low-psychoticism sub-groups were most different from each other on the following variables, in order of importance: degree of superstition, quality of religious experiences, and the feeling of being psychologically incomplete most of the time.

Using the same technique, but first dividing the sample into high psychoticism, low to intermediate psychoticism, and non-psychoticism sub-groups, showed that the following variables best differentiated the sub-groups: superstition; the positive quality of remembered "high points" or peak experiences in one's life; expressed criticism in the parental family; degree of imagination; feeling that it is very difficult to love others; quality of religious experiences; degree of problem-solving ability; feelings of destructive anger; the trusting-suspecting personality dimension; religiosity; and reported poor concentration. In this solution there was one curvilinear, or inverted U-shaped relationship: the low psychoticism sub-group had experienced an unremarkable quality to their lifetime high points, the intermediate psychoticism sub-group had experienced a good, positive quality to their lifetime high points, and the high psychoticism sub-group had experienced a very poor quality to their high points.

These variables can be combined in order to predict into which group any new eccentric would most naturally belong. This can be accompanied with an overall rate of predictive accuracy of approximately eighty-five per cent. In this particular instance, correct classification was not the primary reason for having recourse to computer-aided mathematical analysis. Rather, such an analysis points out not only which variables are relevant, but also those that are latently or more obliquely associated with the possession of schizophrenic-like features. This would pertain especially to the people in this sample, but perhaps also to other individuals who resemble them psychologically. These latent variables, or "co-variates", included the rated severity of any stressful life events experienced; the degree of creativity and originality; expressed criticism in the parental family directed at the eccentric as a child; an interest in politics; dramatic swings of love and hate; an interest in science; the quality and number of spare time activities; and younger chronological age. These co-variates may or may not be causally implicated in the inception or maintenance of schizophrenia-like symptoms. These co-variates nevertheless are important in building up an evidence-led mosaic of psychological concordances between schizophrenics and eccentrics. Using this information, it would then be possible to compare these findings with what is already known about "true" schizophrenic disorders.

By and large, eccentrics do not lose touch with reality. They have excellent insight into their behaviour. However, if schizophrenia and eccentricity share more than superficial similarities, findings from the latter might usefully be extended to the former, and to be informative in ways not possible to achieve by looking at one group in isolation. Positive empirical evidence from the field about one group might also apply to the other. This is implied by continuum/dimensional psychological models, ranging from healthy normality through to overt mental illness.

One obvious similar factor has to do with the amount and nature of expressed emotion in the immediate families of schizophrenics, and how it has been shown to be related to relapse [42, 43]. This bears some similarity to the picture presented by the eccentrics, in which their schizophrenic-like symptoms are more likely to emerge in those whose family life contained a general atmosphere of perceived criticism. This is compounded, in both the schizophrenic and the eccentric cases, if the criticism is negative and hostile, and specifically directed at, or felt to be focused on, the individual in question. The schizophrenic flees back, or more frequently is taken back, into hospital with a recrudescence of acute active symptoms, whilst the eccentric begins to be affected by similar hallucinations and delusions, though these are of lesser severity. The affected eccentrics' isolated symptoms are milder, less protracted and have different consequences, though they are otherwise essentially similar. They are different from the delusions of most psychotic people in that they are more intimately bound up with the eccentrics' personalities. They are not as distressing to the latter as they usually would be to a psychiatric patient with schizophrenia. Indeed they may be heartily relished by the eccentrics. They become positively motivating, directing at least some of the eccentrics' seemingly boundless energies.

That suspiciousness is involved points to how personality features can become formative in the development of deeply irrational systems of thinking. This presents another point of similarity with certain forms of paranoid psychosis and paranoid schizophrenia.

As in these conditions, it is difficult to work out whether the personality traits contribute directly or indirectly to the delusions of persecution, and whether having had a delusion like this once alters the personality in a generally more suspicious direction. This has always been a difficult issue to disentangle. Kolle [44] described similarly peculiar, reclusive individuals who stood all their lives on the brink of frank paranoid psychosis. However, the eminent European psychiatrist Willy Mayer-Gross pointed out that, faced with such an individual, one could never really tell whether it was the original personality one saw or a personality that had undergone a "weird" alteration [45]. However, psychiatric researchers Anderson and Guerra found little connection between suspicious ideas of personal reference --- quite unfounded ideas that others are referring to the sufferer in their speech, writing or gestures --- and any particular personality type [46]. Part of this may be due to the mysteries of that unknowable inner sanctum of the thinking process --- the mind. On the emotional and non-verbal front, the same might be said about a person emoting or behaving in a particular way. Is the other person's emotional outpouring genuine or an act? Are his protestations based on truth or a lie? The person with paranoia cannot know these things unless he really knows and trusts the other person, and even then he might be led astray.

The paranoid beliefs of the eccentrics were held with almost as much conviction and seriousness as is usual for people who are plagued by delusions. The most commonly voiced beliefs concerned the theft of their ideas, firstly by others, then by the Prime Minister or the intelligence and security services, who might intercept their communications or interfere with them in other ways. As has been seen in recent events, it has turned out that some of these latter beliefs may be based more on reality than these informants could have known at the time.

The Prime Minister or cabinet ministers were referred to personally, sometimes by their first names, as if they had been rivals for so long that they had become like old comrades. Some of these eccentrics' missives to authority figures or politicians were more querulous, verging on the litigious: "If I get my oar into something, I never let go. I write letters to various people to influence and bend their trends of thoughts. Two weeks ago I wrote to Mr. Paton, a Conservative under-minister. I wrote to Mr. Paton and said that he should resign, and explained why. I knew that he wouldn't reply to my letter because I have written this kind of letter before to many different people, but I do this to get results because people don't like being told they are no good. But it will prick his conscience and he will now start to take an active interest in a subject he obviously knows nothing about. So what did he do? He gave the letter to somebody else, who gave it to somebody else, and then a civil servant was told to write to me the usual futile letter that such people always do write, and it is there but for the grace of God go I, because if I had gone into administration probably I would be a lap dog as well."
(Dr A. D. G. Milco, age sixty)

Harbouring superstitious beliefs could provide the underlying habits of thought on which more aberrant patterns of thinking come into being and are then given more credibility. Feeling incomplete, feeling that it is difficult to give love, and rigidly containing destructive anger --- these are mainly the emotions on which such beliefs thrive. This mode of thinking hinges on creating defence mechanisms to ward off dangerous feelings that the person might give in to trusting others. The attitude of distrusting relationships as too unpredictable limits the motivation of such people to make friends. In addition, luck is seen as powerful. The force of destiny, as an all-purpose explanation, is a preferred belief --- in this view, it is more potent than oneself or the machinations of other people.

Superstition is redolent with meaning. It represents more than a perversion of truth. All that a superstition means or implies is interpreted by the believer as true. There can be no more pervasive form of mild self-delusion, and this applies also to eccentrics, and more so for those with mild schizophrenic-like symptoms. No one should feel above the pitfalls of superstitious thinking. It is part of the human condition. Every person who holds a misguided concept is certain of his own rationality, as well as the irrationality of those holding opposing viewpoints.

Otherworldly, uncanny experiences must involve, at a higher level, many philosophical and psychological perplexities. These include the nature of the relationships between mind and body, fact and value, sensory experience and derived surmise. When they do involve lifelong obsessive preoccupations, it is sometimes possible to detect and trace the temporal connections between an individual's interests, attitudes, personality traits, and beliefs. This is shown in the following excerpt, given at full length to demonstrate how the different clues all fit together into a coherent constellation: "I have had a recurring dream almost all my life --- I can take steps up into space. It is fantastic! I can't understand it. I don't know.

"I am psychic. I often get predictive, so-called precognitive dreams. Well, they say I am different because I have these different dreams. That is how I see these Unidentified Flying Objects. They harp on back to this subject . . . it's not . . . some people see them, some people don't.

"People too, no offence to them. God, if I meet them in the street, I can read it in their eyes, and their face will light up, and I have always wanted to ask what they see in me and I never have . . . I don't know what they see but it is almost . . . you pass some in the street, some poor soul . . . I remember them laughing at me . . . they must see something but I don't know what it is. There must be something --- people for some unknown reason start telling me their pasts and I don't know why they do that.

"I don't particularly even like people. A lot of folk get up . . . as if to say, 'Which drain did you crawl out from?' Well, I don't think I belong here, I have been here before. When I was it had something to do with the sea, sailing ships . . . I think I was . . .

"There are some people who have to be in control of a situation, because I know exactly what I am doing. I will take over the leadership of whatever it is --- a road accident, anything. I will take over that road accident in Morningside this afternoon . . . and I will control the police . . . and they will all do as I tell them . . . I don't know why. It has happened in actual traffic accidents. I take over the whole situation --- I am not involved --- and they all kind of jump to it: 'Three bags full sir'.

"I am contradicting myself! I don't have faith in other people. I seem to think I know I can do it better. I think that it is that human beings make mistakes and faults, and they are brushed under the carpet --- I am a very particular person. I never seem to think the other person knows what they are doing --- and somehow I won't go out of my way --- but somehow or other I land up taking control of the other person. I go for an interview for Legal Aid for a High Court case I've been battling recently. I have disputed things that I knew were wrong. The lady said, 'You know, I am supposed to be interviewing you. You have been sitting here and you have been interviewing me!' I said, 'Well, I put you in your place --- you were needing it.'

"I have been asked by a minister not to go to his church, because he knew that one day I was going to stand up and argue with him and he was going to lose. They count the galaxies in billions . . . they count the galaxies . . . and we are in a grain of sand in a big beach in a silver system on a galaxy, and there are billions and billions of stars in one galaxy, and they count the galaxies in billions. There are another forty-five religions and they all think they are right.

"I have always had these beliefs. When I was a wee bairn (child) I used to be outside with my father's overcoat on. I had a telescope and I used to look up at the stars. I just didn't believe. I was sent to Sunday school once and my father asked me what I thought of it, and I told him, and then he slapped my face, but I was never sent back.

"I think there were people here from another planet, dumped here before they blew themselves up, and they have blown themselves up here, and maybe they took them away and brought them back again. Space. Everybody feels they belong to space. You are not earthbound. You look, looking up on a starry night, let your imagination wander . . . I haven't got the imagination . . . it can wander without the imagination . . . you belong to space. If you open a cell door, you don't belong in there, but if you look up at space on a sunny day, you are a part of it, you belong to it . . . not the cell.

"I think it was the challenge at the time away back in the (nineteen) forties. If you mentioned space and objects coming from space, you were a right nutcase, but the challenge was to convince you of the possibility. Why shouldn't there be other things, not with green heads and television masks? I wasn't unique. This idea was either their own experience, or a group of people's experiences, and it started when they were all seeing things . . . other folk seeing things.

"I had bought a caravan and stayed up on a hill called Fantasy Hill. I got an expert to try and trace the origin of the name . . . what it meant, the nearest he could get was the Hill of the Fairies. I don't know why I went up that hill --- it was fantastic! I don't know who the hell it is, but I am never alone. This fellow came to see me once. The sun was shining, I could sense this guy . . . his position --- he was kneeling! I said, 'What the hell is wrong with you?' I made him a cup of coffee. He said, 'I just want to get out of here. Just walk across the hill with me.' Christ, this was a great big grown man wearing trousers. 'You're not a man at all!' I said. Later, a friend, I was telling him about it, he said, 'I visited you up there one night. It wasn't you. You have got beings in that caravan that you can't see . . . I was scared out of my wits. I had to ask my wife to take me home. No wonder that guy in the morning was scared --- you are not alone up there.' I don't think I am."

(Chris, age sixty-six)

The descriptions of these episodic phenomena are very like a series of connected "over-valued ideas". To their bearer, these ideas are seen as mostly natural rather than intrusive, though he can certainly recognise through experience how others might find them strange. He accepts, he acquiesces to the seeming reality of his experiences. He does not mount any intellectual resistance to them. His thoughts and ideas are "ego-syntonic". He did not regard them, when taken together, as senseless or futile; quite the reverse. While able to laugh at the awkward positions his ideas placed him in, he generally regarded them with some gravity.

"Premonitions are not fantasies. They are as real as an intuition about someone you know, how you are made to feel when you are with them. Though your intuitions may not always save you from yourself, there are similar premonitions that come to many of us. Sadly, too many people, thinking themselves sensible, ignore these kernels of hidden secret knowledge. When I became absorbed by the occult, it made a few connections in my thinking, though I reserved judgement when I met some of the charlatans and dupes involved in it."

(Osbert, age sixty-two)

Ideas of the above kind have been seen as impediments to "correct" thinking. They illustrate a depth of consciousness. For those who use such ideas, ordinary practical thinking seems to feel unsafe, or a hindrance. There can be little peace, no compromise, and few feelings of inner security. They are imbued with uncanny intuitions --- knowing without thinking, a kind of knowing that flies in the face of reality. This represents a kind of cognitive distortion, one to which we all may have some access. Every time you gamble or take a risk, or act on a hunch, or follow a superstition, you enter this absurd domain governed by blind instincts and impulses. Why do they occur? To understand logical thinking is not enough. A good starting point might be the reputedly fuzzy, though *intelligible*, thought and language of the eccentric. In a later chapter I shall examine more closely how language influences, and interacts with, thinking.

The unknown "risks" of hereditary transmission

The specific claims made by eccentrics could be their way of attempting to reconcile irreconcilable forces within themselves. Howsoever, they do tend to sound incredible. If their quasi-logical beliefs can be seen as "symptoms" of mild mental illness, as such they are unconvincing --- symptoms on their own do not constitute a syndrome, and even less can one or several be forced to constitute a diagnosis of mental illness. Only *one* informant had a clear psychosis at the time of the interview, and to judge from the evidence of his presentation, he had been in an advanced state of delusional disintegration for a long while. To my knowledge the man in question had never received any treatment for his condition. Had no one in his close-knit mining village realised that there was something amiss with him? On interview, in a state of massive thought disorder, he attempted to bear out his claim to be a real life James Bond by demonstrating (harmlessly) commando throat-cutting techniques, thankfully using only a large turnkey in place of a knife --- with the researcher temporarily placed in the role of "surprised enemy victim".

Where I was able to make direct comparisons, record checks and hospital case note reviews, there was no greater incidence of previous cases of psychosis (at least at a level requiring formal psychiatric treatment) among the eccentrics than would be expected from a random sample of the general population. Aside from the above participant, one woman, in the past, had been treated for a bipolar disorder. However, prior alcohol abuse --- not amounting to alcoholism --- was slightly higher in the histories of the eccentric informants.

A second major finding was that, although thirty-six per cent of the sample could detail a family history of overt eccentric behaviour, frequently in a grandparent, aunt or uncle, their relatives did not have much more mental illness than would be found in the general population. One middle-aged female informant had a schizophrenic son in his mid twenties. One other female informant had a mother who suffered from a single episode of psychosis related to bipolar disorder. These two were the only eccentric informants who had a first-degree relative diagnosed positively for a serious psychiatric disorder. This gives a risk-vulnerability percentage for eccentrics having a first-degree relative with schizophrenia of less than 0.8 per cent, and a similar figure for bipolar disorder. The lifetime prevalence rate for schizophrenia (requiring hospitalisation) is 0.8 to 1.0 per cent [47]. The prevalence rate of serious psychiatric disorder among the eccentrics' first-degree relatives was slightly more than that for the first-degree relatives of the "normal" volunteers in our study, though it was significantly less than that for the first-degree relatives of schizophrenics, people with mixed schizo-affective disorders, or people with other "atypical" psychoses [48]. Three other eccentric people, two males and one female, had second-degree relatives with serious mental disorders, two of which were diagnosed as schizophrenia. The remaining informant had six second-degree relatives with unipolar depression.
(See Table 8).

Table 8: Informants with psychiatrically ill relatives

Informant	Relative	Diagnosis
Female	Son	Schizophrenia
Male	Mother	Single episode of psychosis related to Bipolar Disorder
Male	Two paternal uncles	Schizophrenia
Male	Maternal great-aunt	Schizophrenia
Female	Two maternal aunts, two maternal uncles and two cousins	Unipolar depression

Therefore, although schizophrenic patients have a greatly increased number of first-degree relatives who display eccentric behaviour, people who admit to being eccentric do not have an increased proportion of first-degree relatives with schizophrenia or other psychoses. At the same time, there is also a vastly increased "risk" --- one in three for eccentrics as opposed to approximately one in a thousand for non-eccentrics --- of the eccentric having a relative who is also eccentric. The eccentric relative was usually a parent, grandparent, or an aunt or uncle. There was also one case noted of an equally eccentric brother and sister.

The matter of the assumed family relationship with schizophrenia can be disposed of with comparative ease. For one thing, the eccentric behaviours of schizophrenics and their relatives may be qualitatively different from those of primary eccentric personalities. The actions of schizophrenics are more frequently judged by others as bizarre, meaningless or incomprehensible [49]. It could also be the case that psychiatrists treating or researching schizophrenic patients may have a more sensitive threshold for what constitutes eccentric behaviour than do people in other walks of life. They would be in a state of readiness to pick up abnormal mannerisms and speech. Most psychiatrists have never, or at best rarely ever, met actual "normal" or "well-adjusted" eccentrics. Of course, "adjustment" is a loaded term and a flawed concept, implying one way of being or behaving is better than another. "Well-adjusted" is an obvious value judgement, that the person who uses it as a contrast to some other behaviour is implying that the other is inferior or in some way not as good as the "well-adjusted" way, and that is usually the way of the conformist or of the hypocrite who conveys an outward impression of conformity.

It could be inferred that eccentrics may not share a family relationship in any sense with schizophrenics, though the former may have some features that appear to be similar by dint of their social and cognitive oddness. It is also difficult, though not impossible, to categorise odd behaviours; aside from being statistically infrequent, they are also different one from the other.

The more imponderable finding is the high incidence of eccentrics clearly having indubitably eccentric relatives. What is startling about this is that one presumed mechanism of inheritance is via assortative mating; the earliest stage in this is like meeting like. It is difficult to conceive of this happening with eccentrics, mainly because of their presumed numerical rarity. I reckoned it would be highly unlikely for one eccentric to meet another eccentric of the opposite sex. Despite the potential for mutual tolerance that such individuals might exhibit for each other, it is difficult to imagine such a liaison working in practice, either in social or interpersonal terms. Reproduction might be less likely. There are statistical reasons for this: in assortative mating, one is dealing here with sequential, or conditional, probabilities. Reproducing is an outcome that follows after meeting, feeling mutual attraction, liking and feeling affection, falling in love, and at some point sooner or later in that sequence having penetrative sexual intercourse, eventually producing one or more child.

The most persuasive argument would be in terms of personality traits; a large amount of attraction between people of opposite genders is based on similarity. It is almost impossible to imagine one eccentric, who has spent most of his or her life becoming idiosyncratic, meeting another eccentric who is personally similar. It is also doubtful that, were this to happen, the eccentric in question would find his opposite-sex mirror-image necessarily attractive, other than for reasons of perverse curiosity.

It need then be postulated that the gene(s) for eccentricity, if they exist, while not perhaps being dominant genes, are however "strong", having a tendency to be passed on rather well compared with other extreme or rare behavioural leanings. An estimated prevalence of one eccentric in 10,000 could be explained by postulating a recessive gene, or predisposing gene(s), occurring at the rate of about one in 100. These supposed eccentricity genes would be triggered into life only should a female with one or more such recessive or predisposing genes have a child by a male with one or more of the same recessive or predisposing genes. This would bring about the estimated approximate whole population prevalence of one in 10,000.

Our theoretical assumptions were not borne out in reality. Two couples, with both partners equally eccentric, came forward during the course of the project. Two other female informants had eccentric husbands; however, the husbands in these marriages were unavailable for the research interview. This yields an approximate estimate of the chances of an eccentric-eccentric marriage out of marriages in which at least one partner is definitely eccentric of one in thirty-three. There was a total of six children produced by these four couples. The children of such marriages would inherit the predisposing genes for eccentricity *and* a family environment providing many good examples of florid eccentric behaviour. Including this data into the estimates based on the "recessive/predisposing genes – intermarriage" hypothesis would result in a slightly higher population prevalence for potential eccentrics.

Alternatively, there may be little genetic transmission. Learning across generations, perhaps only learning that it is possible to be different, may have taken place. This environmental explanation also has its complications though; despite the fact that a large majority of the eccentric informants did produce children, very few of their children had as yet shown any signs of eccentricity. It appeared that most of the children of eccentrics reacted against it, opting to become more conventional. Whatever the true prevalence rate is, demonstrable eccentricity of the enduring kind may develop and come to fruition only under rather special circumstances.

Chapter 4. Reveries of Childhood
(The Development of Eccentricity)

Probably all education is but two things: first, the parrying of the ignorant children's impetuous assault on the truth and, second, gentle, imperceptible, step by step initiation of the humiliated children into the Lie.

Franz Kafka, 1936

Many child psychiatrists would believe that anything that produced a staggering impact on adult personality must have its roots in childhood. This can be a rather tendentious argument, and in some quarters has become regarded with suspicion. However, sometimes it is possible to discern trends that recur so often that they cry out for explication. Such is the case in the developmental histories of the eccentrics that were interviewed. They realized that they were different. Sane and intelligent, from an early age they had excellent insight into their mental life.

Case history

As an infant, Bill was left near a doorway of a major London teaching hospital. Mr. and Mrs. A., a reserved and conventional couple, adopted the "foundling" at some point within the following six months.

Mr. A. was an upstanding minor civil servant and his wife was the eldest daughter of an ex-colonial bank manager. Mr. A. had been a spoiled only child who had assumed the role of head of his parental household and wage earner when his father died prematurely. Before her marriage, Mrs. A. had lived a sheltered life. Her role models were a strait-laced mother and an iron-willed grandfather. Both of their families exerted pressure on Mr. and Mrs. A. to have children, and when Mrs. A. was found to be infertile, the couple felt duty bound to adopt. They found Bill to be a model baby for the first several years, but after the adoption of another baby boy, Bill began to show a high level of jealousy. By the time he was brought to nursery school he was a precocious and wilful child. He was disappointed, then outraged, when he discovered that school was not a voluntary experience.

Bill's early childhood was spent in an atmosphere of duty and obedience rather than affection. His parents were joyless and authoritarian, dispensing rewards in an arbitrary way. His upbringing, to him, was a parody of Pavlovian conditioning. Everything seemed to have strings attached; nothing was spontaneous. This made him feel suspicious of his parents, especially when they were forced to demonstrate "shows of affection" for the benefit of family or friends. Bill felt that he could never discuss his insecurities or his feelings with his parents. He believed that they would use his declared anxieties as "ammunition" against him.

At the age of eleven, Bill thought he saw water flowing uphill, and, from that point on, he began to take a contrived stance of having a jaundiced mood and being cynical about the nature of perceived reality. This morose pose in a boy so young further annoyed his teachers and parents. Bill decided that he was good at reading, so he placed himself bodily in the top reading group in his class, and could not be removed or dissuaded despite the protests of his teacher. One of his school reports at this time read: "Disengaged, spends his time staring out of windows, his mind is away with the birds." Dreamy absent-mindedness became second nature to him and he was teased by his fellow pupils. As a result, he became aggressive, and he soon joined a spontaneously formed gang of older boys. This in turn caused him to be summoned to the headmaster's office on numerous occasions. Bill regarded this as the natural consequence of his increasingly violent behaviour, and accepted his role of being the odd one out even amongst the "bad boys".

Bill's unpopularity with authority figures continued into secondary school. In contrast, the science teachers were astounded when he presented them with six-foot-high molecular models of the DNA double helix, and again when he conducted a biology experiment concerned with the origins of life on earth. They were more nonplussed when he pointed out their mistakes. He was unwilling to co-operate in other subjects. His fighting escalated. He circularised the teachers with petitions. He sabotaged classes and equipment. He spent entire lunch hours walking around the playground backwards. At the age of thirteen he made a vow of "purity", his term for celibacy. He set up his own "Anti-Sex League". He also began to show a belief in flying saucers.

Two years later, Bill went on to a single sex school where his obsession for biochemistry flourished. That the school was not co-educational was greeted with enthusiasm; he preferred a school without the "temptations of the flesh", and his parents agreed with this, saying his attitude was "jolly moral". In spite of this, his continued violence caused him to be excluded from all his "O" Level courses, except for science subjects.

Bill became attracted to the local punk and heavy metal music fan group, known locally as "The Filth Club". Its members adulated Bruce Lee, and awarded each other points for various acts of vandalism or desecration. Bill also became interested in military matters, becoming an ardent war gamer, accumulating hundreds of pounds worth of toy soldiers, and building a huge sand table that filled his bedroom. He had three major confrontations at this time with his school's headmaster; these were concerned with his increasing aggressiveness, and at each instance a weapon was confiscated. Bill showed no respect for the headmaster, whom he regarded as poorly educated and self-important, and this opinion was confirmed when he discovered that he had been a physical education teacher. Eventually, Bill was referred to a psychiatrist. He revelled in this, and came to see it as "a most satisfactory victory over authority". In therapy, he interpreted his violence as a way of pre-emptively self-defensive and as a means to obtain status. He read William Golding's *Pincher Martin* at this time, and it was a revelation to him. The feuds with his parents became increasingly bitter. He contemplated, but rejected, suicide.

At the end of his school career, Bill was shaken when he failed his science examinations. This forced him to mend his ways, and he spent a year in near silence. In order to gain some qualifications, he went on to college. He was a solitary student. His only human contact was at lectures. He battled to understand himself better and to think through several of his personal issues.

Bill distanced himself further from others. He deliberately took an anti-patriotic line and joined the Ecology Party, as he felt this was the best way to oppose society. He became a vegan. To prove himself, he endured a three-week long siege on the roof of the college until the authorities agreed to provide him with proper vegan meals.

The next few years of Bill's life were a continuous round of protests and arrests. He lived at the Molesworth People's Peace Camp for up to a month at a time. He was introduced to marijuana by an enlisted man serving in the American Air Force who had befriended him and introduced him to the joys of riding a Triumph motorcycle.

During this time, Bill became convinced of the worth of his newfound anarchist ideas. He formed a cell of his own, called the Anarchist Collective; it lasted for about a year before he was jailed for three weeks for pointing a toy plastic pistol at a mayor he disliked. He called this a "mock assassination". In jail in Pentonville, he resolutely set about fomenting chaos. Being a prisoner gave him more time to rethink his self-identity and he realised that he had swung from a violent counter-culture towards a non-violent anarchist lifestyle, though he still felt that this was unsatisfactory. "It only dealt with my problems of identity from the outside," he said. "It only gave me what to believe, what to boycott; everything was happily prescribed for me and this indirectly addressed my personal psychological needs."

Bill then felt that he should look more closely at his personal striving to be an individual, rather than at more external matters. This made his struggle against conformity less heated and more rational. He has retained his disengagement from much of mainstream society, disliking authoritarian sexual relationships and purposeless luxury, and subsists on a diet largely composed of bread and beans. His earlier choice of celibacy extended into adult life. He completed a dissertation that he had started in prison, and graduated with a good Honours degree in English Literature and Sociology. He has further pursued Peace Studies at university, and is currently studying chemical weapons. At the age of twenty-three, Bill is slowly becoming a happier person, and for some time has been considered by his new friends as eccentric.

First-born children

The first trend discerned was that there was a preponderance of first-born informants in the eccentric sample (see Table 9).

Table 9. Position within the family

	First born	Only child	Other position	Second born	Youngest
Females	68%	11%	32%	18%	19.5%
Males	69%	24%	31%	17.5%	19%

First-born children have always enjoyed a position of privilege in the vast majority of the world's cultures. The rules and observances that underlie their significance in the life history of families and individuals are so common that they have been considered universal [1]. Their privileged position occurs among nomads, hunter-gatherers, and agricultural groups. All kinds of family systems are affected, whether the line of descent is traced through the father's family, the mother's family, or where both lineages are given equal weight. Small-scale geographically limited populations, such as those found in the South Pacific, as well as societies with large numbers and elaborate social structures, like the Ashanti, Mossi, Hausa, and Zulu, all observed first-born privilege. It extended into traditionally literate, more politically sophisticated societies like those seen in India and China. The underlying forces in family relationships may therefore be quite similar in this respect.

In law, the first-born may be the designated heir, by primogeniture, in European cultures as well as those cultures as diverse as the Tallensi, Tikopia, Hindu, and Chinese, and many patrilineal peoples both today and in antiquity. In some, the procreation of the first-born child is itself considered to be a moral and religious duty. It is commonly believed that the birth of the first child confers immortality on the parents. In ancient Hebrew law, a first-born child who was also the oldest surviving offspring was entitled to a double portion of the father's estate. Some cultures believe that the first-born possesses "inherent sanctity"; this belief often shores up political rules, for example, the Polynesian ideal that the chief be the first-born of a line of first-borns [2, 3].

Folk belief, custom and tradition, inheritance laws, and ordinary day-to-day family practices merge to demonstrate the significance of being a first-born child. There is also a preponderance of first-borns among university students and eminent people [4]. Birth order is associated both with intelligence and academic attainment. In one study as many as sixty per cent of a sample of top-flight scientists were first-born children [5]. Interestingly, many such children become overly conscientious and conformist. Factors other than birth order are needed to explain the origins of eccentricity.

Early development

A newborn infant is completely helpless and wholly reliant on parents and other caring people. Perceiving the external world without the aid of any conceptual framework or any way of filtering out extraneous perceptions, he or she possesses a basic subjectivity in the early months, and is also more dependent on internal and external physical cues. In this uncontrolled, intermittently scared and needy state, experiences are obviously experienced, though not particularly remembered, except only residues of vague feelings, if at all, and in the most general indeterminate ways, and then mostly only when their caretakers are exceptionally good overall, or nightmarishly bad. Thankfully, the latter are more readily forgotten with the passage of time, though possibly with a price to be paid later. As all infants grow older, they will have continued to forget, or rather never learned to remember in the ways that older children can.

The developmental changes that take place are the products of mutually interacting influences, attributable to both nature and nurture, which bring about a continuous interleaving of parental preferences and choices, the infant's behaviours, and hereditary factors. In the first year of life, social learning, primarily vis-à-vis interactions between the mother and infant, takes place. This is in the form of verbal and non-verbal dialogues; in this the infant is learning in ways that most probably could not be called fully conscious. In a slow progression of give-and-take actions and reactions, what does come about has several key interrelated parts: the development of reciprocity and intentionality. Earlier mother-infant dialogues tend to be unbalanced, with the mother primarily sustaining the interaction; only later does the infant discover that this is a conjointly cooperative or reciprocal relationship. With intentionality, the infant learns that his actions have effects when he communicates by crying, smiling, vocalizing, gesturing, and that there will be a forthcoming response to these actions.

Gradually, the infant acquires a sense of his separate identity and learns to distinguish himself as different from other people in his immediate environment. As the developmental psychologist Margaret Donaldson pointed out, for infants of this young age, "Awareness grows as differentiation grows." [6] This differentiation is an important cognitive process that permits further growth and learning, including that surrounding personality development. By the age of eighteen months, the child begins to use the word "I". This awareness of separateness, of there being definite boundaries between the self and other, of not being another person or another thing, may continue to exercise the child's mind for many more months [7]. However, parents appear to the child as magically omnipotent, able to fulfil all or most of the infant's needs, and to carry out other actions which no doubt seem miraculous or mysterious.

Reliable distinctions between oneself and others are usually made in the second year of life. At around the age of one and a half to two and a half, the child deliberately does the opposite of what he or she is told. They are learning the uses and the power of the negative, and exercising it in personal ways. As the eccentric poet Ivor Cutler once said, "A child is an anarchist --- he hasn't discovered there are bosses." This marked refusal and disobedience may be a literal testing by the child of the limits of his independence, to see how far he can go with impunity while still retaining a sense of security. By contrast, parents try to control their child as if he or she was an extension of themselves.

First-born children are lavished with attention by their parents, grandparents and by members of their extended families. This was also the case for the eccentrics in this study. The expression of solicitude was the norm. They also entered life with another biological advantage, in that their parents were obviously younger, and presumably that bit physically healthier at their birth than at the birth of any subsequent children. First-time mothers however can be dogged by feelings of inadequacy. With all the joys involved, there is also the certainty of inescapable responsibility. This intimidating prospect can loom large and can hit both parents with a sense of uncertain urgency. Becoming a parent is not only a stressful transition to a new way of life, but sometimes can become a long-running crisis.

First-born children are *usually* more adult-orientated, more conscientious, more achievement-orientated, more affiliative, more concerned with being co-operative and responsible, and more conforming to social pressures [8, 9]. They normally tend to develop stronger consciences than second-born children; they tend to be more responsible, less aggressive, and more intellectually curious [10, 11, 12]. What often begins in early childhood for most children is the bracing questioning, the searching interrogation of either parent, or any relative or teacher who might seem at all accessible and interested in answering. This includes most first-born children, and was more intense and comprehensive for those children who later would become seen as eccentric.

In the course of development, doors are opened and doors are closed, particular options rewarded or rejected at the expense of others. The first-born or only child can learn to cope with the solitariness of his situation --- by inventing internalised other voices in his mind, and/or other people in his imagination. There can be an imaginary friend, an intermittent or ongoing commentator, a passive listener or an entire audience of listeners. As first-born children develop, they show a readiness to express their creativity through intellectual dimensions --- including perceptiveness, curiosity, and an openness to cultural and artistic activities --- and these were strongly related to being first-born. However, too many showed dogmatic adherence to indefensible positions that ran counter to new evidence [13]. This may apply to some of the less creative eccentrics, though not to the majority who were more constructively creative. Therefore, other factors must be influential in changing creative eccentrics away from the customary first-born modes of conformity.

A developing child needs, first and foremost, at least one parental figure who is receptive to the child's needs and emotional communications. Because the parents are inexperienced at being parents, they usually respond to their first child with anxious attention and inconsistency. The first-born child in early infancy is handled in more restrictive, coercive, and emotionally distant ways than is the second-born child [14]. If they are also set apart as only children, there can be additional kinds of solitariness instilled, and different relating patterns can evolve, some of which can continue into maturity.

"Being an only child makes for a lonely childhood. You can come to depend on yourself. You have to learn to think for yourself because you have no one to rub off against, and you go off in directions that people don't think of because you are alone and because you are with adults all the time."

(Dianne, age fifty)

"My father thought I should not mix with other children until I was of school age. So mostly I didn't. On the odd occasion, my mother let some child or other into the garden to play with me, behind father's back. I made sure that they only played with my oldest toys, and even so, I wasn't sorry to see them go. I had a swing at the bottom of the garden and I used to sit on it and sing, but I didn't know half the words, so I used to make them up. [Laughter] Thus mostly my company was my parents, and my childless aunt and uncle, who were neighbours. It might not seem a happy situation to some, but I was entirely happy and contented.

"These adults did not spoil me in that I could have my own way. I was expected to have good manners. If they bought me anything, it was always books, the love of my life. I could read very young. I would draw and read when the adults got together in the evenings to play cards, and half way through the evening when they paused to have a drink, I was allowed to have a small port for being quiet. But I was quiet anyway."

(Iris, age thirty-eight)

Childhood origins of eccentricity

The groundbreaking developmental psychologist Charlotte Buhler made some clever and interesting observations of actual infant behaviour in the 1930s. She also studied the spontaneous creativity of children at play with a variety of materials. To this day her early experiments are pertinent to understanding differences in very young children. In one of these, an adult forbade a child to touch a toy that was easily within reach. All of the one- to two-year old children understood this, and did not touch the toy as long as the adult was nearby, or within sight. As soon as he turned away or left the room, the child began to play with the toy. If the adult returned suddenly, sixty per cent of the children at one year and four months and all of the children at one year and six months showed signs of embarrassment, such as blushing, and turned toward the adult with what was described as a "frightened expression". At one year and nine months the children tended to comply with the prohibition when the adult came back, by returning the toy quickly to where it previously had been placed. However, at two years of age, although the children clearly understood they were disobeying, they invented ways to excuse their non-compliance, for example by claiming ownership of the toy. As Buhler wrote, "After the age of two the child expresses will, insistence on its own rights, and possessive impulses in its relations with adults." [15] I think that what Buhler also showed was that non-compliance precedes non-conformity in developmental terms. I also think that in this non-conformity the first early seeds of childhood eccentricity begin with the children's ability to freely exercise not only free will, but also choice and some early signs of discrimination.

Interestingly, by the age of five, children acquire the ability to think in terms of simple narratives, and to make up fantasies of their own. However, this comes before other, perhaps more intellectually rational, abilities. It is not until about the age of seven that children are able to compare their inner attributes and differences of personality with those of other children. Until then they are usually unprepared to seek out such comparisons, and engage in simpler, more concrete comparisons with parents, teachers, and other children and adults. Picking up the differences between the self and others helps to build up and to confirm the child's self-identity. Figuring out the main differences between other children also helps the child to work out *ad hoc* descriptions and theories about human personality, though not all children go on to develop these into more abstract terms.

While communicating their social and personal values, parents provide and reinforce similar and dissimilar social comparisons. A society's social order, and the interdictions flowing from it, begins to make itself known early, and begins to influence young minds, at first perhaps not deliberately, but sooner or later begins its efforts to perpetuate its core beliefs and priorities, by words, suggestions, demonstration, example, formal education and the inculcation of certain disciplines. Well-founded instances of the latter include the use of foresight, delayed gratification, and simple ethics. All this adds up to a rather prolonged and intense social upbringing, amounting to social programming.

Conforming behaviours normally increase during the middle childhood years. These are created by society through the agency of the family through the concentration of authority and power in the hands of two loving and benevolent parents who have, simply and absolutely, the last word [16, 17, 18].

Children have an ingenuous belief in the goodness and justice of authority, though the duties, rights and privileges parents bestow on them may be perceived as arbitrary. Because many if not all children are sensitive when young, many also have a greater need for the protection, care and concern of at least one parental figure. The ways that adults act towards children may seem unpredictable to them. For the best of reasons, parents tend to control and limit their child's experience to what they consider to be appropriate. Parents want their children to be normal and to progress to be good adults in the light of the values and injunctions of their society.

Children usually dislike and sometimes are made anxious by instability and change. They come to desire the comfort of solid order and firmly structured routines. If responsive parenting is done sensitively to the needs of the child, if the parents forego some of their own egoistic needs for the sake of the child, then they are more likely to adjust what they say and do in ways that will maximise the child's developmental progress. The parents will do this in a more flexible, less authoritarian manner, and will not compel the child to fit into a particularly highlighted preferred mould. They would rather allow the child's potential to be extended in directions guided, at least to some degree, by having the child participate in the process of defining his wishes as he was able to do in earlier interactions to indicate his simpler needs.

Of course, in the main, few young children can conceptualise most of the consequences of their actions. This is not because of their age or developmental stage but mostly because of how they've been treated. The family's ideology as expressed in the home defines and dictates the areas of life that can be attended to, what may be known, what can be safely ignored, what must not be talked about, and what must not be questioned. The nuclear family is the conduit through which cultural belief systems make their initial impressions on the individual child. Appropriate emotional involvement between the parent and child can be an important element in this.

The ultimate parental sanction is rejection, and the pity is that the fear of rejection can take over, can be generalised into over-control and habitual, unthinking conformity. Some families inculcate dependency and helplessness. Until recently, this was especially the case for young girls, affected as they were by the additional complication of sexist attitudes and behaviours. In the pre-feminist past, girls have been found to be more conforming to peer group pressures than boys [19, 20, 21, 22]. Sexism begins early and insidiously. It is covert and subtle.

It would not be wildly speculative to suggest that other out-of-the-ordinary events or situations intervened to bring out any eccentricity in the early years, in both girls and boys. One candidate for this could be gender confusion. The parents of the future eccentrics had often tended to relate to them as if they would have preferred them to fit into a contrary gender role. This would lead to some gender confusion, bringing about androgynous feelings or more pronounced and stereotyped masculine or feminine roles, more frequently than homosexual or bisexual orientations. This also contributed to later feelings of difference, as in the following instances: "Perhaps I was not a typical girl. I was brought up as a boy. When my father came back from the war he was absolutely delighted because I was interested and could do all the things he wanted to do. I was brought up to think like and act like and just be a boy. I enjoyed it. I wouldn't have swapped it. I still enjoy shooting and fishing, and I enjoy the hunt."

(Jean, age forty-seven)

"The difficulty I had, from the age of two, was in meeting my father's exacting, and totally misguided, standards of normality with regard to what was appropriate boyish behaviour. To please him I would have had to display complete imperviousness to my mother's influence. Indeed, I would have had to be more disobedient than I had any inclination to be."

(Alastair, age thirty-six)

"My father had wanted sons, and I really tried hard to meet that need for him until my first brother arrived when I was ten. Actually I wasn't destructive: I think I was merely more aggressive than the average girl in the street and people weren't used to that."

(Caitlin, age twenty-eight)

If and when another sibling is born, there is first the shock of a new situation, one that the psychotherapist Alfred Adler referred to as "dethronement". The behaviour of both parents towards the first-born usually changes after the birth of a second child [23]. The first-born is no longer at the epicentre of his parents' total attention, and may feel cheated out of his exclusive position within the family. This change may involve, sooner or later, a move to another bedroom further away from the security of the parents, or some other sign of "demotion". As Portia Holman has written: "The one most likely to suffer is the one who has just been supplanted from his position as the baby. If he is the first-born, his suffering will be great." [24] Here follows the retrospective experience of a typical eccentric: "You think you're ruling the roost, everyone is always indulgent and happy to see you, and then suddenly this very pretty interloper comes along and she becomes the apple of everyone's eyes. That was dreadful, though what was happening only dawned on me slowly, and so I felt hurt. So, welcome to a childhood full of rejection, hurt feelings and bitterness. I only gained some understanding, some perspective on this, after I grew up, got married and had children of my own."

(Geoffrey, age thirty-one)

Some rivalry between siblings is perfectly normal. If this is based on jealousy or propelled by angry envy, prominence is given to the emotional loss of love and attention that was felt by the first-born child to be his due.

Some first-born children, formerly under a brighter parental spotlight, then go on to learn and demonstrate "higher power tactics" in relation to their nearest siblings, whom they sometimes provoke to the point of aggression [25]. They might not like to share toys, nor even want to take part in proffered reciprocal sharing with the second-born or indeed with other children of their own age. First-born children will continue to strive to maintain a high profile and to be visibly different from the new competitor. They will devise new strategies in order to make themselves stand out more from the new intruder, all for the sake of winning back their parents' affections [26]. This causes them to assert themselves, makes them more compulsively demanding, and is an early spark to their more idiosyncratic ambitions. Sibling relationships and their vicissitudes only influence adult relationships indirectly --- by a step-wise process of one effect influencing the next effect, and so on, until the connection of the earliest with the most recent may seem implausible. The above behaviour might not apply to every first-born child. Whatever a child's position relative to other siblings, they are potential rivals for parental affection and attention. Those children brought up by wise or more experienced parents, or those helpfully overseen by grandparents or by nursery staff, might learn the benefits of cooperative play, mutual sharing, and not always putting themselves first.

A multi-disciplinarian research group at Yale University studying the development of pre-school siblings who were two years apart in age --- seen by many as the least optimal separation in ages --- set out "to study the mutual influences" of the siblings. Though the appearance of the second-born increased the "aggressive drives" of the first-born, if all went well the elder child learned how to cope with these drives and the possibly humbling experiences that might have resulted from them. This could herald the growth of creativity and imagination in the first-born, though there were signs that their ego and ego defences also could be affected [27].

Sometimes childhood quarrels are poorly resolved. Rivalries between siblings can be misunderstood, and things can go awry in unexpected ways for a long while afterwards. The following eccentric woman's forthright account adds a new dimension to the horrible word "brat": "We were all going to the zoo and my sister was downstairs in her carrycot, crying. I had seen my father pacify my mother when she was upset by giving her a cigarette, and it crossed my mind that the same thing would work for my sister. I found a packet and tried to get a cigarette into her mouth. My mother thought I was trying to choke her, and then my father beat me so severely with a golf club that I could hardly walk. What angered me was the unfairness. From then on life became a battle of wits between my father and me, and I cared nothing at all for my mother. I regarded my sister as alien to me. My main priority was SPACE --- I insisted on my own bedroom, and got it by terrorising my sister until she showed intense distress at being left alone with me.

"In order to survive in a disordered household I learned to put on protective clothing: my father believed that 'attack is the best method of defence', and I applied this theory rigorously in dealing with my family. I assumed that they would be hostile to my interests, and accordingly, I devised methods of keeping them at bay. Antisocial behaviour served me well.

"By the time I was twelve I had the upper hand. They feared me more than I feared them. In order not to be left with the thankless task of child caring, I developed a habit of 'non-remembering' --- specifically not remembering where I left them, and abandoning the pram and its contents in various parts of the village. Discerning that mama did not like gypsies or tramps, I assiduously cultivated them, and acquired some useful non-standard education in the process. I was habitually alone in the house without supervision. One afternoon I went out and met a tramp, inviting him home for tea. I took him into the drawing room and made tea for him using the best tea service. My mother came back whilst this was going on, and was pretty annoyed, especially about the tea service."

(Janet, age forty-five)

The first six years of life are crucial in many ways, though not definitive in determining what the child's later personality will turn out to be. Children are able, by the age of seven or eight, to understand the notion of similarity and difference as it applies to individuals' personalities [28]. Their motivation to make social comparisons between themselves and others begins to become apparent as early as four years of age, and reaches a peak between seven and nine years [29]. Further thinking about this facilitates more differentiation and the exploration of possible self-concepts.

More sensitive to their immediate social environment, by the age of seven or eight most eccentrics (at least two-thirds of my sample) realised, or were told by friends and relatives, that they were different. It is how this happened, why they came to believe this, and how they acted upon it that is interesting. It *can* begin simply by happenstance: "The next time I was evacuated Grandma had moved, so it meant going to a different school two villages away. Yet again I became unstuck. The teacher gave me a writing book with sandwich lines in the middle of two wider lines. I hadn't even seen that sort of book before. In London we very often had plain pages and had to draw our own lines. So I said, 'Please, Miss, can I write on ordinary lines?' All the other children sniggered and teacher insisted that I should learn to write all over again like the others."

(Gertrude, age fifty-one)

The underscoring of their differentness can also happen by chance meetings. In this instance, a single remark, said with conviction, touched off three decades of eccentricity: "There was an elderly couple living by us in Bath. They were deep spiritualists. The woman put her hand on my head. She said to my parents: 'Your child is truly psychic.' I remember how that marked me out as different, though I didn't know what it meant at the time."

(Josephine, age thirty-seven)

Or an unusual name can lead in unforeseen ways to be a spur to the adoption of an odder self-identification: "When I was quite young I made a decision that having an unusual name, I was going to damn well be different, and I made up my mind about this when I was about seven: 'I have a different name; I am going to be different.' I am setting out knowing that I was going to try to be different in my life."

(Salome, age thirty-three)

The emotional environment existing within the family during a child's early years affects how he or she behaves toward others in adult life. Persistent parental absence and social class differences can play a part as specific environmental catalysts, as they did in this case: "The years 1942 to '45 (my age then was six to nine) gave me a chance to develop without undue strain because my father was in hospital in India. The same years also left me with a reinforced feeling of being different because we were middle class but the war left us marooned, my mother running a small retail business in a slum area. The children I went to school with did not let me forget that I was different."

(Avril, age fifty)

Most eccentrics, as children, experienced more periods of isolation. This was enforced by circumstances or because they had been ostracised by their peers. They then took steps to defend their still-forming egos by avoiding those situations that were likely to give rise to hurt feelings. If this happened, many found it difficult to sustain good relationships within their social environments. During such episodes they fell back on their own resources for amusement and solace, experimented with their physical environment and ideas, increased their solitary, unshared delight in exploration, and generally extended their range of knowledge. Enthralled by this, they retreated into themselves.

It takes a bit more reciprocal sociality to copy or invent simple dramatic representations and to participate in playing games with other likeminded children. As Peter Gray, a psychologist at Boston College, has said, "If we deprive children of play they can't learn how to negotiate, control their own lives, see things from others' points of view, and compromise. Play is the place where children learn they are not the centre of the universe."

Imaginative play is one of the activities during which creativity first appears [30]. In the capricious sensibilities of early childhood, truth and myth-making can become one and the same thing. Under the influence of imaginative play, children become aware of the differences between reality and imagination, and develop, often with the help of their friends and playmates, the ability to undertake symbolic play. This is matched by their sense of imaginative wondering while at play. This also helps to create complex connections between imaginative productivity and abstract thinking.

If brought up in families in which one or both parents are unpredictable and not attuned to their child's needs, the latter may escape into the relatively more rewarding inner environment of the imagination, even developing an addiction for solitary creative activities [31]. Often such intellectual pursuits became intrinsically rewarding, and lead to increases in the diversity of the eccentric children's abilities, sometimes moving them further away from "normal" children. The following two examples could be thought of as illustrations of how intrapersonal and specific social environmental factors may combine to produce such outcomes: "Did I mention my Martian friend? From about the age of eight I had an imaginary friend from Mars. Sometimes I still wonder if he was perhaps real after all. Living near the Air Force base and being 'right there' during the height of the Space Race contributed to it. Good grief, we had the astronaut Scott Carpenter over for dinner one night. He gave me a ten-inch model of the Mercury capsule. I escaped to my fantasy on Mars frequently. In fact, I'm sure from ages eight to fourteen I spent more time on Mars than Earth. I was thought by my fourth grade teacher to be autistic, though I wasn't because I could come back from Mars whenever it was necessary. I was also very slow at accomplishing tasks, like getting dressed. I was always daydreaming. I liked it on Mars. I had great teachers and knowledgeable mentors there. It is where I learned about magnetic fusion."

(Brenda, age twenty-eight)

"The owner of the house was a retired headmistress. My main recollection is of playing alone and talking to my dolls, dressing them, making up situations and reading. After three years, Miss B. died and we went to another lady. She was over eighty and she terrified me. Her house was utterly dark, with life-size portraits springing out at you from the walls. The poor old soul had senile dementia. She would keep on asking me the same questions, and she called me Phoebe or Melissa. Again I retreated into a fantasy world and read all her Victorian and Edwardian books --- for example, the poetry of Algernon Charles Swinburne from a personally signed edition. It was inscribed, 'To the great love of my life'. I also dressed up in her old evening dresses, shoes, fans, etc. It was wonderful."

(Florence, age fifty-eight)

Not expressed emotion, but expressed criticism

The Russian psychologist Lev Vygotsky believed that development is a series of transformative experiences that employs both evolutionary and revolutionary changes in the growing child. His view of creativity was essentially optimistic, in that he believed that human beings, if they possess the desire and motivation to do so, have the ability to develop their creativity.

Every thought contains a transformed element of feeling. It should also be the case that every feeling, whether expressed or absorbed from interpersonal interactions, contains a transmuted element of related thinking. Many people regard the emotional atmosphere in the home to be of crucial importance in the development of thinking, creativity and personality. This is usually considered a parental responsibility, though as studies of family life have become more sophisticated, interactions with other generations and the child's own behaviour have also been acknowledged as having substantial additional effects.

Research into parental child-rearing practices has been fragmentary. Much of it goes unobserved. There are many diverse forces at work. Psychologists are only beginning to understand the complex ways that these influences combine to bring about particular outcomes, only one of which might be social non-conformity [32]. The acquisition of conforming responses represents an early and significant part of socialisation and of the establishment of personal values.

The range of influences involved is wide [33, 34]. The manner in which parents bring up their child is guided by social ideas of what will be in the child's and the family's best interests, ranging between varying degrees of permissiveness and restrictiveness. Formulae based on child-rearing philosophies and practices less clearly spell out those situations that are, or should be, outwith parental control. Parents' views are further constricted by their own motives, both conscious and subconscious, about being in control of situations that do not warrant control. Parents who fear freely spoken individuality, or the creation of personal privacy and separateness, construct more intrusive approaches in which basic intimacy implies risk, even threat. An accent on parental control in child-rearing is usually related to the formation of conservative attitudes and opinions in their children when they grow up, at least among females [35]. These parental attitudes may then generate behaviours that may be either accepting or punitive. Given that there are so many possibilities for faulty translation of adult performance criteria to actual child-training, parents are often not consistent, smoothly operating child-indoctrination machines, and understandably so.

To shape the child's behaviour, parents have a number of means at their disposal. Foremost of these is their power to reward and punish, based not only on the control of resources seen by the child as desirable, but also on the child's emotional attachment to, and dependence on, their parents. Punishment has been shown to be ineffective, either as a means of eliminating or modifying unwanted responses. It may also have different unwanted effects on different children. One commonly observed effect of punishment is a marked increase in the variability of what happens after it has been implemented. This common form of reinforcement is a less reliable, and therefore less predictable, means of changing behaviour than is more positive, rewarding reinforcement [36]. Child-rearing practices that are negative, unempathic, and coercive lead those children so affected to be more self-centred and ego-bound, and will not expect other people with more kindly motives to help them without gaining something in return [37]. Cooler self-reliance becomes a part of their way of thinking. The possibility of unconditional love becomes more remote, and may be shown in how they go on to relate to others. It is only when they experience friendships and closer attachments as adults that they can learn to put into perspective what happened to them, and progress hopefully to anticipate the needs of others and a more fulfilling emotional life for themselves.

For eccentric children, the primary specific means of parental control was hostile criticism. The most commonly occurring overall atmospheres in their families were neither distinctively warm nor cold. Though strict, the parents were not entirely restrictive, though permissive and democratic approaches were shown less frequently. Boys and girls were treated equally and affected by both of their parents' frequently varying approaches to child-rearing.

Not many adult eccentrics look back upon their parents and siblings with warm or positive feelings. Relationships with family members were generally of an unhappy, though sometimes tenuously affectionate, quality. Muddles over contrasting child-rearing practices, sibling conflicts and mixed emotions in the family conferred on their relationships a special piquancy. Children who would become eccentric expected to be seen and heard, very much so, and ironically they also felt free, or confident enough, to contradict their elders in a time when this would generally draw negative responses. The parents' usual response to this was usually a contingent deprivation of tenderness or sensitivity, with or without separation from the more significant parental figure. Such actions were often painful to each child so affected, though it sometimes could possibly have been the beginning of true communication. Either the father or mother could equally be the source of the resulting critical comments or arguments. Bilateral alliances were not uncommon, nor is it difficult to guess who had been on the sharp end of them. Here follows a cross section of first-hand accounts to give a flavour of what their parents' behaviour was like towards them. When reading these one has also to consider the relative power of children to have a major impact on their parents' lives, on occasion to also dictate the emotional content of their families' lives.

"Most of what I remember was of a critical nature. My mother was very house-proud and I never did anything to her satisfaction, no matter how hard I tried. My personal appearance and hygiene standard were also criticised, as was my poor singing voice."

"My father harboured a hatred of women, so life was unbearable. He came home from work to shout and throw his weight about. To say he was 'Victorian' or 'very strict' would be to grossly underestimate the case. He lived in order to squash the female members of his family, to completely take away any of our freedom to be ourselves. My mother was resentful and over-protective and spent my entire childhood telling me how awful my father was and how awful I was because I was like him. I remember asking myself latterly, 'What the hell am I doing here with these people', and it was then that I began to think seriously about running away from home. Had I carried that out, it probably would have made my eventual break with my family a lot easier."

"Hardly any emotion was expressed violently, though there were considerable unresolved tensions. I heard Daddy in a frightful rage saying he hated women. But all was predominantly stiff upper lip with very little expression of affection, either verbally or physically. My family constantly disapproved of me and rejected me. They failed to relate to me in a meaningful way for as long as I can remember. My father gave me certain insults on the rare chances I got to see him. But I learned from all this negativity. If you believe it, it's like a sarcastic critic, and it's not unlike an abusive father that's belittling you for who you are and nothing else, so if you take it in you can't function. That's what I've learned --- don't take criticism seriously. That approach might not appeal to everyone, though if you're honest to yourself, there's a very good chance people will relate to that."

"Father said, 'You will never be as pretty as your mother.' I've felt cumbersome ever since. I resented him saying that, and retaliated by scoring the side of his old Mercedes with a key."

"I had an amazingly bad-tempered father. Mother and father tended to side with each other against me, as my mother found it easier to keep the near-peace this way."

"My mother had very stern parents who rarely ever cracked a smile or told a joke, so I can't blame her. When she was younger, she was bright and beautiful, though after about twelve years of marriage, she started to live in her dreams of a better life and worked at becoming a survivor. When I was about twelve she passed on most of the discipline duties to my father. Before then I could play one off against the other. One time he took off his thick Army belt to give me a serious strapping. I got maybe ten of the best. When he finished I looked up at him and, through my tears, I smiled, then grinned, and then laughed in his face. That infuriated him. Even the other kids in the neighbourhood said I disrespected my parents. After another misdemeanour, maybe the time I purloined some of my neighbour's tomatoes or broke a window in the back door, he chased after me halfway down the street with some of our toffy-nosed neighbours bemusedly looking on, but he could never catch me. Fortunately, my love of cricket and rugger helped. I could run like the wind, especially when I knew what I'd get if I stopped too soon."

"Critical comments tended to be in the form of sarcasm directed at myself. Sarcasm can be bitter and often hurts more than it was meant to."

"My father, who loved us dearly, showed his affection by being critical of my brother, my mother and me."

"The attitudes of my parents towards me were that I was a worthless female, a kept servant of the family, ignorant and unattractive. This was reinforced continually. I resented the affronts to my dignity. My mother told me, 'You have been so bad that God has sent me a good boy instead.' Underneath, I have not accepted my utter worthlessness. All criticism was directed at me. Nobody else got it. I was responsible for all the evil in the world. There were no endearments, no cuddles, no positive strokes."

"Considerable criticism was aimed my way because I was an unambitious dreamer and showed little talent."

"I was always being criticised but would never understand the nature of the criticism, except that 'success' was always a moral imperative which I somehow failed to satisfy. I was always criticised for not being able to do better. I know that I failed to be a properly behaved child. That was beyond any shadow of a doubt, because later my little brother was under a cloud when he went to school because the teachers still remembered the many instances of mischief I had gotten up to years before."

"My mother was critical. My father was a very placid man. He left it all to my mother. My mother was very dominating and there was also another side to her nature that was very frightening --- she was very diffident. When you realise how cruel she was being, but I mean, to me, she wasn't a cruel person. She was critical in a sense that she wanted us to be good at things, and we weren't good. I remember once when I was a little girl, I was second in the class and instead of praising me she said, 'Oh, second . . .' I always remember saying to her, 'And how would you feel if I had been twenty-second?' I didn't get any praise from her; she was a perfectionist. I think she was more critical of me because she used to compare me with my father, whom she didn't like: 'He tells lies and so do you.' And I didn't really tell lies; I wasn't a compulsive liar. I think she was critical of herself and that would just rub off on us. It wasn't so much that she was demanding; she demanded a lot of herself, rather than actually telling us. She certainly drove us on."

"Mother ruled. We never argued with her. We did as she said without question. If I annoyed my mother she would not speak to me, sometimes for weeks. My mother was always right. I loved my mother in a strange way. My grandmother also rules. She lived in the next street and was stricter than my mother. A real tartar. My mother was often cross with me. There was no sentimentality. I do not remember my mother looking after me at all. I suppose I loved her. I think she bore her very boring life with great fortitude. She never wanted us anyway. I accepted the strict discipline in my home as normal."

"My parents seemed to have been at loggerheads, or even daggers drawn, since the day I was born, and this antipathy seems to have continued unabated."

"I persistently have dreamt about my father in a very aggressive mood, fighting or nearly fighting, quarrelling. He could be explosive at times, and it has taken me a long time for me to get rid of his influence. My father's domination has not been of great use, because he has made me still more seclusive and introvert. Whenever I discovered subjects that interested me, I was meant to learn and have no pleasures. He forced me to study, not play. The quarrels at home were sometimes aggressive scenes, my electric gadgets just confiscated and taken away. Once I was even forced to place an ad and sell my own things!"

"My family was like a school for debating. There were so many verbal to-and-fros going on all the time that my youngest sister didn't even begin to talk until she was about four. Criticism was definitely involved, from both grandmothers, both strong-willed, interfering, highly moralistic women, towards my parents and indirectly towards myself, and from both of my parents most times. This was criticism that wounded, more so than the admittedly deserved corporal punishments. I began to wonder if the criticism might have contained several grains of truth, but whether they loved me or not, that still shouldn't have mattered as much as it did, I now know. Mother kept trying to wrest some control from our father. I could see what would be coming my way had I stayed, so breaking away was necessary. Heartbreaking . . . but necessary. Even so, those two parents, and to a lesser extent some of my younger siblings, set up in me this habit of first always seeing both sides of an argument. The result was, instead of living indecisively, I've always chosen to let my true nature be my guide --- I usually opt for the extremes. I like to tell the truth, in preference to spouting more politically courteous presumptions."

"I had no one to talk to in my teens. One felt simply like driftwood, and it never entered one's head to ask. It wasn't the done thing . . . I received every criticism under the sun."

"Criticism grew throughout my teens but it flew both ways. The criticism directed at me was usually directed at specific actions, like hitting my sister, causing havoc at school, or snowballing motorists. The emphasis seemed to be on acting responsibly."

"Very little emotion was expressed in my family, except anger. Most of this was critical. My family think I am a deadbeat and always have. My parents were divorced in the early fifties and have been indulging in World War III ever since. Megatons of criticism have been directed at me. I am the black sheep. My father considers me a criminal and when I was young he said: 'I doubt he's even intelligent.' So they gave me an IQ test. He then changed his tune to, 'We know you're intelligent but . . .' My mother thinks I don't have a regular job and doesn't believe I know anything about electronics. My father told me when I was seventeen, 'You are lazy and have expensive tastes. The only career I can think of for you, my boy, is living off immoral earnings.' I haven't spoken to him since."

From the above it can be seen that the eccentric children's early rebellions could also be cast as reactions against overly strict parental dominance. A number of them suggested that they themselves had precipitated their parents' efforts to discipline them. There was a modest positive relationship between how much emotion, positive or negative, was expressed and the degree of criticism directed at the particular child in question (r = +.25).

Those families that did express emotion were more frequently critical. There was a much higher, significant correlation between the general level of criticism among family members and the amount of criticism levelled at the young eccentrics-to-be (r = +.58). So, emotional hostile criticism, by itself, cannot adequately explain how eccentricity develops in certain children, though usually not any of their siblings.

If criticism was a family practice, then the eccentric children stood a very good chance of receiving most of it. However, this may have had the unexpected consequence of immunizing them against later similar affronts from other adults, particularly teachers. Aside from that, their parents tended to do little to prepare these children for the inevitable changes that were to come during puberty and early adolescence.

Could the overtly parental criticism be extended backward in time? Can it indicate anything about the quality of parenting during the potentially eccentric child's infancy? I think something of a problematic nature can be deduced, particularly if a parent had been generally less sensitive and more intrusive. Under certain circumstances, the effects of this can begin at a very early age. Peter Hobson and his research colleagues have described how mothers with troubled intimate relationships and confused styles of thinking, sufficient to be diagnosed as having borderline personality disorders, and how they interacted with their two-month old infants. At this age, the infants showed signs of being less able to recover from stress, ". . . showing more dazed looks, and their engagement with their mothers was less satisfying and uneasy." By the time the infants of similarly disturbed mothers were twelve months old, and, as compared with a non-selected group of twelve-month old infants, the former infants were specifically less likely to engage with another person's engagement with the world on a set of social tests [38, 39].

In social tasks interacting with a relative stranger, though not in non-social tasks, the infants, as reported by Professor Hobson, "were less likely to refer to another person when needing things or noticing things, or when encouraged to respond to another person's communicative gestures." [39, 40] From my own clinical and research experience, the above effects would amount to a significant basis upon which at least some eccentric children would become more insular in their approach to their peers, to come to depend less on other people, and prefer to be guided by their own ideas and thinking.

Using one's head with the schoolteachers

Eccentrics, as children, were also adversely affected by their school experiences. This may have begun from the first day at school, when they were taken by their parents to a day nursery or primary school. Some of these children, perhaps the more secure, treated it as the start of a new adventure. Other children experienced this day with feelings of abandonment, that a cheery positive gloss was being placed on what they saw, from their perspective, as a desertion seemingly acutely worse than mere "separation anxiety". Later in their childhoods, their earlier bitter feelings would be replicated in those children who were sent off to boarding schools, and this was often perceived as an inexplicable coerced exile from their families, and they later inferred from this that this was a form of non-verbal criticism, rejection or punishment.

The eccentrics in this study were juxtaposed curiously in schools that from the outset primarily rewarded conformity, punished non-conformity, and subordinated the children's experiences and sense of involvement to the teachers' pedagogy. Worse still, they were subjected to routines of control, condescension, and being made to feel inferior by various attitudes of superiority shown by many teachers. Their entry into the school system was usually their first experience of being benevolently regimented by the wider social order beyond the family. To object to any of this, the children received another bitter taste of conflicts to come, for schooling unhappily turned into a distinctly detrimental blessing for many of them.

I should at this point remind my readers that the accounts of my research participants are retrospective, harking back to educational practices that are now historical, taking place between the years 1938 and 1979. Such practices hopefully may not occur quite as commonly nowadays.

In the course of their primary and secondary schooling, eccentric children threw into question not only general education methods and specific school procedures, but also the content of school work, and sometimes their schools' underlying philosophies: "I first realised I was odd when I went to school at five. I thought the teachers were stupid. For instance, on my first day, they asked me if I would like a drink of milk. I said, 'No, thank you.' They *insisted* I drank it anyway. I thought how stupid the teacher was for asking me in the first place. I could already write my name, but she insisted that I kept a name card on my desk. This would have been all right had she told me the reason was so she could remember my name or so the other children did not feel inferior, but I was not given a sensible reason. The teachers were always insisting on you going to the toilet when you didn't want to, etcetera. The reason I felt so odd is because other children seemed to accept that all this was quite normal, but I did not. I thought the teachers stupid and that was what made me feel odd."

(Janet, age forty-five, measured IQ 150)

There was a broader question the eccentric children felt needed to be answered, whether or not teachers fostered a trained incapacity for critical reflection, and if they did, as they thought, that needed to be more widely recognised. If the eccentrics are to be believed, their teachers did not teach with intellectual empathy, that is, they seldom tried to explain or understand different or opposing viewpoints. The teachers, in putting forward their lessons, came across as being far too factual and categorical about issues that were more subjective matters of belief, opinion and judgement. There was the right way to think --- that was their way --- and little else. Contradictory voices reportedly would not be listened to, or heard.

In some classrooms, spontaneity was stifled in the interests of a felt need for order and firm discipline. The teachers' primary aim was to defend against change, to control their pupils, and by so doing instil in them attitudes of submission, docility, and deference. Aspects of their pupils' behaviour, verbal and otherwise, mainly ones irrelevant in the assessment of their intellectual potential, were often employed, seemingly engendering self-fulfilling prophecies [41]. The punishments that were meted out by parents, teachers or other pupils for being different or behaving differently could easily establish a fear of non-conformity. The correction of mistakes, if not accomplished with care, could provoke anticipatory anxiety. In general, what was learned was that responding differently from other people could produce anxiety as a consequence. Like much social conditioning, this anxiety can generalise to the point that the expression, perhaps also the thinking, of different opinions may arouse aversive fight-or-flight drives and associated feelings. From the teachers' viewpoint this would be positively reinforcing --- the classroom would be made orderly, under control, and its daily rituals maintained rigidly.

Creativity and curiosity were often bounded by the availability of work materials and a one-dimensional work ethic, and also by rules governing the exact placing of objects in the environment. Many forms of control placed on creative activities were de-motivating, and could have had a detrimental effect on creativity and the quality of artistic production, and on subsequent related intrinsic motivations and exploratory activities [42, 43, 44]. Even certain rewards can have similar effects if they place undo pressure to perform in a specific manner

[45, 46, 47, 48]. Rewards, if perceived as diminishing self-determination and thereby undermining autonomy, or of inducing an unnecessarily competitive element, also can have a negative impact on self-esteem [49, 50, 51].

Schools serve a multitude of socializing functions. These include spelling out and rewarding those social goals broadly endorsed by the wider society of the time. Teachers, guidance counsellors, and administrative staff collaborated together in this, and acted as intermediaries with those exerting leadership and social control in the adult world. Teachers' unsung successes often involved instilling positive values and performing other vital communication interface services.

Transgressors, eccentrics or other rebels, have been launched on early careers of ascribed deviance, scarred by labels and pseudo-diagnostic evaluations that hampered their progress through primary school and beyond. Sometimes the label was based on a series of mistakes by teachers, and compounded by the cruelty of other children. These errors and cruelties may themselves be based on some trait in the individual child involved, that then becomes blown out of all proportion over the years. The relevant question should be, "What do we want children who happen to be different to believe about themselves?" Following up on that is to better understand what children want from their many educational experiences, and how that might diverge from what responsible adults think is best for them.

Pupils should be encouraged to discover the implicit models in their own minds. Very young children find that thinking, and subjects akin to ethics, philosophy and psychology, can be fun. However, as competing influences for their attention took over, certain forms of learning seemed more of a chore, of work given to them that they didn't regard with the same kind of joyous self-initiated curiosity that they once had. With good parents and good teachers, their earlier attitudes of discovery could have been recaptured. Whenever and however they achieved that central option led them to realize many further choices, to progress, to open up further options for themselves.

Creativity is facilitated when that involves children working autonomously and towards their own goals [52, 53]. Originality represents a departure from conformity. Many of such deliberate attempts to overturn orthodoxy can produce fruitful, though unexpected, results [54]. How many teachers, even today, provide the impetus and self-confidence to support their pupils' creative flights of imagination?

In several respects there is sometimes an evident overlap between childhood eccentricity and intellectual giftedness [55]. The psychiatrist Kazimierz Dabrowski identified certain characteristics, which he called "overexcitabilities" or "supersentivities", most of which I have found to be shared by both eccentric children and gifted children. These are rapid speech, impulsive behaviour, competitiveness, compulsive talking, compulsive organizing, the appreciation of beauty, deep curiosity, love of knowledge for its own sake, love of problem-solving, avid reading, probing questioning, theoretical thinking, independent thinking, vivid dreams, good senses of humour, magical thinking, love of fantasy, daydreaming, having imaginary friends and detailed daytime visualization [56].

In Britain, precociousness has incorrectly been perceived as problematic and a liability both for gifted children and their parents, and is seen this way by some teachers and psychologists. In a peculiar way these children's advantages are too often seen as disadvantages.

Eccentric children's kind of divergent creativity, because it did not conform either to what was expected, or indeed what was wanted, has been poorly recognized and sometimes actively thwarted. The following narrative is from a gifted eccentric with a very high intellectual capability: "When I was four I began attending a nursery school, but I never felt the slightest inclination to play with the other children. One day my mother took me to see the headmistress, who had asked to see us. 'You'll just have to face it, Mrs. E,' she said, 'your son is a simpleton.' A few days later I remarked to my grandfather, 'Grandpappy, I'm a simpleton!' My mother was furious, and told me never to say such a thing again.

"At primary school I found it very difficult to communicate with other children. I spent most of the breaks standing on my own in the corner of the playground. Whenever I tried to socialise with my fellow pupils, I was amazed by their pettiness, by their selfishness, and most of all by their hypocrisy. I cried often, and children who are prone to crying are never popular at school. My four years at secondary modern school were probably the most miserable of my life. I had been bullied rather badly before, but now I was beaten up, kicked, spat on, and humiliated in a hundred other ways every single day. The so-called justice and punishment system meted out at my school was far from perfect. I couldn't handle authority, and there were several teachers who taught everything not by individual discovery but only by recourse to their greater authority. There could be no justification for what they put me through. At the time, it undercut a lot of their Religious Education teaching. They taught a lot about moral principles by which individuals were supposed to be guided. The hypocrites! What I really learned is that if a child is presented with unexpected brutality from his fellow pupils and unjust treatment from a teacher, he will be less likely to believe that justice will always prevail, or that it will always come about even-handedly and equitably throughout one's life. Incidentally, because of this, I never went to university."

(Rick, age thirty-four)

Admittedly, this account is one-sided. It would be salutary to try to imagine the points-of-view of the teachers and other children concerned in the above incidents. For the sake of balance, it is fair comment that sometimes the eccentric child is the principal determinant and lone perpetrator of mischief and misbehaviour. Some of their miniature revolts were far from hidden, and bearing in mind their chronological age, can best be savoured from a quiet retrospective distance. Such is the case with the following person, whom some would say exercised an excess of self-determination: "I could tell the time and also read fluently before I was two. I learned to write early as well --- long before normal school age. This was a policy of my parents, but I did not disagree with it. I enjoyed opportunities for learning, even reading adverts, street posters, and sauce bottles.

"When I was six, it was decided to try out some form of schooling for me, and a local school was chosen. It was private, co-ed, and smelt of wet clothes, disinfectant, India rubber and disinfectant. I think I spent about half a term there, if that. The first problem arose because I could read and write and felt bored in the kindergarten. To amuse myself I dared the children to drink ink out of a fountain pen I had that had a hole in it through which you could suck up the ink. Not surprisingly a lot of them became sick, and my mother was asked to discipline me. She couldn't. I had no respect for her.

"During this very short period I managed to recruit a 'gang' of village children, mainly boys, who came home with me after lunch and water-pistolled passers-by from our front garden. A maid left because of this, and the school asked my parents to remove me because of my disruptive influence. The next school was just down the road, but it was no more successful. I was bored and spent most of my time in Matron's room. The war closed this school. I had been there for less than a year. This left only two other schools in the village. One was a convent school; the other was the village school. My mother was implacably against the village school for all the usual middle class reasons, and my father was against the convent school because he feared religious indoctrination, but (he) was the weaker of the two and gave in. It didn't last long.

"Within one term my parents had been formally asked to remove me, and the list of offences was quite varied: first, coming to school improperly dressed. About this time I started to walk barefoot everywhere --- I can't tell you why --- I enjoyed the experience for its own sake, but there was an element of 'sez you!' towards my parents, who had the humiliation of sending maids and sundry members of the household between the house and the school searching the gutters for my cast-offs. Punishment, even severe beatings, had no effect. I was developing a will of my own. Second, I was leading my fellow pupils into sin. This simply meant that I asked them --- incredulously --- if they *really* believed in the Virgin Birth, etcetera. Third, I was failing in obedience. Sent to the chapel, frequently, for talking in class, running in the corridors, not addressing the nuns properly, not standing up for the Mother Superior, etcetera, etcetera.

"From the age of eight all formal education stopped. My father educated me himself with the aid of sundry governesses and tutors. When I asked too many questions, the latter seemed devoid of equanimity. None of them lasted the pace for long. The procedure was simple: no curriculum --- any question I asked would be dealt with. Education on demand. I had almost total freedom of choice: no one had the stamina to battle it out with me if I chose not to study something, or chose to study something else. A couple of years after my war ended we moved and I considered my childhood at an end."

(Miriam, age fifty-three)

Many eccentrics feel bitter about their education or complain about particular teachers' failures to involve them. To say the least, their experience of school was negative, and often contrary to what they thought they wanted. Teachers tended to ignore what they felt and what they said. The teachers were also often reluctant or unwilling to speed up the tempo or complexity of their brighter pupils' instruction, even when it was patently warranted. Here follows several examples of this taken from my interviews with the eccentric informants:

"I was not stretched or pushed at school and I was presented with lessons which were incredibly easy. Needless to say I became lazy and bored and retreated into myself. One of the reasons for my introversion was the fact that I now attended a school to which people of no intellectual ability were sent. What followed? Five years of the same. I seemed to drift further away from my contemporaries. I couldn't get out of school quickly enough."

(Jimmy, age thirty-two)

"A lot of teachers in my primary school did not recognise my potential --- another reason for thinking them stupid. They tried to treat me as an ordinary child, which I was not. My mother later sent me to the local grammar school. Here I did not think my potential was recognised and therefore I did not bother working hard. I wanted someone to say, 'You are different. I recognise that, and it is a good thing.' I felt different but my teachers told me that the reason for this was that something was wrong with me, and that I suffered from some sort of character deformity that made communication difficult. For it was in this way that I felt odd --- I felt unable to communicate with others in a way that I would like. Conversations always lacked depth. I never fell in with any particular group. If I said what I thought, others might ignore it, laugh at it, or simply fail to understand it. That problem still exists today.

"I wrote poetry, dreamt of sailing off to Tahiti, and pursued what I daringly thought at the time to be deep philosophical issues when most of the other lads were kicking around footballs. Thanks to a P. E. teacher and a vindictive headmaster, I was expelled from an academically-minded selective school, ostensibly for repeated disobedience by breaking some newly-imposed rules. Things changed, in retrospect mostly for the better. When I went to a grammar school, I think my self-awareness was positively heightened because several good teachers challenged my more premature understandings of life, philosophy, and history. They did it by pushing me to consider other possibilities above and beyond those I had developed throughout my previous prejudiced tuition."

(Leslie, age forty)

Ordinary schooling techniques generally tended to militate against the attainment of individual enquiry. Children were urged to be goal-orientated and competitive. Competition could have reached such an intense degree that it may have undermined the very purpose of education itself. The eminent mathematician G. H. Hardy believed, for instance, that the competitive examination for the Mathematical Tripos to establish the most prestigious "Wranglers" among Cambridge students effectively wiped out creative mathematics in England for a century.

With high levels of competition that were not always necessary, it was easier for teachers to stress the importance of deferring gratification. The excitement of discovery was discouraged. Any element of enjoyment was remorselessly squeezed out. Usually, only serious classroom activities were permitted. Interactions with the "outside world" were reserved for special occasions, as if it would be too untidy or confusing to illustrate what the process of education was really preparing young people to do.

Less structured situations were avoided; these would expose the average pupil's inability to cope independently, without cues, without spoon-feeding, without the artificial cushioning of partly irrelevant curricula. Boundaries, between what was considered to count as education and what was not, were maintained, not to divide social reality, as Ivan Illich claimed, but rather to suppress thoughts of social or political change [57].

Schools fostered chains of conformity. Teachers were made to feel that the maintenance of order and control was the principal priority from which good education flowed. Their competence was judged by how well they controlled their pupils, and by how quiet their classrooms were [58, 59, 60, 61, 62]. In such settings, a failure to conform led rapidly to labels of deviance sometimes followed by corrective actions --- punishment, guidance, referral to health practitioners or social workers, treatment, suspension, and expulsion. Non-conformity was reduced or transformed into a range of pathological disorders: attention deficit and hyperactivity disorder, conduct disorder, school phobia or school refusal, and so on. Such labels were attached to non-conforming children quite readily.

Seeing only their outward dreaminess, teachers categorically misunderstood the inherent positivity of some of their young charges' strength of imagination. What was most wrong with the school was inverted: the school authorities neatly reversed the situation by blaming the victim. Young people were turned into scapegoats for being young, and the conditions contributing to their difficulties were never addressed directly by the people most responsible for them. By so doing, the teachers avoided the need to question the social milieu that they created and in which the child had been inextricably bound.

Inventiveness and fantasy in their young pupils constituted a threat to the teachers' morale, and possibly the achievement of their desired disciplinary and pedagogic goals. Schools were not geared to change or to confront changes in society. The eccentric and gifted children who remained wouldn't hesitate to tentatively correct teachers, or amplify what they thought they were trying to explain. This could lead them into challenging or further cross-questioning, not out of disrespect or arrogance but simply to find out more. Here follows four examples of these phenomena:

"For three years I got the strap twice a week for bad writing. One teacher first berated what I was trying to do, and then she drew an orange on top of mine to show me how to do it. I was crushed. I failed every art exam in secondary school, but became a certificated junior teacher myself. The continual pressures of being one of the crowd subverted my individual development."

(Julia, age forty-one)

"My family sent me to school in clothing from my dancing class, to wear it out, so I wore velvet jacket, lace cummerbund, with bells on. I discovered I was short-sighted and so had to wear glasses. My grandmother put shredded garlic in my shoes and wolf's bane in my locket necklace to ward off germs, but also I suspect, evil spirits. My family would not have me inoculated against any disease, and the teacher made me stand on my desk while she poked fun at me, and the rest of the class laughed. Whilst all this was going on I simply looked down my nose at them and felt superior."

(Mina, age forty-three)

"Well and truly indoctrinated in three different faith schools by the time I was fourteen, when I realized what I had been taught to be the voice of Satan's minions was really my own internal voice, a part of me, and that the still small voice of Conscience was also my own voice and a part of me, did I feel free to cut loose and rebel. Soon afterwards, I was peremptorily and totally unfairly expelled . . . for the first time."

(Ralph, age forty-four)

"I was always daydreaming. School was great when it allowed me the freedom to create, but when I had to conform, I usually refused to, which got me into a lot of trouble. Schools are one of the types of places in the developed world that practically everyone attends in their life, and where simply talking too much is actively discouraged and sometimes punished. Holding independent opinions, especially taking a certain view that is different from the one purveyed by a teacher, is not exactly cherished either. Several times I felt I couldn't take it anymore and ran away from school. It was about this time that I blew up a garage with my rocket fuel experiments, and started correcting my maths and science teachers. In 1967, I got into trouble because I told one teacher there were two planets beyond Pluto, and that there were many more moons in orbit around the major planets in our own system. He could accept the possibility of moons, but not extra planets. I told another science teacher that neutrons are not actually neutral, but are positively charged, and negated by the more negative electron. Naturally I was thrown out of class. I really deserved what I got."

(Gabriel, age thirty-three)

The nuclear family's Alcatraz

The adolescent years, maximally befuddling and often seemingly indecisive, explode with angst, premature disillusionment, and what appears to many parents as gratuitous rebellion. This is so common that Anna Freud once went so far as to assert that adolescent rebellion is essential to becoming a "well adjusted" adult [63]. This was probably an exaggeration, if not a mistake, and has since been overturned by a body of reliable research evidence [64, 65]. A major finding from these subsequent surveys was that fourteen to twenty per cent of teenagers never showed any form of rebelliousness, but nevertheless went on to be perfectly normal adults. Anthropological fieldwork also indicates that rebellion is not shown by adolescents in all societies [66]. Therefore, teenage rebellion is unlikely to be necessary for good personality functioning in later adult life.

Rebellion through joining similar teenage peer groups is a commonplace part of adolescents' struggles to define themselves, though not usually a sign of eccentricity. Many seek out these transitional groups to obtain a personal and social identification that will make them happy. Teenagers converge towards their group's norms; problems arise because their parents do not always like the problematic behaviours their teenagers' newfound norms apparently give rise to. Of course, their parents themselves typically would have grown up with different prior experiences and developed different world-views, much of which they would not, or could not, talk about with their younger adolescent children.

Parents' exploitation of their young children's appropriate earlier dependency sometimes later can become part of an attempt by the parents to make them act in accordance with their greater authority, and in line with their wishes, or to over-control their older adolescents possessively, rather than helping them to develop their appropriate independence.

The greatest revisionists of past feelings --- and memories --- are adolescents. Acquiring a distinct personality often requires some kind of change, and that can include the ability to defy some previously accepted normative behaviours. This often involves rejecting the standards and values of the adolescents' parents and teachers. Some parents, teachers and sundry child-rearing experts have portrayed this negatively, as a war of attrition, with repeated arguments sometimes almost disintegrating former childhood understandings between teenagers and their parents. However, some of these disagreements can turn out to be constructive, even cathartic, for some families.

In their developing minds, adolescents first make advances in their capacity to think about emotions, though this usually comes before they are fully capable of regulating those emotions. For many eccentric adolescents, there was a problematic continuation from the emotional tribulations of childhood into romanticised storms of negativism. Imposed on this was a new range of chaotic feelings and attendant behaviours as their personality development proceeded apace, sometimes seemingly in a haphazard fashion.

Socially, this is the time when acceptance by their peers becomes more important. There can be more than a hint of inward-looking, and outward-looking searching for role models, as well as some narcissism and desperation about this. This is enhanced and fortified by the social media, which taps in to the needs related to the pre-adolescents' newfound feelings about their success or failure in becoming liked.

Eccentric adolescents' major struggles are for the achievement of personal identity and greater freedom, though as much for acceptance, attention or control over others. They begin to ask themselves what having a self-identity might require. They can begin to feel they can choose to be themselves without the approval of their parents or peer groups. Their families and teachers were not at all successful in squelching their sense of uniqueness, or their pride when they began to exercise their early beginnings of individual effectiveness. Parents were less able to inculcate them with the more "mature" stereotyped ideas they had wanted them to take on. The adolescents' hard-won freedoms helped them to attempt to circumvent or overcome the inhibitions and prohibitions placed upon them. They felt they enjoyed the experience of greater autonomy, and also the idea that it may have been within their power to master that autonomy.

Gaining an autonomous sense of self --- a secure self-confidence that whatever one does, it will be from the right motives --- was part of their hoped-for development: "In my mind I was resolved to empower myself to emphasize my right to be myself, though in my heart I was full of what seemed like soaring impulses which made me hover back and forth between my family's wishes . . . what I knew to be about duties . . . and my freedom. When I chose, it was the hardest course, and it was weeks later after I ran away to sea that I began to feel the pangs of homesickness. It was years later that I learned that one needed to strike a more well-tempered balance between responsibilities to oneself and to others."

(Eric, age forty-five)

The parents of young eccentrics could feel incompetent when faced with their offsprings' novel behaviour and ideas. Whether their parents liked it or not --- and they usually didn't --- the eccentric adolescents' courage endowed them early with the ability to stand up for themselves, and to support unpopular peers and unpopular causes.

This degree of self-directedness suggests that these adolescents had attained some personal standards for gauging and for guiding their actions. Young people form standards for judging their behaviour partly on the basis of how people who are important in their lives have reacted to them. There is little evidence from my research to suggest that teenage eccentrics were inherently any less impressionable than other teenagers. It was not only those precepts that had been taught to them that were influential. Parents and teachers not only prescribed and taught standards of self-evaluation; they also exemplified or modelled them by responding to the teenagers' social behaviour.

One could argue, from the research of Gregory Elliott, that, by early adolescence, the eccentrics had grown less vulnerable to the criticism heaped upon them [67]. Good self-esteem also resulted from their diminishing tendency to present a false front to the world. As they matured emotionally, the direct effects of low self-esteem on lying and fantastic fabrication usually waned. Instead, they gained insights into honest comparisons with others and by the social learning that took place at around this time. This was exemplified by what a number of our eccentric informants reported:

"My parents were hardly unusual by the standards existing then on the fringes of post-war sub-London suburbia. Looking back, abstracting from this unpeculiar particular to the general, my upbringing must have been lived by millions of other similar youngsters. However, my combined curiosity and contrariness, or maybe it was a rogue gene, meant that I bounced through my life with, at times, yearning, quizzical all the while, looking for understanding, and always questioning others to the point where I was repeatedly and mistakenly taken for someone I am not. That is the paradox that faced me whenever I cared to question myself more deeply. I chose the paths I took. I don't think I lost my inherent honesty to myself. And I have always tried to remain true to whatever I was feeling inside at the time."

(Saul, age forty-six)

"Watching others' silent reactions for years, and brought up to be the kind of person my parents and other people wanted me to be, I came to understand enough to know that little person who didn't have much of a voice definitely was not me . . . nor was I ever meant to be like that. Now I'm no longer backward at coming forward."

(Abigail, age twenty-nine)

In and around school, popular students who seemingly controlled the significant perceptions of who was popular and who was not were more powerful in exerting social influence [68, 69]. Assessed social desirability, and the saliency of comparisons with others, now became a mainstay for the majority. However, an adolescent who has gained a moderate degree of self-confidence and who goes his own way, unconcerned with popularity, may have found that his peers will then have perceived him as a tower of strength [70]. Such teenagers have a head start in life.

During the first few years of adolescence there is increasing pressure from within and without to develop a coherent personality, one that comprehends personal values and shifting allegiances to people and causes. This is a period in teenagers' lives when they are also learning how to go about asserting themselves and testing the limits imposed on them to see how far they can go. Many eccentric teenagers had begun doing this somewhat earlier than average. Those who were shy and withdrawn were neglected by their peers and emerged from adolescence as social isolates. Self-absorption led to isolation, and vice versa. Many young individualists, confident of their own goals and mastery, and possessed of a strong sense of their own identities, did *not* need or seek approbation from their peers. They were ready for early intimacy, but could, if they wanted, distance themselves from others, avoiding or delaying certain experiences to suit themselves.

The early development of sexual characteristics and sensual feelings was also partly responsible for additional stress, and also for objectionable behaviour that parents could find difficult to control. Those who physically matured earlier tended to break more rules and do so more frequently [71]. These early maturers also ignored their parents' and teachers' prohibitions considerably more often. Early biological maturation may have long term repercussions, particularly in regard to education and personal relationships. Here is a case in point from my sample of eccentric informants: "At the age of eleven I remember feeling sexy. I wore my new summer nightgown into the living room when we had a twelve-year-old boy and his mother visiting. I was promptly reprimanded by my mother, but pranced around in a halter-top in front of the same boy a few weeks later.

"My parents got rather irate with me when I was chucked out of school. That was for going out with choirboys, and my teachers were annoyed with me because my academic standards were not particularly clever. My version was that I thought I was being badly taught. I think I went off and did all sorts of things that my parents did not approve of. They sent me to a preparatory cramming school, but I got thoroughly fed up, frustrated and bored, and got chucked out of there too. That did not please my parents very much and they more or less wiped their hands of me and told me to get a job, which I did. Much to their surprise, and slightly to mine, I worked in a dress shop for a bit. That was fun --- it was interesting, but one did not meet people there that one wanted to meet.

"My mama's ambition was for me to marry somebody landed, early. That would have been nice, but they were all so damn stupid I couldn't stand them. The kind of men I was supposed to go around with were so absolutely awful --- they were all upper class twits and not one of them had a brain in his head. I eventually got married. There again, much to my parents' distress, he was the wrong man, as they thought then. I now know they were correct, but what do you do? You fall in love and marry. You have children, get on with life and if your marriage falls part you get divorced and carry on with life. The biggest problem in my life has been men --- men in the plural and my total inability to say no. If a man wants to take me to bed I tend to say yes, because I am stupid. Men are the problem now."

(Lynn, age thirty-five)

The typical teenager's body image inevitably changed, and this created a heightened concern about the reactions of others. Those not as embroiled in this because they remained self-centred, unwilling to meet some of the needs of others, were likely to receive less consideration by others in return.

However, teenage eccentricity may be adaptive for a number of other reasons. Such teenagers may prefer to be laughed at rather than ignored. In this way, they were assured of some attention, though it may also have helped them to feel distinctive. Behaviour that mocks convention and frustrates people in authority has great potential for fostering confidence about being oneself, and of feeling one knows where one is going in life.

Many parents want to help their children to become independent as adults, and to be what they want to be. Important questions for adolescents of a certain relative maturity are whether they feel controlled or in control of what happens to them, whether they feel a sense of their own purpose or not, and whether they feel fulfilled or discontented in what they are doing. I mention these questions here because so much eccentricity begins in childhood and adolescence, with some dissatisfaction and what would be called alienation had they been adults.

Eccentric adolescents' early ways to demonstrate their confident autonomy was to go against the grain, to antagonise, and to oppose where there may not have been much external necessity to have done so. On the other hand, this self-determination can result in positive self-affirming actions and an ineluctable independence of thought. Their minds were not so much cynically warped by their earlier experiences, but rather these adolescent eccentrics proceeded to reclaim the independence and self-direction of their conscious thinking.

To be autonomous is, in a very basic sense, to be free of external constraints that matter less to the individual. We may all be the products of our culture, but that is no reason why the self should not be free. Democracy can be a very difficult way of life for parents and teachers. Democracy means there is always a potential for resistance.

Young people have been more absolutist in regard to their value systems, and also can be determined to put their ideas into practice. This derives from an astonishing degree of idealism. Teenagers learn that there is a deep divide between the values that are espoused by society and the way in which adults act upon those values. They begin to see through society's covert ideologies, some of which are based on rarely spoken assumptions, and the eccentric adolescent may become better attuned at detecting them. The conflicts of adolescence may sharpen the young person's understanding of what is really taking place behind the scenes. What they can see is the enormous gap between promise and performance. It need not always be that way. Perhaps earlier educational intervention and social enrichment programmes may have helped a number of eccentric adolescents.

Some adolescents are intimidated, terrified of being exposed as different. Some are not happy to hide behind the invisibility that insipid conformity might afford them. Some choose to fight back. This can be uniquely exhilarating.

Chapter 5. Glimpses at Unknown Modes of Being
(The Thought and Language of Eccentrics)

Uttering a word is like striking a note on the keyboard of the imagination.

Ludwig Wittgenstein, *Philosophical Investigations, 6*

Aldous Huxley once estimated, I know not how, that seventy per cent of human existence is dominated by verbal thought and language. Languages, be they verbal or mathematical, are both carriers of banal communication and of radical world-changing ideas. Words, numbers and other vehicles of communication are extremely powerful, and possess the inherent potential for novel configurations and multiple contingencies. Because of that, and for other reasons, the use of language is a far more complicated type of human behaviour than formerly had been appreciated.

Though the ongoing self-concept is one of the most significant elements of human consciousness, how often do people give any thought to the subtleties of its central functions in our lives? Nowadays, people are much less frequently asked by psychologists about how they do their thinking, the *process*, the *how* of it. Introspection has long been out of favour, diminished as a scientific method, though people no doubt do something like it at least on an irregular basis.

Language expresses organically progressing thoughts, and that helps to make sense of the events, random and otherwise, that impinge on each individual's separately ego-bound and individually unique consciousness. It is in the effort after meaning that is communication, both verbal and non-verbal, that we may get to know *what* other people think, but unless we ask we might not understand how they went about making their judgments, understandings, inferences and so on. Private languages clearly do not enable communication, so they are doomed to fail in these functions.

Language is crucial in the process of coming to mutual understandings. How we talk and think about others determines, in part, how we act toward them. Talk, conversation, and discussion act as social glue, and it structures, in part, our perceptions of reality [1]. However imperfectly it is conveyed, language is a social tool.

Language is a complex and systematic structure whose rules, grammar and syntax provide consistent form to our views of the world. It is also the main vehicle for the conscious transmission of a society's ideologies. Society constructs and develops "normal" and "natural" arrangements for what are permissible forms of relationships. By imposing the family's and the greater society's ideas of what it is to be normal, it can also act as one of the milder, though deceptive, means of suppressing alternative visions of what a society should be like.

Some of our understandings might only be partial, some may be faulty or incorrect, or knowable with any degree of certainty because of what other people say, and depends on how they go about phrasing, describing, limiting, hiding or otherwise obfuscating what they know. People often state ideas in terms that are logically contradictory. One also has to listen carefully at times for what a person is not saying as well as what he is drawing attention to by affirming. Nevertheless, language and thinking can provide the means of liberating oneself from having to use immediate visual appearances as the sole basis for making judgements. Both also comprise a system of social and symbolic exchange. We can speak of the sharing of knowledge, and of the products of the imagination, as a shared experience.

A closer look at how eccentrics use this major system of interpersonal communication may give away some important clues about how they think. The varieties of eccentric thinking may also reveal something to us about our more accustomed modes of thinking. What we personally consider perfectly conventional may be generated from the kernels of less than rational psychological processes. Such an approach has helped to elucidate the translation of thoughts into language in schizophrenia.

Without a theoretical context, the idea of all that is called schizophrenia has been called "an idea without an essence". Psychiatry's view of schizophrenia is without any conceptual focal point. It is a set of artificial empirical diagnostic constructs whose boundaries do not encompass and demarcate what is there in nature.

One cannot deny that there are many people who become severely disturbed in what they perceive, think and do. Trying to apply psycholinguistics to this group may appear to be rather like trying to sprint before one can crawl, though there already have been a number of very enlightening contributions to this field [2, 3, 4, 5, 6, 7, 8, 9].

Genuinely deviant language systems can be better understood by contrasting them against that from which they deviate. Eccentrics, because they are more readily comprehensible, may therefore be a good intermediate comparison group, though sharing perhaps some of the thought and language characteristics of schizophrenics.

Schizophrenia sufferers do not abandon the entirety of communication. Their utterances are not entirely devoid of meaning; sometimes they are symbolic and mysteriously informative. However, largely unaware of the severe incongruities and poor logical sequencing in their use of language, their discourse is marked by multiple discontinuities. In their conversation, the regulative links between ideas can appear to be lost. The concepts formed by them are over-generalized, their thinking consequently over-inclusive. Psychotic communications admittedly can sometimes be difficult to decipher, even when heard in context. Shared social meanings are scrambled or, like something out of Alice's misadventures in Wonderland, strategically reversed. As the French psychoanalyst Jacques Lacan pointed out, words and images in schizophrenia do not appear to express a coherent rationality.

On the other hand, those eccentrics who use language in unorthodox ways are not unaware of their inconsistencies and idiosyncratic language usage, but take no pains to avoid them. In some of their language output there were clear deviations from what would be expected to follow from a particular train of thought. A small but not insignificant portion of their thinking was allusive and symbolic. It still remained unified by themes and was internally consistent, and possessed a certain peculiar logic within its own parameters, much like some heightened forms of poetry and expressive art. A smaller number, slightly under ten percent of the eccentric sample, had unusual ways of expressing themselves with figures of speech, remote allusions to spiritualistic texts, and ideas not uncommon in the science fiction and fantasy genres.

Symbols are not relinquished by either schizophrenics or eccentrics --- far from it --- but reveal and conceal, pointing towards, if not fully disclosing, a different ordering of reality and experience. A special kind of power attaches to symbols. Symbols can become imbued with a power that the individual may not possess. The way they are expressed can sound uncanny but are often accessible. Problems in thinking and language are problems of symbols and their meanings. Some anomalous utterances are based on interlocking rogue propositions and burdened with multiple contradictions. Here, for example, is an aberrant language sample from an eccentric who, over some time, gradually had succumbed to an episode of late onset paranoid psychosis: "The present EEC-NATO has ten heads. Until the fall of America and Russia these ten are only significant to the Europeans and Britain, but they can be reckoned the ten iron and clay toes of the figure of Nehruchadnasser's (pronounced Nehru-Chad-Nassers) dream. Who will rise to fill the vacuum left by the exit of the present giants? A definite time would seem to come when Israel made a seven-year pact with this power bloc, which the beast breaks after three and a half years. A person from the pit, Revelations nine-thirteen, could be Nimrod, a Satanist, takes possession of the body bearing the marks, a blind right eye, and a useless arm and his number is 666-Superman --- and he caused an image of the beast with a computer brain to be set up in the temple and no one could buy or sell unless they had the name or number of the beast stamped indelibly on his hand or forehead. A mystic number that appears as a double prophesy. From that time, trade in goods of every description has used money value according to the metal used. When the 'Personality' caused every person to use the number to obtain goods without using coinage, the system is cancelled because, to accept these terms, we accept the Antichrist. All monetary transactions will soon be confined to banks and everyone will use a personal card and number. After this year's census, the computer will name and number every person alive in Europe. All who refuse the name and number are doomed."

(Esther, age sixty-five)

What is it about this nightmarish account that gives it its eerie quality? There must be more to it than a derivative apocalyptic vision. One can begin to get at this if one asks what there is about its language that is *different* from normal language. At a rudimentary level, it is a declaration and a warning. It is highly personal, though it is also enmeshed in beliefs deriving from a fundamentalist variant of Christianity. Some of these beliefs are neither necessarily true nor false, nor are they indeed provable. They are indeterminate, though not to Esther, who gave total credence to every particle of them, and to her explanations, striking as she was in her absolute faith in what she was saying.

There was something else about this material that was so simple it was not immediately apprehended. As a dialogue between two persons, it was a signal failure. Esther had no inkling that the typical listener might not necessarily be particularly interested or share in any element of her expressed beliefs. She would not have picked up any of her listener's non-verbal cues of confusion or disbelief. The presence of a listener would have been meaningless to her; the narrative line would have proceeded in the same way in his absence. He could contribute nothing to it. Esther, for her part, would usually ignore any other person's interjections as well.

When heard the first time, the typical listener would have missed many of Esther's allusions and numerical references. Also, he would not have particularly noticed the partial loss of normal speech transitions and constraints. However, he would have been able to follow the main thrust of her argument, and to grasp the connections. He almost immediately may have "interpreted" the surface message. He may have realised how it was based on present-day worries exaggerated into near-paranoid fears --- how the triumphant powers of technology and/or rampant consumerism may insidiously enslave humanity.

It is not only what is said, but also the way the words are spoken, the social paralinguistics of each dialogue or unintended monologue. The watchful listener may have noted Esther's neutral, detached demeanour. There was a clear disjunction between her genteel appearance and the anguish enclosed in what she had to say. How many times had she recited this same incantation, to herself or to others?

One might then ask why the supernatural was juxtaposed with then-current geo-political and economic issues? Current events were intricately woven into Esther's account, as a kind of proof of her predictions. At the time, bank mortgages, credit and loan arrangements, and the more discreditable practices of financial executives were much in the news. Esther, powerless, living alone and humbly in poverty, had been struggling for many years simply to make ends meet.

To read an unexpurgated transcript of the above only begins the process of understanding the personal import of the narrative for the speaker. Symbols of power are used throughout, the most powerful forces imaginable to the lady concerned --- beginning with a reference to the "present giants" of the dominant superpowers, to the Bible (a particular reading of the New Testament), the horror story ("America's Frankenstein" was later mentioned), the Superman myth, the mystique of what computers might do, and the power of prophecy (read destiny). Not only symbols, endowed with a certain power, were involved. So too were various institutions, particularly those of central governments, because they were seen by Esther to be agents of social control.

The following eccentric's troubles began with his examination of ideas concerning practical political reform, and developed in ways that eventually brought him into confrontation with the individuals whose functions he sought to change. The premises of his arguments invite close analysis:

1. "Freedom is being whittled away by a state apparatus which persecutes dissidents and suppresses free speech and destroys democracy. Many eminent people have warned that grave trouble lies ahead for Britain unless there is reform of the system of government. One of the main problems with the present system is the abuse of power by civil servants and other officials who are not accountable to anyone."

2. "Britain is not a democracy, but a tyranny. Lord Hailsham called the system an elective dictatorship, but in fact most of the decisions in Britain today are not made by elected ministers but by low-minded officials who are unelected, unaccountable, and contemptuous of democracy and natural justice. Neither is the Ombudsman much help."

3. "The tyrannies of public officials, and the other defects in the constitution, are causing injustice and inefficiency, and the result is social disorder and economic decline."

4. "The new democracy will drastically limit the arbitrary power of an oppressive, narrow minded, and dictatorial bureaucracy, which is why the Establishment is fanatically opposing reform by all the means at its disposal. In 1981 Lord Marsh said, 'One of the great things about this country is that there is no problem of anyone being persecuted.' I can show that he was wrong."

5. "A reasonable person would expect that the security services would only be interested in Communists and fascists and other extremists, but the Establishment is so terrified of democracy that it even harasses moderates like me who want to improve the system. The principal security service is called MI5 and it has effective control over the whole of officialdom, including the Police Special Branch. That is why no dissident can look to the police for protection against the lawless activities of MI5. Unfortunately, MI5 lacks the mental capacity to understand that dissidents are the guardians of freedom and the main source of progress. Consider the Chartists and the Suffragettes."

6. "The authorities know that I know. They seem to be afraid that if ever my ideas ever came to public attention, a strong demand would develop for a new democracy, and this would threaten the power of the Establishment."

(Hal, age thirty-eight)

What then is incorrect about the above sequence of thought? Any rational person would first want to be presented with the evidence for several of Hal's opening points. Is freedom actually being "whittled away"? How would one go about proving that assertion? There is recourse to statements by influential people. "Grave trouble" is envisaged for the future if nothing is done. Two dire notions, the destruction of democracy and a coming catastrophe, are placed ominously alongside each other, but are causally connected only by vague implication. However, by citing what could happen, this becomes the reason for persuading people to change, and leads to the next premise, which is more critical of the present arrangements.

Premise 2 unfolds from the fear that some people have had about the relative power of government officials, but then states, as if from first-hand knowledge, that the inner workings of the minds of civil servants are "low minded" and "contemptuous". It is as if the speaker can read the minds of perfect strangers, with, at best, knowledge of only selected specific behaviours and results. There is also the assumption that most bureaucrats hold similar disdainful ideas about decision-making, democracy, and justice.

Premise 3 is the most damaging. It states a direct (though unproven) cause-and-effect relationship between tyranny (never proven) *and* detrimental socio-economic outcomes. Despite not wishing to defend tyranny --- who does? --- one can cite historical examples (for example, some of the ancient Greek city-states, Imperial Rome and Elizabethan England) in which tyranny arguably had the opposite outcomes of cultural advance and relative prosperity for their times.

Premise 4 is stated with the same certainty as the preceding premises, in much the same way as a politician would wish to project his own self-assurance. Many "new democracies" that have been ardently espoused in the recent past have not led to the mitigation of oppression.

Premise 5 uses a combination of two oratorical tricks, the three-part list and the contrastive pair. By using the first he lumps together Communists, fascists and extremists, an idea that may be correct though it is tantamount to verbal abuse. He thereby makes it plain he is brave enough to be willing to attack these targets. By then bringing on the moderate, himself, as the second part of the contrastive pair, he wishes to show that he is on the right side of a fair and just argument, and by implication, a "reasonable person" and "a guardian of freedom". This lead-in, with recourse to apparent reasonableness, rhetoric and the providing of information, attempts to reduce the actual extremity of what he is saying. The contradiction is that he credits the Security Service with the efficacy and power to orchestrate the whole of officialdom, implicitly possessing almost total control, though at the same time lacking the intellectual capacity to understand the purposes and the possible value of dissent.

Premise 6 represents a not untypical worsening transition, from suspicious magical thinking into frank paranoia. Again, the authorities are attributed omniscient faculties to gain secret intelligence, though they are self-referenced to the speaker in a way that suggests the issue is beyond doubt. This is followed by the phrase "seem to be", which conveys as much of note as the specific content following it. The psychoanalyst W. R. Bion believed that particular phrase was employed by deeply disturbed people on occasions when less disturbed people would say "I think" . . . or "I believe" [10]. "They seem to be" refers to a feeling that has been changed into part-perception and part-thought. This proved misleading for Hal, contributing to his belief in an impending disaster befalling the country's democratic system. The "I" and the "authorities" are so thoroughly enmeshed together in Hal's mind, a fair example of a "loss of ego boundaries", that the fears are shown in reality to be his.

Finally, the Establishment is regarded ambiguously. It has great power but can be threatened by a lone individual's ideas receiving public attention. The ideas, and the person from whom they issue, are thereby invested with a powerful quality: Hal's ideas alone would automatically precipitate strong demands from the populace. If that were to be the case generally, civil apathy would be a thing of the past.

Here follows an example that merits detailed comparison with the previous two, not because of its content, but for how the succinct argument is framed, and how it confounds reason.

A.) "I do not believe that there can be any serious argument that punishment constitutes a deterrent to crime, nor that there is a relationship between the severity of sentence and the effectiveness of the deterrent --- of course there is!"

Again, this speaker's opening gambit is based on a debating society device, albeit a more obscure one --- stating the converse, and then voicing the opposite with certainty and gusto. Note also the use of the word "serious", used in much the same way as Hal used "a reasonable person" or "moderates like me who want to improve the system". The worst indictment against this specious reasoning behind this argument is that every year an impressive and overwhelming body of evidence supports the contrary position, which is ignored.

B.) "I do not believe that the general public want lynch law or trial by the press or the media. They do want a society which reflects what they see as the plain truth about the difference between right and wrong, and that one should be rewarded and the other punished."

This premise is cast in contrastive pairs of starkly presented black and white choices. The speaker presents himself to the world as someone capable of firm action and unequivocal resolve. The concept of "the plain truth" is similar to "common sense" for increasing one's sincerity value. Like many homespun notions, both can be contradicted by the reality and the relevance of many physical truths and theories that are counter-intuitive, that falsify and discredit such common-sense "plain truths". By bringing in moral issues of right and wrong, the speaker wishes to present himself as someone strongly on the side of the angels.

C.) "The debasement of currency has run parallel to the debasement of standards. They (the 1960s) were also years of loss of national self-confidence and erosion of respect for Britain in the world."

In this premise, there are two major, and unfortunate, hostages to logic and clear thinking. The first is the use of a fallacious correlational argument. It represents magical thinking, the confusion of propositions about the world with propositions about the uses of language. This demonstrates a feature of what was once called the "primitive" mind, in this case conflating the descriptive, evaluative, identificatory, and status-conferring roles of language [11]. Correlation and contingency are concepts that are notoriously relatively difficult for non-scientists to grasp. There has been a growing realisation, from the work of Sir James Frazer onwards, that in magical thinking there is much confusion between the concepts of similarity, contiguity and causation. Otherwise sensible people also have real difficulties in drawing valid inferences from data based on the relative probabilities of differing events occurring together. Modern anthropologists have indeed taken this further and argued that these magical modes of thought are quite universal, and that there is also a well-nigh universal disinclination for ordinary normal adults to reliably draw correct correlational lessons from their experiences [12].

The speaker also masquerades the fact that the second sentence of premise C is only his opinion. Other critics, commentators and eyewitnesses here and abroad have looked back with nostalgia at the 1960s as a brief renaissance in the cultural life and fortunes of Britain.

The only accurate way to describe this premise is that it combines a fallacious relationship with a half-truth, and is a betrayal of sound judgement.

D.) "In this climate, free expression easily became self-indulgence, sympathy for wrongdoers slipped towards sympathetic tolerance of the wrong itself, love for the sinner slipped into love for the sin."

In the light of the liberties taken with the truth in the previous premise, this last premise is sheer hypocrisy. It also shows other mild impediments to clear thought. Basically, it is the unsupported presentation of an unproven hypothesis, one man's interpretation of modern history. It is better suited to continuing the preceding faulty premises with further rhetoric rather than for exploring whether or not it has any factual foundation. Did any of the hypothetically related slippages put forward actually transpire? From this speaker's viewpoint they did, principally because they were foregone conclusions that had to emerge, predictably, from what went before. It suggests a biased orientation.

The above speaker was definitely not an eccentric. He is the former Member of Parliament for Chingford and coruscating ex-Chairman of the Conservative Party, Lord Norman Tebbitt. The inclusion here, in context, of core excerpts from his 1986 "Poison Legacy of the Permissive Society" speech is not mischievous. It is an illustration of how pervasive these faulty ways of thinking are. It is fair comment to say that most political speeches are not usually analysed in this way.

Despite rational and scientific ideals, despite the wish to know the truth, in everyday practice there appears to be a degree of overlap between the so-called "primitive" and the so-called civilised, between the paranoiac and the politician. In an increasingly secular age, one can expect political eccentricity to replace religious eccentricity as the paramount expression of odd ideas oddly construed.

One major and common mistake is based on an over-reliance on resemblances to make causal judgements. When leaders state such judgements, plausible but erroneous attributions make for multiple misunderstandings.

Such is the power of words, a clever use of them can disguise incorrect thinking of all sorts and make unsound ideas sound beautiful, even wonderfully attractive. This is not only a trick of the charismatic demagogue; unfortunately, benign preachers of all persuasions, trial lawyers, and educated pessimists trying to convince themselves and others, fall prey to such devices.

Thought is affected by language, though the two systems should not be thought of as interchangeable. The interpretation of language structures does not mean that we should necessarily assume that similar organisations exist independently of our thoughts [13]. However, people are often not aware of discrepancies between semantic meaning and what they are thinking, though such discrepancies often do exist. If a language system is imprecise, then the thinking accomplished with it cannot, at least initially, be much better. What can be put into words, numbers and symbols may act as a limitation on what can be thought, or how effectively a thought can be operated on or communicated. Occasionally, the phenomenon of having a word "on the tip of the tongue", or of not being able to express an intuitive concept well, are surface evidences of this. Language has its own modes of working, some that are arbitrary, and some that may affect our patterns of thinking.

Words, signs and symbols can be fuzzy, and sometimes misleading. However, if we tried to limit their use in verbal discourse to only those that are strictly defined and clearly used, much of ordinary communication would be rendered difficult. It's the quality of people's concepts, and their sensitivity to possible misinterpretation, that makes for clearer understandings.

One important function of language is its socially unifying aspect. Sometimes it is used to influence the listener, and sometimes to persuade. The ways that it has been organised are the products of social co-operation over very long periods. Current language can be seen to be at the crossroads of long-term historical and cultural forces, social pressures, and the personal concepts and construing of individuals [14]. Language could be considered to be the primary vehicle by which individuals are able to construe their social behaviour.

There are reasonable grounds for taking the above analysis a step further. Contradiction and irrationality may be fundamental to human cognitive activity [15]. Some people may be more affected by these factors than are others. One large group of investigators at the Johnson O'Connor Research Foundation has found that up to twenty-five per cent of people think in overly personalised, subjective ways most of the time [16]. Such people attend more to what is going on in their own occasionally wandering minds than to the factual realities of the outside world. They follow their own thoughts, extrapolate from their own ideas, apply chance remarks to themselves, and may live much of their existences in a form of inward-looking solitude. It is difficult enough for otherwise "normal" adults to detach themselves from their own subjective experience. Personal feelings may also cloud reality. The important point is that most of us know this, and try to overcome it either by exercising emotional empathy or by thinking our way into other person's point-of-view. How much more difficult this must become for people who live in near-perpetual solitude and loneliness. These states of feeling and being decrease the possibility of exercising, or being exercised by, what is known as intersubjectivity, the linking up of an individual's subjective or emotional experiences with that of another individual.

This interpersonal engagement, this feeling of social connectedness, releases us from isolated subjective experiences that may limit our psychological horizons or otherwise bring about the misconstruing of motives and relationships. Genuine social interchange accomplishes this through an acceptance of other people, and the ability to mount questions and receive answers in genuine two-way communication. The answers, whether they be of the objectively factual type or not, demonstrate a willingness to interact in a meaningful or cooperative way, challenge the other to see things differently, or more significantly to conceive ideas in an unexpectedly different way.

Eccentrics use their solitude very constructively. However, people who pride themselves on their singularity and who are also loners may develop a more idiosyncratic language. The logical, controlling, and inhibitory features of language, which are there for sound social reasons, may exert less influence on some individuals.

It is important for language to be socially intelligible, and to not separate or isolate people. Schizophrenia could be seen as an extreme manifestation of an erosion of the cohering properties of language on thought. While under the influence of a manifest psychosis, it can be very isolating to those suffering from its effects. The speech of the schizophrenic is as difficult to understand by other schizophrenics as it is by mentally healthy people [17]. It is the degree of this linguistic isolation that could separate not only the sign from its meaning, but one person from another. Eccentricity could occupy the middle ground between "normal" subjectivity and schizophrenic subjectivity.

The eccentric lifestyle and way of thinking sometimes has an effect on language. At the simplest level, this might be only a matter of the trendiness, or more frequently the reverse, a reduction of up-to-date usage of the eccentric's vocabulary. The following description from one of our eccentric informants shows the links between personality, social behaviour, and speech. It also illustrates his awareness of what was going on, and his adamant refusal to fit in: "I became even less tolerant of other people and their wasteful, extravagant habits. This is probably owing to living on my own, apart from the tenants with whom I do not fraternise except if necessary, for some time. Now I find most people frivolous, silly and ill-informed. Yet I know this is probably not so and am envious at times of their ability to be silly and have fun.

"This said, however, I do like to laugh and get on well with folk who appreciate my sense of humour. I will go to the cinema or to the theatre to have a good laugh. Too few things now are really funny.

"I resent the changes in language that have occurred over the last twenty years. The in-phrases and jarring improprieties one hears even on the Home Service, Radio Four it is now called. Indeed I seem to become more and more stuck in a time warp, and resent change of any kind. My younger colleagues say that my talk and writing is fustian. I am only conscious of this when I am forced into the company of other people, when people remark on my use of expressions like 'wireless', etcetera, but I don't feel easy with words like 'radio', etcetera.

"I am very saddened by the impoverished vocabulary of many people and particularly the young. Many Scottish expressions which were in current use when I was a teenager are not even understood or are laughed at by the young."

(Evan, age forty-eight)

Sometimes the way of thinking impinges on the way that specific thoughts are communicated. This is much more than a matter of vocabulary differences. For instance, how many people know how a sentence they are about to start uttering will end, or where their words and their implications will take them? Speaking is a collection of mental operations, and some of these are sometimes skipped, speeded up or abbreviated. This can give the appearance of a disjunction or disruption in the smooth, understandable flow of expressed thoughts. It can be an asset or a deficit, either perceived or objectively real. It slows or obfuscates, or sometimes disregards social understandings, and can be as much of a problem for the listener as for the speaker. When this happens, there are sometimes secondary social effects on the speaker. Here is a good description of this: "I am considered to have very odd ideas at times. This is because I do not explain every step of the way. I jump from a discussion on point one to point ten, and leave everyone else foundering. They therefore ignore my point or give me odd looks because they cannot see the connection. This annoys me on two counts: they are so slow, that they cannot see the connection, and I do not like being ignored. I then react childishly, even though I know I should not, it's almost an automatic reaction. I am working very hard myself by this time. If for instance I try to go on to make points two, three, four, etcetera, but others turn out to be always so slow! This results in a degeneration into a squabble and all the intermediate points get forgotten in the heat of the debate. I try to avoid these situations as much as possible. Life is much calmer if I do.

"I find most people extremely narrow-minded, prejudiced, stereotyped, and bigoted. It is rare to find an open mind that actively seeks to find the truth behind the facades. I have found such minds, but most are extremely blinkered. It is this freedom of the mind in me that makes me different from others. They find me a threat. In this respect I do feel I am being normal, and they are all stunted. I have given up the struggle to enlighten their ridiculous situation. Bigoted people will not see reason. Anyway, when I do argue as devil's advocate, I annoy others, who think it must be my actual point of view."

(Cynthia, age forty-two)

Social interaction, and the dissimilar interpersonal styles shown therein, can be an arena for different kinds of discourse. Viable communication often demands variation and flexibility, as well as attention to the non-verbal reactions of others. This affords an approximate template of what the other person may be thinking and what he or she may want to hear.

Eccentric speech can isolate the speaker. Worse still, it can be perceived as having aggressive connotations that might not actually be there. Some eccentric speakers may delight in adopting a belligerent position. Other people's view of this may be coloured by the unusual presentation and approach used. The speaker's attributions about what is going on, though subjective, may be nearer to the mark. The following extract shows an apparent relationship between arriving at original insights in problem negotiation and an apparent language abnormality known as derailment of ideas: "I don't feel a need to be a scintillating conversationalist, most especially when I am lost in thought. I have spent most of my life searching for reasons. It is a compulsion I could do without, for it has often led me into conversational exile, in other words, into the aloneness of isolated thought. Because I see things in a different light, I am in constant conflict with my fellow antagonists. I have tried to come to terms with my predicament by concealing most of my thoughts and theories from my compatriots. In this, I can survive, but in a vacuum.

"A lateral or corkscrew thinker can't easily communicate his thoughts, for he is governed by that which, in the first instance, does not make sense. Debating a problem, he may switch to many things that appear to have no bearing on what is being questioned. Nine out of ten I will lose . . . for I have entered a different wavelength. On the surface, the others may have partially resolved the problem, but by that time I'll know what made the problem a problem in the first instance, and will be seeing it in a totally different light. These constant breakdowns in communication, these difficulties in proving an argument, take their toll . . . unchecked, they could lead to a total withdrawal from society.

"The aura of beauty around the real world prevents me from turning my back on the chaos and disorder in it. At times, I do feel the temptation to leave the human race to its materialism, but for some unknown reason my conscience will not permit a retreat into absolute seclusion.

"I question my own integrity. I often doubt my own sincerity when seeking the truth. I ask myself, what makes me think my thoughts are so superior to that of my peers? The answer to this troubles me . . . it undermines my confidence in what I believe to be true. This distrust in myself is counterbalanced by my reasoning being proved correct. My predictions do come to pass. There is only the power of reason and most of us have it . . . if only we would take the time to use it. But frustration is the reward for insight. With this goes a feeling of guilt of not having been able to steer circumstances towards better goals. This is borne out of the belief that all things are related to one another."

(Gerald, age forty-seven)

The speaker is unsure, at least once, of whether to use the first or third person singular. This example also shows an interesting conjunction of his imperfect awareness of a communication disorder with quite expansive superiority feelings, and if not wholly omnipotent, certainly fairly self-referencing.

Sometimes a single event, for example an episode of altered consciousness, can affect the way one thinks. This begins as a significant experience in people predisposed to be subjective. It confirms them in their subjectivity, and it influences their thought inasmuch as they become aware of, and prefer to use, intuition and other methods of thinking derived, at least in part, from a special altered state. This is fairly independent of language, though the predisposition for subjectivity is conveyed in a language full of images allied with inexpressible transcendental feelings. Some eccentrics entertain the possibility that an extraordinary mystical dimension parallels our own, and may be reached, though specifically how and why that can happen is often communicated awkwardly. This may be because certain code words and symbolic concepts take on special personal meanings. Here is one such effort to express them: "Please excuse the semantics, but if people do not define what certain words mean to them, accurate communication becomes even more hit and miss. Unless another person actually experiences this state beyond the space-time curtain, it is not possible to communicate it exactly.

"Who hasn't at some point looked back on their own life and speculated on whether they've made the best of it all? For me, it happened as I was walking across a field admiring the velvet black silhouette of Scots pines backed by a pink moon rising through an orange, yellow, green, duck egg blue, twilight sky. Just past the wee loch, a farmer's pond was filled with evocative inky black water due to its natural peat lining. Simply seeing this scene was like a switch was thrown. It set off a breathtaking chain of associations and combinations of ideas. I suddenly changed from an 'I' experiencing an aesthetic delight to purely being that which I observed. Simultaneously to the big switch-off of the space-dimensional view one normally has, time, in the sense of my own remembered past, present and anticipated future, was replaced by a continuous instantaneous Now. Penetrating into it was like a dragonfly brushing across the surface tension on the top of a pool of water.

"The immediate consequence of this was a feeling of ineffable peace. All memory of past experiences, good or bad, all concern or hopes for the future disappeared. There is no need to guess. There is no need to question. This is all knowing. All knowledge of how things actually are existed here, without thought or any doubt whatsoever. This was an overwhelming experience. One knows and one knows that one knows.

"As waking consciousness began to return I became aware of being spatially just above my head, from which viewpoint one realises the qualities of knowledge arrived at through thought. As I returned finally and fully I found that I was still walking, became aware of myself thinking again and the real superior reality of this universal consciousness became a truly amazing memory . . . like a spiritual orgasm."

(James A., age thirty-five)

The extraordinary thing about this explanatory narrative is that it is couched in paradoxical modes of thought, used by this individual for the statement of themes of great complexity. Similar representations of this sense of being outside oneself have been traced as far back as classical Greek antiquity [18]. These feelings, transmitted culturally, are persistent over time and across many different types of cultures. They happen to eccentrics, though not to all of them. This does not mean that ordinary ways of thinking are relinquished. Such experiences can enhance the eccentrics' more mundane perspectives derived from ordinary linear thought-processing. In James' psychological context, he has attained a way of judging and fairly balancing evidence from external sources with intuitions from within.

James' account sounds, at first, similar to someone philosophising retrospectively over a spontaneous attack of depersonalisation and/or derealisation. These are the technical terms for feelings of unreality and strangeness concerning, respectively, one's own person, and one's surroundings. They are not uncommon experiences in a range of conditions, including fatigue, severe anxiety, phobias, and epilepsy, as well as psychosis. They are also the most realistic way of explaining many out-of- body experiences. However, little attention has been paid by psychologists to how these private visions are interpreted by individuals, how they become elaborated into all kinds of meaning, from "oceanic feelings" and experiences of "astral projection" to "proof" of the soul's immortality. As we have seen, there are other causes why an individual may ascribe, and metaphorically disperse, some of his feelings into the natural or supernatural world.

Less attention has been directed at understanding how such feelings, experiences and interpretations may change the way a person thinks. The following excerpt from an eccentric converted to new ways of thinking and behaving, at least in part, by such an experience, is pertinent. It illustrates how the resultant new way of thinking then structures later sensations and feelings: "From my modest human perspective I have to acknowledge that we should be embracing our mutual responsibilities to the planet and all its peoples, and to the natural world. When I am among the trees I am on a natural high and love to smell, hug, kiss, and feel them. Before, I used to enjoy chopping them down, when I still held some of mainstream society's views. [Interviewee shudders]. I was arrested by a police patrol here in the suburbs not long ago when I was doing my thing. They thought I was a dangerous escapee from a mental institution.

"It gives me a thrill to come to some new understanding of any part of nature, from the sub-atom to the universe. I have become spiritually attached to the biosphere. But I hate entering the city people's environments, the urban haggle, lie, pose, pretend, and hack-away-at-each-other lifestyle. Yet I remain emotionally attached to the idea that the galaxy belongs to the *Homo sapiens* line, despite having not long ago seen an Unidentified Flying Object with my own sceptical eyes.

"Looking at all the wonderfully diverse animate species, we can see that three have developed a truly communal lifestyle: the ants, termites, and bees. *Homo sapiens* is taking the same route in modern cities very rapidly now. The clincher has been the appearance of single mothers, single breeding females and children supported by the community. The big leap is coming soon. Females will come to outnumber males much more. It's the point of no return in evolutionary divergence. It's here now.

"What is weird to me is that most urbanites have this delusion that they are free, but it is really only the freedom to dash around the heap, communicating with others constantly, like all the other ants. I want to freely evolve.

"We have another primate brother. Fruit bats. This really tickled me, as I'd always found their bodies to be strangely attractive, sensual in a fashion that no other animals are, and this used to induce guilty and abundantly perverted feelings in me. How jolly marvellous to have a relative that can fly! It provides me with a sense of not being earth-bound and lessens the envy one feels towards the birds of the air."

(Philip, age thirty-two)

The above passage illustrates how themes can perceptibly shift, each developing to a certain point, then slipping to a related one. Not only *what* Philip is saying is unusual, but also the way in which he is saying it.

Close analysis of what such people say is an indirect way of studying their thought processes. This method consists of asking each informant about his meaningful experiences, and recording verbatim samples of the ensuing monologue or discourse for further systematic psycho-linguistic analysis. Its broad aim is to understand consciousness in relation to each person's life situation, and to view the thinking not as a set of separate bits of isolated phenomena, but as an interconnected whole [19].

I obtained a ninety-minute tape-recorded speech sample from each of the persons in our study. Two raters, both with postgraduate training in linguistics, independently evaluated the speech samples using the Scale for the Assessment of Thought, Language, and Communication (TLC) published by Professor Nancy Andreasen [20].

The TLC instrument defines eighteen subtypes of thought, language and communication disorder, and has been found to be reliable. The subtype definitions rely heavily on the naturalistic observation of language behaviour. Most of the time, language behaviour involves a dyadic interaction between a speaker and a listener, and a disorder occurs because the speaker fails to follow a set of rules that are conventionally used to enable listeners to understand him easily. For instance, when the speaker fails to take the various needs of the listener into account, the result is usually a communication disorder. According to this definition, the following items from the scale are rated as communication disorders: poverty of content of speech; pressure of speech; distractible speech; tangentiality; derailment; stilted speech; echolalia; self-reference; circumstantiality; loss of goal; perseveration; and blocking. The concept of language disorder was invoked for those specific disorders in which the speaker violates the normal syntax and semantic conventions that govern language usage. These are incoherence; clanging; neologisms; and word approximations. The use of neologisms --- invented words so individual as to usually be incomprehensible --- sometimes indicates a degree of creativity that is not always under one's self-control. The concept of thought disorder comprises those disorders in which thinking seems aberrant. These include poverty of speech, which is aberrant because thought seems not to occur or to be vocalized. The second of these types of thought disorder is illogicality, which represents aberrant inferential processes. By using the TLC scale's operational definitions I was able to compare the eccentric sample with values for normal subjects obtained by the scale's originator [21]. (See Table 10.)

Table 10: Frequency of thought, language and communication abnormalities

	Normal people (percent)	Eccentric people (percent)
Poverty of speech	5	15
Poverty of content of speech	1	0
Pressure of speech	6	38
Distractible speech	3	0
Tangentiality	2	28
Derailment	32	6
Incoherence	0	0
Illogicality	0	6
Clanging	0	1
Neologisms	0	0
Word approximations	2	0
Circumstantiality	6	28
Loss of goal	18	9
Perseveration	8	0
Echolalia	0	0

Blocking	1	2
Stilted speech	1	2
Self-reference	1	33

This turned out to be quite an intriguing comparison. The major point to note is that the communication disorders of eccentrics are best understood as communication differences. One can say this because not all of the normal-eccentric comparisons place the eccentric at the abnormal or deficient end of the scale. Also, fifty-eight per cent of female eccentrics and forty per cent of male eccentrics were clear of any language abnormalities. Qualitatively, a typical listener can often understand and comprehend what an eccentric is getting at. Rather, it is the way that an eccentric arrives at his point that is different. Usually even the worst instances can be deciphered.

The increased frequency of pressured speech (speech which comes out so rapidly that it has a driven quality) and circumstantiality (speech which is minutely detailed and sometimes excessively embellished, or with empty verbalisms), both components of a factor designated "Fluent Disorganisation", gives to much eccentric speech its over-talkative and long-winded quality. Acute literary observers previously have reported similar versions of this. Two characters in Paul Theroux's *Mosquito Coast* --- the visionary inventor protagonist as well as the fundamentalist missionary --- had these characteristics. Mark Twain was also aware of these tendencies of speaking. He wrote, after hearing of a revolutionary fanatic who had been inciting Americans to invade Canada, "This person could be made really useful by roosting him on some lighthouse or other prominence where storms prevail, because it takes so much wind to keep him going that he probably moves in the midst of a dead calm wherever he travels!"

Pressure of speech produces an increase in the volume of spontaneous speech when compared with what is considered socially customary. The individual talks rapidly and is difficult to interrupt. Ideas and perplexing trains of thought, seemingly thrown in haphazardly, pour out. Though speeded up, simple questions that could be answered in only a few sentences are answered at great length. The answer may take many more minutes than expected, and indeed may not come to an end if the interviewer does not interrupt the speaker.

A circumstantial pattern of speaking is very indirect and delayed in reaching its target idea. The speaker brings in many tedious details and often makes additional parenthetical remarks that may not be relevant to the topic in hand, or to the specific context in which he is speaking. When interrupted, the speaker often continues to talk, usually loudly and emphatically.

"Fluent Disorganisation" is not due to received misunderstandings. With the eccentrics it arose usually from them having a lot to say, perhaps not having had the opportunity to express their ideas so openly for some time, combined with a more intellectually playful attitude in social interaction, occasionally missing some of the non-verbal signals of social mutuality.

The human voice itself, and its characteristic emotional expressiveness, also has a telltale pattern. For instance, in schizophrenia what has been described as "strange intonation" occasionally occurs in a minority of patients. The eccentric informants in this study showed the following voice pattern. Pitch was sustained at a moderately high level. Timbre was moderately blaring. Inflection went irregularly up and down, but was upward overall. Rhythm was irregular. Enunciation was somewhat clipped. Taken in its totality, this vocalisation pattern is suggestive of a number of different emotional states, including joy, cheerfulness, anger, and impatience. My clinical impressions of the eccentrics studied would tend to favour a combination of ongoing cheerfulness and impatience. Also, some of the more problematic forms of these individuals' speech and language showed that they might not be sensitive to their immediate social contexts.

A particular sample of eccentric speech may show a number of abnormalities, many of mild degree, though when taken together, these clearly differentiate it from other speech patterns. The following verbatim excerpt shows at least seven different types of disorder: "I have since resolved to actually Sherlock Homes a manuscript, anticipatory, of many practising psychiatry, this conjectural profession, none to date have concentrated their probes into the mind's cognitive faculties, which . . . I suspect . . . is . . . as it were, a high octane, rather than the typically average petrol . . . that circumstance, IQ, and health, is responsible for neurosis. Is it a key to the wonderful fulfilment of this gift of life? Whiter light needs darker shadow. The greyest gap in psychiatry is that it must accept creative individuals are left to stew in their own portentous juices to work out their eccentricity unaided.

"Your trained mind could tolerate my ineffectuality of knowledge. You may gladly have the bones of my lifetime journey. Biology made me an ineffectual creature-spirit, brooding over chaos. I longed to be an artist. My sensitivity turned into 100 per cent pacifism, befitting my physical unmanliness, deemed cowardice. So be it . . . I did not make myself . . . my errors may have compounded my naiveté lack of worldly-wise. To add fear to fearfulness is cruelty. Thought has been a permanent friend . . . and enemy . . . to try and reason with lifelong regret of ignorance of life and how it is lived. Why is the one word always with me?

"Inflationally richer in ertz [ersatz?] money, and to have learned what little impact the born introverted mind has on society, the eccentric can be consoled of their bijou part through life, which the gregarious have made less secure than the simplicity of my childhood. No earth could be more wonderful, no altruism, so trampled by the sheer forces opposing peace . . . and harmony . . . which the populist mind, chooses as its rights. Why I even got into the pod of civilisation's green peas, ancestry alone knows." (Brendan, age sixty-six)

At a subjective level, there was much poignant poetry in Brendan's heartfelt outpouring. At several points the associative threads became slightly unravelled (derailment). The tempo of his speech was moderately speeded. The words he used were quaintly phrased (stilted speech), and several unfinished clauses ran into new ones without full logical connections between them. The middle paragraph also showed mild sub-clinical self-reference. There was one questionable example of clanging, a comparatively rare pattern of speech in which the sounds of particular words partly determine the choice of a following word or words. There is only a single occurrence in the last two sentences ("peace", "pods", and "peas"), albeit a fairly tenuous one.

The above passage demonstrates how a number of mild to moderate language abnormalities can add up to give a distinctly odd ring to the possible meanings conveyed to listeners. Outside the artificial situation of a research interview, some people might tend to lose patience with such a speaker. This may be because conversational skills have had to become more efficient and utilitarian in modern life. Peer group pressures force us to conform even in conversation. There is not much room for overly original, ornate or flowery language these days. Looked at in this way abnormal language may become attenuated by the nature of ordinary language, which is very much taken for granted.

The woman who produced the following passage was given short shrift when she consulted a counsellor about a personal problem. Normal forms of discussion, including confessional forms of psychotherapy, became impossibly time-consuming, confusing and without effect because of her rambling prolixity. Beneath this she had great reservoirs of emotional warmth and creativity that were obscured by her normally pressurised speech, jarring derailment of ideas, and loquacious circumstantiality: "Heady stuff, this ... and then, looking back, when I was sixteen, through my father's work he met a very, very educated man who was a dietician in a hospital, and he had twin boys, one of whom had rheumatic fever, and he knew he was going to die. I didn't know he was going to die. His father wanted his son to meet me because I was musical --- it gets around --- I had a reputation, and I sometimes remember this chap because he influenced my life. I fell really in love with him in a truly platonic and . . . sentimental way . . . he put his arm round me once.

"I didn't look at another man for years and years, but I had no confidence in this relationship and I knew nothing about sex at all, nothing --- no facts of life. I just adored this chap and couldn't have a job and I remember he introduced me to music and gave me some books and he sent to Paris for this, and this has been my most treasured possession, but that was a very big highlight in my life. I must tell you something as it is important about this relationship but I remember it was very funny because I was very fond of him, but I remember those things. Before I tell you what he did, I have memories of being beaten by my father, and he cut my thigh and I have memories of my mother coming in at night and bathing my wound. I don't know why my father beat me . . .

"He took me to the Giant's Causeway and said, 'Whatever you wish you will get,' and then he would take me into town and buy me toys, so I have those happy memories. So therefore my mother . . . This relationship with this chap was entirely innocent because I was a late developer. This is a relationship which I find really marvellous and he did mean to have a wife then, I didn't hear from him but then I heard that he was engaged to a schoolteacher, but I understand now that he wanted to get married, but I was only sixteen. I was slightly hurt and I knew that the girl he married wasn't musical, and I think very deprived."

(Susan, age forty-seven; elapsed time of speaking --- 1 minute, 42 seconds)

The average listener's attention would sustain at least one jolt on hearing the above. This occurs when the narrative of the main anecdote is suddenly replaced by a more dramatic one. Before the listener can work out the reason for the enigmatic transition to the incident of the beating, he could also feel a little frustration at being unsure whether the speaker was referring to her father or to her boyfriend. This would be due to a delay in clarification.

These difficulties are slips at the highest level of control over language processing. The earliest difficulties to interfere with the production of coherent discourse occur at this level of sentence-to-sentence linkages, and may be perceived as errors in maintaining topic direction, as errors in establishing major and minor role characters and clear lines between events, and as errors in achieving unambiguous cohesion between clauses. Narratives usually provide enough clues within themselves to provide most of the information needed for the listener's comprehension. If no explicit specifying ties are provided by the speaker, the listener is compelled to supply his own, somehow. Too much, and yet not enough, information is there. What is there is unintentionally cryptic. These problems could indicate that the verbalization of traumatic events were not well integrated within the individual's remote memories. Attempts to signify meaning can sometimes produce further misunderstanding. Associations flow together almost automatically, though too swiftly. This mildly disrupts the stream-of-consciousness, and the flow of speech, at times. This poor degree of overall inter-relationship between narrative strands then makes the planning of future discourse and intentions difficult to sustain.

The degree of derailment of ideas was *negatively* correlated with creativity, though only for males, and only to a modest extent ($r = +0.31$, $p < .05$). These language derailments then, if anything, mildly interfered with creative responses and ideational efficacy, though only usually for the male eccentrics so affected. People who do this frequently lurch disjointedly from one topic or viewpoint to another without preamble or forewarning, sometimes losing the focus on what they initially were saying. Researchers Armstrong and McConaghy have described this kind of allusive thought and language as a normal personality characteristic; they found that it occurs in a good proportion of university students [22]. These researchers also found that it is associated with verbosity (perhaps related to pressure of speech), poor attention, and poor concept learning. An allusive thinking style with unusual word associations also has been found in many highly creative people, and in some other people with "lesser" creative gifts [23].

However, derailed communicative themes were not common amongst eccentric speakers. They occurred significantly less often among them than among normal control subjects. How then should this "communication disorder" be properly conceptualised? It could be considered that this is, at least in part, garden-variety digressiveness. The ability to digress could be regarded as possessing some positive, co-operative social value. The Belgian linguist, Patricia Niedzwieki, working at the Sorbonne in Paris, scrupulously accumulated experimental evidence that favours this hypothesis. She linked digression to sex differences (men digress less), emotional responsiveness, and constructive non-linear thinking. Judith Hall at Johns Hopkins University, in reviewing a hundred and twenty-five previous studies, has provided evidence that lends weight to this idea [24]. Men typically make more use of conversational pauses to put forward their ideas, and also interrupted more frequently.

If these studies and assumptions are correct, some eccentrics may be *deficient* in appropriate digressiveness. If difficult-to-follow derailments occur along with other communication disorders, then the overall impression might be that of *too much* variation in content. This may cause adverse effects on the listener. When it comes to the attribution of meaning, allusive thinkers bring in relatively peripheral concepts, introducing partly irrelevant and more unusual associations. The outcome is that more information is presented, but the network of associated ideas may become less accurate, less succinct, and therefore less effective.

Here are three further examples that illustrate these difficulties. They demonstrate a range of ideational derailment problems, pressure of speech, circumstantiality, tangentiality, and the occasional outright contradiction. All three are, admittedly, borderline instances:

"Always looking to immortalise my history forever. . . . I had my Alaskan Husky puppy's skin tanned and the pelt hangs on my front veranda . . . I've asked that my own carcass is to be freeze dried and mounted over the fireplace . . . coming from the philosophy of each of us being the centre of our own universe and *everything* that we are I am conscious of, I am responsible for. There are no accidents. There is no blame. There is only choice."

(Felix, age forty; elapsed time of speaking --- 25 seconds)

"No, I have never acted in Edinburgh. I was telling you I collect autographs, and I had been wondering about taking a few to some of these old folks' places and getting an epidiascope and showing them on the wall. I have quite a lot of interesting letters. I've got one from Lord Lovat (Chief of the Clan Fraser of Lovat and a prominent Commando leader during World War II) recently and Len Murray (the trade union leader) . . . all connected with

Malcolm Campbell for instance . . . a chap at church gave me his autograph . . . he had got Campbell's autograph when he was at university. A friend and I have been getting little things about Campbell. Also the *Titanic* . . . My father was a golf professional . . . Mr Q. was an Englishman living in America, and he told father he was going on the maiden voyage on the *Titanic* and Dad said not to go on it . . . he had a feeling . . . he never told him but he always felt he should have told him. So they are down in Davy Jones' Locker those (golf) clubs now. That is one reason I went to Harlands and Wolf shipyards in Belfast because they built the *Titanic*; they gave me some photographs and drawings as well recently. Beautiful drawings."

(Joseph, age sixty; elapsed time of speaking --- 55 seconds)

Interviewer: "Are you a collector?"

Informant: "Yes, I do . . . the collection comes down to this: . . . If someone says to me I have a rhyme for your CB broadcast . . . my first answer would be . . . did you? . . . Or the question would be . . . did you do it yourself? Now I am interested if he or she did it themselves. . . . It doesn't matter what it sounds like, what is of interest to me is what it sounds like, but it is more important that they did it themselves. If it is something, say Wordsworth . . . then I am sorry, I am not interested. I am only interested in the immediate . . . what you or yours experience. If I want Wordsworth then I suppose I would go and get him and explain it to myself one way or another, but I don't want that, but I do want this one. That is the difference . . . I collect that . . . I don't collect Wordsworth, but I do collect the aspiring or the clever.

"I will take anything --- virtually the most prosaic thing and I can kick it into a story, for instance, verses really to me are little stories, it just so happens that I put them into verse, maybe one verse. If so then these are the most difficult because you have to get a beginning, a middle, and an end, all in one verse --- if you have got more --- I take any subject like that . . . My goal is to bring culture to people."

(Leo, age forty-five; elapsed time of speaking --- fifty-five seconds)

Tangentiality was observed comparatively frequently. In this, the individual replies to a specific question in an oblique or irrelevant manner, again in a way that may not be an adequate response or an appropriate reply to what has gone before in the specific context in which he was speaking. It refers only to replies to questions, not to transitions in spontaneous speech. The verbal reply of the informant, talking past the point or around it, may be related to the question in a distant or almost unrelated way, and places an emphasis on a part of the question that is incidental or a trivial aspect of what was originally asked. In general, the effect on the listener has been described as "frustrating" [25]. Politicians being interrogated by the media or their opponents often use this ploy to divert attention from the fact that they are not providing a genuine answer. Not wanting to give ammunition to their opposition, this disdain for openness is usually based on avoidance. This is especially the case when they are faced with having to provide an answer that might be construed as too difficult or embarrassing for them personally, or for their party colleagues.

Eccentrics showed tangentiality more often than the normal control subjects, and more so than did people with mania, schizo-affective disorder, and paranoid schizophrenia studied by Andreasen [20] and Andreasen and Grove [21]. Usually it was only of a mild degree of severity in the eccentrics, and may not always have been used intentionally. There was a significant *negative* relationship between tangentiality and measured intelligence ($r = -0.37$, $p < .05$), though only for male eccentrics. More intelligent male eccentrics were less tangential, and less intelligent male eccentrics tended to be more tangential. Tangentiality was not related to creativity.

This chapter would be incomplete without saying something about the high proportion of eccentrics who showed extreme self-reference. This communication disorder is one in which the individual repeatedly refers the topic under discussion back to himself when someone else is talking, and also refers apparently neutral topics to himself or his own experiences when he is talking. This cannot be properly evaluated on the basis of a diagnostic interview alone, since the subject is specifically then asked to talk about himself. However, this may be observed validly during informal conversation about neutral topics; there was much scope allowed for this in our full range of questions. More oddly, there was a handful of eccentrics who, while highly self-referencing, consistently referred to themselves in the third person singular. For male eccentrics, but not female eccentrics, there was a significant *negative* relationship between self-reference and intelligence ($r = -0.38$, $p < 02$). In other words, more intelligent male eccentrics tended to be less self-referencing.

For female eccentrics, but not male eccentrics, there was a significant positive relationship between self-reference and creativity ($r = + 0.36$, $p < .05$). Creative female eccentrics tended to be more self-referencing, and less creative female eccentrics were less self-referencing.

Eccentrics are not only more self-referencing than normal subjects, they are also much more self-referencing than any of the carefully diagnosed clinical groups of mentally ill patients interviewed by Andreasen [26] or by Andreasen and Grove [21]. All comparisons between eccentrics and these patient groups showed a statistically highly significant difference. Such a finding could have occurred by chance less than one in a thousand times.

There is only one other large category of people who possibly may be as highly self-referencing. These are children, who have a tendency to use more first person pronouns than do schizophrenics [27]. Could the eccentrics' apparent high levels of egocentricity and self-concern simply represent their retention of a childlike and innocent vision of themselves and their worlds? On the other hand, Albert Einstein once admitted that his commitment to science was a way of relinquishing a view of life based upon the powerful centrality of both the "I" and the "We" in seeing the world [28]. Looked at in this way, becoming more "mature" in terms of objective judgement may hinge on developing accurate empathy.

One important aspect of empathy may be conceptualised as an appreciation of what someone or something means to a person. This represents a fundamental part of many human transactions. Playing a role is an instance of empathic behaviour and it subsumes an understanding of the ways in which people other than oneself might feel or think or behave in particular circumstances. Role-taking represents a special form of discrimination learning. To the degree that this is selective and organised one is able to make more confident attributions and inferences about other people's feelings.

Another factor thought to be responsible for empathy is the arousal of some form of interpersonal motivation: affiliation, love, nurturance and altruism have been put forward as likely candidates. These potential effects of empathy are an emotional response elicited by, and congruent with, the welfare of someone else. For these to work, one would have to be able to experience another's emotions vicariously, to the point of sharing in them.

Excessive self-referencing may accentuate any other disadvantages in shared communication. This may be commensurate with impaired empathy, and a concomitant insensitivity to social cues. Verbal means may distance us from the immediacy of knowing other people's intentions. Language disposes itself through words, usually without much reference to subtle distinctions. It requires the speaker to authenticate himself by an accepted accommodation that entails engaging with standardised codes, semantic systems and arbitrary constraints.

When we employ our feelings and do not rely exclusively on stereotyped concepts, we may come to know the working of other minds more insightfully. In this, spontaneous feeling transcends cold logic. The logical process is fairly impervious to the vitality that comes from self-realisation and other-realisation. The nuances of personal significance, the fine-tuning and connotations of relationships, for instance, are still sometimes untranslatable. However, boys and eccentric men tend to rely more on their intellectual capabilities to exercise accurate empathy [29]. In this study, empathy and intelligence were moderately correlated for male eccentrics (r = + 0.46, p < .01), though not for female eccentrics. Women in general, whether eccentric or otherwise, are more consistently empathic and more accurate at decoding non-verbal communications than are men.

An inability to shift as necessary from one role set to another suggests that the individual is using a limited repertoire of responses for a wide range of different situations. This inability to make effective social discriminations has been noted by clinical observers studying similar kinds of loners, for example, those believed to have either schizoid personality or Asperger's syndrome [30, 31, 32]. Some eccentrics are more at ease when the appropriate social responses are more predictable. This particular variety of impaired empathy is not so severe as to adversely affect primary attachments with parents, though it may impair social affiliation and some interpersonal relationships.

About forty per cent of the eccentric sample had a definite impairment of empathy. This might be a function of stable personality attributes [33]. One connection like this would be the finding of a negative relationship between empathy and narcissistic personality [34]. This may be partly due to an inability to construe people in psychological or abstract ways, or using other than concrete concepts [35, 36]. This could also be understood in terms of the inverse relationship between intelligence and impaired empathy found in male eccentrics.

I also found highly significant correlations, for both sexes, between ratings of empathy and independent ratings of rapport (for males, r = + 0.85, and for females, r = + 0.94). This represents more than an obvious recasting of similar terms. Accurate empathy refers to the nearness, or otherwise, of an individual's interior matching between what he thinks is going on emotionally within another, and what actually is. Among its outward manifestations are the communication skills demonstrated --- not only talking clearly, but also listening perceptively. Rapport, on the other hand, is a direct measure of the overall success of this: how closely two people simultaneously understand each other, how well they both synchronously identify with each other's feelings, and how much mutual liking this engenders. Jean-Jacques Rousseau put a description of this distinction rather nicely, though differently, in his *Reveries of a Solitary Walker*: "To judge of the speeches of men by the effects they produce is often to appreciate them wrongly. Apart from the fact that these effects are not always felt and easy to understand, they vary as infinitely as the circumstances in which the discourses are held; but it is solely the intention of him who holds them that gives them value and determines their degree of malice or good will."

Rapport had more to do with personal qualities and personality. Intelligence played a lesser role here; correlations between rapport and intelligence, and between rapport and creativity, were not significant. Female eccentrics with good rapport could be distinguished from those with odd rapport, primarily in terms of greater stability for the former and more ongoing anxiety admitted to by the latter (according to 16PF Second-Order Personality Factors). Male eccentrics with good rapport were tenser than male eccentrics with poor rapport, and also tenser than female eccentrics with good rapport. However, in terms of their speech, language, and non-verbal communications, the eccentrics showed little overt sign of anxiety during their interviews.

The impression these differences made on the other person in the conversational dyad is that female eccentrics with poor rapport appeared to be wrapped up in thinking about themselves. Male eccentrics with odd rapport came across as being full of their own importance, not given to suffering fools gladly, and with an element of antagonism just below the surface. In contrast, eccentrics of both sexes with good rapport impressed others most with their gentleness and disarming friendliness. Their effortless and chatty conversation and outgoing array of social skills put others at their ease.

Thirty per cent of female eccentrics achieved above average rapport, whereas only twenty per cent of male eccentrics did so. Poor or odd forms of rapport were in evidence in fifteen per cent of the interviews with female eccentrics, and in thirty-five per cent of the interviews with male eccentrics.

When both impaired empathy and odd rapport were rated for a female informant, in every case these were associated with personality problems, uncertainties about their sexual orientation, or personality disorder. This sub-group amounted to fifteen per cent of all the female eccentrics.

Proportionally twice as many male eccentrics were rated for both impaired empathy and odd styles of rapport. Two of these informants had a questionable or ambiguous presentation, or a history suggestive of untreated mild mood disturbances. The remaining male eccentrics showing both impaired empathy and odd rapport had few psychiatric symptoms or other dysfunctional personality traits.

It can be seen that a relatively high proportion of eccentrics probably are hampered in their interpersonal relationships and in other social arenas by their odd communication styles. Most of the eccentrics did not realise that the tenor of their discourse was different from others, in some instances remarkably so. Looked at objectively, the communication difficulties and secondary misunderstandings of eccentrics could occasionally be problematic for those affected.

Chapter 6. No Masters of Silence
(Eccentricity and Non-Conformity)

"That the middle class, which was to receive such a terrible importance for modern history, is capable of no self-sacrificing action, no enthusiasm for an idea, no exaltation; it devotes itself to nothing but the interests of its mediocrity. It remains always limited to itself, and conquers at last only through its bulk, with which it has succeeded in tiring out the efforts of passion, enthusiasm, consistency."

Bruno Bauer, 1843

The last century witnessed a stark form of madness, that of state-directed terrorism. During the Holocaust and other genocidal slaughters there were so many collective and individual acts of barbarity that their cumulative hideous effects could have paralysed the positive spirit of humanity. The cold fact is that individuals not too much unlike the rest of us perpetrated many single acts of callousness. After World War II, many social psychologists turned their attentions to elucidating what made people conform in groups, though as individuals, and later, what made people obey orders and go on to carry out inhumane deeds.

The major emphasis was on conformity, and an enormous body of rather artificial research was generated, much of it of a high order of excellence. The experimental procedures used were scrupulous. They were sometimes backed up by some observational data collected in what psychology students call "The Real World". The major findings were re-checked and replicated. Their theoretical underpinnings, where they existed, were exhaustively examined and refined in the light of discrepant research or more elegant conceptual analyses.

However, the dominant approaches were one-sided. Conformity involves a change of behaviour, belief or thinking to align oneself with those of other people or with known normative standards. By concentrating on conformity, social psychologists had largely neglected to look at its alternatives. The major theme was conformity, and the major emphasis was on why, how and when people change their behaviour to be more similar to others [1]. This was strange, because the obvious evaluative judgement being made was that conformity to majority opinion and behaviour could be a bad thing under certain circumstances. It is also the case that those who habitually conform are not always tolerant of others, or at ease in rejoicing about non–conforming individuals' ability to find novel possibilities in their lives.

The view was that the key social pressure is the implicit wish to not be viewed as on the fringe of a social group. However, this did not take into account how artificial and temporary most of the resulting *ad hoc* experimental groups were. Often, the psychologists that devised the experiments managed arrangements that had the outcome of persuading or pressurising people to conform temporarily, even when the majority of the group was wrong. Other experimental social psychologists looked at obedience forced by pressures from authority figures, to see if these pressures could temporarily overcome the strictures of conscience and ethics.

Over the years, much less attention has been focused on those people who deliberately wish to be different from others, and on the lawful conditions to which such people do not conform. There is a need to understand the motivations, beliefs and thinking of such people. Less is known about the specific situations in which non-conformity flourishes. Not a lot is known about those people who consistently behave in non-conforming ways. We cannot begin to estimate what proportion of people could conceivably have the strength of character to challenge social assumptions or indeed the wider society. This is quite a telling gap, made more surprising when one discovers that the modal response in most conformity research (and perhaps other psychological research) is actually some variety of non-conformity.

In the quintessential experimental paradigm, initiated by Solomon Asch, most of the subjects' actual responses were the correct ones, despite the majority verdict of the experimenter's confederates, who were deliberately acting untruthfully by agreeing on an erroneous alternative [2]. In this classic study of simulated perception, a series of students judged two lines of different lengths to be the same length. A minority of the real (non-confederate) subjects, manipulated by the experimenters and their stooges, and perhaps guided by their own inner needs to be seen to conform to group norms, did comply and agree. At least in the short term, it appeared that their inferred needs to be accepted or well liked overruled the evidence of their senses. Did they deceive themselves as well as being deceived?

In the original experiments and many that followed, the manipulations introduced were of very short-term durations; like some illusions, the effects, if any, may have lasted only for minutes. The effects could have been confounded by differences in both social and visual-perceptual sensitivity. In order to achieve a design that permitted group comparisons, stimuli and topics were selected that could not have been central to the subjects' main preoccupations. In most cases, the subjects' more personal preoccupations were not elicited, and therefore passed unknown.

The irony is that, though it is impossible now to tell exactly what was going on in the early experiments, as a cautionary tale on the power of people's needs to conform, they did stimulate many further significant investigations. It is more than odd though, and it may be a direct, massive denial --- what Walt Whitman wisely called "the terrible doubt of appearances" --- that these studies successfully diverted attention away from all those many types of behaviour that are the opposites of conformity.

So what is known about non-conformity? We cannot talk properly about it only in terms of its opposites. There must be more to it than simply a "reduction of conformity" [3]. Conceptual analyses have posited the rough shapes that it may take. In defining the other pole(s) of the conformity dimension, researchers have come up with terms like independence, counter-conformity, anti-conformity, and creative personal dissent, as well as non-conformity [4, 5, 6, 7, 8, 9]. Patterns by which these hypothetical summary traits could be contrasted were also put forward [6, 7, 10, 11].

The typical subject in most psychological experiments is usually unrepresentative. The conformity experiments were largely accomplished with young college students acting as the experimenter's confederates and the experimental subjects; both were at least chronologically immature, with little experience of life living on their own. Much of the non-conformity exhibited could as easily have been due to residual adolescent rebelliousness, rather than that based on decision-making of a more adult type.

The experimental tasks provided were usually dichotomous. With the notable exception of researchers Santee and Maslach there was usually only one way open for the subjects to not conform [9]. Negotiations and non-conforming compromises between the subjects and the confederates were disallowed. These experiments were therefore not realistic analogues of social situations in which there would be a greater diversity of optional responses.

Experimental responses were further limited because simple binary decisions rather than qualitative judgements, were requested. This constrained the subjects' responses to only a single dimension of a problem. It also compelled them to assume a passive role of simply reacting. Taking positive action, such as generating alternative answers or outcomes, was disallowed.

The choice that usually was faced by the experimental subjects was between unpopularity and being wrong. Ultimately, this confused any attempt at subsequent evaluation; the important question of motivation was obscured. The experimenters assumed that the behaviour shown represented in microcosm the differential weights placed on each subject's internal balance of motivational forces. The critical behaviour could have reflected a choice to renounce the group's normative responses, though it also could have been an adoption of the correct or the popular position. Would it not have been better to simply ask?

If the above critique is correct, we should be circumspect in our interpretation of this important body of research, and especially about what can be inferred from it about non-conformity. (See Reference [12] for a helpful meta-analysis of further studies based on Asch's line judgment experiment.) What is known about non-conformity by inference and deduction is fairly scanty.

Gender differences in conformity?

To begin with, the evidence for gender differences is inconsistent and equivocal. Three groups of earlier researchers [9, 13, 14] found that females tended to conform more than males, though researchers Seybert and Weiss found that females were not differentially reinforced by escape from an aversive situation of intermittent non-conformity any more than were males [15]. It could be assumed from this latter study that the female subjects found non-conformity no more threatening than did the male subjects.

Studies from the 1950s and into the 1960s concluded that women in general were more likely to conform than men. In those decades, there was much conformity to stereotyped notions of what was to be seen as "natural" behaviours, as defined both by social and gender roles. And individuals maintained stereotyped models of their social and gender roles. It is undeniable that, in the past, social pressures for women to conform have been stronger than for men, predisposing women to the development of a greater awareness of normative behaviours. Social attitudes and prejudices played a major part in this. Older women, brought up when gender roles were less fluid and more inflexible, were significantly more conforming than older men when being watched and when an experimental task involved the subjects forming impressions of group members' likeability. Among younger subjects, there were fewer gender differences, or none [16]. However, it was found that there could have been experimenter gender bias involved in most, if not all, of the earlier studies -- all the experimental researchers then were male [17]. In many societies worldwide, females still possess less political and economic power than do males.

Using the technique of meta-analysis to summarize sixty-one previous conformity studies with group pressure and twenty-two conformity studies without group pressure showed that in 62% of the former and in 86% of the latter there were actually no gender differences [18]. Further studies confirmed that conforming behaviour in women was affected by group pressure, and more so if the experimental subjects were in face-to-face contact with the experimenter's confederates who were trying actively to exert influence on them [19, 20, 21]. Furthermore, another group of researchers found no gender-based differences or interactions related to conformity across a range of different situations [22]. It also did not seem to matter how much social support was provided; females were no less prone to conform than were males.

From the early 1970s onwards all kinds of creative and otherwise conventional women enabled themselves to break away from what was increasingly perceived as the treadmill of female existence, employing more flexible conceptions of gender roles, and by so doing became more self-reliant and independent-minded. This was at a time when it was becoming clearer that there were clearly better social learning explanations to augment and often replace the older genetic/biological explanations for gender differences in behaviour.

More recent research in the twenty-first century shows subtle shifts towards less frequent female conformity [23, 24]. Field studies show more complexities. For instance, in actual pedestrians' behaviour, conformity to group pressure and compliance with legal prohibitions could be observed directly [25, 26]. In this work, women were shown to be no more compliant than men, but were somewhat more conforming. Furthermore, individuals with higher self-esteem are better able to resist the impulse to conform to the majority opinion, even under highly pressurised conditions [27].

It is also apparent that gender roles and attitudes towards sex differences in non-conformity have been complicated by what was believed to be so-called "appropriate" or stereotypical gender roles and/or gender-based behaviours [20, 28]. On the other hand, researchers Spence and Helmreich found that their student subjects claimed that they would respect and admire "a masculine, competent female" [29]. However, the results of another experiment contradicted this finding, and this was particularly so for male perceptions of women's behaviour [30]. Male subjects responded to non-conformity on the part of a female by refusing to permit her to influence their task-orientated decisions, by actively showing their dislike of her, and by rejecting her as a potential collaborator. Males, on the other hand, were seen as more influential and more desirable co-workers the more frequently they violated normative procedural rules. A female's "abrasiveness", perceived as being both irritating and a violation of gender role norms, was more than sufficient to motivate other research subjects to discredit her and/or deny her competence and credibility.

It is currently seen that any remaining gender differences in conformity are due to specific cultural values and attitudes, social roles, and sexist thinking. Strictly gendered sex roles are still causes for concern in some quarters. However, it also could be said that, perhaps because of the Women's Movement and associated feminist ideologies, women have become more accepting of less orthodox lifestyles. Karen Prager found that "finding one's true self" enhanced the self-esteem of women (and probably always had), and that newer non-traditional areas of identity development are becoming more important determinants of a fulfilling life [31].

Viewed in this way, conformity would be the consequence of inadequate opportunities to be self-directed. This too was the view of the following eccentric informant: "I explored the world on my own terms. Marriage was something else. It meant you were not independent . . . you have to submerge yourself, and try to please others, which is not easy for me. To be a successful wife you have to give the whole of yourself to your husband, then he would be happy and you would be subservient. In my view, mediocre men prefer submissive, subservient and blandly smiling women who will willingly subordinate themselves, often to the neglect of their own genuine needs. Such women are so without minds of their own, they must feel they exist only in the eyes of other people, men and women. I could never put myself completely into such men's hands. I would feel like a puppet jerked about on the end of many strings. I could never give my inner self to anyone. I cannot completely trust anyone, I suppose. I am scared stiff of being taken over and not being able to think for myself. I have become a going-my-own-way sort of woman. And as a woman nowadays you may have to be subversive to succeed; in professional life you just can't rely on your colleagues to do the right thing by you simply because you deserve it."

(Julia, age fifty-one)

Eccentric non-conformity

As far as personality correlates and personality differences are concerned, research has failed to find global personality characteristics that are consistently associated with conformity [32, 33]. However, a positive relationship between non-conformity and ego strength has emerged [14, 34]. There is also a slight indication that dominance is negatively related to conformity [35]. This was corroborated indirectly with a small (though statistically significant) positive relationship between self-abasement, an approximate opposite of dominance, and experimentally demonstrated conformity behaviour [36].

Most other studies have not demonstrated any correlations between a given personality measure and conformity, and others have found minimal correlations. There has been no consistent pattern of correlations with personality dimensions across comparable studies, nor is there much evidence of individual consistency across the types of situations devised by experimental social psychologists.

In general, conformity, and by implication non-conformity, appears to be exquisitely situation-specific. When group pressure is exerted, research subjects seem to register, and act on, subtle differences between differing presentations, whether that is based on content, the presence or absence of support from a single ally, or informational feedback from the experimenter [22]. There is, for instance, a dramatic change towards non-conformity if a single truthful dissenter is present [37, 38, 39, 40]. It would seem that, if one wished to predict non-conformity in average university undergraduates, it would be better to know about their immediate social environments than about their gender or personalities.

Autonomy varies with the context; a person can be independent in one situation but be dependent in another. Like conformity and non-conformity, autonomy is extremely situation-specific and context-dependent. People are made to become unnecessarily dependent on society's benefits by the various social controls that are placed upon them --- from well-intentioned beneficence through mild prohibitions to outright repression. In this view, that is the essential nature of the process by which people become inculcated into what their society wants, into what are seen as appropriate social values and behaviours. Specific types of societies have tended to restrict the field of conscious possibility.

The social context is never static. Perceptual awareness and experience are dynamic. Over the long term, people assimilate into their conscious minds various social strictures and mores. Conformity in the face of novel experiences remains highly structured by the influence of significant others, and by the group's collective social fantasies. Some viewpoints are held tightly, others are relinquished for more convincing reasons or more powerful reinforcement. It is therefore incorrect to think of independence as a trait residing exclusively within individuals. If particular circumstances are altered, some of the people who conform in one situation may not conform in another.

People, be they agents of society or not, also force other people to accommodate themselves to a particular vision of the world. That is the nature of social control. Newly invented personality diagnoses by the psychiatric establishments of some countries, for example, so-called "Oppositional Defiance Disorder", clearly shows how non-conformity can be negatively weighted and made to appear devalued.

The above social controls may be less applicable to eccentrics. Counter-conformity and anti-conformity, seen as having the purpose of challenging a relevant social group, are manifest in deliberate and steadfast rejection of attempts to influence the individual. Eccentrics, though they do not pay much heed to external social influences and attempts at persuasion to change, do not usually or necessarily have as their primary purpose the direct challenging of social groups.

Happily, eccentrics tend to overlook or bypass the limits of convention and conformity. They seem to thrive by living on the frontiers of experience rather than within the cosy parameters of conventionality. Sometimes they remain steadfastly beyond the need to follow some of the commonplace rules of social organization, and in some instances even show contempt for the rulebook in question. This can be problematic, as various unspoken rules are much in evidence throughout the entirety of the interpersonal and social fields. Lifelong ventures of this kind cannot be easy.

It might be informative to contrast the actuality of the eccentrics' lives with the experimental studies described above. Eccentric non-conformity may be more enduring and unchangeable than that seen in those studies or elsewhere. Eccentrics' behaviour may be much less situation-specific; their lesser need for social acceptance, and their scepticism about its relative value, speaks volumes. Their efforts to fit into one or another social order only emphasized their more separate individuality as outliers on the fringes of society. They habitually demonstrated a more general trans-situational disposition to resist group pressure. They refused to let themselves be led by others in ways they think are fundamentally wrong.

Societies are not aggregates of individuals pursuing their various isolated ends, but rather are systems in which people work together cooperatively toward common goals. The modes of thinking in a particular society, as inferred from verbal communications, especially about moral and ethical questions, tend to conform to the belief systems of the dominant culture. Cultural groups exploit prescribed systems for filtering and interpreting the everyday experiences of their realities. By informing awareness, socially conditioned experience is exposed to strategies for increasing conformity. The way language is used in news reports and disguised non-impartial comments, the discussions that may follow from them, and the social priorities shown and denied, are factors in supporting and maintaining the *status quo*. In a similar fashion, the making of meaning is culturally determined in conformist societies, and supposedly more often individually determined in more open, egalitarian societies.

Membership in society may mean different things to different people. For eccentrics, society is found wanting, though sometimes capable of being corrected, rehabilitated and otherwise improved. They find it bland, boring, organized around work, hierarchies, business, and advertising, the latter of which they consider to be equivalent to "brainwashing". A significant minority see the political system as an exercise in cynicism and despoiled by short-term goals, as opposed to inspiring and based on higher ideals and principles. They exclude themselves, or are excluded by, one or more social/political institutions, and should they join a club or party, often find themselves to be unwilling to go along with the leader's ideas or dominance, and immune to their charismatic appeal.

Eccentrics are not taken in by the "bully pulpit" sometimes used by politicians or the mass media, nor are they persuaded by the advertisements and publicity schemes of celebrities. Eccentrics are more individualistic; therefore the presence of agreeing social support or feedback may be irrelevant for them. They don't give a hoot about what other people may think about them. They are unmoved by social pressures, particularly attempts at persuasion by recourse to authority. They are likely to circumvent such forces. They may refuse to do things in the ordinary way, and may take an oblique stance in regard to taken-for-granted understandings. Surely, although they are inveterate non-conformists, they must have some kind of understanding about the assumptions made by people who do conform.

Non-conformity and non-compliance is an undercurrent underlying many of the eccentrics' guiding principles. These principles may be more important to them than other common motivational needs, for example, for affiliation or conspicuous consumption. The level of commitment to their ideals and ideas is so high that appeals based on "common sense" often are rejected out of hand. The above factors were generally demonstrated by the tenor of Vincent Van Gogh's eccentricity in those long periods of his life when he was not psychiatrically ill. His general attitude was best summarised when, with striking self-awareness, he wrote, "What am I in the eyes of most people, a nonentity, an eccentric, or an unpleasant person --- somebody who has no position in society and will never have; in short, the lowest of the low. All right then --- even if that were absolutely true, then I should one day like to show by my work what such an eccentric, such a nobody, has in his heart."

Eccentrics may not stop short at milder challenges to authority but may proceed to civil disobedience, as for instance Henry David Thoreau did on a point of conscience when he went to a court of justice and then to jail for not paying his taxes. Such challenges might lead to political activism and/or individual civil involvement with causes or particular issues: "I just don't accept the authority of the state the way other people do. And I just don't understand why people are so apathetic about things that are happening to them. Groupthink should never be able to supplant the call of individual conscience. Conscience arises from the imagined condemnation and praise of a person's peer groups, but what of an appreciation of an individual's responsibility? It's quite a British thing to have taboos about discussing certain uncomfortable subjects. I attack my typewriter as soon as I see something in the newspaper that takes my imagination or I feel requires criticism, and I fire off letters to the newspapers. I have no tolerance whatever for censorship. If more people took an active role in such ways of resisting authority, there would be fewer attempts at 'enforced amnesia' to cover up human rights abuses. Thank God for freedom of the press, and use it. I always tell people to be more open to change. And I usually say no to other people's rules and restrictions."

(James B., age forty-seven)

There has always been a need for analyses of the manifold expressions of social conflict, opposition and strain, and of ways of resolving them. It is by making a stand against something that an individual's true character sometimes may emerge. Protracted revolution against society is never an easy endeavour. To do it alone may seem practically impossible. Yet the contemplation of this is part of the eccentrics' ethos. That some of them are intellectual rather than practical revolutionaries makes them no less dangerous. It can never be more than a subjective value judgement that affords the ideas of a Karl Marx any less dangerousness than the activities of a Vladimir Lenin.

The revolutions of most eccentrics are peaceful and in miniature. The kind of permanent non-conformity displayed by eccentrics might be defined broadly as a series of expressive acts that invert, contradict, abrogate, or in some fashion present an alternative to commonly held cultural codes. These acts have both symbolic and practical aspects. Non-conformity is essentially an attack on control and regimentation, on closed systems, and is concerned with the potential reversibility of parts, or all, of the established order. It deploys a novel disrespect for received structure and authority. It does not produce a stereotypic reproduction; instead, it assigns new functional values to old oppositions, and can trigger unprecedented courses of events.

People are more likely to blame abnormal dispositions for behaviour that clearly deviates from social expectations. The concept of differentness is a social one. Societies have the ways and means to paper over their basic social inequalities. In the manufacture of abnormality, a full spectrum of various behaviours can be deemed to indicate something pathological within an individual, rather than considering the nature of the social nexus in which that individual lives. This process of selective ignoring and denial, and the use of propagandistic camouflage, undermines the true understanding of what is going on. The more unusual a deviation in behaviour is, the more likely it will be perceived as potentially disruptive, dangerous or threatening in some way [41]. Those whom people decide are negatively different, and especially those who interact less with other people, can become objects of fear.

In addition, judgements of condemnation, however fair or unfair they may be, are part of the normative policing of cosmetic social agreements. Working under these, there are those people who, wearing masks of self-righteous indignation, feel compelled to search out deviance in all its Hydra-headed forms that may possibly offend, rather than welcoming any novel increase in the diversity of opinion and creativity. In Britain and its far-flung former colonies, the repressive and often persecutory Puritan mindset was continually reinforced by various proscriptions that made it all too clear what was thought to be "appropriate" standards for living an upright life [42]. There is narcissism about taking offence upon simply hearing the expression of a so-called "outrageous" idea, whether the idea is said in jest or in witting provocation. After all, what gives one individual's sanctimonious judgments the privileged high ground of moral authority? Persecutory judgements by the self and by others may underlie what R. D. Laing, brought up in a hard Presbyterian environment, referred to as, ". . . this almost complete holocaust of one's experience on the altar of conformity" [43].

Clear relationships have been found between the rated disruptiveness of certain types of unusual behaviour and the amount of social rejection that may stem from them [44]. Paradoxically, there is a high degree of tolerance on the part of individuals within the general public for extraordinary behaviour [45, 46]. Members of the general public are fairly reluctant to label much of this behaviour as mental illness, and the notion of eccentricity offers an alternative involving less social stigma.

My research shows that most eccentrics are aware of their differentness, and of society's stereotyped reactions to them. Indeed, their struggles to be different tended to positively transcend the stereotypical roles others sometimes tried to impose on them, despite what that may have meant in terms of their personal fulfilment. Eccentrics cleave to their differentness as a given that continually needs to be proven in action or defended in words: "I am aware *all the time* of being very different from other people. I think I succeeded early on in retaining my individuality. Now I feel a need to better integrate myself with people, because I find that there are lots of people I do like. I meet a great many people through business and social activities and generally feel I know much more about them than they do about me. Some people have found this difficult, and so far I have learned to adapt to other people almost instinctively. I am still usually the only person doing whatever it is I am doing --- particularly with business ideas --- and they seem to work; so my eccentricity is perhaps more a view from outside than from inside."

(Anne, age forty-five)

"On the whole I don't have much of an opinion of the public at large. I think people are terribly mundane and they conform all the time and I don't want to. I don't want to be a lawbreaker, but I do want to have that spark of something. I'm very self-opinionated; I make up my own mind about many things. I've always wanted to be different. I am however unshakable in my beliefs and in lots of other ways. When it came to the crunch, when there was something I knew I *needed* to do, I was surprised by how I could be so stubborn, so determined. All I have to do is stay with it, trust my instincts, and keep looking behind the masquerade that is modern life. I also know that the more society represses things, the more it invites transgression. It seems I've been getting invited a lot of late."

(Robert, age thirty-seven)

However, like anyone else, not every instance of an eccentric's behaviour is deliberate, though little of it is regretted: "For myself, I define eccentricity as being able to behave as a free soul within a pressurised society. I remember wondering to myself while listening in Sunday school to a lesson about our duty toward others, 'Where is the *I* in all this?' Unquestioning deference to those who believed they knew more than most folks --- that was what was being demanded, however humbly and graciously. Later, I witnessed the same kind of thing being done by more successful and powerful people. Falling into line without raising objections did not come automatically to me as I think it did to many others. I only propose, never impose. I am eccentric by reversing the conformist attitude within the law, and by not wanting 'things', eg., dressing for colour and comfort, and not fashion. I unwittingly drop clangers because of the way I see things."

(Jane, age forty-seven)

Eccentrics will put up with ordinary life, but they don't like mass culture --- that is, believing what everyone else believes. While equating eccentrics with geniuses and aristocrats in her largely anecdotal sketches of eccentrics she knew personally, the poet Dame Edith Sitwell wrote that eccentrics are ". . . entirely unafraid of and uninfluenced by the opinions and vagaries of the crowd." She was right about that. Eccentrics refuse to have their opinions shaped to fit current fashion, no matter how out of step they may seem to be. The eccentrics' disregard for up-to-date fashion, which they view as facile manipulation by advertising people and a sterile over-concern with passing fads, has not been altogether lost on those who control these "trivial" activities. As the French couturier Coco Chanel said, "In order to be irreplaceable one must always be different." Eccentrics see trendiness as being yet another eminently dispensable element of modernity. Wildly anachronistic, eccentrics either feel they are ahead of their time or would prefer to live in an earlier age. To them, fashion setters help to perpetrate an ongoing hoax. Advertising and mass communications are seen as ultimately stultifying tools of the marketplace. An eccentric medical practitioner in our sample, for instance, commented critically: "Assuming that life as we know it continues, in the absence of nuclear warfare, I am very concerned about the brainwashing patterns which are coming about as a result of TV. For example, one of my patients said, 'I hope that the TV doesn't go on strike, because then there will be no advertising and I won't know what to buy'. Poor soul."

(Dr. Charles U., age sixty)

Eccentric non-conformity is more than just a reaction against the prevailing *status quo*. It is liberating, and requires a degree of courage to sustain --- true iconoclasts know that often the objects of their ridicule are cherished by the majority. This knowledge does not modify their zeal to flaunt the conventions they feel are bizarre, silly or mistaken. Power and potential personal popularity has little impact on the eccentric. The associated requisite bravery is felt to hinge on the self's very identity and achievement of integrity: "Trying to be more like others can be disorienting. You see, I usually know what I want. When I was younger, I learned to look more closely at myself and to appreciate things on my own terms. I find that most people are more dependent on others' opinions than I am. All their mainstream lifestyles, and the certainties they spout, leave me cold. It's as if they're too willing to follow some kind of Identikit version of how people ought to behave. That's not for me. I refused to play their game. If by playing the game I might have had a chance of getting what I wanted, I might have tried harder, but what would I have been compelled to sacrifice?

If I were to give up on my own attitudes, I'd be concerned I'd lose my independent-minded self-concept. Liberation is better. I'd rather be an outsider. If anyone tried to control me, they might as well forget it. To be true to one's self, and unafraid whether one is correct or not, this is much more admirable than the paltry cowardice of surrender to conformity."

(John, age fifty-nine)

This kind of antithesis is posited for good reason. When the struggle against conformity involves a crucial part of someone's personality, this then demands that no concessions be made on the basis of other people's hostility. Eccentrics have few qualms about such matters when they are on the offensive. They know what they are against with as much conviction as they know what they are much more positive about: "No, I wouldn't care very much whether people talk about me or laugh about me or not. It is how I feel that matters, not what other people think. I for one feel strongly that nowadays people are devalued, dehumanised, reduced to the status of ciphers by the present amoral social climate, an analogue of an Arctic wind in summer. They are good, brave or bad people, but in everyday life behave like a herd of cattle. When somebody from a more cosmopolitan culture finds himself trapped in a community of inward-looking people who despise him simply because he is different, and their universes of discourse have almost nothing in common, he will feel lonely. Individuals require intellectual stimulation, and I cannot get away fast enough from the barrage of pop music, advertisements, and the general decadence and self-indulgence. For this, I am certain that people who don't really know me well disparage me as some kind of old-fashioned fuddy-duddy throwback to an earlier age."

(Donald, age forty-four)

There is a powerful and fully conscious need to excoriate much of what has gone before, and any sense of there being an accepted truth disintegrates like a mirage in the face of such critical onslaughts. When this impacts, and impact it must on other people's awareness, unpredictable things happen.

The slanted diatribe becomes part of the eccentric individual's private self-consciousness. In one-to-one interpersonal relationships, there is occasional distrust, hostility, and the effects of mutual bewilderment: Believe → claim → reaction → counter reaction → reciprocal alienation → further mystification. As one eccentric informant explained it, "I get bad vibes from people when I tell them about me, about myself. They think I'm mad, but I know that I'm an oasis of naturalness in a plastic world. Each person's consciousness is a thread in a multi-dimensional matrix, and worthy of close individual attention, undistracted by the decadent goo-gaws pushed at us by advertising and bread-head money addicts. Let's stop accumulating and start assimilating, I say."

(Lenny, age twenty-three)

Transgression and Taboo

Many people, at some point in their lives, participate implicitly in similar polarised monologues. They embrace given meanings from their social environments, and while these reference points help shape what they may become, it becomes less possible to incorporate these points without contradiction. Parental authority specifically encourages and sometimes forces compliance, amplifying societal belief systems, dogmas, and stereotypes that are frequently founded on rather questionable assumptions. In many traditional cultures, socialisation processes are more uniform than in our own, and individuals conform more consistently to internalised feelings about what is correct behaviour. Shame-based cultures are nourished in societies in which there are strong feelings favouring mutuality and unity, and in these cultures the threat of sanctions prove more effective. Contradictory splits are handled by the implementation and vigilant adherence to taboo.

Adherence to normative behaviour takes it's meaning from prohibitions. What charges taboos with power is that it is known that people do transgress, however rarely, even against the strongest proscriptions. The word *taboo* derives from the Polynesian islands of the South Pacific. There it means what is forbidden on pain of a ritual sanction, that a penalty is believed to be brought about by the performance of a forbidden act. If a taboo has not been broken, then it becomes superfluous. However, there have been a number of these strong prohibitions, based on ancient and arcane superstitions though still extant today, for example, the taboo against twin siblings in some rural areas on the Indian Ocean island of Madagascar. Related to a putative curse on the family or community, mothers of twins face the choice of abandoning their children or being ostracised.

Between the taboo and its denial comes the transgression of individuals. Some translate their notions into action. To transgress against a taboo corresponds, by way of counterpoint, to behaviour that could bring about grave danger, madness or, at the very least, severe social repercussions. The behaviour prohibited also is often plainly illegal. What possible significance can a taboo possess if its sanctions are not patently manifest? Taboos attempt to order natural phenomena that society finds it difficult to prevent by other means. As such, taboos have a bearing on the social ensemble, though they also can be understood as proscriptive justifications for existing and enduring power relationships.

Transgression is strictly prohibited because they reveal real, though fleeting, desires. Questioning of the taboo seldom arises; to do so is usually also forbidden. The inviolate nature of an injunction has several effects, the most far-reaching being the sealing off of avenues of change in the conceptual and critical faculties of those who believe. As William Blake's character Los says in *Jerusalem*, "The Spectre is the Reasoning Power in Man; when separated from Imagination, and closing itself as in steel, in a Ratio of the things of Memory. It thence frames Laws and Moralities to destroy Imagination, the Divine Body, by Martyrdoms and Wars."

The products of this are rigid control practices and fewer contradictions, both in and between people. A system of social relations may become slowly transformed into a mechanism that enforces rigid control over individual freedom. However, order never fully takes over, nor could it. Cultures at different stages of development may require different controls in proportion to their level of adaptation and civilized lawfulness.

Taboos and concepts of sexual sinfulness, usually impossible to comply with entirely as long as there is a carnal, animalistic side to human nature, are implemented to engender feelings of shame and guilt. Within this context, some functions of society and religion are primarily suppressive and repressive.

There is so much repugnance associated with some taboos, such as those concerning incest, that a biological foundation for some of them is credible. Observation of primates in the wild has led to a consensus that an endogenous inhibition is "built into the wiring" [47, 48, 49]. In reaction to something as abhorrent as incest, formidable prohibitions and punishments justifiably are put in place to counteract it. Anthropologists and other researchers have shown that worldwide reactions to incest are remarkably similar across a wide range of human cultures. Most repulsion is reserved for mother-son incest, slightly less for father-daughter incest, somewhat less for brother-sister relations, and less still for relationships between near-cousins [50]. This unambiguous detestation of incest, as elaborated into cultural and religious taboos, as well as by laws and other social strictures, serves important health and evolutionary functions. Heterozygous genetic populations have a survival advantage over more inbred populations. As well as preventing the obvious immediate and long-term harms involved, the taboos motivate exploration beyond the extended family, propelling people into new relationships with genetically different, and sometimes culturally different, social groups [51].

The dual nature of taboo, the conjoining of the sacred and the sacrilegious, encapsulates every kind of power relationship: parent over child, male over female, leader over followers. However, there are also some beneficial effects that flow from specific instances of non-observance. The injunction "Don't look!" becomes flexibly transformed to a weakened taboo or norm that may be broken at a later stage in a child's development [52]. The ban, where applied, engenders curiosity. Some religious proscriptions sometimes can impact on the entire economic life of a community, its agriculture, fishing and healing beliefs, for instance, as was the case for the peoples of the Malaysian peninsula [53]. Other sexual and menstrual taboos are known to have problem-solving functions as well as supporting magical beliefs and religious indoctrination [54]. Any rite of passage, any crucial turning point in the life cycle, can require some kind of taboo observance.

Taboos, as seen from either a social or an evolutionary perspective, have a regulating function. Taboo observance is a way of helping to maintain good social relations and avoiding conflict. Transgressing a taboo violates both specific laws and in-group security. It also undermines primary decision makers, particularly those who arbitrarily compel large numbers of their people to serve with blind subservience.

Social and cultural norms

Despite an apparent cross-cultural diversity of social arrangements, cultures share common origins that are repeated and self-replicating. It may be the case that a society must replenish itself by becoming somewhat more heterogeneous in its beliefs. Original heterogeneity obviously must begin somewhere. Fortunately, of all the animal species *Homo sapiens* displays by far the greatest plasticity of behaviour. The proper question to ask may be how cultures, and individuals within cultures, do eventually manage to throw off the shackles of ultra-conformity that were put in place originally to constrain rapaciousness and anarchy. It shows the strength of a society by how much eccentricity it is willing to condone.

History is replete with societies whose institutions have become so frozen and so unyieldingly stratified, that they inhibit or frustrate change. At the individual level, the conformist must, on many occasions, hold himself back, and by inhibiting himself so habitually, has to defer allowing his true self coming openly to the fore. Because of this, he may find himself managing a more enduring false front, or repeatedly placing himself in a false position.

To adapt sometimes forces specialisation, which can then ossify past the point of optimum adaptability. Stability fulfils multiple needs and functions --- security, dependability, and more enduring group identities. Its unintended consequence may be that no one dares to challenge the group's underlying assumptions. Norms are susceptible to repeated, arbitrary manipulation by powerful sub-groups. Thus, appeals to patriotism and national identity can derive, with different connotations and shades of meaning, from very different political parties. How else could norms survive for long periods, through changing and challenging conditions, and sometimes when they have become dysfunctional?

A norm inherently strengthens social solidarity, and so, to challenge a norm undermines the cohesion and continuity that those in control feel society needs. Cohesion is such a constant feature of society that it is almost taken for granted. It is so important to the maintenance of all that is revered, that it could be seen as a prerequisite for society itself.

The significance of social cohesion can be gauged from a list of functional societal prerequisites proposed by one influential group of thinkers [55]. At least five of their nine prerequisites --- shared cognitive orientations, a shared set of goals, a normative regulation of means, socialisation and social development education, and the effective control of disruptive forms of behaviour --- are related directly to unifying a culture.

These "prerequisites" can be criticized as reflecting little more than the value judgements of scholars deeply enmeshed in a conservative hierarchy. In general terms, people often superimpose their value judgements on different individuals in, and beyond, their immediate social networks. Social scientists can never isolate themselves effectively from their own personal history of social shaping, and the preconceptions that derive from it. It is logically defensible to argue that a type of society more transilient and more improvisational than our own could dispense with one or more of these social cohesion and regulation "prerequisites", and still function adequately on its own terms. Certain given assumptions seem to have culturally conditioned our thinking. Experience over time may introduce false limitations into our thinking.

Social structures are not immutable; there is discontinuous change in both time and space: revolutions, breakdowns, and seemingly inexplicable disjunctions. The examples of innovative and unusual personalities are one of the sources of behavioural and social changes. Such people seem to come in serendipitous clusters; the nature of their appearance does not suggest any apparently lawful pattern. A series of interactions between singular personalities and particular types of culture is both more appealing and more complicated. This thesis has its proponents, among them the eminent social theorist Raymond Firth [56].

Such considerations call for new investigations and new theories to explain how a majority of individuals in a society come to respond positively to cultural pressures, and how there comes to be as much perceived uniformity. Both societies and persons may have many more ways of being than have been experienced. There may also be a concatenation of individual acts and organisational weaknesses that can precipitate later deviance or innovation.

We are not simply the producers of institutions; we are more frequently the products of them. By holding onto mutual cultural values may help to explain the how, though not the why, of stable forms of conformity that, to the majority, become ego-congruent and satisfying. However, this might not offer an adequate explanation for major transitions and rifts. When a culture thwarts those who carry a burning wish to not conform, some typically human response will be forthcoming. If society's suppression of this or other human needs is sufficiently draconian, this response may force a more powerful turn toward the restructuring of the culture in question.

The vices of a culture can become stylised as its virtues. A culture stands or falls by how balanced or strictly applied are its taboos, and how open to misunderstandings it is. If a culture is ultimately stronger --- more vigorous though not necessarily healthier --- than a composite of its more resilient protesters, it may attempt to remake them in the likeness of its ideal. Such a culture may wish to foster or prescribe particular ways for individuals to behave, and even what they should think. Non-conforming individuals may need to live in obscurity or go underground, or choose to rebel in many different ways.

Drastic departures from accepted standards may not disrupt a society's functioning if those controlling it channel, subvert or otherwise destabilise the dissenters. Culture and personality need not always fit. For long periods, an important group with revolutionary ideals can appear to co-exist within a dominating culture, as for example a group like the

Solidarity movement did within Poland when that country was dominated by the totalitarian Soviet Union. Many peaceful protests have not been against something, but for greater choice, for more alternatives, and fewer restrictions on basic human rights.

There are rules throughout differing societies that dictate how people live. The strategies of people are seldom committed to a consistent reliance on rules, because the rules are often replete with ambiguities and outright contradictions. So-called cultural imperatives contain openings and loopholes, and sometimes allow for new interpretations to accommodate specific situations. Or, as the novelist and biographer Penelope Fitzgerald once noted, "Rules are defined by being broken."

Eccentric non-conformists are figures of rebellion who manifest their need for liberty, especially if it has been denied to them. A rebel looks at the world and sees an injustice that he feels the need to react against in order to expunge it or change the social order that brought it about. On the other hand, the eccentric rebels, as he or she has chosen to live, by opting out, by coming at an issue in a roundabout way, or by propounding so radical an alternative vision that people think it is preposterous.

The eccentrics' projects are based on a series of deliberate decisions, and the actions that flow from them. Each new turning in the project is a leap in the dark. It is the eccentrics' projects and attitudes with which he becomes most closely identified. Their projects become ones in which they are personally very involved, and which gives value and point to their lives. In the most literal sense, a criticism of an eccentric's project very easily becomes an attack on his integrity. The real defence of an eccentric is that he recognises that many people harbour wishes and fantasies that they feel unable to indulge. He knows those wishes are there because he feels free to act on his.

A characteristic feature of being human lies in the ability to become an object to oneself, and the thoughts we develop towards ourselves are commonly referred to by such terms as "self" or "self-concept". This may first show itself in the presentation of the self in society, and is most likely to be judged as a self-conscious strategy in which there is usually a clear intention to be different from others. One of the choices that flows from this is to be knowingly eccentric.

One of the significant limitations to a person's interpretation of his actions is that furnished by social conventions. By making experience follow conventional courses, more personal meanings sometimes are avoided, and more conventional social responses and ways of relating to others are put in their place. The behaviours of those so affected are guided by what they think they are supposed to do in a range of situations. This leads them to be particularly susceptible to depend on external ideologies in defining themselves and others. Instead of thinking for themselves they are prone to rely more on consensually approved beliefs and behaviours.

The typical eccentric wants to cast off the more mundane inhibitions of thought and action that many other people feel are for the good of themselves or others. Free will, or the freedom to be one's genuine self, to eccentrics, is not an intractable, maddening problem; it is an essential fact of life. Eccentrics are not necessarily either selfish or self-centred, and often perceive their motives as essentially altruistic. Their lives are based on the conception of themselves as free and responsible agents. Their atypical endeavours, be they judged worthwhile or not, are indeed on the fringes. They have ambivalent attitudes toward standard views of morality. Furthermore, they have doubts and qualms that absolute moral strictures are justified, especially when they interfere with an individual's attempts to achieve a meaningful project or a meaningful existence.

The enhancement of selfhood sometimes means not going along with the crowd, nor placidly accepting integration into the world of prescribed social definitions. There are oftentimes opportunities for self-definition that are missed because of social and underlying psychological factors. When eccentrics find themselves defined by others in ways they find demeaning or otherwise unacceptable, they are at first surprised. Later, on reflection, the unvoiced but perceived threat to their integrity that this other-definition implied weakens their trust in other attachments they may wish to form. This may leave some eccentrics in situations that are fraught with ambiguity.

Little is it appreciated that by broadening the boundaries of our freedom we may set off chain reactions that eventually may not only expand our consciousness but also our horizons. Eccentrics could be important models of this progression. They are potent symbols of unfettered freedom of spirit, enquiry, and change. Their radical activities within or outside the confines of the body politic seem to trouble them little. They show that disobedience need not become a legal problem or a rightful part of a psychiatric pathology. Indeed, in circumstances of unfairness, civil disobedience is positive, potentially leading to remediation and restitution.

I am in awe at the diversity of human nature. I reject the notion of men and women tied to their fates, be it by genetic or environmental means. Such an idea, eccentrics also think, may rob them of their future development as well as their essential dignity. Such men and women are concerned with pushing forward, with remaking their possibilities. Therefore, I am left to regard them as free and imbued in the active process of becoming.

Intellectually, coming to self-understanding makes sense as a creative exercise in its own right. The eccentrics' creative exercises become one of the means to this goal. Deep change can be attainable. Simply by being themselves, eccentrics are happy to refuse to be dominated by the dominant beliefs and ways of believing seen and heard in their given social milieus, as if they were destined to point up society's accepted absurdities. Their willingness and ability to seize the chances that life's experiments present them with is a good measure of our liberty.

Chapter 7. A Rough Reality to Embrace
(The Personality of Eccentrics)

"A man has as many social selves as there are people who recognize him."

William James

Quite clearly, almost by definition, eccentrics are people who do not easily fit in to society. So why should there be any expectation that they could be bracketed any more neatly into any exciting personality theory or framework of what constitutes a valid self?

Eccentrics can be seen as exceptions, whether the emphasis is on motivation, thought, or on how so-called normal personality supposedly functions. For themselves, many eccentrics show an intellectual appreciation of, and sometimes a fascination with, their radical exceptionality, and occasionally exalt in it.

As those who work in the mental health field know from experience, normality, even as an ideal, is a convenient fiction. It is important to stress how much judgements of normality are often social definitions, based themselves on the quality of one's own interpersonal rapport and social relationships [1]. Many people will admit to possessing within themselves various vexing aspects to their personalities, and many people believe that such elements cannot be fundamentally altered.

Another view is that there are infinite parameters of individuality, that the only significant limit to an individual's perception of his actions is that prescribed by social convention. In other words, a sense of possessing a significant self can arise not only out of our social interactions. The study of eccentrics can let us see what the implications of this are for our conceptions of the self in various social settings. I found that the self-concepts of the eccentrics "anchored" their entire ways of thinking about people, much the greater part of their socio-psychological conceptual systems. On the other hand, non-eccentrics anchored their equivalent conceptual systems much more frequently on their experiences of other key people that they knew well.

A social application of Role Theory might shed some light on the nature of the eccentric's essential incongruity [2]. An analysis of the different ways people may diverge from their given personal roles shows that no single "misfit" category is specific to eccentricity. There is much overlap; up to four or five of these general sources of differences may be linked to eccentricity, sometimes within the same individual. The people in this study are living confirmation of William James' above dictum.

Eccentrics are unquestionably misfits in terms of their motivations and value systems. It is less certain whether or not they are misfits in terms of their own identities. They are aware that differentness is a crucial element in their make-up, though may be unsure of some aspects of themselves because of their individual unpredictability. Like many non-eccentric people, eccentrics may disavow certain aspects of their personality. However, their insecurities about their identity only very rarely approach the levels of adolescent or neurotic personality conflicts. They may also be malfits through performance --- in instances where their education has not matched their innate intellectual gifts, or where circumstances have forced them to work under strictly rigid regimes. Some eccentrics are also misfits in terms of motivating incentives: some may wish to achieve significantly different objectives, or none at all, though others have fairly conventional goals --- fame, fortune, and credibility. Very few eccentrics are misfits by way of skills or capacities.

This kind of approach, when used descriptively, rapidly leads to a cul de sac. It does not enlighten us about the causes of eccentric attitudes and deeds. It runs out of explanatory power, possibly because eccentrics do not seem to fit any of the main strategies of self-presentation [3]. These are ingratiation, intimidation, exemplification, supplication, and self-promotion. Unfortunately, except for the latter, which is indulged very infrequently, these categories are irrelevant for describing, or generalising about, eccentric lifestyles. Eccentrics expend much of their mental energy in the types of stimulation where concern about self-presentation is low, including in those situations that absorb the individual in wholly involving intellectual challenges. Eccentrics, like everyone else, can freely choose how they present themselves to others in a variety of contexts. The types of strategic considerations designated above are largely disregarded by those who are, above all else, concerned with their authenticity and integrity.

This second failure to find a viable scheme based on social exchange theory led me to construct some new objectives. The first of these was how to discover the criteria people apply in judging other people to be exceptional. I could then go on to compare our data on eccentrics against each of these. I doubt whether the criteria I have adopted are comprehensive, or ever could be. The seven that I have discovered so far are those that I think, on rational grounds, are relevant to this issue. It should be said that exceptionality, as a concept and as a way of seeing human nature, is a rather odd chestnut itself. We think we recognise exceptions, though often these judgements are based on partial knowledge, or intuition.

My seven criteria by which a person could be regarded as exceptional are as follows: extremity, rarity, the possession of special attributes, the possession of unusual combinations of attributes, doing ordinary things in extraordinary ways, the violation of the "rules" of what we think we know about normal personality, and lastly, disordered or abnormal personality.

Extremity

Most people are near the average on most dimensions of normal personality. When given a valid personality test, very few people indicate extremely high or extremely low scores on any given trait. The first thing we can look at is the proportion of eccentrics with extreme levels.

On the test of normal personality used in this study, the 16PF, extreme levels are represented by standard scores (or stens) of 1 or 10 on a ten-point scale [4]. Such very low or very high levels on any dimension of personality are obtained by only 2.3 per cent of those taking this test. This is considered to be relatively uncommon, if not quite rare.

Less is known about *de facto* special or presumed extreme groups, such as eccentrics. Such analyses are long overdue, if for no other reason than to assure oneself that the bedrock concepts of descriptive and inferential statistics, such as those to do with the normal distribution (bell-shaped curves) and probability assessments, also apply to the intangibles of human nature. The larger numbers of the bulging middle positions surrounding the central tendency or average do not rule out the wild diversity at the extremes. In the natural sciences, it is well known that unexpected things can, and do, happen at the extremes --- thus *high* energy particle physics, *low* temperature physics (super-cooling, super-conductivity), *zero* gravity effects, etc. Why then shouldn't this tendency to bizarre and exotic effects at the extremes apply with equal force to human personality and the workings of the human mind?

As can be seen in Table 11, the eccentrics surveyed easily broached, many times over, the expected 2.3 per cent threshold for extreme values on the majority of the test's personality dimensions.

Table 11. Numbers of eccentric informants with extreme personality traits

16PF	Personality Factor	Males	Females
E+	Dominant, assertive	7 (9.6%)	20 (35.5%)
B+	Intelligent, bright	10 (13.5%)	7 (12.5%)
N-	Forthright, unpretentious	9 (12%)	6 (10.5%)
L+	Suspicious	7 (9.5%)	6 (10.5%)
M+	Imaginative, bohemian	9 (12%)	4 (7%)
H +	Bold, venturesome	6 (8%)	6 (10.5%)
A -	Reserved, detached	3 (4%)	8 (14%)
O -	Self-assured, placid	3 (4%)	7 (12.5%)
Q_2 +	Self-sufficient, resourceful	9 (9.5%)	2 (3.5%)
Q_1 +	Radical	2 (3%)	5 (9%)
I -	Tough-minded, hard	2 (3%)	5 (9%)
Q_3 -	Follows own urges	4 (6%)	3 (5%)
Q_4 -	Relaxed, tranquil	3 (4%)	4 (7%)
G -	Expedient, disregards rules	1 (1.5%)	5 (9%)
Q_4 +	Tense, frustrated	6 (8%)	1 (2%)
H -	Shy, timid	4 (6%)	2 (3.5%)
C -	Affected by feelings	4 (6%)	2 (3.5%)
F -	Serious	2 (3%)	3 (5%)
F +	Impulsive	2 (3%)	3 (5%)
C +	Emotionally stable	------	4 (7%)
I +	Tender-minded, sensitive	3 (4%)	1 (2%)

(Note: Percentages in brackets represent the proportion of males or females in the study sample possessing the trait in extreme degree (a standard score, or sten, of 1 or 10). Seven males and one female were each also extreme on eight other variable traits, one apiece. None were of extremely low intelligence; none were extremely trusting; and none were extremely socially dependent.)

The other related question that arises is just *how* extreme can extreme be? It is believed that people possessing more than one extreme score on a personality test are statistical rarities [5]. Many eccentrics had very low or very high scores on more than one personality dimension. To begin to understand this second quantitative issue, one should reference this unusual group against a range of other more or less unusual groups. In other words, the real question should be: how extreme is this group in comparison with other groups of people of similar age and social class but with dissimilar problems? To do this, I therefore compared the eccentric group to three other groups from whom I had previously collected extensive personality data, including that derived from the 16PF personality test [6].

Independent psychiatrists had diagnosed those in the first of these groups with long-standing neuroses prior to referring them to clinical psychologists for assessment and possible treatment. The second group were composed of reputed "persistent patients", also called "hypochondriacs", people operationally defined as having a physical symptom for which no known physical illness had ever been found by numbers of consultant physicians over many years. The third group had a definite physical illness, diagnosed by physicians and confirmed by consultant rheumatologists, that of rheumatoid arthritis. (See Table 12.)

Table 12: Proportions of informants in each group with multiple extreme scores on the 16PF

Group	2 Extreme	3 Extreme	4 Extreme	5 Extreme	6 Extreme	7 Extreme
Neurosis (n = 32)	8 (25%)	2 (6%)	3 (9%)	3 (6%)	----	-----
Hypochondria (n = 29)	1 (3%)	1 (3%)	2 (6%)	----	1 (3%)	-----
Arthritis (n = 26)	7 (27%)	2 (7.5%)	1 (4%)	----	----	----
Eccentric (n = 130)	26 (20%)	17 (13%)	13 (10%)	2 (1.5%)	1 (0.75%)	1 (0.75%)

As can be seen in Table 12, there is a modest excess of eccentrics with three or more extreme scores in combination, when compared to people with chronic psychological disturbances or physical pathologies that are painful, deforming, and sometimes depressing.

There was not a necessary, nor even a mild, relationship, between the presence of extreme personality traits and the presence of personality disorder. Those eccentrics with personality disorder had only a few more extreme traits overall than did those without personality disorder. There were specific areas of extremity though. Those with personality disorder were *six* times more likely to be extremely suspicious and *five* times more likely to be extremely untroubled by guilt than those without personality disorder.

Rarity

As mentioned earlier, an approximate estimate of the prevalence of classic full time eccentrics in the population can be provisionally placed at around one in ten thousand. Due to the unorthodox sampling techniques and to the initial imprecision of definition, the margin of error could be as much as fifty per cent to either side of this estimate. In other words, the genuine eccentric condition could be as rare as one in fifteen thousand, or relatively less rare at one in five thousand. There also may be many more people who share some, though not all, of the features of the dyed-in-the-wool eccentric.

Eccentrics are much more than chance mutations or flukes of human nature. Probably many more people have the potential or predisposition to be eccentric than ever have the opportunity, bravery, and effrontery to be so.

Special attributes

A person's special talents often mark him off for unusual consideration by others. They also may form, in part, a basis for the development of real individual differences.

Eccentrics do possess special attributes. An eccentric's curiosity knows no bounds. (See also Chapter 8, section headed "Into unlimited curiosity") If, for instance, a non-eccentric individual wanted to know more about electricity, he might simply read a book on the subject or look it up on Wikipedia. An eccentric would read more and to a greater depth. He might also call the local electricity authority, and arrange to observe a power generator in operation to see how it works in detail. Then he might knock on the door of a physics or electrical engineering professor to ask seemingly naïve and abstruse questions about his favoured topic.

Such total immersion in a subject, sometimes to the exclusion of almost all else, can lead a person to identify closely with the subject and the personalities of the other characters involved in it. This is more than empathy; it may be obsessive empathy --- the eccentric does not stand aloof from the subject of his admiration, but feels a sense of communion with that knowledge base, object or person.

One eccentric had become so absorbed in the study of the Robin Hood legend, and liked the character so much, that he legally adopted the name by Deed Poll. This man wore the traditional green costume, complete with longbow, arrows and feathered hat, seven days a week. Ironically, he earned his living by installing bank security equipment and automatic cash dispensers. He subsequently has returned periodically to Sherwood Forest, living in a well-camouflaged tent for a good part of the year.

Since completing my formal research, I have also heard from several dissimilar individuals with the same subject in common. There is the feminist Robina Hood, a woman with strong views who seems to be making a point. Otherwise an accepted academic, she is more interested in cross-dressing than the redistribution of riches; she enjoys the effect of donning the greenery and striding purposefully around her local area.

Two more realistic pretenders co-habited in a caravan in the Lake District, on the shores of Lake Windermere. Until a final showdown with a very tolerant pub landlord, Robin St Claire and his trusty companion Maid Marion could often be spied, in their full regalia, drinking and captivatingly regaling all and sundry in the New Hall Inn (known locally as the Hole in the Wall) at Bowness in Cumbria.

Less ostentatious is John Goodheart, who eschews the dressing up except on special occasions. However, he insists that he is related to an actual historical Hood upon whom the legends were based --- Robin, Fitzodo de Locksley. After years of patient heraldic investigations, Goodheart, a bespectacled and mild mannered civil servant, has taken his case to the European Court of Human Justice to explain why he claims the title Lord John Pope-de-Locksley, K.O.T.O.

Other interests can become an eccentric's favoured topic. That of Dr. Alan Fairweather is the potato --- its history, how to clone it, how to grow different types with different qualities, and so on. He wrote his doctoral dissertation on potatoes. His diet consists wholly of meals of two pounds of potatoes, topped off with a chocolate bar, the occasional vitamin pill and many cups of tea. He has consumed this type of meal for more than thirty-two years. He doesn't believe in livening up his plate with chips or mashed potatoes, either. They are always cooked the same way --- boiled in their jackets. "Potatoes provide all the nourishment I need --- I can't be bothered to cook anything else. It doesn't get boring," he insisted. "I usually have a good heap of them."

Alan needed little encouragement to expound on the socio-political repercussions of this vital tuber, or alternatively the best way to cook the hundred or so varieties --- "Plunge without peeling into boiling salted water, after twenty minutes juggle them around in a hot dry pan to make them fluffy". As an Inspector for Scotland's Department of Agriculture and Fisheries, he was fortunately well-suited to his expert professional role. His working holidays took him to Peru, Bolivia and other South American countries --- ostensibly to study the humble spud in its native environments. "I suppose you could say I have a potato-centric view of the world," he said.

When back home in Edinburgh, Alan sleeps on the floor of his study, renting out all four bedrooms of his large home. "I've never seen the point in having a special room set aside to spend thirty per cent of your life unconscious in, or having this special piece of furniture which has to be got into" he said. "I use a sleeping bag, and sleep wherever I am."

Eccentrics are also blessed with a phenomenal, though sometimes unorthodox, sense of humour. One aristocratic woman, an artist, showed up for her interview with a plastic lobster on a leash trailing behind her. When I asked her what this was about, she replied matter-of-factly, "It's my mascot, a pet that doesn't need feeding." Another woman, sixty-six years young, was a frustrated dancer. After completing her interview, she asked if she might demonstrate one of her exotic dances. Before the researcher knew it, she stripped off her dress to reveal an Edwardian bathing costume and began dancing around the room.

For eccentrics, such zany behaviour is nothing new. The biggest city in Scotland, Glasgow, once known as the second city of the British Empire, had one of the funniest eccentrics among its many other natural humorists. This was A. E. Pickard (1874 - 1964), a millionaire with a heart of gold. It was in one of his music halls, the *Panopticon*, that a sixteen-year old Stan Laurel and a young Archie Leach (later known as Cary Grant) made early appearances.

Pickard was as rich as Midas. It was said of him that he could "start a party in an empty house". He once shouted at an interviewer, "Does Glasgow belong to me? Of course it does. When (the music hall entertainer) Will Fyffe began singing it belonged to him I was going to take out an action against him in the Court of Session." He was nearly right about his ownership claim; as a property magnate, the only landlord who owned more property in the city was Glasgow Corporation. He never evicted a tenant and gave generously to his tenants and other people who needed help. He also gave secretly to many charities.

At his home named "Golden Gates" there were eighteen Rolls Royces, only one of which was fit to drive. He was the first man in Glasgow to be booked for a parking offence; late for a train, he had parked his Rolls in the middle of Platform 8 at the Central Station. Later fined £1 for this unusual parking violation, he paid with a £100 note. After World War II began, A. E. built an air raid shelter in the garden of one of his city centre mansions. It was cone-shaped and festooned with bright neon lights and could make an easy aiming point for the Luftwaffe. When air raid wardens saw it, they immediately looked shocked. A. E. was delighted to see their reactions, and he said, "The Nazis wouldn't dare bomb A. E. Pickard!" A forerunner of Screaming Lord Sutch of the Official Monster Raving Loony Party, A. E. stood for Parliament as the Millionaire Party candidate for the proud but impoverished Maryhill constituency.

Then there is John Ward, a former librarian and engineer with a gift for whimsy. Wearing a huge multi-coloured bow tie and Elton John-style white-framed glasses, with his white hair shooting upwards as if electrified, he describes himself as a freelance "Junkist Inventor of the Unusual". His inventing began with his attempt to paddle across the English Channel for charity on a "craft" made out of four bicycles and four oil drums lashed together. However, the seas on the day proved to be "too choppy by half", and reluctantly he had to turn back.

When John was starting out, he confided, "I have known so many people who are absolutely burnt out from trying to push an idea, so I said to myself, 'Forget about it. I could be practical, but no, I'll go to the funny side.' " As his title implies, he creates various fantastical and delightfully humorous contraptions from objects other people have thrown away. One of his first constructions was a "Jungle Bus", which was soon put on display near his previous home in Northamptonshire. On the day the Prince and Princess of Wales were married, John celebrated the event by welding together three bath tubs to make a boat for his four children.

For months afterwards, John beavered away with piles of household junk and a mini car gearbox and engine. Well-meaning friends and total strangers turned up on his doorstep with donations of broken household appliances. Local businesses contributed hundreds of pounds of faulty goods. Finally John unveiled the fruits of his hard work --- a fully functioning, fully equipped simulated Moon Buggy, described as "Chitty Chitty Bang Bang on acid". In appearance, it was like something from a *Star Wars* movie set, with flashing lights, sirens and a mind-boggling array of Heath Robinson-style gadgets and instruments. Taken apart, it consisted of an old bed, a number of hairdryers, several vacuum cleaners, a wicker linen basket, and bits and pieces from, among other things, a milk float, a tumble dryer and an old pram. "It is a shining example of a load of old rubbish," John said, with tongue firmly in cheek.

One of his madcap machines looked like a cross between a torpedo mounted on wheels and an autogiro-helicopter. He spent three years constructing it from an old motorcycle and sidecar, adding the front end of a scooter, two wheels off a mini, a tailplane, rotor, and wings made from a gate-leg table. He ended up with a five-wheeled machine twelve feet long, eleven feet high and nine feet high, so big that it was too big to go through his garden gate. Sitting in it and smiling broadly and wearing a mask and a clown costume as I surveyed its wings, fins, stabilizers, multiple propellers and its small engine mounted under the cockpit built into the back of the fuselage, John said, as his suburban former neighbours looked on bemusedly, "There's so much waste in the world, so I like to put rubbish to good use," he said, adding disarmingly, "I call this model the Wogan after (the popular radio presenter and prolific chat show host) Terry Wogan, because, like him, it's always there. I think it will prove popular." He then added, "A lot of people say I'm into my second childhood, but I don't think I ever got out of my first. Getting carried away is the bother of invention."

John has also "worked" as a professional wedding guest, built the world's only three-wheeled Robin Reliant fire engine, and, using a catapult of his own devising, masterminded and attempted to set a world record in the national cabbage-hurling contest he founded. About the latter event, he remarked, "It actually amazed us, we didn't realize it would go global . . . by the interest it has generated around the world." His other inventions include a mobile church baptismal font (described as a "go-anywhere christening device, complete with a thermostatically-controlled water vessel, self-levelling castors, and inbuilt towel dispenser"); an electric spoon; a giant bird feeder; a musical frying pan ("one verse of 'Heartbreak Hotel' or 'The Yellow Rose of Texas' and your egg is ready"); a hand-held barbecue; an automated hair washing module that operates on the same principle as a car-wash; and the electric bra-warmer. In inventing the latter, John was simply responding to the cold climate of rural central England. One can only imagine the scene at Belfast Airport when John's baggage, containing many of his more portable inventions, was examined as he was traversing the thorough security checks shortly after the Irish Troubles had come to an end. I witnessed this myself, and can say that the customs officers and stern-faced policemen were convulsed with laughter the deeper they probed.

When asked to explain his behaviour, John told me, "An eccentric is someone whose modus operandi is not linear. I prefer the 'funny' side as opposed to the 'hate' or 'frighten' side of life as that is easy to do as you need no effort to be nasty but to get a laugh from somebody takes a certain know-how (if only I could find out what it is!) and while I perhaps don't 'click' at times with the odd one or two folks, perhaps three even!, I get an overall result because I like the challenge, as without challenge why would we bother? . . . I sometimes have as many as four or five ideas buzzing away at any given time --- at this time, there are three 'in motion' but each one is geared for the GF --- the Giggle Factor. Life is just one big giggle, and it isn't equipped with an instant-replay button. I'm just trying to cram as much fun into it as I can. People have always said that I have a great zest for life.

"I get a response even going shopping, as I can change the process into an adventure of sorts as I can 'paint' if you like the situation and then carry on with the input of the sales assistant as being my 'straight man', but he is unaware of that! And within minutes the whole place is giggling away --- no smut, no foul language but just good honest banter.

"On the other side of the coin, like it or not, I now find myself in the position of being my own worst enemy as was proven a couple of years ago when I was invited on a local radio programme and the response was, they tell me, that I overshadowed the supposed radio presenter who was basically inadequate as he had never come up against anybody like me. It was all a bit of a rum do. I am supposed to be a 'natural', I am told, as opposed to another churned out sausage machine standard issue BBC presenter with a charisma bypass, and I was looked upon as a threat of sorts as this guy could not handle doing anything 'ad lib', and was unable to think on his feet in real time terms."

John, like a number of other eccentrics, firmly believed in the value of retaining his childlike joy, maintaining a playful attitude, and not only in joking around and exhibiting his sense of humour. This relates to the eccentrics' ways of developing creativity throughout their youth and adult life. As the cult comedian and eccentric Ivor Cutler observed, while blowing bubbles off a London rooftop toward the people in the street below, "Life is to play games. If it gives pleasure, do it --- that's my touchstone." Or from an educational viewpoint, the prominent cognitive psychologist Jerome Bruner referred to play as "that special form of violating fixity", emphasizing the importance of play as a way of acquiring flexible repertoires of skill that can be used as young people continue to develop.

Caught up in their humour, eccentrics have occasional lapses from good taste because, unbound by social convention, they have rather pointed comments that they feel compelled to make when the occasion arises. They are more extreme and exuberant in the expression of their witticisms. An Oxford-educated Jamaican man with a surreal philosophy about life's various adventures, for instance, would turn up for interviews for manual labouring jobs for which he was patently over-qualified dressed up in top hat, white tie and tails. He explained this by saying, "The way to avoid being flushed down the toilet is never to conform to straight society's values." His companion, surprised by his own comparative staidness, said, "If everyone carried on like you, the world would go to the dogs." To this his riposte was, said with a look of slightly wounded bafflement, "It's the squares who traffic in wars, they are the ones sending the world to the dogs."

Eccentrics use hyperbole with abandon. For example, one eccentric living in Derby proclaimed this opinion to his amazed drinking companions: "The only things of value that so-called civilisation has ever produced are Napoleon brandy and Mozart." For some unknown reason, this enraged the stunned publican, who showed him the door, allegedly saying, "Keep your bolshie face out of my place."

Comprehensive in the range of their humour, eccentrics are fairly exuberant in its execution. How other people see and think about eccentricity often turns upon what they find funny, or not. Not everyone is moved to mirth by the following hair-raising narrative: "My brother's friend is eccentric. He collects suits of armour and Indian ornaments, lives in a large Georgian mansion, and has some strange habits. His mildest kind of practical joke is to push a dish of meringue trifle into the face of the chief lady guest at a smart dinner party in his home, having first asked her to 'smell it to see if it is off.' There is an oubliette under one of his dining room chairs and any boring guest is seated over it and dropped into the wine cellar when he can stand no more. His coup de grace was the miniature bomb that he planted inside his son's birthday cake, which he detonated when his boy blew on the candles, covering all his little friends with icing. The man's long-suffering wife had then to clean them all up, then somehow explain and apologise to their parents after the party."

Eccentric humour is far broader and more varied than the immature practical joke. It extends across the range known to students of the art. It can be used to bring other people fairly briskly to understand some truth about reality, or more usually, register an outspoken opinion:

"Natural evolution has progressed to the human brain and Nature is having to be cruel in order to kick its butt into real kindly action."

"I maintain that politics at all levels has an alarming number of 'lost souls' with, frankly speaking, severe brain disorders. Hard science also has more than its fair share."

Some eccentric humour shows a wholesale disregard for social conventions. Those who are strongly anti-authoritarian use their humour to gently ridicule people who might customarily have expected a degree of deference. Some of these eccentrics tend to be shy to the point of near seclusiveness, and to withdraw gingerly from social situations if their barbed wit stirs up aggressive feelings. Eccentrics who are more self-confident prefer to express their feelings through whimsical irony, and sometimes in mildly self-deflationary ways, such as: "I weigh fourteen stone, ride a bicycle but can't dismount, so I have to ride past my cottage and fall off into the grass bank fronting the sea wall. My pottery consists of mice in ballet dresses perched on trinket boxes, comical frogs wearing top hats, and bonnets perched on pottery apples."

(Jeanette, age fifty-one)

The funniest eccentrics are those who do things with a straight face and are blithely unaware that they leave people convulsed with laughter and tears in their wake: "My mother could always be relied on to do the unexpected. Her real forte was staircases. She ripped them out or re-routed them with gay abandon. She waltzed the good one round the house for five years --- never of course having it fixed. The only way to the second and third floors was by outside ladder. In my sixties, I can still shinny up a ladder three stories high. Finally, she chopped the house in half before the staircase finally came down --- she took it with her when she sold the house.

"Mind you, I don't think I could persuade removal men to try to take a concert grand piano up a spiral staircase. She persuaded them it could be done --- after each abortive attempt she plied them with whiskey and they took a piece of the piano. When they all accepted defeat we had three legless removal men and a piano, also minus its legs, lid and pedals.

"Then the fun really started. She wanted to call the builder to re-route the staircase. How he did it I don't know but by nine o'clock next morning my father had procured a carpenter and a mobile crane. The window was taken out and the piano duly installed. Why she carted that piano around was like everything else: never explained. One thing was certain. She never learned to play it. As she was surrounded by beautiful things, it wasn't one-upsmanship."

One of the study's eccentric informants was a stage, radio and television humorist, among several other occupations, and by the time we met he had already been perceived as one of the godfathers of alternative comedy and had garnered something of a cult following. I was keen to find out about the source of his humour and how his sense of humour worked. This was his reply: "I use the unexpected. I use the false premise. Pith and paradox. My humour is a social way of treating despair. The funny things are minor tragedies, like the hot water bottle bursting in bed. Or two poached eggs slipping off the plate onto my lap. I then phone my girlfriend and if she laughs like mad, I know I'm home free. I correlate and synthesise. Creatively, I write in bed at 1 A. M., or in a public place, where I am seen writing, and pitied for trying to be seen to be important. I let words come to the surface, and craft the aesthetics of them, disregarding the content, trusting my unconscious to supply me well, which it does. But I feel alienated. I belong to a minute band of people who look with a child's eye. We are seen as anarchic, a possible menace of all things. It's like living in a madhouse. I jump from one field to another, always one step ahead. I seem to have tried out most creative forms, in response to the negative reactions of all around me. So I've spent my life proving my worth. What a personal waste! I'm very egocentric. I'm desperate to belong and feel loved and lovable. Why do I go on, the world being what it is? I think I'm just myself, and in doing so create problems for myself in society. Ninety per cent (of people) don't really know what I'm on about. For a fleeting moment, when they hear me or read me, they wake up and stop being zombies. Parts of my appearances were banned in the 1960s by the BBC. Some people find me fascinating and even wish they were me, to have my mind. Bloody fools."

Many eccentrics are quite happy creating their own peculiar worlds. Given their odd and ironic sense of humour, a tendency toward hyperbole and usually stunning optimism, the results are often striking. They may have stumbled onto a new universal law: contemporary life expands to accommodate the amount of daring and fun put into it.

Unusual combinations of behaviours and attributes

Eccentrics in history appear, at first glance, to be better at these remarkable combinations than their modern counterparts. About half of the former were eccentric in two or more different ways. For instance, no one knew what to expect from the likes of Gerald Tyrwhitt-Wilson, the fourteenth Baron Berners (1883 - 1950). Aside from being a musical genius and a novelist of merit, he dyed his pet pigeons shades of pink, wrote scatological verse, built a folly in the grounds of his ancestral home, and entertained his friends and his white horse at a formal tea party at his mansion in Berkshire. His friend and fellow composer Constant Lambert recounted how Lord Berners had developed a special technique for keeping unwanted strangers out of his railway compartment: "Donning black spectacles, he would, with a look of fiendish expectation, beckon in the passers-by. Those isolated figures who took the risk became so perturbed by his habit of reading the papers upside-down and taking his temperature every five minutes that they invariably got out at the next station."

The other half of the eccentrics in British history were motivated by only one very single-minded purpose, be it frugality, finding peace in solitude, or being universally kind, and then taking that goal to extremes. Inadvertently, their behaviour would make people wonder. For instance, all that Thomas Birch wanted was to emulate Isaac Walton --- to become a complete angler. A librarian at the British Museum in the eighteenth century, Birch's ambition led him to disguise himself as a tree in a costume carefully designed to make his arms look like branches and a part of the fishing line a floating blossom. History does not tell us how successful he was at catching fish, though it does record that he frightened the living daylights out of passing walkers whenever he spoke or moved.

The modern inheritors of the historic eccentrics' mantles concentrate their efforts on somewhat broader repertoires of outrageous behaviour. Some are quite peripatetic, finding ways to innovate at work while keeping their friends and acquaintances perpetually off guard and wrong footed with a dazzling neglect of what others might think. As knowingly described by Francis Bacon, "Whatsoever affairs pass into such a man's hands, he crooketh them to his own ends."

John Slater was such an eccentric. He walked some three thousand miles along the very edges of Scotland's rugged coastline, and in doing so managed to raise about £1,000 for charity. He subsequently became the only person ever to have walked from Land's End in Cornwall to John O'Groats, Scotland's northernmost mainland point, in his bare feet. During this long trek he wore only his red, white and green striped pyjamas, making him appear to be a perambulating Christmas tree. Throughout this adventure he was accompanied by his loyal pet Labrador, Guinness, who sported two pairs of home-made suede bootees. After four months and many minor escapades, he limped into John O'Groats, where a crowd awaited him. "I'm seldom speechless," he said, "but I just stood there without a word. I thought to myself, 'It is possible. You can if you think you can.' "

Prior to these exploits, John's occupational career had been somewhat chequered. As a young man, he had served as a Royal Marine commando but, as he told one reporter, "There came a time when I lost interest in learning how to kill a man with my thumbs." Afterwards, he worked as a Royal Marine bandsman, lorry driver, steward on a luxury yacht, waiter, carpenter, painter and decorator, residential social worker for special needs children, salesman, insurance broker, public speaker, health food advocate, and charity fundraiser. Such a history is reminiscent of Ferdinand Waldo Demara, the Great Imposter, except that John has always remained true to himself.

John's diet consisted mostly of brown rice. He once volunteered to spend six months in a cage at London's Regent's Park Zoo as a human exhibit to help raise funds for leukaemia research and Giant Panda conservation. The zoo authorities "short-sightedly and foolishly declined". He then lived with down-and-outs in London, so that he could help them and learn more about himself. Back home, he appointed his other dog, Tiny, to be a Director of his limited company.

When I first encountered John, his blazing blue eyes, salt-and-pepper beard, denim outfit and large floppy hat gave him the look of a beachcomber, which indeed he was. This was at the time when he sometimes temporarily resided in a cave below the coastal cliff on which his home "Driftwood Cottage" was precariously perched. The Gaelic-speaking locals who knew him when he lived there in Wester Ross referred to him as "The Englishman". He lived in a stunningly beautiful location. I could see the dark silhouette of the Isle of Skye off to the west. Seals frolicked through the waves offshore, occasionally sticking their heads out of the water and peering at John as if they understood his peculiar behaviour. What was unfortunate about John's cave-dwelling episodes was that his favoured caves flooded with seawater at high tide.

"I am I my self and, without wishing to sound smug, because I'm not," he said, "I am the person that I want to be, and above all else doing things that mark me out as being more than a little bit distinctive. Some of the things I've done would get me locked up in other countries. Why do I do all that, you ask? There is a cathedral-like silence in caves which helps me to think and work things out. I'm addicted to harmony, peace of mind, restfulness. There's so much spending on the quality of death and nothing on the quality of life. While I'm here, I'm nursing all this terrific idealism, always thinking about what I can do next. I gave a friend of mine a brand name for his new wholemeal bakery --- 'Thoroughbread'. And why hasn't someone marketed a unisex deodorant called 'Every Body', as I suggested . . .?"

On the occasion of his third marriage, his new wife insisted that he desist from his cave dwelling and live with her properly in their marital home, a modernised stone-built crofter's cottage. John then turned his hand to making furniture from driftwood on a commercial basis and ran a one-man tourist service called Busybus. John's lifetime goal is to raise a million pounds for charity. His motto is "Wag your tail at everyone you meet".

Other eccentrics will quietly invent a satisfying niche compatible with their intellectual attributes, and remain in it stolidly and brilliantly, preoccupied for long periods. Rhea Shedden followed this pattern. From her early childhood in Cologne, Germany, she was told that she was special and unusual. She was an only child until she was twelve years old. "One was always made to feel wanted and loved and cherished and treasured." Her mother remarried when Rhea was thirteen, and her stepfather attempted unsuccessfully to cajole and groom her with various bribes and then to sexually abuse her. Because of her intellectual and athletic abilities, she was invited to join the Hitler Youth Movement and the Nazi Party, but immediately refused both offers on moral and ethical grounds. "How could anyone presume to control me? My stepfather tried, my teachers tried, my husband tried, the state tried. I'm the only one who controls me." Rhea later obtained a degree in Languages and in Education from the universities of Cologne, and after World War II, postgraduate degrees from Dundee, London, and Edinburgh, and continues to study all day long, every day. Her measured IQ is at least 165. When interviewed she said, "If I know the truth, I can cope with it. I would be full of brilliant ideas . . . then people would befriend me and then pinch my thoughts. Mentally I'm firing on all my 2,559 cylinders. Twenty-four hours (in a day) isn't enough for living --- now if I were twins! or quadruplets! Or if I could clone myself, what fun I would have!"

The cider-loving and louche Jake Jonathan Zebedee Mangle-Wurzel is more difficult, by any standard, to place in a conceptual frame. On the long side of his farmhouse at Salendine Nook, Peat Ponds, outside Huddersfield, West Yorkshire, large lettering proclaimed THIS IS, and the gable end completed the message, THE CRAZIEST COTTAGE IN CREATION. A smaller sign read "Department of Culture Shock --- Visitors Welcome --- Eccentric Offers Only Considered --- This is the house that Jake built . . . You are about to witness a unique watershed in your life's experience." The exterior of his house was surrounded on the ground level and on the first floor deck with rows of multi-coloured toilet bowls, chamber pots, plant pots, hand-painted flowerpots, and various paraphernalia. Jake couldn't explain why he placed a "classic" Morris 1000 automobile on the roof of his house, though a rooftop Victorian bathtub functioned as part of a homemade internal water-wheel system. Inside, his home was cluttered with memorabilia, unfinished mechanical projects and miscellaneous objects that didn't seem to serve any particular purpose.

Jake possesses a robust though quickly changing mercurial temperament. He is six and a half feet tall, with striking blue eyes, a bushy red beard, long greying hair tied back with a bow. He usually wears jeans, a thick turtleneck sweater, a rawhide jerkin festooned with badges and epaulets, knee high silver Wellington boots, and a bright red headband under a three-cornered sea captain's hat from the early nineteenth century. The impression he makes is that of a down-at-his-heels piratical-looking Cavalier. His elderly Triumph motorcycle has two masts --- the mainmast bears a lightning rod on top and the mizzenmast a Union Jack; strung between them is a clothesline festooned with Jake's well-worn long johns.

Jake was born John Gray in the Yorkshire village of Marsh. As a young man, he realized that his sense of self was relatively unformed, and that he was without an identity he could call his own. "I trained as an engineering draftsman," he said, waving his arms about from side to side, "then served three disastrous years in the Royal Air Force. After that, I tried all kinds of work, but it was an endless treadmill, and nothing gave me a sense of meaning." He felt compelled to shake himself free of that drab chrysalis.

During the first two decades of Jake's adult life, there was evidence of increasing alienation. He was not happy about how others had made assumptions about his identity, about how he ought to be living his life, and how he ought to behave. Those were assumptions he was not willing to accept. He began to believe that he had to change himself, and this would necessarily entail finding new ways of dealing with people. He changed his name, eventually emerging as a curious hybrid, a gadfly flitting from issue to issue, and stinging those in positions of power whenever he found them to be overbearing. Disarmingly frank, Jake told me, "When I turned forty, all I knew was that I'd been searching for something and not finding it. My old name hadn't done me much good, so I invented a brand new one and settled back to see what happened next. Once you've got the seed of growth you've just got to keep going and see where it leads you. Everything else changed. These were the early days of inspiration, perspiration and incredible mental and physical energy. I turned my life around by becoming eccentric, started re-creating my house, and surged off into a happier state of being. I liberated myself . . . and realized that if I became able to live like a free man it would be better for me and those close to me. I figured at first it could last just a few months, and then a day came and I pulled myself up short and said, 'Well Jakey, at least I've had six months of damned good fun.' But since then I've been going strong for many a moon. It's an extraordinary achievement, if I do say so meself. Sure, I'm a buffoon. But I'd like people to think of me as a serious commentator. I am an old-fashioned guy who believes that we should not hurt people, lie to them, or use them. I might act as daft as a brush from time to time, but a lot of what I do holds up an example to others who are like me, who, like me, want to tweak the tails of those who think themselves our betters."

What Jake discovered was the possibility of making, through his own actions, fundamental changes in his personality and lifestyle. As he went on, he soon became more willing to brazen out the quizzical, re-defining looks that people who had known him as John Gray then began to give him. His new conception of himself could not always prevent his former alienation from occasionally slipping out. When this happened, he would verbally try to scandalize others with outrageous acts or slyly mocking comments. It was said that in doing so he had "a rare talent for annoying self-important people in power and causing enmity."

By the time I first met Jake he could ably differentiate himself from other non-conformists and eccentrics he had met, sometimes befriended, and sometimes "inadvertently" insulted. He also provided many reasons for his actions; these can be summarized as oppositional and mildly confrontational, and self-reflective as he also began to see through and point out the hypocrisies of the many "phonies" he encountered. Throughout his interviews there was a remarkable absence of self-justification, self-blame or of blaming significant others. He occasionally came out with outright bragging, for example, "I've done an in-depth study. I know more about religion than the Archbishop of Canterbury, or the Pope." This particular boast partly may have been based on the fact that one of Jake's grandfathers was a notable English atheist who had left many writings that Jake later re-discovered and studied with earnest enthusiasm.

Jake's primary aim is to lead a happy life in his own way. In essence he has created for himself an entirely new, though sometimes a little bizarre, identity, and has become the friendly custodian of his own myth. Indeed, once he had changed from his former more conventional lifestyle to his eccentric one, he did not attempt to inhibit or conceal any of his newfound beliefs about himself from anyone who would care to listen. They amounted to the deliberate transformation in his fundamental philosophy about life.

For most eccentrics, one thing leads to another, and then they become quite transported, carried away by the prospect of a crucial discovery, attaining a significant self-revelation, or becoming a success in some way only hinted at in their daydreams.

About half of the eccentric women and three-quarters of the eccentric men clearly possessed a number of special talents and attributes, and expressed their delightful giftedness in a variety of ways.

Slightly more than a third of the informants also felt that they contained within themselves at least one other personality that was different from their more usual personalities. This suggests an assumption that some social psychologists believe to be incorrect, that people have only one personal identity. At the very least, many people have multiple identities based on their social group memberships.

For the women in this study who voiced the idea of containing another personality, that was perhaps no more than a secret wish, and they described this other personality most frequently as being uninhibited, sexy, and successful. For the men, their preferred alter egos were described as being *more* self-confident, adventurous, and successful. This may have been these eccentrics' way of saying that they wished to be more extraverted and outgoing. In addition, the females could have been expressing an urge to be even less hampered by the dictates of convention.

Doing ordinary things in extraordinary ways

Two men, looking very serious, and dressed in formal white tie and tails, are playing classical music on motorcycles. Not while sitting on them but by actually producing quite musical notes by treating the various parts of them as percussion instruments. This is an obvious eccentric complex of behaviours, but it does not necessarily mean that the men involved had eccentric personalities. It could have been an odd experiment, a challenge, or a bit of harmless fun, following Oscar Wilde's advice that "One should always be a little improbable". Not all unorthodox behaviour can be called eccentric.

Two eccentrics I studied improvised musically in unusual ways. The less eccentric of the two merely employed an instrument central to the folk tradition of one country to play the folk music of another country. The second eccentric played jazz on an assortment of old bones from anatomy school skeletons.

Doing some perfectly ordinary act in a perfectly extraordinary manner has always been a hallmark of the true eccentric. Sadly though, adult education has never really benefited from the example provided by John Alington (1795-1863). Firmly believing he had a responsibility to broaden his employees' horizons, he transformed the islands in a lake he owned into a scale model of the known world. While his farm workers rowed him around the different countries he lectured them on introductory geography. Prior to taking them to London for the Great Exhibition of 1851, he required them to construct a large-scale model of the streets of London between Hyde Park and King's Cross. After many practice walks resulted in failure, a chastened though wiser Alington declared that they were all too unintelligent to be trusted not to get lost, and cancelled their outing.

Francis Waring (1760 - 1833), the vicar of Heybridge in Essex, had an altogether different attitude to his calling. He read his church lessons at breakneck speed, gave a very brief sermon, no more than a quickfire series of aphorisms, ran down the aisle, leapt onto a fast horse and rode at a gallop to repeat similar efforts at two other churches. His everyday domestic arrangements were no less peculiar. Though not poor, he furnished his vicarage with rough-hewn logs rather than chairs. His children ate their meals from an interior trough beside the split log dining table. At night, Waring and his "darling spouse" slept in an enormous wicker cradle suspended from the ceiling, slowly rocking back and forth.

In a similar vein, Lady Margaret-Ann Tyrrell (1870 - 1939) ploughed her enchanting though contrary way through both her and her husband's career. Supremely absent-minded, she was devoted to her grand scheme to research and write a new kind of parallel history. In terms of her presentation, she was ahead of her time in tracing simultaneous events in all parts of the world from 2000 BC until her own time. With so many threads to chase, annotate, cross-reference and connect, it was small wonder that Lady Tyrrell was prone to absentmindedness and little social gaffes, such as mistaking the future George VI for her husband's private secretary. She also charmingly conversed for several hours with Lord Birkenhead under the misapprehension that he was the Turkish Ambassador. During her husband's diplomatic posting to Paris, she preferred to avoid most official functions. Ensconced in the uppermost branches of a tree in the Embassy gardens, she was better able to concentrate on her "magnum opus".

The modern counterparts of such eccentric people can be relied on to find alternative means to do things that others usually accept unthinkingly. This could involve eating and sleeping arrangements, housing, ways of writing, transport, and the conduct of interpersonal relationships, in fact almost the entire gamut of human activities.

Such behaviour usually occurs in the context of a deliberately altered lifestyle. For instance, Andy, at age twenty-four, decided to avoid city life. Leaving his comfortable middle class family home, he went to live for some time in the bombed-out shell of a house in Northern Ireland. Its previous occupant was a reserve police officer killed by the Provisional IRA. Andy grew all the food he needed in a large organic garden. He travelled everywhere on a huge, odd-looking tricycle of his own design, carrying all his camping and cooking facilities with him, as he said, "distance no object". By choice, he became a recluse and a deep green environmentalist who selectively followed certain aspects of the Taoist religion.

Andy was the eldest of five children. His mother's first baby died, and Andy's birth was a difficult one. He was a sleepy, independent, determined child who also tended to cling to his mother. He walked and talked early, and was a quick learner. However, he performed poorly at primary school; this was later attributed to boredom.

Andy was treated over-protectively, though he had kicked against "the system" in his early years. He started his "change in course" when he was thirteen years old. He was happy while alone, though dictatorial with his friends. He seemed over-confident and unafraid of everything, staying out of doors all night if it was foggy. He converted the family garage to a room of his own, and then shut himself off from everyone, even refusing to be photographed. As he became more impatient with people in general, his relationship with his family progressively deteriorated. He deliberately "went wild", walking to school barefooted in order to harden himself, and drove the family's Land Rover quite erratically around the countryside.

This long-running phase began when Andy tried to live permanently in a tent in his family's back garden. This had been a success for him, and by stages he progressed to the point where he enjoyed pitting himself against the elements on the mountains of the Lake District and the Scottish Highlands, walking very long distances. In Ireland, he became known by his friends as "the Yeti" or the "Abominable Snowman". Aside from tending his crops and herbs, he also wrote tongue-in-cheek letters to newspapers under historical names like P. Kropotkan or Gerard Winstanley. Several years later, Andy became reconciled with his family, and was described by his mother as "happy, warm, giving, optimistic and open".

A number of eccentrics show the first public indications of their eccentricity by being *against* some fixture of modern life. Several people in our sample were vehemently anti-automobile. One of them would intentionally dart out in front of cars to make his point. Another would drive a milk float too fast through city streets. A larger number, twenty of the eccentric informants, were opposed to most of the tenets and practices of modern medicine. Ten of these have acted on their beliefs to the point of becoming complementary or alternative medicine practitioners.

If not active as healers, eccentrics can also become proselytisers. Stanley Owen Green (1915 – 1993), a famous "sandwich board man" in the West End of London, was in this mould. He was greatly affected by a Sunday school teacher who said, "Don't listen to dirty jokes. Walk away from them." Stanley went on to become steadfastly principled: "I've always been a moral sort of person. I've spoiled my life by being too honest. I refused to do dishonest things when expected to do so on two occasions and lost good jobs that way". He worked in the Civil Service and local government, though at the age of fifty-three decided to devote himself to publicising his theories. He once accused the British Broadcasting Corporation of "spreading indiscretion, indiscipline, and indecency". Cycling twelve miles to and from Oxford Street six days a week on a daily diet of porridge, home-made bread, steamed vegetables and pulses, and a pound of apples, he was routinely faced with mockery while carrying his placard. It read: "Less Lust, By Less Protein: Meat Fish Bird; Egg Cheese; Peas Beans; Nuts. And Sitting." At home, he would use an antiquated printing press to run off hundreds of his own pamphlets. As well as selling these to the public for a nominal amount, he sent copies to five British Prime Ministers, the Prince of Wales, the Archbishop of Canterbury, and Pope Paul VI.

Ann Atkin, a potter and artist who creates huge abstract "spiritual paintings" on the scale of Picasso's *Guernica*, is also well-known for her gnome, elf, pixie and fairy sanctuary, which she launched in 1979. So far, there are thousands of these garden creatures, small ones, large ones, and intermediate-sized ones on display around her wild flower garden, in the surrounding beech wood and also throughout the interior of her West Putford, North Devon home. Each year countless visitors trundle down the winding rounds and don a peaked, red gnome hat to see Ann's gnomes peeping from behind tree stumps, fishing, playing chess, making music with various instruments, kissing other gnomes, sleeping on beds of moss, and more or less looking appropriately gnomish. "It doesn't matter whether you are six or a hundred and six, this is a place to come and forget your cares," said Ann. "I wanted to create a place that was an antidote to modern life. . . I am sixty-three and fit as a fiddle, apart from a back injury from transplanting a tree fifteen years ago. And I have been happy all my life." When I first met Ann, she presented me with a knitted hat of the brightly coloured, pointed type as worn by gnomes. I didn't realize it immediately, but she too was dressed as a gnome. There was something discordantly philosophical and mysteriously gnomic about her observations on life.

Some eccentrics go about their lives far from the glare of publicity. Eve, at seventy-seven years old, is a tiny, frail lady who has always had an abiding sense of fun. Although she sees superstition as regressive if allowed to direct one's life, she practises a form of extrasensory perception by "reading" whatever intuitions she feels when handling an object belonging to the person consulting her. Her life has manifestly been one of constant development, though she humbly minimised this: "I used to be a Moaner Lisa whenever I had a problem. I have really changed very little from my infant school days, where my inability to absorb knowledge and a lack of a retentive memory still haunts me. I don't conform. I don't know why. Tolerance is my creed. My religion is a constant effort to have my ego removed painlessly.

I'd have it removed with chloroform. I'd squash my ego because it's a very disturbing thing. If I could, then I would be absolutely free to think of other people all the time.

"Two years ago I was at my worst with arthritis pains and I was putting paint on the walls in the most fantastic designs. Now I knew that there was something wrong with me, I shouldn't be doing this, but I seemed to get something out of my system by doing it. It made the room look like a theatrical setting. My family looked at it and looked at me as if to say, 'We've got a right one here.' But I covered it up. I felt better after that. Perhaps it was another form of catharsis. I have kept myself alive on eclectic thoughts, and that is a lazy way of living, but those thoughts saved my sanity."

A quarter of the eccentric sample did ordinary things in extraordinary ways, thus fulfilling this criterion of exceptionality. This basically had to do with greater variability in behaviour. To understand this one should bear in mind that such variability can give one an enriched sense of personal identity. Whether this engenders a different organisation of personality features remains to be seen.

Violations of the "rules" of "normal" personality?

Although the laws of acoustics, for example, are not broken by cacophony, not enough is known about normal personality to ascertain what constitutes normality. One cannot justifiably speak about laws of personality precisely because personality has so many presentations, is so changeable, and is, at heart, intangible.

Those individuals who are attuned to the nuances of their own personality have been found to be more responsive to social cues for particular behaviours, and are therefore *more* variable in their behaviours than those with less self-awareness and self-knowledge [7]. This would apply to both eccentrics and non-eccentrics. While behavioural variability and diversity may be seen in some quarters as problematic, it can also be a valid expression of an individual's ability to simply be himself.

Individuals are not thrown randomly into social environments to which they must acquiesce, but in many instances manufacture and structure their field of experiences as they define its vicissitudes, develop their capabilities, and find their limits. They can also have an effect on their social environments. The extent to which people's actions potentiate their will, desires, primary motives or perceived lived experiences, will have some effects on their future behaviour and their more enduring personality traits.

People come to include values and qualities in their self-concepts in proportion to the degree that these are perceived to be under their control, or have become associated with their intentions [8]. To render oneself anomalous is to choose to risk the possibility of being removed from the vast majority of those with whom one could be compared. Civilisation can encompass these forms of private and restrained dissent. However, I believe there is more to being eccentric than antipathy towards mass organisation and planning, and the many other bugbears that such people find objectionable.

The concept of normality, while superficially not difficult to grasp, turns out to be quite slippery. The word normal derives from the root *norma*, or rule. Since *norma* etymologically once referred to a T-square, normal is that which bends neither to right nor left. It may designate the attainment of a happy medium, though it can also be a value that is attributed by virtue of personal evaluative judgements. This is why agreement about what is normal can be fraught and weighed down with reservations. It is as if our image of the world is in part a display of our values.

Those people imbued with power can identify and define what they think is normal, especially in terms of social norms. One can also have ideas about what normal means without there being a consensus vision, or even knowing how such views had come about.

It had seemed that statistics could provide a more neutral, value-free way of deciding such issues. Statistical normality has been defined as that which departs from some ideal value only as far as some measured upper or lower limit of functional demand [9]. Translated to distributions around an average value, normal is included between plus or minus one standard deviation to either side of the middle value [10]. This means that about sixty-eight per cent of any population would be assuredly considered "normal" on whatever variable is measured. The absurdity of this notion becomes apparent only when one realises that this categorizes the other thirty-two per cent as "abnormal".

Yes, this is absurd, yet at the very least it could be a way of showing which variables may be different in one specific group of people when compared with another group or with the general adult population. Human characteristics that can be measured on a quantitative scale allow each individual to be assigned a numerical score that he may or may not share with other people in the same population. The personality traits of each individual in several population samples can be placed along numerical scales and the central tendencies of the populations compared.

The eccentric sample significantly diverged (by greater than one standard deviation) from the British population norms on only two 16PF personality test dimensions --- that of Dominance/Assertiveness (Factor E, the eccentrics' mean score was 7.5, standard error 0.2) and that of Imaginative Disposition (Factor M, the eccentrics' mean score was 7.5, standard error 0.15).

The Dominance/Assertiveness factor describes someone who enjoys controlling as well as criticising others. A person such as this relishes being in command, faces up to challenges, and may have a superiority complex. Assertiveness tends to be positively related, to some extent, with social status, and is somewhat higher in established leaders than in followers. Someone high on this factor will be considered to be confident, aggressive, stubborn, headstrong, pugnacious, vigorous, adventurous, insensitive to social disapproval, and unconventional. He or she so endowed would profess belief in his or her own capabilities [11]. There is a possibility that assertiveness becomes altered somewhat with age, affected perhaps by frustration or mellowing. This holds true for the eccentrics to a limited degree, inasmuch as there was a modest negative correlation between assertiveness and age ($r = -0.23$).

The female eccentrics in the study were more assertive than the male eccentrics, and more assertive in general than British females. Such high levels might imply that these women were rebelling against the many conventional female gender role stereotypes they had faced. After all, the original idea of a stereotype involved notions of behavioural and attitudinal inflexibility in the face of discrepant information. It is still seen to be more socially acceptable and sex-appropriate for males than for females to express opposition, even today. It is unexpected to find this degree of general and specific rebelliousness in females; it runs counter to past roles based on previous cultural expectations. This could be construed as the eccentric women's rejection of their socially devalued female roles. Many of the female eccentrics reacted strongly against perceived sexual discrimination, some at an age and in a time when such behaviour was considered to be "not the done thing", and therefore unexpected of them. Such obviously rebellious females seriously challenge the privileged power and status of their partners, husbands or other significant males. As one of these women confided, "I think I give out sort of challenging vibes which a lot of people can't cope with."

This sex difference is more impressive when one remembers that the average age of the women in this study was forty-seven. This means that their assertiveness probably predated post-modernist feminism, and that it may have been higher when they were younger, or has not been subject to any age-related frustration or mellowing effects.

Women stepping farther and more radically away from what others expect of them may be given the label of "madness", perhaps in an attempt to control them by negative means [12]. Alternatively, individual women may conceive of themselves, or designate themselves, as eccentric, and thereby neatly sidestep the degree of stigma they might otherwise receive. This then could become a definitive act of liberation.

The Imagination factor is the one mentioned by the creators of the 16PF as the best marker of eccentricity. That it is significantly elevated in this sample provides a neat piece of cross-validation. Persons who score high on this factor are described as self-motivated. They tend to become concerned with major issues, with essentials rather than details. They can become absentmindedly distracted, and the core of their absentmindedness is based on intense subjectivity. At this level of subjectivity they are deemed to be unusual individuals unlikely to fit into a limited lifestyle. These are reckoned to be people who often seek unique courses throughout their lives.

The reactions of subjective people are fundamentally personal. Honestly self-centred, and proud of it, they rarely fall in line with another individual's point of view. They act out monologues derived from unfolding dramas of current events, usually in their own minds. In so doing, they vaguely fail to comprehend the opinions of the majority. They do not care to sacrifice their sense of integrity by colluding with elements of mass culture. Subjective people therefore stick to one viewpoint for a longer period of time than others who are considered to be more objective. The former may elaborate their viewpoints more frequently, and come to look into each and every of their favourite subjects more deeply. This can be accompanied by hyper-attention to apparently less important aspects of a problem. They see significance in things that others would pass over.

For eccentrics, this subjectivity may be based on a tendency to perceive reality through their more autonomous and singular ways of thinking, and more in accord perhaps with their dreams and wishes. Their interests occasionally lead to playful situations punctuated by spasmodic expressive outbursts. With their unreliable approach to practical matters, they may not always be accepted by others on their own terms, though they are generally unconcerned about this.

Younger eccentric informants, those under forty years of age, scored significantly higher on the Imagination personality dimension than did older informants (Univariate F-ratio 6.4, $p < .01$). However, creative activity, drawing on many imaginative sources, depends to a certain extent on having encountered rich and varied experiences throughout the whole of one's life, and is in part dependent on having at one's disposal the cultural tools necessary to work flexibly toward fulfilling their goals.

To help understand which eccentric individuals come to possess a more imaginative flair to their personalities, it is possible to make use of a rather complex sequence of mathematical equations. This technique is known as multiple regression. This showed that those eccentrics who are more imaginative are also those who are more emotionally sensitive and tender-minded (Personality Factor I+). This is the most significant single factor, and the correlation between imagination and sensitivity is one that often occurs among non-eccentrics too. With their sensitivity allowing them to take a wider overview of human variation, such people tend to be less judgmental. Such sensitive people are described appropriately as kindly, gentle, introspective, with a love of all things cultural and aesthetically pleasing. They can also be impatient, pervasively emotional and sometimes emotionally labile, and can thrive on dramatic situations.

Some of the contradictions concerning the sensitivity personality trait in this context are more intriguing than its more usual associations. In the days when gender roles were rigidly defined, sensitivity was said to be more oriented toward "feminine" inclinations. This clearly seems to be at odds with my earlier finding, that eccentrics, and especially eccentric females, are much more assertive than their non-eccentric counterparts. It is also the case that, second only to sensitivity, assertiveness is also a very good predictor of an imaginative bent, at least for eccentrics. Assertiveness and sensitivity are usually not sympathetic bedfellows, unless the assertiveness is measured and appropriate.

The second surprise is that people who are emotionally sensitive usually come from indulgent, overly protective families [11]. Some of them, as they developed, had become unusually sensitive to implicit communications or non-verbal signals. This may have been the case for eccentrics, though their family environments also ladled out criticism, an emotional form of criticism often directed at the future imaginative-sensitive-assertive eccentric child. This rich seam of family criticism was also picked out by this research project as a predictor of imaginative personality.

There are other predictors too. At first sight, the propensity for daydreaming --- the playing out of a sequence of events as mental images --- may be seen as another way to express an imaginative personality. Visions of Walter Mitty and Billy Liar to one side, daydreaming is a talent that many older children choose not to adopt and that more adults never put to practical use. Daydreaming is also implicated in another triad of predictors, which in turn was also related to schizotypal experience --- excessive religiosity, the belief that one can carry on two-way communications with God, and a pervasive style of emotional criticism within the family home.

One other point --- despite the relative youth of many of them, these people had experienced lives that were studded with an interesting array of positive life events or "high points" rated by them as the best moments in their lives. Here follows a representative list of some of them:

- Being placed in charge of an important archaeological excavation.
- Translating *Alice in Wonderland* into Latin.
- Being accepted into Mensa, the high intelligence club.
- Founding Densa, the average intelligence club set up possibly to mock Mensa. The former's motto is 'Too stupid for words'.
- Passing the professional examination to become a doctor, after six years' private reading and without formal instruction, having previously been expelled from medical school.
- Winning a design award.
- Finding God.
- Building a house.
- Making a science fiction prediction in 1934 that became a reality in 1945.
- Going hang gliding.
- Making political speeches to hostile audiences, and winning them round.
- Commanding a regiment on the North West Frontier, successfully waging a non-war.
- Transmitting psychic healing.
- Climbing Morocco's highest mountain.

- Being born.
- Acknowledging and sharing in the beauty and logic of nature.
- Getting into the army in 1939 as A1 with one leg three inches thinner than the other.
- Becoming an international authority in a very minor field.
- Stowing away on ships.
- Prospecting for gold and bushwhacking in the Australian outback.
- Flying solo to Canada and Africa.
- Taking revenge on the school bully forty-six years later.

The positive nature of these peak experiences was in turn related to the eccentrics' perceived ability to solve problems ($r = + 0.39$, $t = 4.43$, $p < .001$), and their greater number of spare time interests and activities ($r = + 0.30$, $t = 3.41$, $p < .01$).

It is important to not only look at single personality traits and behaviours in isolation. Most people's real personalities are a more or less organised and interactive composite of a variety of traits. While there are practically infinite permutations of kind and degree possible, most studies of normal personality distil this down to an arrangement of four or five key dimensions, or second-order factors. These arrangements usually are attempts to find a more realistic view, and can be a way of understanding what is happening to the organisation, be it static or dynamic, of the components of personality.

This was accomplished by a complex, mathematically elegant correlational procedure known as factor analysis. Many aspects of personality, attitudes, interests and behaviour are related to each other. By factor-analysing the degree of these relationships by this technique one can extract the main factors underlying the group of traits measured, and then compare them with accepted views about personality. A properly conducted factor analysis sorts out those qualities that go together, and can also be used to eliminate superfluous variables. It therefore captures a clearer picture of quite complicated material and can show which personality traits define the best-fitting personality description. Also, the relationship, or "factor-loading", of each trait to each personality factor allows an assessment of the degree to which each trait contributes its import to each factor. One is then in a good position to identify those dimensions that can help to explain the basic underlying personality dynamics. This procedure can be used as a tool in an exploratory investigation, such as this one, to see how one group of people compare with a representative cross section of the population, comprising usually many thousands of individuals.

Just as the discovery of a scientific law rests on the possibility of demonstrating the assumed lawful relationship in different investigations, so too psychologists ought to be able to rediscover fundamental human factors across different investigations. In factor analytic studies, this kind of replicability is known as factor invariance. Personality factors can be difficult to replicate because, among other reasons, the organisation of factors, or factor structure, may differ among different groups of people [13, 14]. Second-order factors, derived by repeating the procedure on first-order factors, tend to be relatively more steadily invariant when based on the same tests given to different types of people [15].

Perhaps it would be contrary to reasonable expectation to find the same pattern of factors emerging for eccentrics as for other groups of people. To the extent that the eccentrics' factorial personality composition may be *different* would be another, more indirect indication of the substantive degree of their exceptionality.

The method of factor analysis used was that of Principal Components, with a Varimax Rotation. This was applied to the data from the 16PF Personality Test. Factor analysis enables the researcher to determine the minimum number of dimensions or factors that can best summarise the relationships of the data by noting the "grouping together" of the traits, their correlations and factor loadings. It attempts to lay bare the assumed hierarchical structure of personality and to unravel its basic dimensions. How far a particular first-order factor is related to a higher second-order factor can be determined by the correlation between them. This relationship is known as the "loading" on the factor. The Varimax Rotation procedure usually provides a more psychologically meaningful presentation of the complex inter-relationships within and between these personality dimensions. As is common practice in such studies, only factors with a statistical "eigenvalue" above unity were considered significant. The solution provided five superordinate, or second-order, factors, accounting cumulatively for two-thirds of the total variance, or variability, in the eccentrics' personalities. Table 13. shows the organisation of these factors.

Table 13: 16 PF Personality Test Factor matrix

Factor	Factor Name and % variance	Factor loading	Mean (average)	Standard deviation
Factor 1 (17.3% of the variance) Stability versus Anxiety				
Q4	Relaxed vs. Tense	.82	5.20	2.33
O	Confident vs. Apprehensive	.78	4.82	2.26
L	Trusting vs. Suspecting	.69	6.38	2.07
Q3	Uncontrolled vs. Self-controlled	- .48	4.66	1.80
C	Emotionally unstable --- Mature	- .80	5.24	2.12
Factor 2 (16.8% of the variance) Introversion versus Extraversion				
H	Shy vs. Venturesome	.72	6.04	2.43
F	Reticent vs. Enthusiastic	.72	5.58	2.21
A	Aloof vs. Outgoing	.60	4.55	2.02
E	Submissive vs. Assertive	.53	7.44	2.18
Q2	Group-Dependent vs. Self-sufficient	- .75	6.83	1.72
Factor 3 (12.4% of the variance) Intuitive Independence of Thought				
M	Practical vs. Imaginative	.78	7.35	1.82
E	Submissive vs. Assertive	.58	7.44	2.18
N	Naïve vs. Sophisticated	- .76	4.07	2.07
Factor 4 (10.5% of the variance) Tender-minded versus Tough-minded				
I	Tough-minded vs. Sensitive	.77	5.88	2.46
A	Aloof vs. Outgoing	.43	4.55	2.02
Q1	Conservative vs. Radical	- .73	6.17	2.09

Factor	Factor Name and % variance	Factor loading	Mean (average)	Standard deviation
Factor 5 (9.5% of the variance) Low Superego Strength versus High Superego Strength				
G	Expedient vs. Conscientious	.83	4.7	1.82
Q3	Uncontrolled vs. Self-controlled	.61	4.66	1.80

The first two second-order factors, Stability versus Anxiety and Introversion versus Extraversion, have occurred repeatedly as the two largest personality factors in a great number of investigations. Both are not substantively different from previous solutions. More stable people tend to be generally satisfied with themselves and their lives, and can aim towards achieving their goals, whereas more anxiety-bound people tend to have a degree of maladjustment and possibly are negatively adjusted socially. Those who are introverted tend to be shy, somewhat interpersonally inhibited and self-sufficient, and can tolerate, sometimes even enjoy, keeping their own company. On the other hand, extraverts are socially outgoing and less inhibited, and also more likely to follow their more immediate impulses.

One intriguing observation made here was that when the data was broken down between male and female eccentrics, it was the female eccentrics who were more stable and less anxious than their male eccentric counterparts. This is not what has usually been found in most studies of male-female differences, whether these were based on community or clinical samples. In addition, the most consistent finding for all psychiatric patient groups in similar factor analyses has been a low score on Factor C (Ego strength or Emotional stability). This was not found for this group.

The third second-order factor, interpreted as representing Intuitive Independence of Thought, is somewhat different from prior parallel derivations. Part of this difference is due to gender differences in Factor N (Naiveté versus Shrewdness). It was liable to "wander", as it is related to Extraversion for women, but was more related to Intuitive Independence of Thought for men. In addition, Factor N has a low (+.30) but *positive* relationship to Intuitive Independence of Thought for women, but a high (-.75), very significant negative relationship for men. It is not only variable, but also different across the genders; in other words, its influence relative to other factors could be gender-specific in regard to eccentrics.

Factor N (Naiveté versus Shrewdness) is known to be associated with a vague way of thinking, and this resonates with the thought and communication abnormalities discovered amongst eccentrics. It is also associated with a socially awkward, blindly trusting spontaneity that echoes the elevated incidence of unguarded self-disclosure styles amongst young schizoid adolescents [16, 17]. Is it mere coincidence that the compulsively confessional Jean-Jacques Rousseau (1712-1778) or the plainly spoken and forthright Henry David Thoreau of Walden Pond, luxuriating in solitude though openly hospitable to strangers, have been seen as ideal models of eccentricity? It is brilliant egomania to say that you belong to your self, though that sounds childlike in its negation of the Machiavellian cynic's way of thinking. The positive qualities attaching to this naiveté are caring genuineness and utter directness. The downside is that it feeds into an outspokenness that can cloy and annoy.

The fourth second-order factor, Tender-mindedness versus Tough-mindedness, usually refers respectively to people who are more likely to be rather more gentle and involved with artistic orientations, contrasted with those who are more resilient, decisive and involved with entrepreneurial orientations. However, in the current research it is perhaps not as straightforward to interpret as it at first appears. It is confounded by significant gender differences on all three first-order traits involved. The males in this study were more tender-minded than the females, while females were more radical and experimenting than the males. Factor A (Aloof versus Outgoing) was different across the genders in two ways. This factor was related to Tender-mindedness only for females, and more to Extraversion for males. Also, the females were more aloof and reserved than the males. As in many other studies, older informants were more conservative. Personal preferences were also involved: while sensitive individuals gravitated toward non-radical religious experience, those with a rigorous mind and experimental attitude had interests of a scientific nature. No evidence for a relationship between Tender-minded versus Tough-minded attitudes and psychotic symptoms, thought disorder or communication disorder was found in the course of this study. The single fragmentary exception to this was a statistically significant correlation ($r = +.31$, $p < 0.001$) between 16PF Factor I (Tough-mindedness versus Sensitivity) and mystical-religious experience.

The fifth-order factor, Low Superego Strength versus High Superego Strength, is composed of two first-order factors that primarily involved the eccentrics' adroitness at rule-breaking and their willingness to ignore rules. This second-order factor had a positive relationship with age, older informants being more guided by the dictates of conscience. It was also related negatively to impulsiveness, irresponsibility, and the expression of destructive anger.

Overall, eccentrics scored highly for Independent Thought and low on Superego Strength. The real surprise was that the normal factor pattern of the 16PF test emerged from this trial of eccentricity as robustly as it did when applied to this extreme group. It is with just such a group as this that one might expect to observe some demonstrable collapse of the basic assumptions of personality assessment. This did not happen.

Personality disorder

A persuasive case could be made that some personality deviations do not exist, particularly in the light of historical changes and cultural differences in what is judged to be deviant. It was a crime, for instance, in Viking Iceland for a person to write poetry about another person, including complimentary ones, though only if the verses exceeded four lines. The English peasant of the fourteenth century was not allowed to send his son to school, and no one lower than a freeholder was permitted by law to keep a dog. The following have at different times been crimes in Britain: printing a book, professing the concept that blood circulates through the body, selling coins to foreigners, keeping gold at home, and buying goods on the way to market in order to make a profit.

Therefore, it would be an error of judgement to define personality disorder solely in terms of social maladaptation or law-breaking. To do so would be to accept the idea that an individual must subscribe to his society's rules, whether those rules are right or wrong. In this view, there can be little individuality based on ethical premises. The good citizen is seen as infinitely malleable in regard to laws, customs or propaganda that can bear down on him, being forced to accommodate himself or herself to society, be it an oppressive or an enlightened one. The converse of this flawed notion is that if the society is offensive, if its means fall short of justifying its goals, it should be denied any right to define right and wrong. This is what Martin Luther King so eloquently meant in 1968 when he said, "Through such creative maladjustment, we may be able to emerge from the black and desolate midnight of man's inhumanity to man, into the bright and glittering daybreak of freedom and justice." A decision about the point at which a society reaches the stage that unlawful action ought to be contemplated involves a value judgement of weighty ethical complexity.

Further conceptual confusion about personality disorder has come about because morally objectionable behaviour has been confounded with dispositions of the person. Behaviour that is unacceptable in moral or socio-cultural terms is neither necessary nor sufficient to identify a personality disorder. In this matter, unaided clinical diagnoses have in the past been fairly unreliable [18, 19]. This remains a troubling source of torrid controversy for clinical psychiatrists and occasionally for the general public, usually during criminal law proceedings. As to validity, it has not always been easy to distinguish between what is true and what is merely believed.

In practice, the assessment of personality disorder can be defined only by the identification of enduring behavioural patterns that permeate a person's adult life, and especially in the area of interpersonal relationships. They represent a set of pervasive maladaptive traits showing their first signs in late childhood or early adolescence, though they only solidify into more fixed patterns of behaviour in later adolescence or early adulthood. These behavioural patterns become resolved as more enduring personality traits and persist undiminished at least into late middle age. These traits reinforce inferences drawn from observations and show a degree of consistency in behaviour across a range of situations. Abnormal traits constitute a basic aspect of the affected person's usual functioning. They are concerned with the "how" of behaviour.

It should be emphasized that individuals with personality disorder, though they are frequently assessed and dealt with by psychiatrists and clinical psychologists, do not necessarily suffer from any known mental illness. While the various types of abnormal personality described by psychiatrists are represented amongst some of their patients, there is no reason to believe that many of those in the community with such personalities ever seek psychiatric help or are disordered to the extent of being socially incapacitated, or necessarily are the cause of distress to others.

When this study began, there was no way of knowing whether eccentrics were personality-disordered, and if they were, in what way. It could be that when people call someone "eccentric", they are simply mistaken. They may know that something is amiss or different, though not the specific nature of the abnormality. Eccentrics in the community may also be essentially different from those who have come to the attention of clinicians. On the other hand, eccentricity and personality disorder could co-exist, either coincidentally or in an intricate relationship with other aspects of personality.

Personality disorder does not usually confer any particular advantage upon an individual. Many people with personality disorders are not in harmony with their social environment, and people who are in contact with them may not feel in harmony with them. My general impression of the individuals I met was that their personalities were anything but pathological, that their positive traits outweighed their problems. However, impressions can be deceptive.

Advances in systematic classification and the more extensive use of consistent terminology, definitions and diagnostic criteria have greatly helped. The overall diagnosis of personality disorder has achieved, over more recent times, respectable reliability and reasonable predictive validity [20, 21]. The development of a standardised interview schedule, the Personality Assessment Schedule [22], offered the opportunity of studying the relationship between personality disorder and eccentricity. This schedule involves an interview in which twenty-four personality variables are rated quantitatively. Each informant subsequently can be classified into one of five broad categories --- antisocial, dependent, inhibited, withdrawn, or normal. Within each of the personality disorder categories there are a number of personality types. These were initially obtained by using a computer programme originally derived from a large-scale cluster analysis of extensive clinical personality data [23].

With this system, when two personality disorder types receive an equivalent rating for the same person, a hierarchical method is used to obtain the primary personality disorder diagnosis. This method is based on Professor Peter Tyrer's exhaustive work with the Personality Assessment Schedule (PAS). His evidence suggests that significant social maladjustment is more frequently produced from those with sociopathic personality traits than with schizoid personality traits, with the traits of the other personality types in between. This is presumably because the characteristics of sociopathy are by definition more likely to be antisocial in the broadest sense. (See Table 14.)

Table 14. Personality disorder classification by PAS (Percentages in parentheses are the proportion in each diagnostic category within the female and male groups.)

Category		Females	Males
Antisocial	Sociopathic	1 (1.8%)	3 (4%)
	Explosive	---	1 (1.3%)
	Sensitive aggressive	---	1 (1.3%)
Dependent	Passive dependent	3 (3.5%)	1 (1.3%)
	Histrionic	---	---
	Asthenic	---	2 (2.7%)
Inhibited	Obsessional	3 (3.5%)	5 (6.8%)
	Anxious	---	1 (1.3%)
	Hypochondriacal	---	---
	Dysthymic	2 (3.5%)	---
Withdrawn	Schizoid	4 (7%)	6 (8%)
	Paranoid	---	2 (2.7%)
	Avoidant	2 (3.5%)	2 (2.7%)
Non-personality disordered	Normal	43 (77.2%)	50 (67.9%)

As can be seen, the majority of eccentrics had no personality disorder. Of those with personality disorder, those with schizoid personality disorder and obsessional personality disorder were somewhat better represented than the other types. Schizoid personality disorder is usually distinguished from schizotypal and paranoid personality disorders by the prominence of social, interpersonal and affective deficits in the absence of psychotic-like cognitive and perceptual distortions [24]. The ten eccentrics with schizoid personality disorder showed few moderate or severe affective deficits during their interviews; nor were such deficits apparent in the biographical or family histories they provided.

Commensurate with data provided from interviews using the Personality Assessment Schedule, twenty-eight per cent of the entire eccentric sample had a recognisable personality disorder. This compares favourably with a larger sample of neurotic patients studied with the PAS, in which as many as forty per cent were found to be personality-disordered [25]. Also, the passive-dependent category is significantly under-represented among eccentrics, as compared with the latter study's neurotic patient group. To put these figures in perspective, epidemiological studies in the community suggest that between eight and ten per cent of the UK population suffers from a personality disorder [26].

There is more to this story. There are at least three other varieties of personality disorder not covered by the PAS --- these are the narcissistic, borderline, and schizotypal personality types.

Some eccentrics' self-presentations seemingly approached the classic descriptions of patients with narcissistic personality disorders [27, 28, 29], though this was not a consistent feature. The key outward sign of this personality type is an inveterate feeling of great self-esteem, a grandiose vision of one's mission or personal significance to the world. For true narcissists, achieving their very high goals becomes essential to their psychological balance. They are aggressively ambitious, and if thwarted in their attempts to control their aspirational destinies, become disproportionately angry. Their signal over-reaction to criticism springs naturally from the above, as do the excessive demands they make on others. Their self-absorption indicates a way of coping with their deeper concerns, which has to do with their loss of sufficient attention from others. Beneath their superficially charming facades, they tend to disregard others, or feel contempt for "lesser mortals". Genuinely creative ways of living are diminished primarily because narcissists make unrealistic demands on other people, and the ways that they go about doing that.

A number of the eccentrics were only narcissistic in the simple adjectival sense, though this was a fluctuating feature. The quality of their personal relationships was in no way as impoverished as the clinical diagnosis would normally imply. Eccentrics shared a few of the ancillary traits of narcissists: a sense of unbounded possibilities, and recurring themes of lost opportunities and unfulfilled potential. Both eccentrics and narcissists may also embrace fanatical causes, though from different underlying motivations. The telltale indication of this is that some narcissists can get caught up in enthusiastic discipleships, to the point that psychoanalysts talk of their sense of identity being merged with that of their leaders. Eccentrics only very rarely place themselves in such roles; they abhor being followers. It is doubtful if any self-respecting eccentric could be more than temporarily seduced by someone else's charisma.

By the use of objective measures, ten people in the study, six females and four males, received an assessment of narcissistic personality disorder. This diagnosis occurred as frequently as did schizoid personality disorder amongst this sample. Six of these individuals, three males and three females, had not received a personality disorder diagnosis on the Personality Assessment Schedule. Narcissistic personality disorder occurred in conjunction with "secondary" traits and behaviours of borderline personality in five individuals. This is of interest because several clinical theorists have sought to establish close connections between narcissistic and borderline personality disorders [27, 28].

However, there are few links to be found between borderline personality disorders and eccentricity. They seem as far apart as it is possible for two personality categories to be. Arguably, the two categories are poles apart in many ways. People designated as borderline have a range of social and emotional problems and specific types of behaviour: an unstable but not absent sense of reality; an impaired self-image and personal identity; tempestuous and non-enduring relationships; building up a person as an ideal only later to treat him or her contemptuously; intense mood swings; temperamental angry outbursts; and self-damaging behaviour and suicidal impulses [30]. Their trains of thought become markedly derailed and consequently their conversations often seem to lack coherence. Borderline personality pathology may be one of the more severe and negative personality-related conditions encountered clinically [31, 32]. On the other hand, eccentrics are only rarely seen in a clinical context and are imbued with many positive traits. Only one informant in this study, a male, received a primary diagnosis of borderline personality disorder.

Superficially, eccentrics have been thought to bear perhaps more resemblance to those with a non-disordered schizotypal personality. Some eccentrics, no less than a fifth and no more than a third of the eccentrics studied, shared three characteristic ways of functioning with the latter:

a. Magical thinking, for example, superstitiousness, beliefs in clairvoyance, a "sixth sense", telepathy, and that "others can feel my feelings".

b. Odd communication styles, for example, circumstantial, digressive, tangential, over-talkative and overly elaborate.

c. Suspiciousness and mildly paranoid thinking ("I don't feel but know that people have been against me."). In general, this is not strong among most eccentrics. It may represent milder suspicions of the motives of other people. As evidence of this, their suspiciousness was not robust enough to push their scores for 16 PF Factor L (Trusting versus Suspecting) far above average levels. However, earlier research has shown that those people who score more highly on another related measure, the more clinically-orientated MMPI Suspicion cluster, tend to express their impulses, value their sensations, and have an active imagination, their thinking often dominated by feelings and fantasies [33].

Although eccentrics possess several atypical ways of thinking, their perceptual experience is usually abundantly unimpaired, and sometimes gifted.

Only one informant in the study, a female, received a primary diagnosis of schizotypal personality disorder, and that was of mild degree. Therefore, there are insufficient grounds for retaining the mistaken clinical lore that more enduring eccentricity and schizotypal personality disorders are closely associated. Furthermore, this individual, and also the ten individuals shown to have a schizoid personality disorder, did not show any of the neuropsychological markers that have been observed in schizotypal personality disorder and schizophrenia, such as cognitive dysfunctions and deviant smooth pursuit eye tracking movements [34, 35].

The inclusion of these three additional personality disorder types brought the proportion of eccentrics with personality disorder up to thirty per cent for the female informants and thirty-five per cent for the male informants.

Looking closely at only those eccentrics with personality disorder, seventy per cent of the females and fifty-four per cent of the males fulfilled strict diagnostic criteria for two or more personality disorder categories. This could be indirectly indicative of their personal complexity, or their idiosyncrasy. Three female eccentrics attracted thirty-one separate personality disorder diagnoses between them. Six male eccentrics attracted thirty-nine separate personality disorder diagnoses between them. It is not uncommon for patients with severe psychotic illnesses to be given a number of personality disorder diagnoses [36]. However, none of the above eccentrics was mentally ill, not even mildly so. It is common to find that individual patients meet the criteria for several supposedly distinct personality types [37, 38, 39], though no one as yet understands exactly why.

The only clues that this research study can offer are that, first, the three female eccentrics with personality disorder diagnoses in multiple categories had one thing in common: a primary diagnosis of narcissistic personality disorder. Second, the six male eccentrics with personality disorder diagnoses in multiple categories had a primary or more frequently a secondary diagnosis of borderline personality disorder. Because of the relative severity of narcissistic personality disorder and borderline personality disorder, it has been considered that those two diagnoses should be given precedence. However, as to the latter, only one informant in this study received a primary diagnosis of borderline personality disorder, and he also showed secondary schizoid and passive-dependent features.

A likely explanation for the problem of people with more than one personality disorder diagnoses is that people with narcissistic and borderline personality disorders are inherently more disturbed. Because of this it may be necessary to subsume a number of other personality disorder types to adequately describe the full reality and uniqueness of their personalities. Little wonder that these individuals are recognised as eccentrics, both by themselves and by those close to them.

These clues present at least two alternative explanations. The individuals affected could have had covert mental illnesses, though this seemed unlikely. However, the correlation between personality disorder and thought disorder (by Present State Examination) in the entire eccentric sample was +0.27 (p < .01). This is believed to be a low estimate of the underlying relationship. (The reason for this is that this correlation is uncorrected for attenuation, and a standard correction therefore should be applied when the data covers a restricted range. This was the case here: the majority of the informants had either no personality disorder or mild personality disorder and also had low or mild degrees of thought disorder.) In addition, there was a significantly greater relationship between personality disorder and formal thought disorder for female eccentric informants than for male eccentric informants. This coincided with an even greater relationship between personality disorder and communication disorder (by the Thought, Language and Communication scale) for female eccentric informants. (See Table 15.)

Table 15. Personality disorder and communication disorder (by TLC scale)

	Non-personality disordered	Personality-ordered
Females	36%	100%
	(2.0)	(5.2)
Males	63%	70%
	(2.9)	(3.9)

(Percentages refer to proportions in each group with communication disorder. Numbers in parentheses refer to each sub-group's average communication disorder scores.)

These relationships between personality disorder and with both formal thought disorder and communication disorder respectively are significant. This was the first time that they have been discovered to exist together in certain types of individuals, and so demonstrated.

As would be expected, eccentrics with personality disorder are at a disadvantage in a number of ways compared with eccentrics without personality disorder. The former were less curious, less original as judged by independent raters, and were demonstrably more superstitious. They also had received more consistently negative reactions from other people, at least in terms of frequency, by as much as fifty per cent, than did eccentrics without personality disorder.

Is there more than one type of eccentric?

A related question that has often been asked is whether or not there is more than one distinct type of eccentric. The way this question is posed refers to the underlying psychology of eccentrics, rather than trying to group them in line with their specific, sometimes very different, types of interests and behaviours. Having collected overlapping data sets covering normal personality and personality disorder; a comprehensive range of psychiatric symptoms; and many other psychological and biographical variables --- in all 120 variables on each of the 130 informants, or 15,600 separate data points --- my research team was in an excellent position to begin to answer this question. However, as I knew, every particular data set collected from different types of people will produce a different solution, depending on what types of data go into the analysis, and its quality, which is generally based on its reliability and validity.

My first task was therefore to reduce the number of variables to as few factors as possible, whilst retaining the crucial elements of what had been found. To do this, I performed a factor analysis that included every variable measured. A Principle Components factor analysis with a Varimax Rotation was used. To resolve where to stop extracting factors, Professor Raymond Cattell's "Scree Test" was used. This solution reduced the hundred and twenty variables to twenty-six factors, which accounted for ninety-five per cent of the total variance from the interviews and various psychometric tests. (See Table 16.)

Table 16: Factor analysis of the entire dataset

Factor	Variable	16 PF Factor		Factor loading
Anxiety --- Stability (18.1% of the variance)	16 PF	Q4	Free-floating anxiety	0.77
	PAS		Sensitivity	0.73
	PAS		Anxiety	0.71
	PAS		Vulnerability	0.64
	PAS		Introspection	0.62
	Item		Feeling incomplete	0.59
	16 PF	O	Guilt proneness	0.58
	PAS		Irritability	0.56
	Item		Dramatic love and hate	0.56
	16 PF	L	Suspiciousness	0.55
	PAS		Aggression	0.54

Factor	Variable	16 PF Factor		Factor loading
	PAS		Pessimism	0.53
	PAS		Hypochondria	0.52
	PAS		Lability	0.50
	PAS		Childishness	0.44
	PAS		Rigidity	0.38
	Item		Feeling empty	0.35
	Item		Loss of positive images	0.35
	Item		Difficult to love	0.34
	PAS		Suspicion	0.30
	16 PF	Q3	Ability to bind anxiety	- 0.54
	16 PF	C	Ego strength	- 0.62
Shy submissiveness (8.9% of the variance	PAS		Shyness	0.68
	PAS		Submissiveness	0.50
	PAS		Feelings of worthlessness	0.46
	PAS		Conscientiousness	0.43
	PAS		Impulsiveness	- 0.32
	16 PF	E	Assertiveness	- 0.49
	16 PF	H	Boldness	- 0.75
Religious beliefs (7.1% of the variance)	PSE		Feeling Close to God	0.85
	PSE		Receiving Communications from God	0.80
	PSE		Religiosity	0.77
	PSE		Religious delusions	0.68
Education (5.6% of the variance)	Item		Education	0.83
	Item		Social class	0.78
	Item		Depth of thinking	0.39

Factor	Variable	16 PF Factor		Factor loading
	Item		Interest in science	0.35
	Item		Amount of reading	0.32
	16 PF	N	Shrewdness	- 0.34
	Evidence		Spelling errors	- 0.39
Perceived difference (4.9% of the variance)	Item		Difference from others	0.80
Psychotic experiences (4.3% of the variance)	PSE		Special arrangement of things	0.69
	PSE		Visual hallucinations	0.69
	PSE		Auditory hallucinations	0.65
	PSE		Thought broadcasting	0.31
Future orientation (4.0% of the variance)	Item		Future of self	0.44
Concentration & emotional deficits (3.7% of the variance)	PSE		Lack of concentration	0.64
	Item		Remembered hurt and anger	0.40
	Item		Destructive anger	0.38
	Item		Negative reaction of others	0.38
	PAS		Impulsiveness	0.37
	Evidence		Spelling errors	0.31
Extraversion (3.6% of the variance)	16 PF	A	Outgoing	0.58
	16 PF	F	Happy-go-lucky	0.52
	16 PF	H	Boldness	0.40
	Item		Interest in politics	0.31
	16 PF	Q2	Group dependency	- 0.74
Thought interference (3.2% of the variance)	PSE		Thought withdrawal	0.83
	PSE		Thought blocking	0.46

Factor	Variable	16 PF Factor		Factor loading
	PAS		Optimism	0.33
Tough-mindedness (3.0% of the variance)	16 PF	Q1	Experimenting	0.65
	16 PF	E	Assertiveness	0.53
	16 PF	I	Tender - minded	- 0.56
Thought transfer (2.6% of the variance)	PSE		Thought echo	0.68
	PSE		Thought broadcasting	0.65
	PSE		Thoughts controlled	0.37
	Item		Curiosity	0.34
Imagination (2.5% of the variance)	16 PF	M	Imaginative	0.74
	16 PF	G	Expedient	- 0.41
	16 PF	N	Forthright	- 0.44
Directed criticism (2.4% of the variance)	Item		Criticism in the family	0.79
	Item		Criticism of the informant	0.69
High points (2.3% of the variance)	Item		High points	0.73
	Item		Problem solving	0.51
	Item		Spare time interests	0.44
Worries and problems (2.3% of the variance)	PSE		Present worries	0.72
	Item		Biggest problem	0.43
	PSE		Paranoia	0.32
Dependency (2.1% of the variance)	PAS		Dependency	0.53
	PAS		Resourcelessness	0.42
	PAS		Pessimism	0.37
	Item		Daydreaming	0.33
	16 PF	Q3	Lack of control	- 0.36
Telepathy (1.9% of the variance)	PSE		Thoughts read	0.64

Factor	Variable	16 PF Factor		Factor loading
	PSE		Repetitive thoughts	0.39
	PAS		Optimism	0.33
	PSE		Visual hallucinations	0.32
	Item		Negative reactions of others	0.32
Callousness (1.8% of the variance)	PAS		Callousness	0.78
	PAS		Suspicious	0.32
	PAS		Irresponsible	0.31
Superstition (1.8% of the variance)	Item		Superstition	0.78
Originality (1.8% of the variance)				
	Item		Originality	0.63
	Item		Imagination	0.43
	Item		Repetitive Thoughts	0.39
Special privileges (1.6% of the variance)	Item		Special privileges	0.69
	Item		Future of world	- 0.34
	Item		Interest in politics	- 0.39
Feeling difficult to love (1.6% of the variance)	Item		Expressed emotion in the family	0.53
	Item		Difficult to love	0.41
	Item		Destructive anger	0.31
	PAS		Childishness	0.31
Creativity (1.5% of the variance)	Item		Creativity	0.59
	Item		Vivid dreams	0.54
Disinterest in sport (1.5% of the variance)	Item		Disinterest in sport	0.56
Interest in science (1.3% of the variance)	Item		Interest in science	0.59

(16 PF = 16 PF Personality Test factor; PAS = Personality Assessment Schedule of Personality Disorder; PSE = Present State Examination of psychiatric symptoms; Item = Interview Item Answer; Evidence = Physical Evidence.)

Many of the factors contributed very small amounts of variance, though all those shown above were statistically significant. The above twenty-six factors themselves were then factor-analysed to obtain fewer, more reliable and stable second-order factors. (See Table 17.)

Table 17: Second-order factors

Second Order Factor	First-order factor (number and name)		Factor Loading
AA Neuroticism (25.1% of the variance)	1	Anxiety	0.70
	2	Shyness	0.69
	17	Dependency	0.59
	15	High Points	- 0.53
BB Psychotic experience (17.8% of the variance)	18	Telepathy	0.92
	6	Psychotic experience	0.60
	10	Thought interference	0.36
	3	Religious beliefs	0.30
CC Intellectual aptitude (15.5% of the variance)	26	Interest in science	0.96
	4	Education level achieved	0.62
DD Extraversion (12.6% of the variance)	9	Extraversion	0.86
	20	Superstition	0.75
EE Tough-mindedness (7.3% of the variance)	8	Concentration deficits	0.42
	19	Callousness	0.40
	25	Disinterest in sport	0.40
	11	Tough-mindedness	0.39
	26	Interest in science	0.27
	7	Future orientation	- 0.57
FF Creativity (6.9% of the variance)	5	Different from others	0.69
	24	Creativity	0.63

Second Order Factor	First-order factor (number and name)		Factor Loading
	12	Thought transfer	0.40
	21	Originality	0.38
GG Borderline / Narcissistic Personality Disorder (5.4% of the variance)	22	Special privileges	0.74
	23	Difficult to love	0.47
	1	Anxiety	0.32
	10	Thought interference	0.32
HH Imagination (5.2% of the variance)	13	Imagination	0.77
	14	Directed criticism	0.27
JJ Worries and problems (4.3% of the variance)	16	Worries and problems	0.70
	1	Anxiety	0.29

(16 PF = 16 PF Personality Test factor; PAS = Personality Assessment Schedule of Personality Disorder; PSE = Present State Examination of psychiatric symptoms; Item = Interview Item Answer; Evidence = Physical Evidence.)

The results of this second-order factor analysis were quite interesting. Factors AA, BB, DD and EE correspond to well-recognised personality dimensions: Neuroticism, Psychoticism, Extraversion and Tough-mindedness, respectively. This was not surprising because the Present State Examination and the tests of personality and personality disorder were major parts of the comprehensive information collection achieved during this research.

There are also two incidental points of interest that came out concerning Factor DD, Extraversion and Factor EE, Tough-mindedness. The first of these, Factor DD, was the finding of a relationship between extraversion and superstitious ideation and various anomalous experiences (paranormal assets, telepathy, alien abduction, etc.). Extraversion has a significant relationship with the amount of sociability and gregariousness that an individual experiences and enjoys. Superstition of course is socially communicated. Also, some people who are more sociable are also more superficial in their interrelationships with other people, and may well be interested in, or admit to, superstitious beliefs, depending on their particular social context. The superstitious individuals in this sample of eccentric people also tended to have personality disorders, six of whom were in the antisocial category, as well as eight with obsessional personality disorder, ten with schizoid personality disorder, and one with a schizotypal personality disorder of a mild degree of severity. These were people who usually experienced much less individual control as a result of adverse childhood experiences, and in adulthood experienced more insecure attachments and were susceptible to greater personal loneliness. These individuals had some issues about what might be called the tensions between personal separateness and social relatedness.

The second point, this one concerning Factor EE, Tough-mindedness, was a modest relationship between tough-minded attitudes and scientific interests. Factor CC could be tentatively identified as an Intellectual Intelligence/Aptitude factor. The results here showed that a strong interest in science was one of the best markers of high intelligence; science subjects are often seen as amongst the most difficult at all levels of achievement. As noted above, those eccentrics with a rigorous mind and experimental attitude gravitated towards interests of a more scientific nature. Also, intelligence was the best predictor, in this analysis, of the individual's academic achievement, and that an interest in science was highly correlated with this.

Factor FF surely represents Creativity; the connections with the psychotic-like Thought Transfer factor and feelings of difference from others are of note here. The remaining three small factors are self-explanatory. However, in Factor HH, a linkage has been evidenced between hostile emotional criticism in the family and inner imaginative experience. This broadens the ambit of both of these areas --- it might be said that expressed familial emotion clearly does not always have adverse consequences, nor are all its effects limited to the possible exacerbation of schizophrenic symptoms. This lends weight to the thesis that expressed emotion directed towards an individual is not directly causal but may have more indirect effects, perhaps leading to escape or avoidance leading to solitary loneliness and then, in some individuals, to lone imaginative pursuits. Only in a few predisposed cases would this process regress in a pathological direction and degree toward thought disorder and bizarre symptoms.

In any event, the nine second-order factors were sufficiently psychologically meaningful for the next step. This was to perform a cluster analysis of the entire sample of eccentrics. This cluster analysis showed that there is basically only one type of eccentric person. The primary cluster accounted for ninety-two per cent of the variance amongst the informants. There was a small second cluster consisting of only four male and two female informants. Also, there was a sole "isolate" eccentric who failed to be subsumed in either the primary or secondary cluster. However, these last seven informants were not qualitatively different from the other eccentrics. This was shown by their proximity to the main primary cluster, and that they were (in a statistical-psychological graphic representation) in the same quadrant in two-dimensional factor space. They were quantitatively different on the two major second-order factors of Neuroticism and Psychoticism. These seven informants were somewhat different from the main body of eccentric informants in that they showed somewhat more of the core markers of neurotic withdrawal and/or psychotic-like thought disorder.

This was the first time that a clinical psychologist has examined what constitutes actual exceptional personality from multiple perspectives, and with concepts drawn from a number of cognate disciplines. Although the organisation of traits into first-order factors, and first-order factors into second-order factors, assumed a fairly normal configuration, the other six criteria of exceptionality proved to be pertinent to understanding eccentricity. The great majority of eccentrics fulfilled at least two of these six criteria, and many of these individuals fulfilled more than three of the criteria.

These exceptionality criteria were applied mostly to the eccentrics' mental states, personality and related behavioural indicators. The overriding impression to be drawn from this analysis is that being an exception is far from handicapping. To the contrary, it can be seen to be quite a positive attribute for most of these individuals.

Our human potential, the possibility to change for the better, has been treated with disbelief by cynics and pessimists. To become a self-actualised person is to exercise a unique prerogative of life. It is brilliant egomania to say that you belong to your self. The mark of this profound single-mindedness in the face of resounding conformity is the exercise of that individuality in everyday life.

A desire to fulfil whatever elements of individuality the person feels are as yet unrealised, and the resulting striving after it, is shaped by one's personality, and the continued behaviour that flows from this arguably shapes personality further. Selfhood depends on the assertion of identity, whether this is done to defy the forces of power, or of control by others, or even garden-variety tedium. To this end, one can pit oneself against enforced order, soulless organisation and uniformity. Eccentrics do this, however much their social environments may be indifferent to their personal experiments in subjectivity. In terms of personality, it may be creative to burst free of the seeming constraints of behavioural conformity. By so doing, the floodgates of creativity may be opened.

Chapter 8. Detours before Obstacles
(Creativity and Eccentricity)

"I am certain of nothing but the holiness of the Heart's affections and the truth of the Imagination."
John Keats

It sometimes appears as if contented conformity limits exploration and innovation. I would not go as far as that --- there is not a necessary connection between non-conformity and creativity. However, a high proportion of prodigiously original people have been described, in their time, as eccentric. A cursory list of creators so identified by their peers and contemporaries hints at the staggering implications of this connection --- Alexander Graham Bell, Lord Berners, William Blake, Lord Henry Cavendish, Charlie Chaplin, Salvador Dali, Emily Dickinson, Thomas Edison, Albert Einstein, Ronald Firbank, Benjamin Franklin, Sir Francis Galton, Vincent van Gogh, Percy Grainger, Charles Ives, Edward James, James Joyce, T. E. Lawrence of Arabia, John Lennon, Hugh MacDiarmid, Franz Anton Mesmer, Yoko Ono, Dorothy Parker, Beatrix Potter, George Sand, Erik Satie, Sir Clive Sinclair, Dame Edith Sitwell, Stanley Spencer, Henri de Toulouse-Lautrec, J. M. W. Turner, Sir Barnes Wallace, Oscar Wilde, General Orde Wingate, Andrew Wyeth, and Ludwig Wittgenstein.

Definitions and concepts
Concepts of creativity do not present as many conundrums as do those of eccentricity. The former have had much more research addressed to them than the latter. They have received a great deal of impetus from the scientific pandemonium created by America's failures in the early days of the Space Race. Even then, psychological researchers could at least turn to over fifty years of theoretical work in the field of creativity.

Early speculation posited two complementary intellectual processes to explain the workings of the creative imagination --- dissociation and association, and analysis and synthesis [1]. This notion corresponds with the field observations of Richard Rothe [2], an Inspector of art and drawing in Vienna's education system. He distinguished two basic approaches to art: "The first type builds up his drawings or sculptures out of separate parts, as one would build with bricks. This is the 'building type' in contrast to the 'seeing type', who proceeds quite differently by moulding the form he is aiming at out of a single piece. He holds in his hand the piece of clay with which he is working and turns it round and round whilst at work. Whilst he is working he thinks of a definite figure in a definite posture." It would be tempting to speculate that these different approaches could represent more than stylistic preferences. They could be early orientations towards either inductive or deductive reasoning, or intuition over cold analysis. However, it has been established that a person's general intelligence alone does not produce creative activity [3, 4, 5, 6, 7, 8, 9, 10, 11]. The distinction is really between intelligence and imagination. They are separate factors. This was what the physicist Niels Bohr may have been driving at when he gently admonished one of his students by saying, "You are not thinking, you are just being logical."

It is important to be able to explain the how and why of creativity. Theories in the twentieth century had mainly been derived from two disparate sources: those informed by the insights of psychoanalysis, and those from early work in the related fields of cybernetics, computer science and Artificial Intelligence.

Theories deriving from psychoanalysis placed great emphasis on warring struggles inside an individual's psyche, or between contradictory needs and unconscious unfulfilled wishes. In this view the creative individual is wracked by conflicts within his mind that are practically irreconcilable. The process of creation emerges from this almost as a by-product. The associated definition of creativity stresses the point that partial resolutions of inward-looking struggles force the making of novel, unexpected mental connections [12, 13].

These ideas led to the further exposition that what is most worth salvaging from these experiences is specifically those remnants of vague hunches that some would call disordered, or in a slightly more kindly way, archaic or rudimentary. This was followed by a definition of creativity as adaptive regression, a temporary return to more primitive modes of thought (so-called primary-process thinking) for better self-understanding or in the wider service of society [14].

On a related tack, I. A. Taylor saw creativity as the ability to perceive the environment with an elevated degree of plasticity, combined with the ability to communicate clearly any resulting unique experiences [15]. The plasticity of the human brain shows itself in its responses to new learning and experience, and especially in continual open-ended creativity. These views converged at some point with the more problematic notions that creativity can be fuelled by psychotic-like experiences derived from fasting, sensory deprivation, the experimental use of psychedelic drugs, meditation, or by other esoteric means. Clearly, the original idea had turned back upon itself, no doubt inspiring controversial commentators like Timothy Leary and R. D. Laing.

Other behavioural scientists, drawing on published accounts about high-powered inspiration, and on direct observation of gifted individuals, were coming to some quite contrary opinions. This alternative viewpoint defined the creative process as one of development toward greater subjective organisation. Brewster Ghiselin gathered the first-hand accounts of this process from eminent artists and scientists [16]. In these accounts it appeared typically to follow the four stages initially put forward in 1926 by psychologist Graham Wallas [17]. These were mental preparation, incubation, illumination and verification.

In the preparation stage, the individual recognises that a problem requires solution, or that a particular idea or theme is a fitting subject to be exploited. This stage includes the time in which the problem is being delineated and during which the individual works to develop the skills and knowledge necessary to solve it, helping to formulate what seems to be the best questions. The individual selects which aspect, which bits of information, should be given priority over others, then concentratedly works on these, while the rejected elements are shunted off, though these can be retrieved or can otherwise break into awareness later, perhaps as an "afterthought" or concealed in a dream or an altered memory. There is often an intervening period characterised by frustration. This feeling becomes acute when the obvious preparation and background research has been done, while the solution remains elusive. In this interregnum, often filled with feelings of exasperation, there is a good deal of undirected emotionality, restlessness, doubt, and transitory thoughts of abandoning the quest.

In the incubation period, the whole matter and associated information sinks into the subconscious, and the mind continues to work upon it in some mysterious, poorly understood way.

In the illumination stage, a solution abruptly emerges into full consciousness. No one knows how long each of these stages might take --- there is great variability from person to person, and from one field to another. It is now possible, by both electroencephalography

(EEG) brain wave techniques and functional magnetic resonance brain imaging (fMRI) to study the neural correlates of illumination or insight and its antecedents. As seen in these studies, that special *Eureka* moment, as previously thought, is the culmination of a series of brain processes [18].

Finally, in the verification stage, the solution is put to the acid test: empirical work is implemented to test and possibly invalidate the new hypothesis, and possibly compare it against any existing alternative hypotheses.

This model accentuated the plausibility and meaningfulness of the creative product, which was defined as "a presentation of constellated meanings" [19]. If an intellectual idea has potential, it should resonate productively with other ideas and have implications for related areas. Further extrapolations will lead to further questions, new directions and unexpected departures. This is related to the idea that the creative mind is one in which a problem, acting as a stimulus, evokes material from various experiential areas [20].

The study of heuristics and exploratory activity emerged as offshoots from the AI and decision-making schools, and its techniques were seen as various forms of procedural know-how. For some mental operations, including information feedback and routine decision-making, computers are in part analogous to human thinking, more especially for all those processes that can reduce incoming information into binary and other mathematical forms.

The definition of creativity that emerged from studies in cybernetics and decision-making characterised creativity as a special case of problem-solving activity [21, 22, 23, 24], and related it to risk-taking. Psychologists later found the latter factor to be bound up with personality traits like extraversion and sensation-seeking. A willingness to take an unconventional approach, persistence, and the level of difficulty of the initial formulation of the problem were also related to successful problem-solving. Creative people have a greater openness to experience, are more versatile [25], and are able to choose combinations of factual or theoretical elements drawn from disparate subject domains. A broad diversity of interests has been advised by previous thinkers, for example by the mathematician Henri Poincare, as a corollary of attaining creative insights [16]. Because of their greater openness to new experiences, creative individuals do usually possess a greater variety of interests [26], and are able to use these experiences to beneficial effect.

My concept of creativity is that it encompasses effective empathic problem-solving. It is a cognitive-behavioural potential that cannot always be realized. Involvement, sometimes a deep immersion into a particular topic, demonstrates the significance of this for wanting to understand something more fully [27]. The part that empathy plays in this formulation is that it represents a transaction between the individual and the problem. The individual is seen as displacing his point of view into the problem, investing into it something of his own intellect and personality, while drawing knowledge from the nature of the problem. He no longer identifies these problems solely with objects, or with their attributes, but rather identifies himself with the profound depths of the problem. The closer one can come to this ideal the better. Georges Braque expounded on this in regard to artistic creativity: "One must not just depict the objects, one must penetrate into them, and one must oneself become the object."

This harks back to ways of thinking that extend far into humanity's deep prehistoric past. Paleo-archaeologists have studied the 32,000 year-old cave paintings at the Chauvet-Pont-d'Arc cave system in the Ardeche Gorge in south-central France and other ancient works of art at the Lascaux cave in the Dordogne. The paintings found there --- of lions, rhinos, mammoths, horses, bison, deer, ibex, bears, and owls --- are extraordinary and beautiful. Jean-Michel Genesie, the project leader at Chauvet and Lascaux, has said, "What is astonishing is how naturalistic the drawings are. The animals seem present, real. Every day in the cave is amazing. I look at the horse panel (a dense charcoal composition of twenty animals) a hundred times a day. I feel like I'm in a sanctuary."

The eminent scientists working at Chauvet have identified the artists' fundamental modes of thought, which have been designated as *fluidity* and *permeability*. Both were different from modern ways of thinking. The first of these more archaic forms of thinking, *fluidity*, means that people did not see barriers between humans, animals, plants and other elements of the natural world. The affected prehistoric people are now believed to have lived in a rather solipsistic state in which there was little differentiation of "self" from "other". They were tribal, clannish people, deeply embedded in their small social collectives, with perhaps a little less self-awareness but more group awareness and group care.

The anthropologist Claude Levy-Bruhl used the term "participation mystique" to point out the close connections people have with their social environment when they are unable to clearly differentiate themselves from it. Individuals would never want to go it alone; to do so would be to perish. A group mentality of maximally integrated teamwork, sharing and mutual support was profoundly embedded into the human hunter-gatherer psyche. Elements of these group modes of thinking, bound up with sociality, are still with us today, and are briefly felt today during religious ceremonies, well-attended entertainments, mass-attendance sporting events, and occasional political rallies of charismatic leaders. These feelings are the opposite of the modern alienation and sense of anonymity at being "lost in a crowd". Instead, the individual person gives oneself over to the same emotions that are almost inseparably experienced by the larger group.

Humanity's early art was a means of communication between humans, with their immediate ancestors and possibly with their future descendants. It was also possibly an early realization of the differences between representation and reality. As hunters, providers and defenders of their familial groups, perhaps they were seeking to assert some kind of magical power over their prey by creating images of them, and perhaps performing collective proto-religious rituals. These early peoples' understandings did not allow for strict categories or lines of demarcation between any individual parts of their world, blurring the distinctions between this world and the unseen world of the spirits. Human beings were seen as being interchangeable with other living beings, and the behaviours and properties of everyone could be adopted freely by various growing things and creatures great and small, for example, trees were believed to be able to "speak" to people, or the souls of eagles or horses could flow through and intermingle with the spirits of people. *Permeability* was rather like this, except it had more to do with the imagined interactions between entities living in the natural world with those of the supernatural sphere, and there was seen to be a great deal of movement between each. In the great majority of ancient cultures there was a complex of dream-related preoccupations centered about the use of dreams to seek and control supernatural powers.

More involved rituals that developed in more recent historical times may have been based on understandable atavistic wishes to get away from the limitations of the self within small tribal groups. Still, the natural world was permeated with the spirits of all those who had gone before. For example, an Australian aborigine rock painter told an anthropologist, "I am not painting. The hand of a spirit is painting." For those who can see the above connections that may or may not exist, both of these archaic ways of thinking are similar, though not identical, to the loss of ego boundaries and some of the first rank symptoms of schizophrenia mentioned in an earlier chapter.

I would suggest however that it is the solitude of mind and the ongoing eccentricity of creative people that is the key to their ideas and problem-solving, rather than the micro-psychotic experiences or coincidental mild thought disorders that occasionally overtake a minority of them. In modern creativity, being totally engrossed in a subject or problem means that there is tremendous commitment to understand it; this involves the recognition of few limits and leads to a shift in the individual's point-of-view. In some cases this deep empathy was the intentional strategy employed, and can appear quite extreme by everyday research standards. For example, the architect Kiyo Izumi purposely took LSD in order to apprehend the perceptual distortions of schizophrenia [28]. This was done not out of idle interest, but to identify as fully as possible with schizophrenia sufferers in order to design their living environments. Quite apart from setting off a shift in consciousness, and moving away from one's usual patterns of thought, this general approach is all about "getting inside the problem". It is a special instance of participant-observation, beginning with the subjective internal state and working outwards. In Izumi's case, it resulted in a host of specific design solutions. The controlled use of a psychedelic substance was the means to accomplish this. This example is used only to illustrate a wider approach that many effective creators take without recourse to any chemical help. It seems as if many of them can dip into their subconscious minds almost at will, and are also able to return with unusual associations and insights, also at will.

Towards these ends, various components of the overall creativity factor may be exercised. These components are originality (the uniqueness of a response); fluency (the productive quantity of output); flexibility, or adaptability (a spontaneous willingness to attempt and to modify various solutions, not being tied to any one solution); and elaboration (improving the initial idea or applying it in other content areas). The significance and use of these components depends on the individual in question, his past experience, his environment, and the specific task demands of the subject and the type of problem.

Like eccentric people, creative figures also run the risk of marginality [29] and of not being taken seriously by others in the general culture in which they find themselves. Creativity necessarily involves at some stage a rejection of at least part of what has gone before. Like eccentricity, much of creativity remains shrouded in mystique and mystery.

The assumption of much of the above research, one that I share, is that creativity can be perceived and learned. If we knew the fine detail of what actually transpires in the mind, especially during the incubation and illumination stages, many more people could model their thinking on those fortunate few who are prolific and original. At the point of beginning this research, I was aware of the links in my own reasoning --- if creative people are eccentric, by painstakingly interviewing eccentrics, one could tap a rich new vein of unexplored knowledge, thereby approaching the subject from a different direction. It is my contention that our lives would be better if we understood more about the mystery of the creative gifts.

Eccentric creativity

Are ordinary eccentrics creative? The answer is an unequivocal "Yes". Their lives are generally improvised and experimental. Knowing them makes one think that what the French philosopher Jean Baudrillard once proclaimed is true, that everyone has more ideas than they actually need. Eccentrics feel compelled to create. Their poetic singularity of imaginative thinking in the face of their sometime marginal reality is distinctive. Do they or their works fulfil any of the above criteria of creativity? By self-report, at least two-thirds of the eccentric sample believed themselves to be creative, original or highly imaginative. (See Table 18.)

Table 18. Cognitive qualities of the eccentric informants

Creativity			
None	*Low Average*	*High Average*	*Pronounced*
7%	27%	57%	8%

Imagination			
Unimaginative	*Low Average*	*High Average*	*Pronounced*
2%	15%	65%	18%

Originality			
None	*Low Average*	*High Average*	*Pronounced*
34%	31%	20%	15%

Daydreaming			
None	*A Little*	*A Lot*	*A Great Deal*
26%	18%	40%	16%

Nocturnal Dream Vividness Low	*Mild*	*Moderate*	*High*
14%	13%	14%	59%

Curiosity			
None	*Mild*	*Moderate*	*Pronounced*
1%	8%	49%	42%

Depth of Thinking			
Superficial	*Slight*	*Fairly Deep*	*Very Deep*
---	15%	62%	23%

Problem-solving Effectiveness			
Ineffective	*Effective*	*High Average*	*Very Effective*
2%	28%	65%	5%

On further examination, the eccentric informants were indeed creative across a broad front and in practically every modality. There were a number of visual artists, poets, short story writers, novelists, and radio and television writers. Indeed, in a large-scale survey I helped the Yahoo internet organisation to conduct in 2005, eccentricity was perceived to be thriving best in the Arts --- by about a quarter of a cross-section of the British population sampled. This was higher than for all other fields of human endeavour, including science, comedy entertainment and fashion.

Other eccentrics in my research turned their creative efforts to science and invention. One man had founded an entire new religion. In addition, most demonstrated a clear insight into the very questions about creativity asked of them. Several anticipated further questions, and extrapolated from these to their own understanding of this subject, thinking up follow-on implications and questions, as for instance, the following contentious excerpt shows:

"Are all creative people --- artists, Christian mystics and reformers, Jesus, Buddha, thinkers such as Wittgenstein, etcetera --- eccentrics? Their attitudes are often seen to be at variance from the more conformist values of whatever society in which they are loosely embedded. Are the traits of non-conformity essential for an individual to be a reformer or creative individual? Is the truth or meaning, as expressed in the writings of such philosophers, religious reformers and artists, then not really external, universal verities as is so often assumed, but merely expressions of an eccentric attitude of mind? I know that artistic people are often in the advance guard of the coming age because of their sharp awareness of reality, and even idolized for their free-ranging and far-seeing insights, though as far as practical matters go they may not be so good because their minds are elsewhere. Could it be that these individuals do not in fact widen the limits of our own conceptual realities, but merely act out their own karma in their eccentric traits? Are they, in other words, not authentic, but merely charlatans, and their insights irrelevant to the conformist, socially conditioned lifestyles of most people, and merely concerned with eccentric, alienated styles of social and psychological integration?"

(Hubert, age forty-two)

Before we approach more questions, it may be best to demonstrate the varieties of eccentric creativity. Here, by way of example, are seven representative poems produced by seven very different eccentric individuals:

Perceptions
I saw a star fast falling,
My companions were surprised,
I thought of wonder calling, a spaceship undisguised.
But then I thought its nature,
A gift for me to see,
I wished for all our happiness,
That was its prize for me.
The girl who walked beside me,
Stood silent looking on,
The girl next to her couldn't see,
She thought it was the Bomb.

(Moira, age thirty)

The Cotswold Way
The path was edged with rusting maple
Shining gloriously in the late sun
Little bloomed but Greater Knapweed
And Old Man's Beard
Tangled in the thorns;

Sandy patches scratched
By night animals
Bare bones of rabbits
Drying in the air
Here great piles of hedgerow
Cut down for ease of passage
And burned areas with
Remaining ash.
Upwards the path rose
To present a splendid view
Of hills and hollows
Coated in russet
And bullocks silhouetted
Against the sky.
Continuing on through gates
To open fields with
Scattered oolite rocks
Stone walls proclaiming
The Craftsman's skill
Enclosing rich ploughed soil
And knots of trees
Giving shelter from
The winds
Sighing lazily
As the path reached the road

(From *Cousin Joan's Reflections*, by Joan R. Gilmour)

Love among the daffodils
Tell me the shapes behind those eyes
That catch this blinkered male
In chains of stares and fettered
States of silence when beneath
His own bewildered gaze
There lies that cubist flare
Of beauty ---
                    Yet
Beneath the eyes
There lies a subtlety of flattery
That blends the moment's hour
To a static second when blue
Electric stares become moments
Of decision to declare
In conscious thought,
            this indiscretion.

(Daniel, age thirty-seven)

Spaceflight One

The kinetic windsong glows with the keening
Of rockets blazing into macrocosms
Of unbewitched mysteries, and careening
Through revved, oblique supernova blossoms,
Intercosmic man, stripped from the leechtide
Inheritance of bleak sundering havoc,
Where the bloodspurting warwords are crucified
And shackled in the black cesspool zions
Of our guilty hearts, to spring like rampant lions
Onto the heraldry of shame. Souls sing
Hallelujah. The searing blasting pylons
Of ultratensile steel jerk through an astral
Continuum of stars, hurtling constellations
Flashing through the lightning void like vast castles
Splendid and far in the infernal equations
Of convulsed and celestial zodiacs,
Of blinding primal fires and Magellanic Clouds.
And succumbed in the bold bare momentum
We shoot forward, spewing maelstroms like shrouds
Along a wake inconceivable as grief

(Nick, age twenty-seven)

Why me?

Have you ever been possessed by an inner power
Which seizes every part of your being
Dragging it screaming through agonies and ecstasies
Into a dazzling light of understanding?

Have you ever experienced an infinite power,
Storming through a lifetime in a second,
Working at fever pitch all day and night
Without a thought of sleeping?

Have you ever been terrified of your own power?
Stricken by a crystal clear vision
Of things we are not supposed to know
Feeling able to answer every question
The Universe can throw at you
Except for "Why me?"

(Brian O'Donnell, age forty)

Undergraduate Blue Note

To walk into a never-ending whirlwind
    And stand in the eye.

To ride that sugar train to nowhere
    And get off.

To fall off the end of the world,
    And bump your head
                   (Gus, age twenty)

Revelation

I looked at myself in the mirror
At my image so mothy and mild,
And there was surprised to discover
That the person I saw was a child.

Not a heavenly babe but a hellion,
(The truth I confide to this verse)
In a permanent state of rebellion,
Who kicked at the shins of his nurse.

All the effort to scold him and mould him,
All that trouble to make him a man
Was an idiot tale that was told him,
Since he turned out to Peter Pan.

From that first paroxysmical screaming
It always has been much the same;
It was all just repetitive dreaming
But I felt I was somehow to blame.

And though it may all have been dreaming
And the sum of the sense not a lot,
I am free of contrivance and scheming
And free of the things I am not.

So I spring from my pond like a mallard,
The water sheds bright from my back;
I quack on quick wings my quack ballad
And return with a gratified quack.

These insights are just an illusion,
It really doesn't alter your fate;
The sense of release a delusion,
You learnt it all when it's too late.

But I'm glad that I looked in the mirror
At my image so mothy and mild,
It's a crossing of one little river
So to be, slightly more, reconciled.
(Mr. Anonymous)

Writers of prose, psychologically inhabiting diverse time periods and places, were also much in evidence, covering a broad range of subject matter. Their works included a published romantic novel by a mature author, a comprehensive guidance manual for young school leavers, a television play about government corruption, three pieces in praise of the English countryside, and a non-fiction books on the links between the shape of the guitar and Greek poetry, feminism made easy, locomotives, the White Rajahs, buses of the English Midlands, wild orchids, shepherdesses, the Golden Mean, how to square the circle, Sulahman III, and much more. In sum, there was enough material from these eccentrics to keep a small publishing house in frenetic operation for several years. Space permits only the inclusion of the single following synopsis. It is for a science fiction novel and typically does not shy away from issues of controversy or the possibility of offending peoples' sensibilities.

Man from the Shroud

The narrative concerns the attempts of a biologist to create one clone of Jesus Christ from residual DNA misappropriated from the Turin Shroud. The idea was inspired by a passage in the book *File on the Shroud* by H. David Sax.

My story is set in an "alternative future", one in which the Germans had won World War II. The biologist, Julius Rosen, embarks upon this dramatic project because he believes it to be the only solution to prevent the world descending into barbarism.

Rosen, of Jewish heritage, still commands a considerable reputation, a fact that allows him some freedom of action to continue working. A comparatively successful assassination attempt --- far more successful than actually happened in reality --- leaves Hitler a physical wreck. Bormann, Goebbels and their heinous Nazi confederates, fearful of their own position, attempt to replace Hitler with an actor. This works but only up to a point. However, it is good enough until another scientist suggests that Hitler could be "repaired" using the latest transplantation techniques. Rosen is ordered to become involved in this work. He doesn't greatly care about the outcome of this research, as long as he is given time to pursue his ideas.

This attitude changes dramatically when he visits Palestine and witnesses the degradations of the indigenous and transported populations. Palestine has been set up by Germany to show the remainder of the world that the Final Solution is not seen to be necessary now that Hitler is out of the way and Germany is no longer at war. Rosen believed the German propaganda that the Jewish people deserved to live in their historical homeland.

The brutal treatment by the SS that Rosen witnesses re-awakens an awareness of his Jewish heritage. He conceives the idea of cloning Jesus and sees the outcome as a method of liberating Palestine and later, Europe.

The cloning experiment appears successful and the result grows into a peculiar individual, a person with no sense of identity, and as such is perfect for the project. He is indoctrinated with one single aim, to liberate Palestine. He achieves a measure of success, as a terrorist leader causing considerable bloodshed. The Nazis discover the plan and make the fatal mistake of allowing it to proceed, arrogantly assuming that it will fail and discredit

Christianity. They play along with the scheme, and go as far as staging a "mock crucifixion" after the Jesus clone is captured. Their plans go disastrously wrong, and "Jesus" survives. It is too late for anything to be salvaged from the experiment. For the Nazis, from that point on their downfall is only a matter of time. They had sown the seeds of their own destruction.

(Alan C. Arno, age thirty-eight)

Among the female eccentrics there were six poets, six short story writers, four novelists, four artists, six musicians or singers, three professional actresses, and one elderly and very vigorous prison reformer. In addition, there were six professional research scientists who worked in the following fields: archaeology, neurophysiology, artificial intelligence, botany, forensic chemistry, and marine biology. Among the male eccentrics there were four poets, fourteen writers, fifteen artists, one architect, and seven musicians. There were also seven research scientists, working in the following fields: astronomy, artificial intelligence, botany, biological gerontology, and zoology.

As a percentage proportion of the total number of male and female eccentrics, the only major difference between the genders was that male visual artists were relatively over-represented.

In quantitative terms, the eccentrics' high level of creative activity is spectacularly different from that of the general population. However, qualitative judgements concerning their actual abilities and the value of their work cry out for individual attention. There can be little doubt that their fluency of ideas, and the translation of these ideas into creatively clever output, is prodigious. Also, their talent is not apparently restricted to a specific medium, topic area, or mode of representation --- at least twenty-one per cent of both male and female eccentrics exhibited their skills, to benefit, in more than one modality. They also had unusual combinations of creative endeavours, for example, astronomy with photography and music, and unusual combinations of leisure pursuits, for example, gymnastics with electronic engineering, or painting and radio work. On average, this sample of eccentric individuals had about five pet preoccupations, more than just hobbyhorses or projects. These very much involved them deeply and provided them with many fascinating interests. These interests focused their imaginative tendencies to some degree. Some of these eccentrics found areas in which they could test their controversial ideas; others sought likely ways to meet like-minded acquaintances.

Using Osgood's Semantic Differential technique [30] to compare and contrast the perceptions of people in the community, independent raters were given extended language samples of creative and less creative eccentrics to read. The raters did not know the nature of the study, and were "blind" to how creative each eccentric individual was. This showed that the creative eccentrics were rated more positively in general than the less creative eccentrics, and were also seen as psychologically more robust and more active than the less creative eccentrics. This may reflect to some degree the positive evaluations that the creative eccentrics had given themselves at interview. It was also independent corroboration of the impressions that the creative eccentrics gave to their interviewers.

Empathy does figure in these eccentrics' imaginative approaches. This is used not only for general problem solving and technical matters; it also occurs in the interpersonal realm: "I'm a great believer in creative spontaneity, in responding to the moment. My imagination, it's fairly vivid. I see it as a way of emancipating and expanding consciousness. I find it easy to imagine how it would be to be in others' shoes. Sometimes this can be distressing, so I stop."

(Jenny, age thirty-three)

"I can put myself in the position of someone suffering, and feel their sorrow. In my imagination, I can get right inside a character. For instance, I can imagine I am someone else in a futuristic world, in the position of a survivor."

(Keith, age forty-three)

"I do have a very vivid imagination. It is not always a good thing. It is extremely useful for my writing, as I can imagine situations and take it from there. I can see an everyday incident, such as two people meeting, and, because of their actions, I can start to imagine what they are saying or put them into a different, dramatic situation. If I see a stranger looking particularly unhappy or upset, I can weave a story around the person to account for it. My imagination places me in situations where I am articulate, or romantic, or really quite sexy, or becoming the centre of attraction. I can get lost in my imagination like some writers starting out get lost in the twists and turns of their plots."

(Val, age fifty-one)

"I am trying to become a novelist with a fresh and maybe subtle perspective, by observing people as they are, without any preconceptions about how they should act. I can put myself in another person's place, which I think makes me a sympathetic kind of person, and also makes me able to act. I can see ahead and anticipate a variety of consequences along many possible dimensions. I didn't succeed at my writing at first, but that didn't deter me for more than a few days."

(Sheila, age fifty-two)

Despite these abilities, it is a paradox that this is an area many eccentrics do not fully exploit, usually preferring to be social loners, though not being averse to a good argument. While being able to see both sides of an issue, they will not be swayed by others' efforts at persuasion, and will quite adamantly press their point home with more regard for it than for their erstwhile opponent's feelings.

Eccentrics also dislike attempts by others to persuade them to think or do something differently. Obsessional resistance in the face of opposition shows how crucial their underlying ideas are to these creative eccentrics. Their more assertive reactions are reserved for those detractors foolhardy enough to criticise their creative work. Their conviction about the value and truthfulness of their creations can surmount the discouragement originating from other peoples' more conventional perceptions and "prosaic" criticism. Such attitudes are more likely to be encountered from eccentrics who have carried their childlike openness onto a more adult plane. Somehow they had managed to preserve elements of their earlier and more innocent sensory and intellectual capacities, and did not succumb easily to the pressures imposed upon them by people around them with more accepted or accustomed ways of thinking.

The individual manifestations of the eccentrics' happy obsessive preoccupations can be related to the human mimetic faculty [31]. This could be seen as pertaining to the eccentrics' hypothetical ability to imitatively self-represent themselves, or their natures. Seen in a more enlightened light, this could equally refer to their tendency to create themselves afresh in more unexpected ways. They have many goals, some of which may on occasion be motivated by the desire to preserve their personal integrity. Acting freely and decisively with terrific vitality, they are, by trying to be themselves, heroic examples of the social construction of the self.

Creators might talk of creative struggles, but also occasionally of the joys of discovery. There's a mystical element to eccentric creativity, and there's a humorous element about it also. Wittiness and humour have been positively correlated with creativity [32, 33]. The temporary liberation from the bounds of rational thinking, as in dreams, is common to both humour and originality. From the age of six onwards, there are modest and consistent positive correlations between humour and creativity ratings or test measures [34, 35, 36]. Humour and creativity share a similar source, and that source is the clash of incongruous ideas, or the way of expressing them. Good jokes make people laugh, and sometimes think.

The clash of ideas also helps create further wonderful ideas. Many eccentrics actively seek out incongruities, looking to explore and possibly exploit them in some way. The resolution of incongruity, if successful, can lead to positive creativity and problem solving. There is a chain of potential causes and effects. Humour and joking relaxes people. For many, this reduces rigidity in thinking and enhances spontaneity, which in turn leads to less fixation on a single solution or a single means to reach it. This, along with the beneficial priming of incongruous ideas, enlarges their cognitive network and thereby facilitates creativity. This is a way to help integrate and possibly resolve the opposing elements of a problem.

Eccentrics explore seemingly irrational ideas through their use of humour. For them, humour has the power to liberate them from more everyday worries. Adopting a humorous attitude frees up the eccentrics' view of everyday reality. Satire works by exaggerating human realities. Wit sometimes turns predictable ideas upside down, and a playful sense of fun can be an unquenchable source of delight.

Eccentrics believe that almost everyone else perceives the "realistic" world in a boring way. However, other people can be ambivalent about those eccentrics with less appreciated behaviours, and sometimes those gifted individuals who are perceived to be situated on the periphery of mainstream society.

Certain eccentrics' forceful attitudes can also foster a more combative style in response to criticism that perhaps occasionally comes too close to the bone for comfort. Here is an example of such an "intense disputatious argument", known as a *flyting* in Scots, meaning to scold or rail at. (The word is derived from the Old English word *flitan*, meaning to wrangle. It is of early Germanic origin, related to the Old Frisian word *flit*, meaning strife.) It is from a celebrated poet and eccentric, whose style, techniques and influence were parodied in a satirical pamphlet from an eccentric critic who disagreed with his unique style and what he regarded as the poet's "foolish following" by the Scottish nation's intelligentsia:

12th March 1964

Dear Sir,

My attention has just been called to your booklet. I do not know any reason why you should get away with your stupid vituperation and lying about a writer --- or number of writers --- whose shoelaces you are unfit to tie, and I certainly do not intend to let you off. I will make it my business forthwith to find out precisely who you are, and then, if, as I am told, you are a school teacher I will call a meeting of the parents of the pupils, of any school in which you may still be teaching (a job for which you are obviously monstrously unfit), and at the same time I will issue a pamphlet dealing faithfully with your booklet and distribute that to these parents and to the press and others; these steps will ensure publicity in the national press.
Yours sincerely,
  Hugh MacDiarmid

At this point we should draw back from this well-deserved flamboyant riposte from a renowned poet with international stature to a philistine's mocking criticism.

Problem solving, planning, chunking, remote associations, and meditative relaxation

Evidence of humankind's apparent need and dangerous ability to attempt to control nature is all about us. This is nurtured by the concept of volition, by which the exercise of free will and willpower enables us to resist given assumptions and the realities of natural laws.

Be that as it may, people have much more complicated systems of thought for explaining mental events. Using these personal modes of thinking, they are not too happy to explain all cases in terms of general rules or laws, or in a coherent way from one new instance to another. By falling back on "common sense" theories of human nature, people prefer to deal with individual cases one by one. Bearing in mind that eccentrics are active in making the identities that they present to their social environments, it may be illuminating to ask what they do actively in their inner worlds. What are their imaginations like? What do they do specifically to be able to create? At least some of their creativity could be presumed to be conscious and deliberate, and if so, there might be discernible strategies.

First of all, there are a series of actions that are reeled off in preparation for the creative process, with the purpose of easing the individual into the requisite frame of mind: "When I need to solve a problem, I go walking and get away from its immediacy, indulge in sex, read up all the data, then do something quite different and write notes, especially very early in the morning when my best ideas are most usually apt to come."

(Jennifer, age forty-seven)

These procedures will differ from one person to the next. The above self-report also shows the distinctive element of *intentional indirection*: quite clearly, Jennifer goes off on a seemingly irrelevant tangent in at least three different ways, though with an intent to come back to the problem in hand. This indirect approach can also be used at other stages in the creative process.

The next step involves some degree of planning. A range of contingency plans are modelled, and considered: "I go about solving problems analytically, sequentially, logically, and generally with the aid of colour-coded 'pro' and 'con' tables. I tend always to see myself as living at some point on a flow chart, and mentally draw lines to bring out the current exigencies. I may also consult the *I Ching (The Book of Changes*, a venerable divination system from China, couched in terms of social interactions, personality and stages of the mind, in the form of sixty-four hexagrams), mainly to bring in a random factor, to help me assess my response to it. I am very deductive."

(Jane, age thirty)

There can, for some, be as much pleasure in the general forward planning, or expectations based on prior improvised experience, as in the execution: "You might say I love my work, and though I know this sounds self-satisfied, I can assure you I am not. I do keep reaching higher, and in doing so I've also had some happy accidents in my life. I've always made it a point to do work that I enjoy, and enjoy the work I've chosen to do, to find something meaningful that gives pleasure to me and to others. What more could I ask?

"It is a changing condition, I think, of reverie, letting it take me where it wants, allowing my feelings to take over and flow, and my artistic instincts to guide me. I always hold my breath and hope that the previous time taken studying, sketching, sorting out my intentions, trying out differing possibilities of form and colour will help me create something novel of value, something that might approach that rare transfiguring moment. If, by doing something like that, you commit to something wholeheartedly, it's freedom from the self, it's doing something beautiful for many other people, most of whom are strangers you'll never meet."

(Edwin, age forty)

"I like creating things. My imagination is very vivid. Too much so. I always cross my bridges before I come to them! The imaginary impressions in my mind's eye are more interesting than my performance of my actual work could ever be. If there is some project in view, I always imagine that something unpleasant will prevent it from happening. I like doing things, and that I enjoy tremendously. I always think of the worst thing first. If it happens, then I'm prepared for it. If it doesn't, then I get a pleasant surprise. A real turn-on."

(Gena, age fifty-seven)

This preference for planning potential solutions to problem areas in detail, this predilection for troubleshooting at an early stage before the act of creation begins, is in the context of an habitual personal approach with an emphasis on long range planning: "I spend a lot of time in what is really long term planning of my life and work. This involves imagining what I would do under certain circumstances, and trying to keep all my options open. When I make my decision, it is then put into practice and may involve manipulating other people's behaviour."

(Jennifer, age forty-seven)

The heart of the creative process is about the apprehension of newly appreciated possibilities. Some of these novel perceptions and ideas may be types to which most people might have little direct access. The beginnings of such ideas are often poorly defined; they are inchoate cognitive experiences for which there might not be appropriate words available.

Amidst this chaos there may be a number of automatic sub-routines that easily could pass unnoticed in the turbulence and excitement of novel idea-making, were it not for the thinker's insight and ability to abstract some of the key features. Making unusual connections has been called the foundation of originality. It has been known for quite some time that the making of associations, some that would be remote [37], some innovative, and a significant but smaller proportion innovative *and* feasible, might be crucial in this. This case of making permeable associations could stand closer examination in the light of a few clues derived from the creative eccentrics: "My thinking has inputs and frequently there are large chunks assembled, put together already. But few people I meet can put the same range of ideas together in the same way I do until I tell them how."

(Tommy, age thirty-three)

This way of schematising possibly related events and longer thought sequences into "chunks" facilitates the processing of information by integrating it, thereby increasing the overall information-processing efficiency: "I can involve and interrelate facts which are distant from, and don't, in the first instance, have any relationship with the main topic, but which later on can fit it quite well."

(David, age thirty-six)

This ability to make remote associations is neither necessary nor sufficient. Furthermore, it may be more highly related to conventional verbal intellectual skills, or convergent thinking, than to divergent thinking. However, it contributes to a fantasy life of singular intensity and what appears to be a deeply meaningful irrationality. A merely associational theory of divergent thinking is probably inadequate, and would perhaps be ordinarily valid only at higher levels of expertise [38, 39]. It is a richer and more complex process, considering that it may involve the working through of individual facts and findings, perhaps combining them in some meaningful way, to connect them to other facts and findings but also educated hunches and intuitions, and then possibly to find the appropriate images, metaphors or principles, and then knit those together into novel concepts.

It is probable that eccentric creators are only loosely repressed. They reject repression as a concept, and in practice are less inhibited, more informal, and bohemianly unconcerned and radical [40, 41, 42]. Because of this they can sometimes remove the remaining restraints upon their partially semi-conscious inclinations. There is still some repression remaining inside, and still rules in the world outside, and the oppositions these set up cause repeated frustrations. A half-formed idea eventually is dredged up. There is a flash of insight, a creative outburst, an emotional release from pent-up frustration, and it is this that may in part energise innovative individuals [43]. Because of their sporadic pattern of inspiration --- often coming in sudden flashes of realization --- their creative process is unpredictable and manifests itself in an under-controlled and sometimes indirect approach: "Occasionally my imagination goes into overdrive, a sort of spiralling spin, generally tangential to what I'm supposed to be doing. My imagination is not usual. When other people will be thinking about, say, opening a vacuum flask on a picnic, I may well be thinking of a pleasant Kierkegaardian-type dialectic which will lead to a cute paradox in which to amuse myself with."

(Jane, age thirty)

Such people, despite being temporarily less emotionally constant and also sometimes distracted, are still capable of using their feelings in relatively effective ways. They may not appear to others to be "well adjusted" in reference to prescribed psychological parameters and definitions, but are adjusted in the broader sense of being potentially socially helpful and indubitably personally happy. Their creativity contributes to their feelings of relaxation, happiness and fundamentally reduced stress. The result is an instinctive form of intellectual response, becoming a powerful conduit for understanding. This too can be by the indirect approach, as the following man commented: "I can sometimes see to the heart of a problem, by using an intellectual form of 'peripheral vision'; looking directly has little effect, but looking indirectly works much better. If I look at a complex device, by knowing its purpose I could recreate it one step at a time."

(Eddie, age thirty-eight)

On the surface, such statements may sound a little boastful. This attitude might be beneficial if one is continually challenging "the system". Once one gets past this, there is a richness of insight into the eccentrics' motivation: "I seem to be imaginative across a fairly wide spectrum. In literary terms this reflects a pleasure in the creation of structures and a love of words. In the more practical elements of life, it may reflect a mind that does not necessarily accept the validity of learned knowledge. I have considerable scepticism about most received wisdom and a consequent general readiness to think for myself.

"When I was a child, I couldn't get over to my parents how important to me it was to act on the stage. Nevertheless, they had seen me taking off with stories made up out of my imagination, taking a role as a storyteller, and playing several parts myself, each with a voice I thought I had made distinctive. I did all this earnestly and with precocious conviction. With others, I wouldn't necessarily take the lead role, though I was a leader, a kind of immature director, critical commentator, and master of ceremonies rolled into one. My own scenes I made splendidly melodramatic, so much so that I think it carried over into real life.

"Bringing you up to date, there was much excitement when I began my most recent project. For two solid years I could think of nothing else. I could sleep for only four hours every night, however exhausted I felt when I woke up. I would wake up at four in the morning and work simultaneously on my novel and screenplay. It took over. It had a life of its own. It gave me plenty of room for my own imagination and my own voice to take over. It was as if I had become an actor capable of playing many parts. I was on a roll and I didn't want to get off it. I felt like something wonderful within my mind had been released. I had no idea I could have worked so hard and feel so delighted at the end of the day.

"Much of what I was doing then found an echo within me, seemed familiar to me, and I was able to re-play past events in my mind and wonder what had really transpired, and then I could re-write these past events in different ways, from different angles. New light was cast on these old happenings. I was thinking of people I have known . . . what they had meant to me. I found myself sometimes wishing things had turned out differently, that I had been a bit more insightful at an earlier stage. What was good was that I could recollect vividly the feelings I had experienced in these meaningful personal relationships. Little did I know at the time that this was going to be turned into a different form of expression. Throughout this exploration I seldom thought that this was going to become my first novel. It seemed to have followed on naturally from my broadcasting and journalism, as part of some perfectly understandable, coherent sequence. This work gave me much satisfaction. If I'd conceived of doing fewer idealistic endeavours I wouldn't think I'd have remained faithful to myself or to my finer principles."

(Tony, age fifty-five)

Eccentric non-conformity extends beyond the usual forms, and it can also question our assumptions about the basis of what we know, why we know it, and how we come to know about it. These people are trying to describe a very real difference in outlook, and its attendant effects. One effect of this is their further separation from the people around them, most of whom are far from like-minded. Another effect is the disillusionment that this brings about: "I can find very few people who seem to think on the same lines as I do. They seem to demand an anchorage of some kind while I do not."

(Cyril, age seventy-four)

It can also happen the opposite way --- adverse feelings about the community can engender in the eccentrics a need to maximise their differences from it, and their feelings of differentness. They separate themselves from those they dislike and would like to shock, and sometimes this produces further alienation: "I tend to make decisions very quickly. I like doing it on my own. I would rather stew on my own and have only myself to blame for the end results. I think everybody else is daft and I am normal. I can have dotty ideas. I hope desperately that I am different from the rest of Edinburgh people. I love the city, but Christ, I hate the people. They are narrow-minded and parochial, they have tunnel vision and the rest of the world does not exist (for them).

"I like doing research on things. Part of the fun of writing my three books was the research: I don't like accepting facts unless I am sure they are correct. So yes, I am creative, because I can't bear looking at the same old unchanging things. I like to make something different. Boring is a word I use a lot."

(Henrietta, age fifty)

For some, creative functions become ends in themselves, and so addictive that although they occur naturally and automatically the bearers of these gifts develop special techniques to regain their privileged access to these special states of mind: "My imagination seems to operate all my waking time. I seem to notice much that my friends ignore. If walking I will be playing with my peripheral vision or trying to feel the texture of the earth beneath my feet. I often deliberately deprive myself of sleep because I enjoy the heightened awareness this brings. I have always thought laterally, and most people have found me strange in this."

(Barry, age fifty)

This strangeness is more than skin deep. There is more to this than the acts and incongruities mooted above. In eccentric creativity, there is a moderate relationship between the eccentrics' degree of originality and their overall mild levels of thought disorder. These two variables are sufficiently related to comprise a separate factor in the factor analysis of the eccentrics studied. (See Table 19.)

Table 19. Originality factor	
Variable	Factor loading
Degree of originality	0.63
Imagination	0.43
Repetitive thinking	0.39
Overall Thought Disorder (by PSE)	0.39

(Note: It should be remembered that the higher the coefficient, or factor loading, the more important is that variable in comprising the psychological meaning of that factor.)

A good deal of the creativity demonstrated was intentional, understandable, and proceeded from elegantly simple techniques. One of these methods involved being quietly and dreamily meditative: "I came to be creative by observing shapes in clouds, and by reading and listening when having to lead a quiet life as a child. And by really being contemplative. Any and all of my creativity has been close to nature. Creating seems more interesting and absorbing. Beauty has such a wonderful side to it that I want to tell everyone about it, I really want to share it with them and show it to them in as unadorned a form as possible, to those who can perceive as well as I and to those who might be able to see, with some help, what I can see."

(Joan R. Gilmour)

The connection with meditation and other forms of waking reverie has been found elsewhere. In one study, highly experienced female meditators exhibited higher scores on objective tests of visual-perceptual originality than did those with only an interest in meditation, or those with intermediate levels of experience in its practice [44]. An alternative explanation with experimental backup [45] is that meditation induces relaxation, which in turn is a good condition for increased theoretical risk-taking --- the so-called "Risky Shift" towards heightened originality and flexibility. Because eccentrics are much less affected by stress and its resulting anxieties, they may be more relaxed in general and therefore better able to get themselves into a relaxed state before and perhaps during the creative process. During deep relaxation brain activity is still taking place. According to those who have undertaken brain-imaging studies, such as Professor Andreasen and her team at the University of Iowa, "the brain never rests". Their work also demonstrated that associating words, images, concepts, and memories of past experiences in thinking allowed various assemblages of brain cells to "converse with one another in a free and uncensored manner" [46].

The research team led by Colin Martindale of the University of Maine conducted an EEG study that showed creative people produced more brain waves in the alpha range when performing creative tasks [47]. They also found that such people exhibit more right cerebral hemisphere EEG activity than left cerebral hemisphere EEG activity during creative performances, and that this pattern was not found in less creative people. Alpha waves are neural oscillations of a low frequency (7 to 14 hertz or cycles per second), and are associated with relaxed activity in mind and body. They may be a significant indicator of when and where in the brain active coordinated networking is taking place. In addition, the complexity of EEG activity is higher when individuals solved tasks that required divergent creative thinking, more so than during intelligent convergent thinking tasks or than during mental relaxation. The strong increase in EEG complexity underlying the generation of novel ideas has been attributed to a greater amount of possibly competing interactions between massively interconnected brain cell assemblies [48].

It may well be that creative problem-solving is preceded or accompanied by lower levels of cortical arousal, shown by an increase in alpha wave power, as suggested by Austrian psychological researchers Fink and Neubauer [49]. They believed this increase in alpha wave activity indicated that the individuals in question were focussing on "internally generated stimuli" --- thoughts and images --- rather than on the external environment around them. They also found that during more original creative responses, as opposed to less original responses, there is stronger task-related alpha wave synchronization. Perhaps this was another way of indicating greater brain cell interactional complexity during effective creative work.

The other major clue that Joan Gilmour's above excerpt reveals is the tie-up with the use of visual imagery. This turned out to be very significant, and in unexpected ways.

Imagery and vivid dreams

"My mind works in a series of patterns, a scheme of ideas. Stripping objects of their detail to give one picture. In order to recognise an object, the mind must have somewhere deep within itself a picture, an image. The mind is constantly sifting information and constantly analysing the world into these patterns. The rate at which these patterns fall into place gives you a measure of human emotions. Two disparate images which are not normally put together are put together by the mind to produce a completely different idea. By doing so you experience a sensation of delight, a feeling that means something."

(Ryan, age thirty-three)

This theory of visionary looking, developed independently by one of the eccentric informants, and tellingly related to particular emotional states, quite properly accentuates the importance of visual imagery in the creative process. Psychologists have alluded to this repeatedly [50, 51, 52, 53, 54, 55, 56, 57]. So too have a number of artistically oriented poets of the twentieth century, such as Ezra Pound, who wrote, "The image is not an idea. It is a radiant node or cluster; it is a . . . VORTEX, from which ideas are constantly rushing." It is also known that verbal metaphors evoke images, and can be conveyed through the further use of imagery.

Mental imagery plays an important role in memory, dreams, and waking fantasies, and has an influence on our perceptions of the world about us [58, 59, 60]. Like much of visual perception, the use of imagery is an active process. Imagery plays an integrative role in what can be imagined, doing much more than interpreting what can be seen. Fantasies, like dreams, can be very instructive in learning about the psychological worlds of individuals with differing levels of self-awareness. For those who consume the products of the imagination, be it artistic or scientific, the creator's use and conveying of imagery clarifies what they are trying to communicate and understand. As the Russian writer Ivan Turgenev said, "A picture may instantly present what a book could set forth only in a hundred pages."

It is important to emphasise that an image can be active, and it operates on other concrete and abstract ideas within the mind. It creates, by synthesis, conceptual analysis, symbolism and modelling, new forms of information. These can then be transmitted to other areas within the brain. Because mind and brain shape behaviour, imagery can be understood by reference back to what the individual has experienced in the past, and forward to what he wants to do in the future. The mind can therefore access and accept ideas of creation, the beginnings of new thought worlds, sometimes out of relative chaos. It can be concerned with particular elements of human experience, as in this example: "I used to run through a long sequence of thought or imagine a long adventure. I visualise intellectual problems and my personal philosophy. I use a form of metaphor to 'play with' or analyse situations. My visual metaphor for the interactions and inevitable conflicts of people is of so many spinning tops intent on maintaining their own motion but bumping into each other. And its appropriateness is in the relative indifference of the tops to each other."

(Paul, age thirty-eight)

It is likely that a person's conscious control over his imagery abilities might also be important to his creativity. As early as 1893, the eccentric Sir Francis Galton noted that, among people able to have mental images, there were tremendous variations in the clarity, flexibility and mastery they had over their conscious visual images. Psychologists Durndell and Wetherick found a link between imagery control and results on psychometric tests of divergent creative thinking [61]. This was borne out by what many eccentric informants reported spontaneously: "My imagination, and control over it, is strong. If given a topic or cause I can perceive consequent images; and I can also produce my own topics. I have a belief that something may be technologically feasible and then find indications why. I imagine anything, then ask --- 'what system could it be in? What are the linkages?' I then extend the logical possibilities for as far as they will go, and beyond, into darker, nefarious, subterranean areas. I do this best in a semi-sleeping, half-awake, slowed-up reverie, which I first found full of angst, frustration, and half-remembered ideas. I now greet it expectantly, warmly; it sometimes comes out after lunch or at a concert, with my eyes closed, but this can't be planned for. What happens is similar to the famous case of Salvador Dali's having received strange images in dreams after he had eaten some Camembert cheese."

(Matthew, age forty-two)

Psychological research shows that most people think using verbal means. Eccentrics have a greater tendency to think using visual images, or a combination of visual and verbal means. Because of this, eccentrics are often flabbergasted by the discordances between what they see with their eyes and what they imagine, and between appearances and reality.

The most frequently mentioned aspect of imagery in the eccentrics' detailed descriptions was that of image vividness. There is previous research that shows a significant correlation between image vividness and divergent creative thinking [62]. This vividness amounted to well-preserved eidetic imagery of sparkling clarity. Eidetic imagery is a way of mentally representing objects and events that has many of the characteristics of actually seeing them. It is related to the lay concept of possessing a "photographic memory". More precisely, it is the ability to project upon a blank screen a picture after its removal from view and to focus precisely on any of its details. Here is an example from an eccentric informant: "I can see faces, wraiths, shapes, forms, etc in designs on wallpapers, carpets and such like. These stay in my mind after I shut my eyes, and sometimes after I have fallen asleep, I can see them in my dreams. Most times, this allows me to have an almost perfect photographic memory over long periods of time."

(Val, age fifty-one)

This capacity is often well-developed in young children but, as one grows older, it gradually fades for most people. It is quite common in children, but rare in adults. It comes to be lost as the person acquires a more abstract method of processing information.

Some of the eccentric informants were very vivid imagers. They could, with their eyes shut or open, clearly "see in the mind's eye" a play or story enact itself as if being presented to them. Due to their practice and experience, their skill became quite accurate. Outwardly, they might appear passive, as if in a cinema watching a film, but a lot is going on in their minds. "When my wife speaks of any happening or location I see it in colour, and vividly. I describe to her what I imagine and she assures me that the picture is correct."

(Sylvan, age seventy-four)

This imagery can be in sensory modalities other than the visual. It need not necessarily be only a matter of passive reception, but can be actively worked on, manipulated, and changed: "I can hear harmonious sounds as they arose out of the silence as I listened in the grotto in the garden space. It was a vague pulsing rhythm like a heartbeat at first, growing clear as I focussed and concentrated. From that time on, I can imagine a visual or sound effect, then work to create it. When I am reading, I can visualise, hear, feel, smell, in my imagination. Words stimulate my imagination as well as sound, colours, etcetera. I can see ahead and really anticipate consequences."

(Sheila, age fifty-two)

The movement and action of the images can become extended to the point where series of them fuse, and precipitate further images, become blocked temporarily and fuse together again, until the imagery is almost impossible to follow and "dances before the eyes". Some images become transformed playfully into speculative hypotheses; some are enrolled to enlighten other people's understanding. Just like dreamers, who on awakening, attempt to make sense out of the images that come unbidden to them in their sleep, so too did the eccentric imagers attempt to interpret, and operate on, their waking images. Just as dreams only can be rarely controlled, the ideas related to these images also can have a wild, elusive quality, sometimes only representing vague associations of events and feelings from the past. However obscure the connections between them, they also can provide access to the boundless domain of the imagination. The difference between creative people and non-creative people might be that the former use different parts of their brains, and that these function in somewhat differing ways.

The human brain is formed into two well-integrated cooperating hemispheres, left and right, each with quite different functions, though richly and complexly joined together by more than two hundred million nervous fibres --- these are known as the cerebral commissures, also called the corpus callosum. This is a really wondrous structure, involved in a number of different functions. Not only is it engaged in the transmission of brain signals from the left hemisphere to the right hemisphere, and the right hemisphere to the left hemisphere, but also some of the fibres can inhibit certain inappropriate signals from crossing over, again in both directions. Other fibres act like traffic lights, helping to direct signal transmission, regulating and coordinating which streams of signals should take precedence for other more specialized functions. The cerebral commissures have also been found to be concerned in the maintenance of sustained attention, or vigilance. This is important in how accurately we may perceive incoming information from the external world, and our ability to think in a more concentrated way.

Although there may be a variable degree of mirrored re-duplication possible for some functions in both cerebral hemispheres, there may also be some spare capacity for certain tasks in both. For most right-handed people, the left hemisphere is dominant for language, and perhaps is naturally dominating in other ways too. It is predominantly verbal, rational, analytical, and deductive. The right brain, on the other hand, among its many functions, helps control things artistic, intuitive, improvisational, spiritual, and roughly inductive. It dreams and fantasises, helps one to recognise people and objects, and to find one's way around familiar terrain, and to solve jigsaw puzzles, maze tests and Rubik cubes.

When one's right brain is more actively involved --- whether you are sketching, writing or daydreaming --- you become immensely absorbed; the more of that freely flowing absorption there is, the more likely that one's sense of time may be lost, and in this state, colours seem more alive, and one can feel contented or uplifted. Eccentrics are similar to persons of genius in this respect, though a higher proportion of geniuses have longer and better formal educations and possibly also differ in the amount of rational power and work their minds can exert.

Albert Einstein said he thought in images, not words, and trusted his tremendously powerful, instinctive intuitions for understanding what was really going on in the natural world. His theory of relativity began by his imagining what it would be like to ride a shaft of light into outer space, and what it might mean, *in relative terms*, to walk forward on a train that is also moving forward at a greater speed. "Imagination," he once said, "is more important than knowledge."

Vivid daytime imagery and vivid nocturnal imagery in dreams share much in common. Higher levels of dream recall have been shown to be associated with more vivid voluntary images while awake as well as more frequent use of visual imagery [63]. When rapid eye movement (REM) sleep, which is when most people dream, is experimentally suppressed, some people show an intensification of sporadic eye activities at the onset of the delayed REM-sleep state. These coincide with much more vivid dream imagery, and more activity in the dream that would provoke eye movements similar to those seen in waking life. This is not the entire story however; for example, some people occasionally report dreaming just before they've been awakened from non-REM sleep.

There are also considerable similarities in content between naturally occurring daydreams and nocturnal dreams obtained by wakening subjects in sleep research projects. In both, people often feel at the centre of events or to be participating personally. Such comparisons show continuity in themes and current concerns between waking thoughts and images and sleeping images. For example, personal anxieties experienced while awake, such as being inappropriately dressed, being lost, letting someone down, or being late for an appointment, can re-appear in dreams, especially those involving social interactions [64, 65]. Occasionally, emotions may appear heightened or incongruous.

Self-awareness while dreaming seems to be initiated by noticing positive and negative feelings, and by the perception of personally defined oddities within the dreams [66]. I was able to obtain reliable assessments of the emotional content of the dreams provided by the eccentrics, and two colleagues compared all these dreams independently and blindly to the dreams of a matched control group of community volunteers. This showed that while eccentrics, as a group, had very similar proportions of joyful/elated dreams, angry dreams, and sad dreams as the non-eccentric control subjects, there was only a very low proportion of eccentrics showing surprise in their dreams, less than five per cent doing so. This lack of surprise may be because the eccentrics tended to remember their dream images very well, and also paid greater attention to their waking images and to those images seen in their dreams.

In addition, the eccentrics had significantly more anxious or fearful dreams than the non-eccentrics, more than four times as many, forty-two per cent as compared to about ten per cent in the non-eccentrics. Though only a very small number of the eccentrics reported anxiety or fear in their everyday waking lives, they still would have been exposed to the sporadic stresses of living generally non-conforming lifestyles. Plato had argued that a person who in waking life denied his emotions would suffer occasional startling dreams of an anxious or shocking nature. Perhaps that is the price that eccentrics pay by repudiating a more emotional way of responding to adverse life events, or by remaining calmer when others would be more affected by stress. Howsoever, no more than ten of the one hundred and thirty eccentrics studied were found to have mild or moderate anxiety in the past months on interview with the Present State Examination. (See also Reference [67] for other quantitative data on dream emotion).

Dreams can sometimes appear to be real and mainly conform to life-like experiences, though this varies greatly and there are often detectable differences from waking states of perception. The experience of dreaming is rather like being immersed in an alternative reality, and that is probably one reason why dreams have been thought of as having some kind of similarity or connection with waking hallucinations and delusions. However, there is obviously nothing intrinsically pathological about dreaming [68]. Sleep itself is not a total interruption, but a transition in the form of the flow of consciousness. Our mood during the previous days, our waking imaginativeness, our predominant concerns, and various bits of information we pick up about people in whom we are interested, are all significantly correlated with how we depict others, and ourselves, while dreaming [69].

It is important to emphasize that the brain normally works as a coordinated neural network. However, in four to six episodes every night for about a quarter of one's time asleep, the mind/brain lets down its guard. EEG brainwave studies suggest that during visual dreaming the right and left sides of the brain are far less integrated [70]. Instead, the two sides work more independently, more so than at any other time. The electrical activity of the cerebral commissures that connect the two hemispheres is greatly reduced during REM sleep [71]. When this partial disconnection occurs, the dominant language-orientated left-brain is less able to affect what goes on in the image-laden right side of the brain. However, this stage of sleep is the closest to being awake, though the brain stem blocks any bodily movements. Neuroscientists working in this field hold the impression that networks of associations stored in people's memories may become looser in the dreaming state than in wakefulness and that this too perhaps favours creativity [72].

People who have suffered injuries to the right side of the brain report that they can no longer experience dreams [73]. Also, dream recall has been found to correlate better with mental imagery abilities rather than language facility, as assessed by psychometric tests. However, in dreams as in daily workaday reality, there is an easily bridgeable gulf between words and images, as can be seen in some of the surrealistic artworks of Rene Magritte. There is other evidence that remote memories used in imagery are also used in recognition, and that dreaming and waking visual imagery share some common underlying neuropsychological processes [74].

The meaning and impact of eccentric dream lives

When and where in our adult lives do we regularly show our greatest omnipotence, and paradoxically, our greatest degree of frailty? The answer of course is at night, in our dreams. What is that space that we inhabit every night when we close our eyes, fall asleep and dream? On the face of it, dreaming is an altered state of consciousness. Although we know that dreams originate in our brains, to what psychological purpose they serve, if any, is, as yet, not fully understood.

Generally, people consider themselves unable to control their own dreams, and that abject lack of mastery may be counter-pointed by how much control and mastery they have, or want to have, in waking life. The initiative to control what happens in a dream is certainly not in the dreamer's power. Things happen to him, and he reacts, and as an actor he is uncommonly tentative, uncertain, lost, buffeted from side to side by dynamic and often unidentified forces. Very few people, and only several of the eccentrics I studied, claimed to have any degree of control or influence over aspects of their dreams. The lack of command over the direction of one's dreams also contributes to why there is such marked variation between the different interpretations different people take away from their dreams.

It could be said that only in our dreams, in our subconscious minds, freed from the constraints of time and place, are we a true reflection of ourselves at a particular point in our lives. Dreams take place within a specific time period, and yet they seem outside of time. Unlike characters in a film or a play, what occurs is so brief that relationships between the dreamer and images of other people who appear cannot be developed as waking relationships can be. Dreams are arranged spontaneously in relation to how the dreamer is feeling, or whatever ongoing part-emotional, part-cognitive personal concerns may be current. Many dreams are chopped up by remembered references to the remote past and to very recent events, a veritable No-man's Land of emotionally-coloured memories, scenes waxing and waning throughout the night. They are full of flashbacks and flash-forwards and brief glimpses, so ephemeral that the coincident feelings are so fleeting that it is often difficult, if not impossible, to make sense of them until one awakens. Even then it can be difficult. Other memories, some meaningful, some not, come forward out of context, often seemingly irrelevant to what is going on in the dreamer's life. To complicate matters, some dream memories rise to the surface readily; others simply dissipate. After wakening, subconscious and sometimes obscure associations occasionally burst into consciousness.

Dreams also show a range of other bizarre events, capriciously scrambling actions and locations, making for uncertainties about space, time and personal identity, as well as fluid misidentifications of faces and places [75]. This has been viewed as part of their unintentional part-concealment. It is common in dreaming to hold contradictory thoughts and feelings, and to see illogical placements of people and objects, as well as shifting and unpredictable changes in scene and content, sudden transformations and impossible things [76]. There is also a pronounced, almost total reduction of voluntary control over the actions that transpire in dreams. Some dream recollections may have been more easily remembered because of the puzzlement that was felt about apparently impossible events, sometimes requiring the dreamer to reflect on alternatives in his life or in particular key social interactions [77].

Dreams are also upset by previews of possible future contingencies, and are "edited" by the dreamer's brain so haphazardly as to often seem to follow random patterns. This fragmentary disarray is either without a story line or is capable of being created into a multiplicity of narratives. This is perhaps why so many surreal or conceptual artworks, however talented and well-informed the artists may be, often look like artlessly constructed collages. However, some dream experiences can be assembled by the dreamer, helped by the patterns that the dreams form, into a more coherent narrative structure [68, 78]. Dreams can provide alternative narrative structures, some wildly improbable, to our consciousness, occasionally working through our waking imaginations and sometimes giving it a diverting lift or taking us temporarily into a divergent reality.

Moreover, dreams can be shockingly uncensored, sensual and sexual, although within the same person they can also be so censored, uncontrollably and against many dreamers' wishes and needs for coherent resolution, that they are frustrated by them so thoroughly that some are quite willing to write dreams off, or to reduce them to nonsensical noise in the neuropsychological "machinery". Though some neuroscientists have also attempted to consign dreams to the category of unimportant side-effect, or to explain them only by their underlying electro-biochemical physiology, the potential meaningfulness of dreams cannot be so easily reduced. On the other hand, there are psychologists who argue, from objective evidence, that the normal state of the waking mind is also that of comparable chaos [79, 80, 81].

Dreams sometimes continue on the main lines of previous waking thought, as a kind of formative re-transcription in visual form. If a dream contains associations with those waking thoughts, strands of those former thoughts can continue into sleep, particularly processing those parts of experience that are actively meaningful or have not reached a satisfactory resolution. Although the form of ideas and thoughts changes from primarily words to primarily visual images in dreams, whatever concerns the person when he or she falls asleep may be carried forward into dreaming. In that context, dreams are there to help us to become more fully conscious of what we need to know.

Dreams can be an essential part of problem-solving. Two psychologists at Cardiff University, Dr. David Fontana and Myra Thomas, have undertaken research that ingeniously demonstrated that a dream's symbolism could produce clues to problems, though the clues were presented in circuitous ways. They gave their experimental subjects anagrams, such as SCNACEDELIHSKR, the solution to which is Charles Dickens. One subject hit on the answer, in sleep, through an elaborate chain of reasoning involving a dream about detectives named Dempsey and Makepeace, then featuring in a British television series. The female star of this programme, set amidst the streets of London, had a hairstyle like the research volunteer's friend, a woman called Carol, that reminded her of Dickens's *A Christmas Carol*, and from this she free-associated the answer. "The interesting thing here," said Dr. Fontana, "is the kind of reasoning used to get from the dream symbolism to the anagram solution. It isn't logical, linear thinking, it's not lateral thinking, and it's not trial-and-error. It exposes a whole different pattern of thought which seems much more linked to intuition and creativity." As evidence, this proves the recurring hunches of earlier psychologists that sometimes dreams attempt to find an interpretable formulation of a problem, and sometimes a way through to a potential solution.

Dreams could be seen as an eventual product of behaviour and lifestyle. They can produce balance in one's mental life, creating order out of disorder. Dreams also provide important clues about an individual's personality, or clues about another person's behaviour, though not pat answers or easy solutions to what those clues might really mean to the dreamer. The exceptional significance of remembered dreams tells us less about one's furtive wishes and more about the sort of person one is striving to become, or trying to avoid becoming.

If human creativity is a socially and culturally mediated activity, as Lev Vygotsky and many other psychologists believe it is, then dreams too must be socially and culturally mediated, as dreaming appears to be one of the sources contributing to creativity. Divergent cultural environments give rise to different key symbols and also reflect habitual rituals that crop up in dreams.

There are many disparate sources of inspiration. Dreams are one such source, however crucial that they may be to the creative process. For some, dreams can help foster a close relationship between vivid imagery and an all-absorbing, concentrated style of imagination [82]. People who had these qualities also had daydreams that contained happier emotional content. There is a positive orientation toward imagination, introspection, daydreaming, and meditation for those who remember their dreams well [83].

From this, one can infer a similar substantial relationship between dreams and imagery to pertain to eccentrics. The eccentrics' dreams were full of images that were readily accessible and memorable to them. This showed itself mainly as a separate and moderately resilient factor in our factor analysis, composed mostly of overall creativity and vivid dreaming, and was also related to the overall degree of eccentricity. (See Table 20.)

Table 20. Creativity factor	
Variable	**Factor loading**
Creativity	0.59
Dream vividness	0.54
Interview Q/A, "Mind dissolving?"	0.29
Degree of Eccentricity	0.25
Daydreaming	0.21

(The higher the factor loading, the more important is that variable in contributing to the psychological meaning of that factor.)

Many illogical events that go unnoticed during a dream seem to demand more attention upon wakening. In understanding a dream the dreamer first reworks it, transforming familiar and strange visual images into communicable thoughts, almost always in the form of words to be sorted out and interpreted. There is a strong tendency for a comprehensible narrative to be assembled from the images seen or the thoughts following from them, and if this happens, memories of these dreams are more likely to persist. Working through a dream --- figuring out what it really means --- is a process of retrospective reconstruction. If done for prospective purposes --- looking forward, or taking memories of the past and using them to make oneself a better person --- psychologically speaking, that is a valid enterprise, whether done alone or "talking them through" with someone else.

People strive to allocate meanings to the images in their dreams, perhaps because their behaviours in dreams are often so different to what happens in their everyday lives. In talking about their dreams, people reveal truths about their most personal feelings and thoughts, hopefully to learn something about themselves or about those people who are knowingly or unknowingly significant to them. This is mainly beneficial because, however they are interpreted, it is those selfsame creative acts of thinking that help us to re-evaluate the meaningfulness of our feelings about other people and our relationships with them. These interpretations are of something impressively and intimately private being made more freely available through the medium of language, and in so doing dreamers can hear back multiple interpretations, opening themselves up to multiple possibilities, inventions and reinventions. The act of interpretation opens up many questions about who we are, where we are going, how we should relate to others, whether they are friends, neighbours, those we like or those we dislike, and these issues, brought into the cold light of day, also have the potential of being repeatedly revised.

In dreams, two of the forces of conformity --- self-control and social restraints --- are almost completely absent. One might ask what happens when the person in question is generally less affected by pressures to conform in daily life?

Dreams occasionally disclose significant bits of information about us, particularly those who fearlessly wish to know themselves better, and this was very much the case for the eccentrics who provided the following dreams. The dream lives of eccentrics, which are very important to them, can give us some insight into the way their minds work, and by extension, how other non-conforming individual's minds might work. For these reasons, the great majority of eccentrics studied were quite happy to share their dreams with me, and were very interested in what I would make of them. Their dreams had never before been interpreted by anyone other than themselves, let alone by a clinical neuropsychologist who could place their dreams in the contexts of the goodly amount of biographical information they also had provided. One should consider the actual content of a number of these eccentrics' remembered vivid dreams, to, at the very least, get a flavour of what they were like. Like other forms of apparent chaos, dreams can be analysed and interpreted at multiple levels of organisation and subject matter. By their often very perplexing nature, there are usually a number of plausible ways to explain and construe them. These presented here are no different.

A. "I once dreamed I was in the trenches in the Great War, handing everyone chocolate bars, to their great joy. As I walked slowly away, it began to snow. On both sides of a muddy and cratered track, there were young wounded soldiers waiting for help, and I knew that I could not leave with my head held high when there were still those men who needed my help. I looked up and saw a million bright stars overhead, and I instantly knew what I had to do. I would stay with the wounded soldiers."

(Mike, age twenty-six)

This at first sight is a deceptively straightforward dream. It reflects a generally good emotional state during the dream and a generous personality disposition. This extends to the point of wanting to put right great hurts (great hurts = Great War) of the past. The incongruity of these wishes results from the contrast between the dreamer's joyous feelings and his underlying expiatory needs, taking upon his shoulders great feelings of contrition for humanity's continuing inhumanity. In his mind, there was a feeling, and an acknowledgement, of his re-doubled resolution to act.

B. "I have had this dream on more than several occasions, and each time I do, it disturbs me. There are three people in a large bath with me and I can't tell whether they are men or women, and I don't seem to care. Suddenly at first, a side panel in the wall slowly opens and we pass through, one by one, very docile we were. However many times this happens, I am always last out.

"Aside from this dream, other dreams mostly happen too fast and I find it hard to remember all but the most vibrant of them. Who knows what I might have missed by forgetting soon afterwards key points of these other more shadowy dreams. When, in the past, I had remembered the overall scene in a dream and the various actors in it, and then worked it up into a poem, sometimes it all came together in ways I hadn't anticipated. This happens all too rarely nowadays. Unfortunately."

(Michael, age thirty-three)

This dream is primarily concerned with the deceptiveness of appearances, though it also contains a clue about gender-role confusions and, possibly, some sexual ambiguity. It could be a dream about being born or about re-entering the security of the womb. These latter interpretations derive from, and help to explain, Michael's recollection of docility in the dream. In the dream, he seems relatively passive, literally a follower rather than a leader. Although he claims that the dream "disturbs" him, its emotional content otherwise seems drastically limited, as if his feelings are separated from his memories and thinking, and as if he doesn't much care about what its meaning to him is.

Another implicit interpretation would place some emphasis on a wish to be able to be in harmony with others, rather than battling against them. To that extent it may be seen as a compensatory dream. It is a metaphor for "going with the flow" or for "letting go", and possibly about losing emotional control.

Because the three people in the bath are presumably naked, and yet Michael cannot tell whether they are male or female, and he does not say whether or not he also is naked, this may have something to do with sexual repression, or breaking free from it. The other people in Michael's dreamt bath are not only anonymous; they are also nondescript inasmuch as he has not described what they looked like or what facial expressions, physical cues or gestures they showed. In classical psychoanalysis, appearing unabashedly naked in front of others as in early childhood, represents a wish to recapture lost pre-Oedipal innocence. In dreams, intrusive images and ideas originating from early childhood are often unwelcome in full consciousness. In such instances, the mind of the dreamer acts to hide, censor or otherwise repress them. Keeping forbidden feelings in check is bound to lead one way or another to the development of defence mechanisms, including in many otherwise loosely repressed eccentrics.

As this is a repeated dream in which the key aspects remain the same, and that on each occasion of seeing it Michael is disturbed by it, this suggests that at this point in his life, childhood anxieties may be re-emerging, perhaps as at his age he will be expected to be taking on more adult relationships or perhaps parental responsibilities. He has not reached any kind of resolution; this impasse is indicated because the dream recurs and remains the same, rather than showing any signs of change. However, their repetition and attendant anxieties should draw attention to the dreamer that something serious is going on that requires thought and perhaps action on his part to provoke real change in his life.

The mind has many ways of evading truths about inner conflicts, as is borne out by this dreamer's recourse to a defence mechanism favoured by eccentric men, that of intellectualisation. Michael's final paragraph above is evidence of this and, in his recollections of how things were better for him creatively then, his willingness to escape into the past. The dreams, acting as "existential messages", are trying to tell him that the dreams, or his anxieties, have no power over him unless he passively and without active attention allows them to possess that power.

C. "I was captured by fierce Japanese samurai swordsmen. To get to a prison camp, I was made to walk barefoot across a pit of bamboo spikes, some covered in blood, some mouldy, some smouldering. I got to the other side of the pit where some of my friends were sitting cross-legged, smoking joints. There were two double-decker buses there that my friends lived in. I was then in a room with two soldiers and a captain. I begged not to be left alone with the soldiers. The captain put a basket of two goldfish between myself and them, saying that the shadow of the fish swimming round would keep his men away from me."

(Angy, age twenty-six)

Interpretations from a pre-feminist era early in the last century probably would have pronounced that this dream is a hidden wish, that Angy unconsciously wanted to be abducted and involved in a relationship with a dominant man, and suggest that she is sexually ambivalent. This interpretation is clearly wrong. Angy's conscious needs and self-knowledge weighs heavily against it. Of course, she also comprehended the meaningfulness of her dream imagery. The device of the spiked pit shows no more than justifiable anxiety, or about the personally harmful consequences that would follow on from her forced submission to another person's gratification of his self-centered desires. Angy may have wanted the fullness of a romantically and sexually fulfilling relationship, though wanted nothing to do with meaningless promiscuity. The heightened passivity of her friends in a drug-induced state serves to emphasize further her feelings of aloneness, because it is clear in the dream that they will not intervene on her behalf or help her. Rape, torture and illicit drug-taking are associated, perhaps because they are all deeply hurtful and wrong. However, the repeated mention of the word "two", along with the word "double-decker", resonates with Angy's concerns: she was acutely conscious of her needs for genuine intimacy with another person, the giving and receiving between lover and beloved.

What goes on within the room derives superficially from Angy's beliefs in the occult, but the latent import is to do with a combination of excitement, fear-laden anticipation and anxiety. This signals Angy's understandably doubting indecisiveness, although she had also been willing to take audacious action when required.

On a higher plane, this dream is about love overcoming fears. The fears concern the duplicitous, sadistic side of evil crimes perpetrated by human beings against other human beings. The love symbolism, repetitively portrayed by both the friends' doubled homes, and by the fragile symbolism of the two goldfish, proves victorious in the end.

D. "I am sailing a large sea-going yacht at night with some other people, strangers. We arrive in a small harbour, and go ashore to a cocktail party with elegantly dressed people and stimulating conversation, but then I am afraid that somebody is trying to steal the yacht, and I go out and single-handedly take it back to sea."

(Arnold, age forty)

This dream is about the anonymity of modern society. This aspect is associated with a distrust of strangers, and this leads on to suspicions about one's original ideas being stolen (a recurrent conscious preoccupation for many eccentric creators such as Arnold). Rather than abandoning ship and opting for a convivial social life, Arnold chooses to abandon the strangers on shore. This dream also provides some resolution: it suggests to the dreamer that he should abstain from social life, with its hidden dangers, and should continue to rely on his own independent resources. It also continues a symbolism of opposites: the harbour represents anything but a safe haven, though the more primordial power of the sea does. There is no easy way, no safe harbour. The message of this dream is that, as Arnold had said elsewhere, "You've got to get on with your life yourself".

E. "I was working at a long Formica bench, 'working' at the prized object, a slightly elongated octagon about two inches long, flat and covered with velvet. There was a second, another prized object, on another bench to my left. It was a pleasant, well-proportioned large room, and two walls were of open work latticed alabaster which let in a lovely glowing, pleasing light. There was a dark brown rosewood frame supporting the workbench. A doorway led the eye to another room with an arch at the end where a small chamber orchestra was playing. This orchestra seemed of no consequence to me. There were about ten or twelve members in it, dressed in green dinner jackets. The orchestra came out past me, and one chap, referring to a blonde pallid youth, said, 'He told the conductor I was marvellous; it's amazing, as I know I made a lot of mistakes.' I consoled him, and said he played wonderfully, as he was wanting me to say, but I hadn't actually bothered to listen. I put my work away and went outside to go home. My youngest child was there and I left earlier than I really wanted to because of her. In the dream, I never actually saw her."

(Anne, age sixty)

This is a complicated, multi-layered dream. The prized objects are this informant's preoccupying, creative life-work projects. They are contained within an elaborate intellectual framework that is conveyed by the architectural detail. The chamber orchestra, seemingly of "no consequence" to Anne, may be a dream metaphor for how professional creative people often deliberately have to blinker themselves from extraneous perceptions in order to focus on their creative work and express their own personal visions. The further irony, or clue, is that, in waking life Anne has much to do with musical instruments.

This dream also establishes the order of precedence between conflicting life roles; only her maternal feelings and close family ties can possibly over-rule Anne's mastery of her creative urges. Her devotion, her committed concentration, and the amount of time invested in her pursuit of truth and academic excellence are also shown by the "prized objects". She prizes her work, and wants to be prized for what she does. She will persevere and not be distracted. It also shows the interdependence of artist and audience, and how honest criticism and well-intentioned encouragement can be at odds. However, the presence "never actually" seen indicates a mother's repressed guilt for not having paid enough attention to her youngest daughter, though this was part of the price Anne felt she had to pay to be prized.

F.   "I have dreamt recurrently that I was an Orpheus-like figure. There is a fishing expedition down a very violent river, but it turns into a continual journey, first across an infinite mossy delta, then into subterranean caves overhung with stalactites."

(Arthur, age seventy-one)

This dream could almost be taken at face value. The surface skein of the narrative is sexual. Symbolic representations for sex and sexual identity in different people's dreams are often associated with the dreamers' predominant long-term feelings about sex. The "infinite mossy delta", in this view, would be the external female pudendum and the "subterranean caves", the vagina. However, the "stalactites" could mean that Arthur feared that the younger female object of his desires might not always be nice or accommodating to him. He may have had some unsatisfactory sexual experiences in the past. The long journey then would be equivalent to a long struggle, only to reach what may have turned out to be yet another rejection. His feelings of inferiority are then transferred from himself to his sexual organs, and to vanquish these feelings, he focuses on the erotic image, thinly disguised, of openly displayed femininity. It might be that Arthur imagined sexual intercourse was going to be great, though it turned out to be less pleasurable, and he repeated the cycle of disappointment to humiliation to inferiority feelings to fixation to seduction to rejection to frustration back to disappointment. These feelings flowed as a stream throughout his rich emotional life, which was basically upbeat though turbulent. It was only when he reached the age of fifty-eight that he found a mutually fulfilling and happy relationship with another woman who he described as his "sweetheart and perfect soul mate".

The interpretation of this dream would only be correct and authentic if Arthur concurred with it, and only if it realistically pertained to a set pattern of behaviour in the past. However, when sexual thoughts are symbolized, as they are here, there is usually a more direct association with what it tells the dreamer about his feelings in regard to his current or recent sexual activity.

This dream also signifies the paralleling of inner journeys and outer explorations. Orpheus descending into the underworld with his lute is aptly analogous to the suffering sustained by artists in dredging up significant and sometimes traumatic material from within. The violence of Arthur's river imagery represents the elemental forces that set in motion his sexual needs, and the dangers to an individual artist in submitting to them. The violence of these forces is reminiscent of Dylan Thomas's poem, "The force that through the green fuse drives the flower".

G.   "I was travelling towards home on a bright day. I passed through local towns coming up the hills in Wales. I came to a pleasant mansion. It had once been a mental institution or workhouse. It has a garden and limestone walls. Some great cataclysm had occurred, but there was a beautiful sense of hope, of a future and present coming and being. I was part of this time and place. Triumph would be too harsh a word for this sense of beginning again. The feeling was more like . . . 'everything not bad at all'."

(P. L. F., age thirty-eight)

This dream shows ambivalence about going home, and probably also about reconciliations in general. This is conveyed in the notion that home can be either a safe asylum or a literal mad house. In the dream, P. L. F. discovers that when he does return home, the experience is a good one. He realises that he should have returned home earlier and/or more frequently. That realisation would mark the end of a struggle. He has made an important decision and, because it was the right one, he is more at peace with himself, or has made peace with someone significant that he has hurt, fallen out with, or possibly left.

This is also possibly a dream about optimistic transformations: a workhouse becomes a pleasant mansion; an enormous disaster heralds a new beginning. This also reprises what happens in creative life. Originality both rends and renews. With more than a bit of wish-fulfilment within this dream, it is carried along on a great wave of euphoria. It is also salient that this is a dream landscape without human figures. This eccentric's dreamworld is one that is empty of people, though almost refilled with his expansive spirit of near triumph.

H.   "Upon being the millionth customer in a shop I won a ticket to Australia. I found myself in an area of sandy beaches. The surf was huge, the dunes giving on to immense forests, the tracks through them dry and dusty, leading to ranches in clearings. In one, a party was in full swing, much pot and wine, music, half-naked figures. In a city, everyone was somewhere else celebrating. Walking through deserted streets, I came to a big de Chirico square. As darkness fell, I became lost and was pursued into a derelict block of flats. To be caught meant death. I escaped via a crumbling fire escape. Upon arriving home to my family, I found no one had missed me, but the welcome home was great."

(Andy, age twenty-four)

This dream begins with simple wish-fulfilment. The creative stimulus in the first half of the dream is seen as orgiastic and celebratory. Andy wanted to travel extensively, and he liked it when he can obtain something he'd been seeking at a discount or for free. His anxiety about the city is due to his prior waking realisation that real life has never been that easy and that as he steps forward into adult life that too will not be easy for him. He also had come to believe that he was not a shallow person and did not need or want to encumber himself with unnecessary material possessions, or for that matter shallow people who "party" pointlessly as a major part of their lifestyle.

The abrupt transition in Andy's dream places the wildness and beautiful desolation of nature in opposition to the emptiness of urban life as soon as the city suddenly becomes depopulated. It is significant that the escape from the city is itself hazardous, though the escape comes full circle, back to the security of his family, where it began. The passing (and incorrect) thought in the dream that Andy's family never missed him means that his dreamt surprise about this belies the warmth of the welcome he hopes to receive, or perhaps knew he would receive. It is from dreams such as this that the return of the prodigal son derives its potent resonances. However, when Andy actually did return, he was not prodigal after all; his family had not even thought of him as prodigal, and they welcomed him back warmly and lovingly. His parents knew he had been trying to "find himself", and in his own way. In reality, Andy was very much loved by his family, who were quietly proud of the way he turned out, and especially of his independence of spirit.

I.   "I was at some queer bazaar. One was taken round narrow rows of excruciatingly boring stalls. I was expecting to be picked up by my sister in her brown Citroen but found my brother instead in our mother's red Audi. We walked out of the dreary street onto a sunny path of grass over blue grit-covered paths. A tiger started to chase us. It sank to a position that we could throw grit in its eyes, and we ran on, it following our scent. We managed to vault over a fence bordering a little stream, but the tiger could not see, so we escaped."

(Mark, age sixteen)

This dream is similar to Andy's transitional homecoming dream with the exception that because Mark was younger, individual family members were incorporated more prominently within it. The bazaar could be equated with Mark's school, or some other social group. Here, the antithesis posed is between consumerist interaction, seen as "boring", and the excitement of survival against the ravages of the natural world. It should be remembered that the oppositional behaviour of eccentrics is not a defect, but rather the consequence of their diverse wills, of them being themselves and making different lifestyle choices. They strive to be faithful to their personally individuating forms of eccentricity.

It should be remembered that many dream images derive from being parts of our true inner selves, and the truths contained in dreams can also involve perceptions about other people. These perceptions may have only been hinted at or rapidly intuited from a specific feeling that may have been doubted, or rationalized, and then passed over, before the mind could properly work out what had been perceived. Learning from such dreams may only come later.

The tiger in this dream may represent his parents' ambitions for Mark, which had the effect of making him feel pressurised. Alternatively, the tiger might really symbolize his fears about growing up and having to be more independent than he wished to be. That the tiger is halted at the stream is related to the superstition about witches not being able to cross water. That Mark felt that he wanted to meet his older sister meant that he had faith in his sister's powers to protect him. His wish was to be looked after by her. The same might also apply to his mother, as represented by his older brother driving his mother's Audi. That there is a similarity between the words "Audi" and "audition" or "auditory" may mean that Mark felt that his mother had not really been listening to him, and he wanted her to hear him better. Because he was thrown into his dreamt adventure with his brother, he was compelled to be brave and active, though this might not have been his first preference.

J.   "I was taking a walk with my girlfriend and went past a house where there was a debutante's party. We walked in and joined the party in the garden. It became familiar; I used to live there. I joined the party for a short time and talked to the girls, none of whom I knew.

"Later a vitriolic attack on my attendance at the party appeared in the gossip column of a national conservative magazine. My boss, a robustly sensual woman, found out about the article and was unspeakably pissed off. I was baffled and confused as I had been at the party for only about ten minutes and hardly said anything, and the article was a fabrication. Why had I been attacked? What had I done? Who had I infuriated so much that *The Spectator* would go to the trouble of trashing me?

"Dreams are somewhat illogical but I could not accept this dreamed persecution, and it troubled me in my waking life for about a month. I talked to friends about it and they seemed terribly nonplussed or bored, and yet my dream seemed so 'real' that it seemed to be a part of my life. Even though I was walking around and sentient I wanted to know what had gone wrong. This dream worried me that it might be prophetic. Needless to say it hasn't been. Although this happened ten years ago, I can still recall the shock it caused me."

(Justin, age thirty-seven)

This dream looks backward to past guilt and forward to possible future shocks. The spur for the dream could have been a commonplace worry, for instance, that people may not be seeing Justin as the nice person he is. This is shown by his incomprehension that strangers could malign him. He is insecure; this gives him a strong need to be liked, and both result in his not being able to take criticism easily, especially if he feels it is undeserved. This is a dream composed of vague guilt and out-of-character paranoia. It is basically healthy. Perhaps he has made a minor mistake in the past, for instance, speaking curtly to a colleague, neglecting to do something, or being disrespectful to his parents. The statement, "I used to live there", gives this away. This probably equates with his parental home. Whatever the real source of guilt was, it has probably been buried deeply in his subconscious mind, and because of this it has been blown out of proportion in the dream. Whatever Justin may have done, he has been ashamed to admit to it, and his mind has come to deny that whatever it was had ever happened.

Other sides of an individual's nature are sometimes revealed in dreams. The contradiction here is that, while Justin acknowledges the illogicality of dreams, thereby projecting an image of himself as a rational man, he also demonstrates perfectly normal feelings of insecurity. This led him to take a single dream seriously and to believe, out of superstitious thinking, that a dream might be somehow prophetic. The repressed wish that energises this dream may be that Justin wanted somehow to outrage his boss, noted for being "a robustly sensual woman" and not a "girl" (as was seen at the party earlier), or at least gain her attention. Preferably, he would secretly have wanted to do this in an especially scandalous sexual manner, believing that this might violate her sensibilities more than anything else, and would thereby precipitate her ire. An Englishman abroad, playing the requisite role of the perfect gentleman in a conformist setting, he was thankfully constrained from acting on these natural subconscious wishes.

K.   "Since Last December, I have had *three* dreams, the significance of which was immediately apparent. There was no need for any attempts to try to work them out. Although the dreams attempted to camouflage what they meant, the meanings were clear. Needless to say the dreams concerned my mother, which comes as no surprise. They didn't reveal to me anything that I already didn't know, but it did demonstrate how our heartfelt emotions had been buried beneath the surface. It was no doubt good that they came out in this way, as a part of my healing journey. The most recent of these dreams was particularly revealing, although the revelation was also about something that I was already aware of. My subconscious was obviously clearing away all the pain. In any event, I fully understand what was going on. It is simply that for me, to have three visual dreams in such a short period of time is truly significant."

(Henrietta, age fifty-one)

This account of three visual and explicit dreams comes from one of the eccentric informants who had comparatively few memorable or visually vivid dreams in her life. These dreams occurred approximately one year after the death of Henrietta's mother. She had been her mother's carer for many years. Henrietta's report is included here to show that when vivid dreams do recur closely together in time, and on each occasion bring out strong emotion, they can have beneficial cathartic effects in the long term process of grieving.

L.   "I have 'serial' dreams in which I dream that I am dreaming, and I can actually threaten others in the dream to kill them by waking up. In a subsequent more numinous dream, I asked these others what they did when I was awake. One of them told me that he was also dreaming and gave me his telephone number to ring after I'd wakened up, but I couldn't remember it."

(Simpson, age forty-one)

Recurring dreams are likely to indicate longstanding preoccupations and emotional conflicts. Simpson suffered from frustrated anger during certain times in his life, and yet he is given extraordinary powers when dreaming. He is sensitive and soft-hearted when awake, and paradoxically gives free rein to destructive urges when asleep. On the surface, this dream shows possibly manipulative tendencies. Generally, dreams with content like this are viewed as overtly omnipotent. That this man's dreams have become "serial" shows that the wish for power, as shown in dreams, can become positively reinforcing. However, these specific dreams were not based primarily on wish-fulfilment, conscious or subconscious. Simpson subsequently admitted to having felt aghast when he awoke after the first dream in the series. A very mild-mannered and gentle person, throughout his life he would be considered to be highly unlikely to hurt anyone in any way. He did, though, have some real contradictions of a different type; these were to do with his creative conceptual art work.

The narrative thread between the connected dreams also indicates that Simpson may be interested in meeting people who are more like himself, people with similar interests in contemporary art. His frustration at forgetting the telephone number is a reminder that the idea of possessing absolute power is flawed at its heart. The power motive, in the course of his dreams, becomes translated from one of threatening aggressiveness to intellectual and social curiosity. Curiosity, of course, has other aspects to it than simply a wish for, or an expression of, undeveloped omnipotent or voyeuristic fantasies.

As it transpired, I discovered that eccentrics were omnivorously curious.

Into unlimited curiosity

There is an unambiguous positive relationship between creativity and curiosity [84, 85, 86, 87, 88]. Eccentrics not only arouse the curiosity of other people, they themselves are exceptionally curious. For many, this is their motivating raison d'être, and can become more important than their desire to be different. Again, they are at variance with cultural norms. In our culture, the expression of curiosity is often strongly inhibited. The main reasons for this are to do with fears of giving offence to others, social embarrassment, or of appearing to be ignorant.

These inhibitions are learned fairly early. Nursery school children with high drives for curiosity are often seen as both initiators of activity and as discipline problems. Curious children are ineluctably resilient in the face of some teachers' compulsions for control. Undeterred after six or seven years of this, those with high curiosity are usually recognised for it, and for their oft-associated greater creativity and flexibility. Visiting educational psychologists eventually come to say kinder things about them, though not at first. For example, one such professional has commented, "Some high-curiosity boys could not channel their exploratory drives in a way that could promote full participation in school learning situations." The way this statement is posed belies the underlying framework of premises. It would be more constructive to ask how the learning situations could be restructured to meet the needs of these children, who quite clearly want to learn new things.

As it is, after age ten, for many children of average intelligence, there is a slow waning in intellectual curiosity throughout adolescence [89].

The powerful drives for curiosity can be modified within the learning environment for the benefit of the child, or to his detriment. This is the stuff of real learning, learning that is potentiated and activated by and for the individual.

Many years of mainly detrimental declines in curiosity must surely affect the differential development of young minds. The secret of the brain's phenomenal plasticity during development, and for the equally astounding flexibility that accompanies it, lies in the extremely complicated ways that brain cells, also called neurons --- eighty-six billion of them --- are linked together complexly.

For many years it was thought that the architectural structure of the brain, down to the position of its neurons, and the way they are interconnected, were laid down and preordained by a person's hereditary make-up, in other words, his or her genes. The many brain cells each may have many extended branches, or dendrites, branching arms of nerve endings fanning out in three dimensions, connecting to numerous other brain cells; between ten thousand and one hundred thousand closely packed brain cells make contact with any one particular brain cell. The dendrites pick up electro-biochemical signals from fibres coming into them and carry it to the brain cell, which then processes it and sends it out. Every one of these nerve cell dendrite complexes is a miniature information transmission and collating system.

Certain classes of dendrites of the cerebral cortex and cerebellum contain small projections referred to as spines or appendages. These spines increase the receptive properties of the dendrites to isolate specific signals between neurons. Increased neural activity at the spines increases their size and conduction, and this plays a role in learning and the laying down of memories, as well as in sensory development. There are approximately two hundred thousand of these spines per brain cell. The dendrites appear to be capable of plastic changes during development and in adult life. In particular, the changes in the dendritic spines are thought to underlie this plasticity. Neurons and larger groups of neurons connect to form neural networks, the shape of activity between the groupings of brain cells continuously shifting from second to second, depending on what one is doing or thinking. The total number of different permutations is almost limitless.

The circuitry of the human brain, in its moment-to-moment flexibility, is surely one of the wonders of nature. The most powerful of electronic supercomputers will still struggle to compete against the performance capabilities of the human brain. For example, early in 2014, researchers used the K supercomputer in Japan, at the time the fourth most powerful in the world, to simulate human brain activity. The K supercomputer still took forty minutes to crunch the data equivalent to just one second of human brain activity.

Human beings have around 27,000 total genes on their twenty-three pairs of chromosomes found inside the nucleus of every cell in the body. Overall, the human brain's extremely large numbers of neurons, dendrites and multiple interconnections comprise far too complicated a system to be dictated by, or fixed by, this relatively smaller number of genes. For every single movement, activity, perception, thought, image, memory, dream, word and group of words there are a multitude of possible configurations of brain cell assemblies thrown into dynamic electro-biochemical movement, ever-changing from second to second. Also, the content and quality of an individual's experiences from the moment of birth onwards influences how well his brain cells interconnect.

However, several studies have linked gene variations that are associated with the neurotransmitter dopamine to both eccentricity and creativity. In 2009, the Hungarian researcher Szebolcs Keri found that highly creative achievers were more likely to have a variant of the neuregulin 1 gene previously associated with schizophrenia [90]. Keri wrote, "Intriguingly, the highest creative achievements and creative thinking scores were found in people who carried the T/T genotype, which was previously shown to be related to psychosis and altered prefrontal activation."

Intriguingly, the eccentrics in my study also tended to attribute hereditary factors as the source of their creativity more frequently than other factors. This was likely to be due to the fact that the majority of the eccentric participants were from the upper middle class, and were brought up to believe that their good fortune was due, at least in part, to "good breeding". (See Table 21.)

Table 21: Attributions of source of individual creativity in eccentrics

	Heredity	Parent's influence	Education	Experience	Effort
Females	43%	13%	7%	4%	7%
Males	41%	7%	7%	15%	6%

An unimaginably complex network of overlapping connections is built up during growth, maturation and throughout most of one's life. It is my contention that the brain learns not by having been laboriously pre-programmed, but by accepting a variety of experiences and by adapting reactions to them by, in effect, trying out different connections within and between the neural networks, until it finds the best ones, the best fits.

Psychologists often speak of such forms of curiosity-related exploratory behaviours as being carried on "for their own sake"; this must mean that they are carried on for the sake of their rewarding associations and consequences.

The sudden illuminating flash of insight can be stripped bare of some of its mystique, but little of its marvel. It is accomplished by semi-automatic processes in the brain; essentially these are maintained by practice and its positive effects, work that is fun for the developing individual, active work, interactive work, conversation, dialogue and debate, and more work. In terms of cerebral economics and energy, the law really is --- nothing in, nothing out.

Curiosity is fundamental to the nurturing of creativity and to the genesis of true eccentricity. Three components of curiosity have been distinguished: general curiosity, venturesomeness, and seeking after experience [91]. This may help to explain a previously baffling finding, that made by the work of Hartmann and Havik, who found a significant relationship between curiosity and exhibitionism on certain psychological tests [92]. This may have happened, as it did with our eccentrics, because some curious people desire so much to "find out" that they actively experiment in the real world, they test out their ideas on others, in front of others, deliberately, and not merely to get their attention, but to obtain their reactions. However, the eccentrics I studied were, by and large, *not* exhibitionistic in terms of their personality, that is, generally self-dramatizing, over-emotional, histrionic and/or attention-seeking.

The novelty of what one produces has been shown to be positively correlated to the degree of complexity of thought one can sustain, and to the readiness to explore not only the outer world but what is going on internally, in ideas and in psychological cognitive analysis. Creative people tend to prefer novel associations; this has been shown with undergraduate research subjects [93]. Novel associations were also quite obviously preferred, and acted upon, by the eccentric people in the present study.

Curiosity can best be described as a general condition analogous to the need to seek out new experiences or to extend one's knowledge into the unknown. This is eloquently attested to by the eccentrics that I met in the course of this study. Interestingly, although the male eccentrics were better at describing their creativity and curiosity succinctly, it was the female eccentrics in our study who objectively were significantly more curious than the males (Univariate F-ratio between the genders = 7.00, $p < 0.01$).

"I believe that a day is wasted if I haven't learnt something --- however unimportant that it is. I've always believed that one has to be prepared to search so that one may learn in order to find out more and better understand. This may sound obvious, but because one has access to the workings of one's own mind, one is also amenable to self-analysis of this new learning."

(Sylvan, age seventy-four)

"If a thing works, I like to know how exactly. I have taken things to bits to see how they work. If I want to find out I go out of my way to find out."

(Bob, age thirty-seven)

"I want to know about everything. I am curious, which also makes me a mine of trivia and useless information. I read a lot, and I listen carefully and continually. Not knowing about something or someone frustrates me. I consume gossip and scandal."

(Julian, age thirty-seven)

"I want to know how everything works. I want to know how my body works, how your body works, and why that leaf becomes green and how the hell that seed produces that flower, or a human being and I are able to argue with, blimey, God --- I have to say, He has made a right cock-up of it!"

(John, age sixty-seven)

"Just about everything arouses my curiosity. It's been a real problem: it's hard to specialise and get something accomplished when *everything* is equally very interesting."

(Eddie, age thirty-eight)

"My inquisitiveness is infinite and as uncontrollable as the curiosity of the domestic kitten. For me, looking into matters as I want is a part of breaking the circuit of control society's higher echelons tries to inflict on those lower down the pecking order."

(Tony, age fifty-five)

"When I was younger, I became aware of how much of our living patterns are conditioned by other people's ideas. That raised any number of disquieting possibilities in my young and still forming mind as I began the seemingly endless process of growing up. I now recognise that there are limits to knowledge, that there are some things that will never be known with certainty or in absolute terms. I am hungry for new information, on what I consider relevant channels. Certain subjects are gently screened out, but nothing is ever censored. The former is necessary if I am not to be overwhelmed by sensory overload. Practical experience is the only real answer to life's puzzles, whether that be about how to grow better Brussels sprouts or how to undertake real explorations into inner dimensions."

(Andy, age twenty-four)

How does eccentric creativity go wrong?

As far as the creative industries of the United Kingdom are concerned, a lot certainly has been going well. The annual value of the creative industries to the United Kingdom economy in 2014 has been put at £71.4 billion [94]. In fact, at least one in twelve new jobs in the UK are now found within the creative economy. It is unknown how many people already in such employment possess eccentric traits and behaviours.

If, as they are, eccentrics are intellectually gifted in many ways --- fervently curious, full of vivid visual imagery while awake and asleep, possessing an above average verbal intelligence quotient (about IQ 115 to 120) --- how can it be that some of their projects misfire? [95]

The answer lies within the very nature of the creative process. It is some of the specific components of the creative process that can go awry, injecting failure into some of the eccentrics' work, failures every bit as spectacular as their known successes. First of all, they are endowed with high fluency: they have very many ideas. However, this causes problems because the ideas themselves, provable and unprovable alike, those far out and others not so unorthodox, are equally highly valued by the eccentric creators. So too are the various methods and processes by which they achieved their ideas.

The eccentrics' embarrassment of riches is the source of a related problem --- that of not knowing which idea to select, to focus on and devote one's energies toward comprehending better. Often, as might be expected from intellectual mavericks, the very worst ideas are chosen, and not only the ones that are counter-intuitive, but also the ones that others would think implausible if not impossible, for example, human levitation, perpetual motion, and squaring the circle. These problems in other contexts might suggest, in neuropsychological terms, a degree of cognitive dyscontrol. This might feature as an ongoing or intermittent deficit in a range of abilities in weighing up evidence, intuitions and pre-existing beliefs. Such problems have been implicated in a number of intellectual operations, for example, decision-making, error detection, tolerance for incongruity, and dealing with internal conflicts. In a culture saturated with sensory and digital distractions, such problems also might have increasingly detrimental effects.

Once having arrived at a subject choice, and posited one or two unorthodox theories about it, the typical eccentric would-be innovator cannot be dissuaded from persistently and stubbornly pursuing that line of enquiry. The curiosity programme is switched on. An eccentric will go to great lengths to obtain information to satisfy his curiosity. He will seek out every news report, book and magazine article about it. If possible he will initiate experiments of his own. He will write to or consult eminent professors, preferring those who have enunciated controversial views. If any of the experts disagree with him, he will still not be dissuaded from following his particular tack. To the contrary, the more sceptical the response is, the more tenaciously will the eccentric defend his ideas and become engaged in the pursuit of proving his critics wrong, redoubling his efforts, and go on working on his project, sometimes for years. In this way, the eccentric can be seen to be far from flexible. Clearly, without a flexible approach either towards discarding an incorrect idea, or changing it, further difficulties can be precipitated. This can be contrasted to adaptive flexibility, in which an individual willingly will make significant changes in strategy, approach, interpretation, or possible solutions.

An eccentric might take a wrong notion several steps further, usually fairly early on. He might over-elaborate his idea prematurely. He might think how it could work in other situations or environments, and work out new applications for his still untried and untested idea.

Some eccentrics stumble upon an idea that others would reject as too obscure or different, then delve into it so deeply that, try as they might to communicate their enthusiasm, everyone is left incredulous. If an eccentric individual does develop an idea into a viable proposition, he or she may communicate it to others in very quirky ways that may be ineffective or indecipherable. For example, there is the case, not apocryphal, of the university mathematician who invented a new and significant equation that he believed would revolutionise the practice of statistics. Upon being invited to present his theory and formulae to a conference of his professional association, he spent the first three-quarters of his lecture describing in great detail how his specific make and model of programmable electronic calculator was the best for doing the work he had done. The time remaining was insufficient for presenting his thesis intelligibly. Follow-up enquiries were more digressive and were belaboured with finicky details, so that even his more patient colleagues came away frustrated, and eventually desisted from enquiring further. This shows how thought and language difficulties can interfere with the communication of creative ideas. On the basis of the present study, the most problematic of these for eccentrics, and probably more so for non-eccentrics, was language derailment, particularly those in which associative threads became unravelled.

Another major stumbling block in the path of eccentric people with many ideas is that some of them can never bring any of their ideas to fruition. Among the eccentrics, there were quite a few who specialised in concocting ideas and selling them as incomplete ideas, or in developing book titles and unedited synopses, or only partially finishing an art work or literary venture. There was always a work in progress, daydreams of what success would bring, and future projects to initiate, "If only there were enough hours in the day"

All of the above happens in scientific work too, and these gifts and attendant problems are so intriguing that the next chapter will be devoted to them.

Chapter 9. Into the Vortex
(Eccentricity and Deviant Science)

"Never refuse to see what you do not want to see or what might go against your own cherished hypothesis or against the view of authorities. Here are just the clues to follow up . . . The thing you cannot get a pigeon-hole for is the finger-post showing the way to discovery."

Sir Patrick Manson (1844 – 1922)

Some creative eccentrics become scientists, and some of these become so-called deviant scientists. The belief in the supposed "fine line" between genius and psychiatric disorder still exists partly because people are increasingly uncertain about the difference between good science and bad science. This may be so because scientists in each of these groups are concerned with the creation of new worlds of ideas, different in important respects to those that had gone before. The positive long-term effects can be quite astounding. Isaac Newton, for example, by inventing calculus, had absolutely no idea that he would be causing reverberations in the British economy that would last for more than three hundred years.

This quest for the masterstroke, one defining characteristic of genius, shows itself in an inspiring stubborn streak, a resistance in the face of overwhelming opposition. Is the eccentric scientist's steadfast conviction of the truth of his creative vision any different from the perceptions, thoughts and convictions of the conventional scientist?

The science community makes and remakes its own history at every opportunity. The creativity of deviant science begins in a state of imaginative muddled suspense. One is almost compelled to reverse August Comte's fundamental sociological principle to read, "Progress is nothing but the development of disorder". Normal science tends to reject that which is vague or indeterminate, since it deceives itself about what counts as real knowledge, and because it has not sufficiently considered what the conditions for neutral objectivity could be like. However much we try to be objective, we are all subjective creatures. Personal factors cannot be completely eliminated from scientific endeavours. The study of "deviant" (read "eccentric") scientists puts the lie to Karl Marx's assertion that humanity poses only problems that it can solve.

Not all deviant sciences are founded on prejudiced beliefs about what counts as a good theory or valid evidence. Nor are all "normal" sciences clear of prejudiced beliefs and other longstanding systematic biases.

There are other uncertainties. Not all deviant sciences are founded on prejudiced beliefs about what counts as a good theory or valid evidence. Nor are all "normal" sciences clear of prejudiced beliefs and other longstanding systematic biases, though they are a part of an ultimately self-correcting process. However, not everyone shares the ideals concerning the beauty and elegance of the scientific method. There is deep distrust not only about the objectives of scientists, but also about their specific procedures, the risks (to themselves and all of us) they are willing to undertake, their underlying belief in the triumphal march of Progress, and how their findings will be used and abused. These doubts are at the heart of every environmental protest, and were every bit as abiding before major disasters like those of Three Mile Island, Chernobyl and Fukushima. Doubt, if not realistic fear, underlies the hard-fought emergence of environmental pressure groups and Green political parties. It is no longer confined to the politics of groups of cognoscenti. The state-orchestrated arrest of thirty *Greenpeace* activists by Russian Special Forces and subsequent charges of piracy were actions with more than emblematic portent.

Many people have become persuaded by anti-science ideas. It is understandable that, faced with science's esoterica, people have nostalgic yearnings for simpler verities. However dispassionate it is, science is seldom generally sympathetic to retrenchment, though it successfully has withstood numerous challenges to its basic assumptions. Radical theories have prompted a closer examination of how new knowledge comes about. Very few of science's notions have come away unscathed from its own process of continuous scrutiny and re-evaluation.

Science does not progress in a smooth linear fashion. If science is free to question how innovatory ideas come about, to be fair the sources of rejected knowledge should also be given some attention. Scientists often simply ignore work with which they disagree, rather than openly challenging it [1]. Neglected work, later rehabilitated in the light of new facts or theories, lends weight to this. One example of this is the gardening hobbyist Gregor Mendel's demonstration of the inheritance of certain traits in pea plants, thus laying the groundwork for the science of genetics. Another case in point is Alfred Wegener's ideas about continental drift; unfortunately, before the advent of the idea of plate tectonics, no one at the time could explain how continental drift worked, and Wegener's writings appeared unconvincing. Such instances encourage myriads of theorists within and outside of science's broad church.

In many sciences, dissent is discouraged, and deference is the norm. Deviant science within the body of institutional science is almost a contradiction in terms. Eccentric and deviant scientists often work as loners, and therefore are less affected by social pressures. If they have not already been ostracised by their scientific colleagues, the prospect of it has little effect.

Error is a significant characteristic of much scientific judgement. The red herring, wrong turning, and blind alley are not uncommon. A false theory may underlie a technological application that comes to be regarded by society as successful. The success of the application does not of itself prove the truth of the theory that led up to it [2].

In analysing the roots of error, like many other judgemental operations, one cannot be wholly objective, however one wishes to be. This immediately raises important implications for the presentation and interpretation of new information and knowledge. The situational context and one's own personal intuitive theories colour interpretations. If, as the philosopher of science Karl Popper [3] believed, our theories about the world may at least in part be "free creations of our own minds, the result of an almost poetic intuition", must scientists adopt a special caution so strong that they take no risks? The answer is, of course, both yes and no --- it depends on the particular stage of advancement, the particular field, and the particular theory.

If the past is any guide in this matter, then clearly, erroneous ways of searching should be encouraged. While many of the early Fellows of the Royal Society were making extraordinary strides, they were also doing some work so without theory or purpose --- other than observation for its own sake --- that it could well be taken as a caricature of science. It demonstrates, if nothing else, how limiting the extreme empiricist position can be. Take, for example, this excerpt from some of their early experimental notes:
1616, July 24

"A circle was made with a powder of unicorn's horn, and a spider set in the middle of it, but it immediately ran out several times repeated. The spider once made some stay upon the powder." [4]

At the conceptual level, Isaac Newton devoted a major portion of his scholarly research to retrieve ancient knowledge from alchemical and other mystical traditions [5]. He believed himself to be recording God's edicts about the great universal laws of celestial gravitation. It has never been easy to separate deviant science from deviant religion, nor from beliefs in the paranormal.

The history of science is peppered with examples of errors fuelling truth. Robert Chambers, a successful Edinburgh publisher, in 1844 anonymously authored a book entitled *Vestiges of the Natural History of Creation*. It applied a law of constant progress and development to geology, to the plant and animal kingdoms, and to the human species. In the latter area, he drew on phrenology, the mistaken notion that mental characteristics could be discerned from the bumps and contours of the human skull. Like Mary Wollstonecraft Shelley's novel *Frankenstein*, Chambers also touched on the idea that galvanic electricity has life-creating powers. Charles Darwin did not regard Chambers as his intellectual forerunner, though *Vestiges* spurred Alfred Russell Wallace to undertake a series of expeditions to seek information on evolution. Wallace was also an enthusiastic follower of mesmerism (hypnotism), phrenology, and their hybrid version, phreno-mesmerism, and later was persuaded by spiritualist beliefs and practices.

It appears that it has always been the case that there is an intimate relationship between pseudo-science and reputable science, with much crossing over of the boundaries and the probable cross-fertilisation of ideas. This proximity, which also causes reputable scientists to react defensively and distance themselves from deviant science, has engendered a degree of circumspection. By way of describing what lay behind this tendency, Blaise Pascal put it thusly, "Imagination --- it is this dominant part in man, this mistress of error and falsity, and more often a trickster than not. . . . But being most often false, it gives no mark of its quality, marking the true and the false with the same nature."

The above movements of thought are characteristic of many processes of discovery. Error functions as a guide to discovery, or as Francis Bacon wrote in his *Novum Organum*, "Truth emerges more readily from error than from confusion". The misapplication of a theory based on a partial misapprehension of what the true situation is guides us to the use of another theory. The transition from an erroneous application of an incorrect theory to its eventual displacement is part of what gives continuity to the acquisition of new learning.

Concepts are often displaced into other situations out of erroneous attempts to apply them to similar instances. Cases in point are the development of the wave theory of light derived from wave theories of liquids and sounds, and the development of theories of atomic structure from earlier theories based on the structure of the solar system. In their time, these theories were not dysfunctional --- they were transitional efforts to arrive at a presumed version of reality. Science is full of such examples, and deviant scientists use these as circumstantial arguments in defence of their ways of working.

Seeking patterns and order in fields of apparent disorder is what many scientists do as a matter of course in their thinking and in their more applied work. The study of science has repeatedly shown that it is the data that do not fit, the provocative questions, and the exceptions to the rules, that signal potential breakthroughs about the nature of the world. Scientists sometimes actively seek out incongruities, searching for resolution or novel understandings of why these do not fit with current paradigms or models. Another approach to science can be seen as the search for misfit data. Experimental method can be regarded as only one way of achieving these attempts, one way among many. The implication of this is that to obtain discordant facts, and information about differences, variability rather than homogeneity within each discipline perhaps needs to be increased.

It turns out that one of the crucial features of true discovery is the ability to switch away from the objective of testing a preferred hypothesis to one of investigating and working to understand an unexpected finding. Over fifty per cent of the new findings observed by Kevin Dunbar in four science laboratories started out as wholly unforeseen [6]. He found that the teams of advanced specialist biologists in question were prepared for the above-noted kinds of eventualities; they had previously worked out a number of significant investigative strategies for dealing with unexpected findings. In the designs of their experiments, they had created opportunities in which such events could occur. They held to the implicit idea that the source of going astray was confirmation bias that arose from being tied to a single hypothesis, and that this diminished or blocked creativity. It had also been agreed that only after repeated demonstrations of the unanticipated finding would they change course and try to conceive new explanations by utilizing more remote analogies, or alternative images, that aided the communication of a novel theory. The big idea was that many different possible analogies or images are involved in working toward a genuine scientific discovery.

Some scientific scholars may look for ideas that are of a "hybrid" or "crossover" nature, attempting to integrate theories and concepts from outside their own particular discipline [7]. Sometimes this generates a fertile source of new knowledge. Deviant sciences sometimes show more variation than do many orthodox sciences, and can generate data and ideas that may turn out, sooner or later, to be useful. Though this kind of marginality can favour innovation, until it is shown to reap such benefits, the status of their originators may be seen as incongruent or questionable.

The philosopher Paul Feyerabend has argued that no single approach to the pursuit of knowledge should be allowed to dominate all others [8]. Rival or seemingly incompatible theoretical approaches should be encouraged, and on the point of methodology, a variety of different approaches should be welcomed. His position was that strict adherence to methodological rules generally does not contribute to success in science. Perhaps within traditional ways of doing science, many workaday scientists may be blinding themselves to other possibilities and not considering what science itself might become if it began to incorporate more diverse ways of conceiving itself.

Feyerabend gave examples of episodes when scientific dogma was overturned, and subsequently regarded as indisputable instances of gaining new knowledge, for example, the Copernican revolution. At such turning points, the commonly prescriptive rules of science were clearly violated by the bringers of the better theories. Feyerabend's philosophy also encouraged tolerance for deviant science, and a full and frank discourse between conventional and unconventional scientists. Conventional science can become used as a repressing ideology, even though parts of it may have begun life as liberating movements. Believing unreservedly in an accepted though soon-to-be deflated theory is seen as akin to accepting a cherished prejudice.

Deviant scientists are often aggrieved at the way a hurried rejection of their pet ideas by a few orthodox scientists can produce a consensus in which the deviant ideas are roundly rejected by those who have little first-hand knowledge of them. On the other hand, deviant scientists should openly allow and help conventional scientists to attempt to test and replicate their findings by using whatever may be considered decent replicable experimental methods.

There ought to be an absolute and free interchange of ideas. The censor's red pencil can have as black an effect on scientific ideas as on political ones, though some limitations and restrictions can throw up interesting alternatives. In science, ideas cannot, should not, be censored. According to Professor Warren Schmaus of the Illinois Institute of Technology, resistance to the formation of new ideas, whatever the source, is truly bad for science [9].

Scientific work normally takes place within an institution and within a particular discipline. Institutions may not always satisfactorily share the same goals as some of their individual members. Each discipline has its own paradigmatic fields within which meaningful forms of enquiry are sanctioned. These sanctioned paradigms are limiting, as Thomas Kuhn pointed out in his book *The Structure of Scientific Revolutions* [10]. These, he wrote, contain "rules that limit both the nature of acceptable solutions and the steps by which they are obtained."

Judgement is situated in the particular context of goal-orientated research activity. The choice of questions that can be asked, and the problems allowed to be posed, reflect the dominant concerns of the time of those scientists who are within a definite social matrix, bounded by social and agreed norms [11]. The ideas of those outside this system should be especially valued for their independence, their complementary orientations, and distance from conformist influences. However, deviant scientists stretch and strain and stress the tolerance and forbearance that may be granted to them. For instance, for the UFO buff, good data are those that have enough concordant points of incredibility to allow comparison between apparently similar incidents. Practices such as this, using only circumstantial instances and a little imagination, because they are adjudged to be "not science", need to be understood psychologically in terms of reasons, causes, and the needs that they meet.

Many deviant sciences flourish because they produce ideas and quasi-experiments that are rewarding and appreciated by those within their various counter-cultures and splinter groups. These benefits are such that when adherents are faced with contrary evidence, their beliefs do not collapse like a house of cards. Facing ridicule for their "crackpot" ideas, they simply change some of their claims to counter one strand of the negative evidence against them. A typical theoretical edifice attempts to explain wide-ranging and disparate phenomena in an interesting manner. "Interesting" often means putting forward a theory that takes a quantum leap into initial strangeness when compared with an accepted theory. One cannot always see the steps in between. The deviant theory sometimes attempts to be at least as comprehensive as its predecessor, and cannot be disproved by contradictory events or experiments because of the nature of its speculative tenets. Some such theorists would abjure normal criteria of evidence or proof by claiming that special circumstances prevailed.

All the above is maintained because it places the true believer, seemingly enlightened or in awe of further notable mysteries, in a more privileged position when compared with that held before receiving his revelation or conversion. More active committed involvement generally requires that the deviant belief can offer solutions to current problems [12], though not necessarily the proximal problem dealt with directly by the belief. For instance, prejudicial racist attitudes have tended to gain strong support in areas with conflict between culturally discrete groups. These beliefs do nothing to reduce the conflict, though they do (wrongly) explain or confirm the believers' convictions that external forces adversely affect or control their lives, causing their failures and disappointments. A leader's scare-mongering rhetoric directed against a minority group legitimises a range of noxious behaviours that previously would have been considered not only deviant, but also deeply abhorrent. Discontents about unemployment and occupational competition are channelled and simplified into racist abuse. This does absolutely nothing to solve the underlying problems, and usually makes them worse.

Theories are the nucleus of deviant and eccentric science. Eccentric science is theory-led. Eccentrics draw pleasure from kicking around ideas that venture beyond what is deemed plausible, often disregarding less exceptional and yet more elegant explanations. To their way of thinking, innovatory ideas need not be consistent with more established or accepted theories. The theories they produce result from an ongoing process in which no assumptions are regarded as sacrosanct.

Theories that generally succeed are those that initially generate problems that no one had previously anticipated, and then go on to explain or predict novel and unanticipated events. This is a kind of predictive validation.

The acid test of a theory is not necessarily its predictive power. It must first and foremost be meaningful, as should the experiments derived from it. Anything that is not immediately intelligible requires explanation.

A good theory should encapsulate a possible mechanism. At all stages of related investigations there should be conscious attempts to formulate alternate working hypotheses, to think of other mechanisms that might reasonably account for the observations, and possibly to structure the information in ways that make comparisons possible. The phenomena that form the basis of the theory should have a meaningful relationship to existing knowledge, though this is by no means necessary. The outcome of derived experiments should also have some systematic format, have a reasonable degree of reliability, and be able to be repeated in similar, and sometimes different, conditions.

Deviant theories, for example those concerning extrasensory perception, psychokinesis, Erich von Daniken's claims that extraterrestrial aliens have influenced human history, or Immanual Velikovsky's ideas about geologically recent planetary catastrophes, did not fulfil the above criteria. However, a lack of viable evidence did not stop many people believing in any of these theories. Many still do. Why is that?

Theories have other functions quite apart from being verifiable or falsifiable. Theories provide intellectual satisfaction, open communication channels, lend themselves to individual enterprise, sensitise people to possibilities almost beyond their ken, challenge ordinary agreed modes of thought, and for some, ultimately affect their social interactions.

Clashes between old and new paradigms are generated and sustained by contrasting social and factional interest groups [13]. Controversies are symptomatic of a divergence of social orientations. Much of science might be seen as falling within the general ambits of ideology, social control, ethics, and politics. Investigations lead to moral choices. The contrasting view is that ideology may make use of science but it has no power to validate or invalidate it. I think that we have to think of an interaction between science and ideology; each feeds upon the other. The elaboration of reality and the establishment of values proceed apace. Facts are relevant within the context of the standards of values supporting them.

For all this, very little is known about the psychology of deviant scientists. Generally speaking, we do know more about conventional scientists. They tend to be less gregarious, more independent-minded, more analytic in their thinking from an earlier age, and prefer to work with ideas and things rather more than with people. Human relations apparently are difficult and uninteresting to many of them. They avoid and are disturbed by complex human emotions, particularly interpersonal aggression [14].

It is my contention that the majority of deviant scientists are eccentrics. They have much in common, and both groups share many of the known characteristics of professional research scientists [15]. Both kinds of scientists are digressive in speech, ideas, and behaviour. The following account is from a highly thought-of, contemplative thinker, a person who admitted to being hard to pigeonhole: "Once I have got a new idea and explored it, I tend to lose interest. A research career for me reflects this. I have come up with a number of interesting ideas. I only follow them a little way. Perhaps I write a brief paper and then I am off. I don't build up a research team on any topic. I have always admired the 'Renaissance

Man'! I like being able to do lots and lots of things a bit but rarely get really deep. For example, I can fence a bit, climb a bit, fly an aeroplane a bit, sketch a bit, talk French a bit, play a recorder a bit. I used to get frustrated and try to *force myself* to concentrate on only one thing at a time. But it isn't me. I was once asked to be Jack-in-the-Green at the Thaxted Morris dances because of my personality!"

(Dr V., age forty-six)

Eccentric scientists are hyper-alert to tangential aspects of problems that others would regard as trivial or unimportant. They search for and postulate significance in things that customarily would not be singled out for investigation. For instance, Professor C. G. Barkla of the University of Edinburgh, who received a Nobel Prize in 1917 for his work on x-ray scattering and polarisation, clung tenaciously to the search for, and belief in, a "J series" of x-ray emissions. He maintained this for over twenty years against a background of informed opinion in physics that his "will o' the wisp" was non-existent. This eventually descended to the level of undergraduate parody ---

"J's a phenomenon known only to the Prof.
On Monday it's working, by Tuesday it's off."

"Prof's looking for kinks and ridges,
Caused by tramcars on The Bridges."

(The Bridges, designated North Bridge and South Bridge, are part of a busy thoroughfare near to where the University's Department of Natural Philosophy was then located).

The J-phenomenon was never found, or proven to exist, and fell into obscurity.

Whatever specific subject comes to be isolated for further analysis by eccentric scientists leads on rapidly to sequences of seemingly disconnected ideas and experiments. Here is a further account from one of my eccentric informants: "For years I have agonised over some phenomena which were aberrations. Allow me to explain. After patenting my orbital engine, I became interested in the possibility of shifting a ten-tonne cement hulled boat over rough ground by manpower and ingenuity. I developed a set of walking feet and horizontal jacks which were secured to the boat, and by turning a cam the boat progressed slowly to the water. It would have worked, but the owner of the boat came into some money and the need evaporated.

"By this time, I was expert in turning my novel circular cams. It stimulated me to ask, 'How fast must the cams be turned before the boat would no longer have time to follow the cam and would in fact be hovering?' I took a guess from a creature in nature that can hover. Namely the blowfly. I found its pitch to be about 64 hertz. I recorded this sound as I released a fly trapped in a cobweb and at the point where he became airborne, and nowhere else, some shot in a horizontal speaker also lifted off the cone, as did some talcum powder on a paper sheet placed over the speaker. I concluded that, at 64 hertz, mass detaches itself from the force of gravity. Now 64 hertz is near enough to C two octaves below middle C. It is the same sound that the Buddhist monk chants his *OM MANE PADME HUM*. It is the sound of the bee and a drowsy summer's day.

"At this point orthodox science screamed with ribald laughter. My ire was up and I set out to solve the riddle. Could this have been no more than resonance in the system? I was referred to a series of science 'nuts'. Characters who talked of sine waves and resonance, and then bird watchers and porpoise fanciers. Incidentally, the 'nuts' are very close to the truth, however narrow were their visual fields. I have surely been put on the Establishment's 'Don't read, just dump' list. I have not decided what to call this work, but a colleague has trimmed it down to 'The Philosophy of Tetrahedronalism and its Tetradental Metaphysics and Metamathematics'. After reading it you will be ready to 'Do the right thing'. You have been warned."

(H. L., age forty-one)

Were this form of thinking not couched in the context of scientific terminology, it would be considered typically schizotypal. Or, it wouldn't be out of the question to consider the above and some of the following descriptions of scientific work as science-based delusions. Just as there are religious and paranormal delusions, it might be the case that scientific thought could also give rise to delusory ideas, for example those that seem bizarre and are considered to be implausible. Other criteria of formal thought disorder might clearly personalized styles of reasoning and overly fluid conceptual boundaries.

However, in scientific work, creative thinking demands the seeing of things not seen previously, in ways not previously imagined. This almost necessitates jumping off from "normal" positions, and taking risks by freely departing from so-called consensual reality. This could place the searcher's sense of self, indeed his mental stability, in some jeopardy, although the revisionist psychoanalyst Erich Fromm has written, "Consensual validation as such has no bearing whatsoever on mental health."

Professional and eccentric scientists are not content only to explore novel lines of research, going into uncharted terrain, but also receive a Puckish delight by doing so using original methods: "It is impossible to understand your personal originality in everyday life before you have realized what are the best ways for you to express it. I'm not too keen to rake over somebody else's failures like a scavenger, nor am I awfully cheerful about using a conventional method, unless it is so outmoded that others have overlooked how it could be used in a new, more interesting way. I deliberately try to avoid ground that's been covered by any of my colleagues. As soon as I recognise a paradigm, when it's not a challenge, when I see it won't have a future impact, I switch off or go to sleep. To my way of looking at things, it is not worth my while to pursue anything derivative, or to cover topics that seem to have no significant implications for the future. If I can't see a whole research programme stretching out into untouched virgin territory, I still worry it like an old bone for details, but usually it hits my 'reject' slot.

"When it comes to calling the shots, that's me . . . I do it. I value my autonomy. I assume that if the standard way would have paid off, some clever postdoctoral research fellow would have accomplished it. At the stage of deciding how to do something, my literature searches are omnivorous, but two-thirds of the material gets discarded. Only something that sparks something in me gets looked into more carefully.

"There are things that can come to be known that are, at first, purely speculative. Those are the things that I seek, that I intend to apply all my knowledge resources and experience towards understanding better. A good question leads on to other questions.

"I'm not a believer, fortunately, though sometimes I catch myself harking back to ideas inculcated when I was too young to know any better. Early on in my scientific life I disabused myself of the need to believe in the many fictions and other old wives' tales that passed for accepted knowledge. I'm a bit of a futurist. Fretting over the past isn't for me. Historical dalliances, living in the past, is hardly worthwhile because we remember the mistakes we have fallen into, the words we had not spoken but should have, and the directions of actions we should have taken but did not. This is the secret of regrets, although there is an effective escape clause, and this is it, it's as simple as it sounds --- If you're back there in the past anyway, make the most of it! Try to see whatever happened to you from a different angle, a more realistic one where you are not the centre of your world, but merely another bamboozled poor sod acting up selfishly and who's getting the wrong end of the stick, and being acted upon by others who really do feel they're central to the scheme of things and you're seen as little more than a bit part actor in their monstrously miniature myths. 'Cause, you see, you never know at the time the significance of what's going on in their heads and where they are in their unfolding development. Do you know what I'm saying?"

(Dr D. C., age forty-two)

"I dislike the *process* of decision-making as it stops me doing what I really like doing: *thinking*. It is known from common experience that thoughts tend to meander, though occasionally some significant bit of information from the past is extruded and flows, connecting up fruitfully, into one's stream of consciousness. Thinking, with lots of time to do it, with a notebook-cum-diary of my thoughts, is what I like doing. I have found niches. I can think new ideas. I am an *enfant terrible*. I enjoy being a little shocking. But I have learned not to be too shocking. Indeed I deliberately keep a low profile to avoid getting *stopped* from doing things. Most theories in my field seem pathetic to me. I don't want to do experiments because they seem to be a waste of my precious time. I prefer inventing things or making theoretical models."

(Dr K. D., age fifty-two)

On this latter point, our interviewee is in very good company --- several of the best experiments performed by Galileo and by Einstein were accomplished as "thought experiments", experiments performed entirely in their imaginations [16, 17]. Things can be thought of along the lines of "what if . . .?" When there are significant blanks, they are filled in sometimes by following a hunch, in their imaginations, and with no little discrimination: "To limit oneself to perceptions, the never-seen, is not enough. You cannot imagine how marvellously satisfying it is to take a shot in the dark, based on what you know, and what you feel to be right, bearing in mind that much of theoretical physics is at first counter-intuitive. These beautiful glorious hunches are not science. They are gut reactions, but they can be checked out by computer simulations and experiments. My wastepaper basket and pending trays are my deductive instruments. My inductive instrument is *(pointing to his temple)* up here."

(Dr. G.R.)

Both professional and eccentric scientists receive great pleasure from intellectual hunches, only exceeded by their joy from inspiration: "When I am in this state, it is heightened arousal . . . it is excruciatingly erotic, but it is more interesting than that. There's the thought in the back of my mind that what I am working on is going to shake up the world, your world, or that at worst, it's going to ripple through the scholarly journals and trigger someone else to think something more significant. That's an incredible turn-on. It gives me a tremendous incentive to get there again. During those periods I dream about what I am working on. It gives me the liberty of a second adolescence. Imagine this impulse --- to hear the unheard, to see, and reveal the unseen, to strip it down to its ultimate, disquieting realness. I don't want to have iconoclastic ideas, but I know that they're the best ones . . . they get a reaction . . . they pique some people's curiosity but raise other people's hackles. Would that I could prod their collective conscience as I can their narrow-minded consciousness. I could rant and rave like this nonstop when I'm in this magical condition, pregnant with impending thought. I believe that if an idea can disturb, it also has the power to thrill and captivate."

(Dr. M. A., age fifty-seven)

Conventional and eccentric scientists part company when it comes to post-inspiration critical analysis. The former scientists can be consumed with doubt, with introspective uncertainty, with reservations about how and why it could all be mistaken or artefactual.

Their internal compulsiveness engages them, quite rightly, to check and re-check their data over and over again. One such scientist, a conscientious research geneticist, acquired the nickname "El Flagello" because of the lengths to which, working sixteen hour days, seven days a week, he took his distinguished soul-searching.

For most eccentric scientists scrupulous attention to validation or confirmation falls by the wayside in the intoxicating rush forward into future conquests. For some, the boundaries of their concepts may be overextended. It can be unfortunate for professional scientists not to regard their findings from a critical perspective, though some scientists become dynamic advocates for their surmises and speculations. Their optimism is almost indefatigable. Witness this brief summary of another scientist's travails: "In the recent past I have been shortlisted for a position writing sales brochures for airships, divested myself of £1200 building and then subsequently dismantling a boat in my dining room, conducted a lengthy correspondence with professors at Cranwell and Farnborough on prone-piloted aircraft, and had a draft patent description on surface-skimming vehicles withdrawn by the Patent Office for review by the Inventions Unit of the Ministry of Defence. Daunted, I submitted one last design for a signature verification system, but became a computer management chap instead. I have some interesting applications for smectic liquid crystal arrays, though the time and inclination are not as easy to find nowadays."

(C. H., age thirty)

Eccentric scientists often come up against other people's rejection of their best ideas. To rationalise this, they may develop subsequent unrelated theories to accommodate the continuous misunderstanding they receive from their target audiences. Here is a typical account of this: "When I set out to produce some inventions, I deliberately chose to cover a broad range --- from a simple special-purpose note stand to an alternative to the Severn River Barrage. I have never had a proposal receive serious consideration from a manufacturer, even my Stock Exchange game. I have written literally dozens of letters about my Innovation Centre idea to various government departments involved in unemployment and education, and to politicians who have had a lot to say about unemployment, and to various notable people who ought to have been interested, and the response has varied between indifference and lukewarm negative interest. The professionally involved are often guilty of arrogant negligence.

"I believe inventors fall into the trap of the perpetual motion machine through the sheer frustration of having perfectly reasonable commercial ideas ignored. I came to the conclusion that antagonism to innovators is so consistent as to indicate some deep-rooted psychological basis. Hence my interest in the work showing that dominant male vervet monkeys behave in a typical fashion, and have an invariable increase in serotonin levels. My theory is that submissive signals are even more subtle than is generally recognised, and that innovators or eccentrics do not conform to the usual pattern which may be based on an obscure combination of many factors."

(Q. U. T., age thirty-four)

The eccentric scientists' progress is strewn with practical obstacles, and also with threats to their egos, and though they might fail to convert many others to their prophecies and utopian visions, their own striving spirit still triumphs: "The university authorities refused to review my thesis although time has vindicated it. Time in fact vindicates a great deal of my thinking. I don't think scholars should be condemned or excluded. It is now almost impossible to get a way-out idea publicised when it is deadly serious, conforms to well-established principles used in another discipline, and is of the greatest possible importance. Eccentrics cannot get jobs in competition with non-eccentrics. I was thrown out of the

Pathology Department for refusing to accept that no doctor can have a beard because of hygiene, so it is 'not cricket' for a research worker to have one. One bearded pathologist went to Cuba rather than shave his off.

"I came to the conclusion a long time ago that if I met me, I wouldn't like me, so I can't blame others for not doing so. Even my children avoid me. I am a very gregarious animal but I can stand being alone. My Social Security was cut off once for refusing to work in a jam factory, so the next time I said I would blow a hole in Oxford big enough to remember me by if they made my life totally unbearable. It gets harder and harder. I seem to have suffered disproportionately in relation to the degree of my abnormality. I write many letters as no journal will normally publish my ideas and I have no other means to propagate them. They're always shocked about something which isn't really shocking. On average, after twenty years, my ideas become respectable. Anything that confers status tends to become sacred, as witness the attempts to introduce laws, valid in physics, into biology. Difficulties of conceptualisation are largely due to the lack of relevant life experience. The professional mathematician has always led the merely well-educated by a larger margin than to any other subject, and they wanted it kept that way. For that reason, the country's economy suffered. I have always supposed myself to have been the victim of a similar process.

"I have never myself experienced anything one would call mental breakdown, yet somehow I have always faced rejection while people with more severe problems seem to be accepted. I was expelled from school, never left a job willingly, had my Ph.D. rejected, my wife walked out years ago, and after twenty-three years, I was forbidden to practise my sport. I remain bloody but unbowed.

"I knew cancer was itself a failure of control. I knew I had to learn it by life experience. I slightly underestimated how long it would take to master. Thirty years later, after continually coaxing nature to reveal itself, I do not satisfy my own standards. I realise I have not got the answer to cancer and my old theory was naïve.

"If my new theory is as naïve as my original theory I can only urge that thirty years is too little to learn the intricacies of control in biology, especially doing it on the dole."

(F. B., age fifty-one)

Chronic disappointments like the above one call up quite fervently held religious feelings. Contrary to the polarisation of popular opinion, scientists have not always been in opposition to spiritual or religious motivations. To some degree many scientists still are not. Isaac Newton, who prized silence and isolation, suffered an apparently psychotic episode that lasted at least several months in 1693. Believing he was transcribing God's precepts about gravity, he felt that God had permeated to the centre of his very consciousness. It could not have helpful when his compatriots started referring to him as "Divine Newton". The haunted-looking John Locke took his Most Knowing Being quite literally whenever he focused on his psychological enquiries into knowledge and experience. The wild-eyed John Ray, one of the founders of systematic biology, described as an "unkempt ecclesiastic without a pulpit", built his science from the ancient theological Argument from Design. He viewed the perfection of the natural world as proof positive of a benevolent Creator, a paternal, infinitely clever watchmaker. Orson Fowler, the proselytiser and driving force behind phrenology, the main mental science of the nineteenth-century, had intended to study for the ministry but opted instead to analyse human personality from the shape of the skull. He did so, sporadically making what appeared to be startlingly accurate "readings".

Modern eccentric scientists share the impulse to cross-breed religion with science. It is no small wonder that there are far more entries in the libraries of the world for eccentric religions than for eccentric people. A great number of new religions and sects burgeoned after the English Civil War, and again when the true impact of the Industrial Revolution was first felt. Was it a coincidence that this happened at a time when many more people were beginning to believe that rational science could bear fruit? Here follows a selection of extracts from modern eccentrics talking to me about some of their religion-science crossover beliefs: "Ideas about life's existential meaninglessness as a series of accidents and coincidences, and the intellectual certainties behind such thinking, these verily leave me cold. I'm very much for grabbing bits out of the Bible and putting my own interpretations on them, one of which is 'the lily of the field neither slumbers nor sleeps', to which I equate 'field' as being electromagnetic field, humming away merrily, 'telling us' things, day in and day out, and that, with a considerable amount of training for mental hygiene, one is able to filter the incoming information for what are good and what are bad signposts."

(Mrs. J. G.)

"My theories came little by little as brainwaves from a spiritual reservoir. From the study of physics I composed a mathematical/metaphysical/UFO theory (the first and only one as far as I know) together with a Creation theory, according to which the expanding universe is not contrary to Newton's law of gravitation. For these, one university called me a querulous scientist. I announced my theory of the descent of man in an extensive syllabus 'Our metaphysical --- Biblical world picture'. It's a pity that most people are not interested or don't understand it because of its conciseness and/or its spirituality. Science is nothing else but devising theories out of a field of knowledge, and that knowledge is an important theme in the Bible. I consider science as the new dimension of Christianity. I became scientifically converted into Christianity. Salaried scientists should not be so anti-Christianlike to deny my theories. They are a good remedy to make other vegetating people think originally."

(Dr C. P., age fifty-nine)

"In psychology, faith is my main interest. At the crazy end of the spectrum, where no one, least of all me, knows if I am right, I have a theory to abolish religious discord. Basically it is that Ezekiel saw a modern Israeli military aircraft, and so did the Persian King Darius. In fact, Christianity was founded by born again Christians, Islam by Moslems, Judaism by Jews. Although it's impossible to get to yesterday, it's dead easy to get to BC time. Space-time is a little like a tunnel diode in four dimensions. Time travel, 'the forbidden gap', is just a matter of energy available, and if two forbidden gaps overlap, bingo, you get to meet Ezekiel.

"Everything you do has been done. To change the past is to wish yourself unborn. The 'god' Krisna points out to Arjuna that he cannot refuse to kill his friends, relatives and teachers in the holy war. Krisna knows he did kill them. To be more precise, Krisna knows he did persuade him to do it, else Krisna doesn't get born.

"My recursive time theory normally rouses animosity or even fear. You would have been fascinated to see its effect on a Krishnerite. I didn't know he was a Krishnerite; I thought he was a fundamentalist Christian or possibly Muslim. Just as an afterthought to the story of the Cherubim, I said, 'In the *Bhagavadgita*, you can see a perfectly ordinary modern yobbo. The sort of man who puts the boot in at football matches. A hooligan playing at being God.' As an experiment, tell me, cold, what he did. It is predictable. He had a book, probably a commentary on the *Bhagavadgita*. I have never before provoked a physical attack. I have been 'rebuked, in the name of the Lord Jesus Christ'. There's always a first time."

(H. C., age forty-eight)

"After ultraviolet, x-rays, and then gamma rays and those little lovelies in atomic piles and explosions and the billion dollar disintegrators of the particle physicists. These may well be the major threat to the survival of mankind. Rather than the nuclear bomb. We see the bomb for what it is. The particle accelerator, to me, seems a much more subtle and dangerous cause of supernova production. I believe the asteroid belt owes its existence to particle accelerators or anti-matter devices.

"When fusion is total, energy is infinite. 'Infinite energy' and 'chain reaction' are synonymous. What the particle physicist seeks is total fusion. Infinite energy. The modern day physicist aims to strip the clothes off of his God, and God will not stand naked before man.

"Plasma is the 'Godstuff', not the God. The God is the ability of the Universal Matrix to conduct its affairs in an orderly thinking way, with memory, plan and creativity, as we know that matrix is so capable. This matrix is infinitely large, totally recognised, infallible, unforgetting but not unforgiving, and infinitely powerful. The patterns found in fractal geometry can be seen in the evidence collected in the new neuroscience of human consciousness. Thus the Godstuff or plasma is fundamentally a never-ending collection of Fracts in a state of Entropy acted on by the God, which is a function of the organisation of the Matrix. A picture of the Universe is thus possible."

(A. B., age fifty-two)

Many eccentric scientists do not need the *Deus ex machina* of time travel to feel ahead of their time. Their retrospective accounts are strewn with claims for their prescient inklings, some of which have been operationalized. Here are some examples of this from the eccentric informants I met in the course of my study:

"Cambridge Corporation now asks its architects to live in their product: an idea I floated thirty years ago."

"I was the first man in Britain to carry a child in a backpack in public and got myself on the front page of *The Times*."

"I was the first person in Britain to listen to radio on headphones in the street."

"I collected cameras and Victorian scientific instruments when labs were *throwing them away*."

"I have been fighting the public authorities, especially my MP, to set up a science for fun project. I feel sure we have to get kids interested in science as early as it is accepted. The effort is too great without enjoyment. It is very hard to get girls initiated into technology on a basis of liking it, not just trying to keep their end up."

"I was maintaining -129° Celsius in high vacuum for fourteen days and nights in 1962 by pumped liquid nitrogen-feedback-controlled cryostats. Were I a Russian the world would have been up in arms. Or if I were a Seventh Day Adventist."

"I am convinced, beyond a shadow of doubt, that the personality survives death. I have irrefutable evidence of guidance and messages from beyond regarding future events to indicate that time and place is an illusion, that the fourth dimension is a continuum, and that the holographic universe is an unassailable fact."

"If you want to see a sample of my thinking, look at the back end of Concorde, in particular, the square exhausts, a totally new breakthrough in gas flow, my idea. (This is true.) I don't think like anybody else I know, and I know why. I have anticipated most of the advances over the last fifty years: continental drift at eight, designed a space suit in 1935, and solved the problem of articulated joints. I know that cold temperature energy won't work and an awful lot more. The world is not against me in any way, but it's terribly stupid most of the time."

Eco-inventions

Some eccentric scientists' ideas are comparatively less speculative and more inventively technologically orientated. These were often triggered by recent disasters and a heartfelt desire to pitch in with ideas to avert foreseeable man-made environmental catastrophes of a similar nature in the future.

One such scheme was engendered by the loss of radioactive gas canisters on the seabed below the English Channel. The eccentric's novel recovery idea was based on location devices; sonic signals and colour-coded dye markers could be actuated when such cylinders would first touch down on the seabed. Rapid location from the air and the prevention of hazard from possible nuclear leakages could be facilitated by his system, the inventor told me.

The same inventor also generated a number of elaborate ideas to clear up and salvage oceanic oil spillages. In his plan the oil slick first would be broken up into smaller particles by unspecified chemical means. Overflying aircraft then would drop many millions of tiny iron slivers encased in polypropylene to keep them afloat. The oil would stick to the floaters that would then be attracted to magnetic plates in long cylinders slung over the bows of six auxiliary vessels. An alternative to the magnetic technique would use powerful electric pumps fitted with bellows mechanisms to provide suction. As maintained consistently by expert marine engineers, there are several difficulties with these plans. The biggest problem is that the formidable volumes of oil usually lost would overwhelm these systems, even if they performed at peak efficiency.

Eccentric scientists and inventors span the full spectrum in the scale of their proposals --- ranging from marvellously fantastic-looking high-performance kites to methods to avert the next Ice Age, which, as the latter eco-scientist asserted, "In random time, may start tomorrow."

This latter plan was first put forward in 1981, before there was much, if any, concern about global warming and the effects of greater amounts of carbon dioxide in the atmosphere. The plan appears a trifle omnipotent, and involved deliberately warming deep seawater by heat induction. Heat-trap buoys would support massive aluminium pipes, reaching one to three kilometres below the surface, in a belt twenty-seven hundred kilometres wide along the equator. Sunlight would heat the pipes at the top. When the interiors at the tops of the pipes became warmer than the surrounding seawater, water inside then would begin to rise and colder water deeper down would flow into the bottom openings of the pipes and continually rise upwards.

This particular technology designer also believed that it would be possible to increase the total sunshine on earth by a modest one per cent, or somewhat more, by placing a belt of spherical mirror satellites into orbit. The test for this system would be to melt the snow and ice boundaries back to their 1940 summer limits. The engineer who designed this system took in his stride Sir Fred Hoyle's warning that such projects could cause an inconvenient rise in sea levels, though he parried this difficulty by proposing the mass construction of sea walls to protect all the seaports of the world. The purpose of this scheme, at the time, seemed eminently laudable and humanitarian --- nothing less than the prevention of the Third World famines that were then projected.

Perpetual Motion

The gold standard, the veritable philosopher's stone for eccentric inventors, is the perpetual motion machine. None of the eccentric inventors that I have encountered have been deterred from trying to design a working model of one, despite the fact that most every respectable scientist in the world would describe such a task as impossible, and ultimately futile.

In concept, it is a machine that, after start up, somehow feeds energy back into it to keep it going. Then a small part of the total energy, it is believed, could be drawn off to perform some task or function, or to transmit energy power to be stored or used elsewhere. Such ideas have appealed to many thousands of people since the dawn of the Industrial Revolution. By 1877, the Paris Academy of Sciences had received so many claims proposing perpetual motion machines, none of which proved viable when objectively tested, and the Academy decided to reject all such machines out of hand.

Essentially, all such gadgets violated both Carnot's First Law of Thermodynamics (the principle of the conservation of energy) and Rudolf Clausius' Second Law of Thermodynamics (the principle that part of the energy associated with every self-acting process must always be dissipated as heat, and also that hot objects always cool to that of the surrounding temperature). As Clausius showed, due to friction, wear and corrosion, all physical processes run down or degrade. It is, as the astrophysicist Professor Arthur Stanley Eddington dubbed it, "Time's arrow".

The problem is not only with the falsity of the basic premise of perpetual motion, but also with a minority of the self-described inventors who continue to put these ideas forward. That some of them are secretive and paranoiac, fearing their ideas will be stolen, probably doesn't help their credibility. Other eccentric inventors, if they know about the above fundamental laws of thermodynamics, treat them derisively and defiantly, as challenges rather than as inevitable limitations. They theorise and act as if one hundred per cent of potential energy equals one hundred per cent of accessible energy, if only the right technique could be found and implemented. Their tenacious denials, made despite overwhelming contrary evidence of ineffectiveness, dwarfs perseverance of the most stubborn kind.

There were four such eccentric individuals who contacted me during the course of my study. This is how they introduced their ingenious notions, abstruse plans and questionable contrivances: "I divided a circle into three substantially parallel segments with two parallel chords. The middle section I truncated with an arc of unit radius through the centre. I discarded the larger part of this and I now had a puck which was slidable between the segments. As I moved this puck across the space during the rotation of the chords, I derived heart-shaped curves. When I used simple harmonic motion or sine curves to plot the relationship it became circular. I was surprised by this for it represented an approach to orbital engines that I had not seen. Others had, but had come up with different solutions to the problem of building and assembling a working model.

"I patented my solution and no one gave any heed to my claims that it was virtually one hundred per cent efficient. I could turn the rotor of a positive displacement pump in a closed housing with complete sealing at 20,000 revolutions per minute, and hold the casing in my fingers, and it barely became warm, and turned much more easily than a roller bearing. Still no interest."

(C. B.)

"Energy formation is a highly special process and applies strictly to wave interaction. This is not because waves are special. Everything is wave-like. It involves the collision of waves.

The collision of wave harmonics and matter waves do not contain harmonics. When anything is involved in collision, energy should be formed, but in the normal collision of waves one wave simply travels through another and to allow two waves to be said to truly collide, harmonics have to be present. In other words, to get any purchase on each other, the waves have to be disturbed.

"It is possible to perform energy-making interactions with the aid of disturbed magnetic fields. Thanks to relativity a wave in true linear motion can be said not to be moving at all. If one now incorporates harmonics and gets two waves to collide, the false motion will be involved in true collision, which in effect should never happen, and so energy is formed.

"Energy for real appears to be a very subtle business and energy level patterns seem to follow a shape. In other words, in terms of the magnetic perpetual motion motor, all one has to do is double the magnetic gap between the stata magnet and the rota magnet. It might work; one has somehow to trick a powerful static force positive motion generator into producing power in a dynamic state.

"If this is the answer it should be possible, with some ingenuity, to split and recombine an electric signal to produce free electricity, and, at say 200 megahertz, the 0.37 joule restriction limits the output rather satisfactorily to seventy million watts."

(K.S., age thirty-nine)

"I have spent some fifteen years now working on a fuelless engine. I am the only one who has any faith in the engine. Perhaps the professors are wrong and I am right. My engine is an underwater water wheel that is always out of balance on one side. The upthrust is greater on one side of the wheel than the other, but you see, it displaces liquid, but does not use any of the liquid. At no time is the water lifted or lowered; you can say that the water always stays where it is, but the lighter liquid, or compressed air contained within the wheel, does move.

"My liquid displacement machine is a mechanical monstrosity, an engineering nightmare, always breaking down. It has a lot of ball bearings and chains on it. It requires much tender loving care and attention. It uses potential energy, ie 'the rock on top of the hill can do work on falling'. I have an ocean full of potential energy that wants to fall, providing I can engineer the means to do it, which I can, although no one *wants* to agree with me.

"I now realise that the ordinary physicist cannot understand my engine because of what I call the 'Pons Asinorum': either you can see it, or you can't. I have had to study their laws of thermodynamics, and the only one that I can find fault with is that there is an equal and opposite force to any force. Apart from that one, I think that all the other laws of motion are suspect. All laws and rules are man-made, and there are always exceptions to any rule.

"If I made my engine available to the (Margaret) Thatcher creature, then I feel sure that she would annihilate the miners. Because I feel that they are my own kind of people, I cannot let this happen. I would not be able to live with myself. I have therefore diversified into designing flying saucers powered by my engine.

(K. F., age forty-eight)

"One day the mystery will be solved. One does feel that the boss of the universe is watching, and just when success is near, one of the laws of creation just pips you to the post. My nearest line of success has been the possibility of forward inertia overcoming gravity. One model which was near working consisted of a ring of 'railway lines', rising and falling around its diameter, of a different width up to the next down-drop. Running on it was a 'barbell', a weight with a flywheel at each end and two sets of wheels set apart so that one engaged uphill and the other engaged downhill. The idea is that the speed gained going downhill carries the larger wheels over the next wheel.

"In fact, the opposite happened, because uphill was easier on the smaller wheels. Although the speed gained was less, it would continue for some distance. I wonder, if made very finely, and numerous different gear ratios tried, how good it could be. Of course, the main snag is that all of the forces --- magnetic, gravity, etc. --- push or pull in one way only. I shall always continue to try."

(P. A.)

Scientists and society find it difficult nowadays to conceive of untrained individuals becoming serious amateur scientists. Some statements made by untutored scientific dilettantes may sound like a string of deliberately enigmatic mystifications, and some indeed may well be. There also have been suspicions, based on fact and on the admonition that if something sounds too good to believe then it probably is, and may be based on a fraudulent get-rich-quick scheme. The idea of "energy for nothing" is akin to selling the Eiffel Tower or memorial rivets on the Forth Rail Bridge. A few perpetual motion merchants, not necessarily eccentrics, are confidence tricksters, "bunko artists" preying on the unwitting and vulnerable.

The general belief of less eccentric scientists is that perpetual motion is a mainstay zany diversion. However, there are scientists who believe that thinking about it can be somehow enlightening. Some of these on the fringes also harbour the suspicion that although perfect perpetual motion is impossible, it can be beneficially approached. Science could, it is believed, "sneak up on it" by gradual degrees. The corollary of this is that close approximations to it will provide greater amounts of power.

Creative Playfulness

On the front of applied science and invention, childlike playfulness still plays a part, and one can never be sure if some eccentrics want to be taken seriously or are "doing their thing" light-heartedly for fun. In a BBC documentary in the early 1970s, Bruce Lacey (born in 1927) delighted in "flying" his improvised flight simulator in his cellar, acting the part of a World War II fighter pilot. He also invented a working radio-controlled automaton, called by its creator "my wonderful robot, Rosa Bosom". On viewing this documentary I was unaware that Bruce was already a noteworthy avant-garde performance artist who had mounted numerous exhibitions, a comedian, a prop master, as well as a stage and film actor. As Rosa clanked and rattled around his cellar workshop, making burbling and chuckling sounds, wheeling crazily past collections of toys, old household tools, "dressing up" clothes, and Japanese samurai warrior armour, in between singing off-key and demonstrating one of his electrophonic musical instruments, Bruce confided to his interviewer, "I used her in a play I produced called *The Three Musketeers*." As his contraption halted and reversed toward him, making intermittent beeping sounds, he said, "I think she needs some adjusting. She operates on the same frequency as cheap Japanese walkie-talkies, and whenever any of the neighbourhood kids are talking over them nearby, Rosa starts to go haywire. I guess I'm a child too, one that never turned into an adult. Adults are too embarrassed to play."

This kind of applied playfulness has also been shown to work extremely well in many of the most innovative multi-national computer-related firms like Apple and Google. It is also known that goodly proportions of computer hackers, reformed or otherwise, are eccentric, and have a high tolerance for ambiguity. They often seem not to mind living solitary, nocturnal lives, in which they are able to mount their ingenious and complicated work free from outside interruptions. Because of their ability to get on the wavelengths of their colleagues in the computing science world, their propensity to innovate, and their penchant for the unorthodox if not the illegal, they are sought out by many internationally reputable organisations. In such circumstances, with the right kind of guidance and leadership, they have made contributions to knowledge about how to defend against illicit hacking and other forms of electronic warfare by devising appropriate security countermeasures and algorithms.

The important question is not necessarily why the United Kingdom has the world's greatest reserves of apparently eccentric scientists, absent-minded professors, and clever inventors. There must be more to this than Britain's broadly individualistic culture, as compared to other more collectivist cultures. We should really be much more concerned with what we are getting right --- in research conducted in the mid-1980s, *more than half* of the new scientific and technological ideas adopted by manufacturers worldwide originated in the United Kingdom [18]. One wonders what riches remain latent, ignored and unexploited?

Chapter 10. Sudden Harmonies
(Summary and Conclusions)

"The heart of man is made to reconcile contradictions."

Essays, David Hume (1711 – 1776)

As my study was the first and, to this day, the only scientific investigation of eccentricity, one of my goals was to arrive at a description of eccentric individuals living in the community. Although the eccentrics were as diverse as one could imagine, they did share some common features. Their characteristic traits and behaviours composed a profile of the "typical" eccentric. In all, there were twenty-five descriptor variables of eccentricity, here laid out in descending order of importance:

- Enduring non-conformity;
- Creative;
- Strongly motivated by an exceedingly powerful curiosity and related exploratory behaviour;
- An enduring and distinct feeling of differentness from others;
- Idealism, wanting to make the world a better place and the people in it happier;
- Happily obsessed with a number of long-lasting preoccupations (usually about five or six);
- Intelligent, in the upper fifteen per cent of the population on tests of intelligence; many notable eccentrics proved singularly bright.
- Opinionated and outspoken, convinced of being right and that the rest of the of the world is out of step with them;
- Non-competitive;
- Not necessarily in need of reassurance or reinforcement from the rest of society;
- Unusual eating habits and living arrangements;
- Not particularly interested in the opinions or company of other people, except perhaps in order to persuade them to their contrary point of view;
- Possessed of a mischievous sense of humour, charm, whimsy and wit;
- More frequently an eldest or an only child;
- Eccentricity observed in at least 36% of detailed family histories, usually a grandparent, aunt, or uncle. (It should be noted that the family history method of estimating hereditary similarities and resemblances usually provides rather conservative estimates.)
- Eccentrics prefer to talk about their thoughts rather than their feelings. There is a frequent use of the psychological defence mechanisms of rationalization and intellectualisation.
- Slightly abrasive;
- Midlife changes in career or lifestyle;
- Feelings of "invisibility", which means that they believed other people did not seem to hear them or see them, or take their ideas seriously;
- Feel that others can only take them in small doses;
- Feel that others have stolen, or would like to steal, their ideas. In some cases, this was well-founded.
- Disliked small talk or other apparently inconsequential conversation;
- A degree of social awkwardness;

- More likely to be single, separated or divorced, or multiply separated or divorced;
- A poor speller, in relation to their above average general intellectual functioning.

(The first five of these characteristics are the most important and apply to virtually every eccentric. Nonconformity is the principal defining trait.)

The need of most people to fit in, to be popular, has never been stronger. At a time when social freedoms have rarely been more wide-ranging, most people want to be the same. Yet it's the differences that make people interesting. Individuality is a distinct mode of being. It is not an indifferent attribute. People are meant to be self-determining. Humanity is unique in the ways that we do not always come to terms with our various environments. For other species, their perfectly valid adaptations are marked by passive responses, or reactions, to their ecological niches. In contrast, people can choose to be different, and choose from a range of environments, physical, social, and psychological.

Though free will is a fact of experience, eccentrics do not take this gift for granted. Eccentrics do more than merely grapple with the existence of free will. Their definitions of the good life generally are not troubled by doubt, nor do they act in more tentative ways. How could they aim for their goals if they didn't already have a feel for where they were going? They engineer their lives in such a way as to repeatedly force its limits.

My thesis is that eccentrics take an active part in forging their own personalities in the direction of greater distinctiveness. While hardly ever denying their eccentricity --- in the light of their evident self-awareness, how could they? --- they well might object strenuously to other peoples' invidious definitions.

Eccentrics usually never change themselves, nor do they hardly ever contemplate doing so. They usually remain true to their own individual natures. Their irreverence toward the strictures of mass culture continually resurfaces. They ceaselessly assert and reassert their fundamental right to be what they want to be. They draw from their inner wealth of experience to enlighten and deepen an intuitive sense of their need for greater personal uniqueness.

In the case of developing self-fulfilment, an individual can attain greater independence. For some people, this may lead to a more intense involvement in life, and a strong sense of purpose and commitment.

Eccentrics can influence people; at the very least they will make you smile with delight. Their actions create a peculiar mixed ambience of quizzical tolerance for apparent absurdity.

Contrary to popular belief, eccentrics show little involvement with fanatical political or religious groups. The eccentric person with a type of extreme personality described in this book should be distinguished from those who are political extremists or who hold extremist attitudes, although there may well be a little overlap. The relationship would be that many political extremists would show some extreme personality features. However, in most instances such extremists would not be eccentric because of their orthodoxy to their more or less derivative beliefs, and conformity to their core group's ideologies and behaviours.

If anything, eccentrics prefer to be leaders or individualistic non-followers working behind the scenes, if they must, rather than followers. They know that to be followers would mean that they might be required to lose their sense of self in order to follow someone else's beliefs or orders. If anarchy did not have such pejorative connotations, eccentrics could be thought of as "benign anarchists".

Because of their ongoing dedication to causes greater than themselves, the lives of eccentrics are full of significance, especially to them. They emotionally invest their inner worlds with meaningfulness, and infused by their enthusiastic intellectual pursuits, they provide themselves with many intrinsically rewarding gratifications. They must find eccentricity rewarding, as there is independent evidence that the personality traits of eccentric people become more pronounced with age [1]. Furthermore, there are higher concentrations of eccentrics around the rural coastal fringes of England, and it is no coincidence that these locales are seen as ideal places in which retired people can find the good life.

Everyone needs to maintain some psychological defences. This is also the case of the individuals described in this book. They used the psychological defence mechanisms of isolation, rationalisation and intellectualisation. However, these tended to be seized upon and developed as much for constructive and idealistic purposes rather more than for defence. Eccentrics did not appear to deny or wilfully negate any of life's unpleasant realities or inevitable disillusionments.

To eccentrics, the commands and injunctions of authority are not in the least bit persuasive. In defiant opposition, the more intellectually endowed have become formidable adversaries of those in authority.

Eccentrics feel no pressure to accept anything that contradicts their perceived or believed experience. Between separateness and relatedness, their personalities allowed them to indulge freely, to the fullest, in the whims and fancies of their vivid imaginations. For them, there is the thrill of possibly discovering things that had not been discovered before, followed by a sense of exhilaration in having one and hopefully more novel insights.

These are people with a boundless lust for life, immoderate men and women who refuse to violate their personal ideals. They do not allow their self-expression to be thwarted, although some feathers may be ruffled in the process. They may fail in any single endeavour, though society wins by their examples and by what can be salvaged from the ideas, problems and questions that they radiate. In many other societies, a deficit in inventiveness is a sure sign of the acceptance of safe compromises.

At the root of eccentricity is a healthy and determined irreverence. Not for the eccentrics are the dangers of obedience. The social hold on them becomes so attenuated that there is little chance that they would ever meekly surrender their indomitable identities. They are not defiant without good reason. Their condition is that of freedom.

Eccentricity in society is essential for that society to have sufficient variety within itself to adapt successfully to changing conditions. People respond by playing active roles, by increasingly shaping and adapting forms and contexts. Individuals and social groups modify their environments to suit their needs. It would be unfortunate if these changes were merely for survival, selfish if for the pursuit of happiness, but full of hope if for the greater common good. The human race's identity is indissolubly linked with defiance against larger forces, suitable challenges for our puny arrogance. Eccentricity can be more than an act of will in a field of artifice.

Restricted social mobility in British society in the past, and to a certain extent in the present, may be one cause for the rise of eccentricity. It remains a startlingly pervasive social class system based on wide and widening economic inequalities, educational opportunities or lack of same, and on differences in speech and manners. Oftentimes those at the bottom of the social hierarchy find it very difficult to be upwardly mobile, and obviously those at or near the top already, are often unable to progress higher or in other fulfilling ways. In the past, people "knew their place", their station in life, and if they didn't act according to their place, regrettably it could end in tears, or worse. There was less choice; rather, "their place" in life was much more likely to be determined by other people. In all of this, the matter of personal choice loomed large. If individuals cannot develop upwards vertically through the class system, and many from all classes cannot, they will still be able however to develop themselves horizontally. One way, of many, to translate this into action, and to bring it to fruition, is to become eccentric.

There are no doubt countries that are more class-riven and class-conscious than Britain, and others that, for historical or political reasons, show a diminution of class- consciousness, although in some of these class exists in terms of old or new money. Most of these countries, with the exception of the United States, do not approach the high levels of eccentricity found in Britain. So too are there countries that are currently less and more conformist. As a personality trait, one would expect it to be randomly distributed throughout the world's various cultures. From my experience it is not so distributed, though this is richly deserving of cross-cultural anthropological research.

Freedom of speech and the possibility of making viable choices are no doubt conducive to eccentricity, if not providing the minimum background conditions for it. Eccentrics believe that we can make ourselves and are capable of making ourselves differently if we so choose. People are able to challenge and push back perceived limits with ingenuity, imagination and determination.

In countries where extremes of behaviour are not appreciated, or indeed are persecuted, it takes more strength and force of character to push back the boundaries or to deviate from the norm. Though democratic countries try to guarantee basic human rights, one feels compelled to pay tribute to those courageous individuals who, by their actions and words helped to make possible these essential freedoms.

It could well be the low-keyed tolerance that was almost taken for granted in the United Kingdom that also provided the fertile ground upon which eccentricity could flourish. In this country, there is a tension between the tolerance of the majority and the vocal intolerance of a relative few, and it is this that brings eccentricity out more so than in other countries. Also, the experimental ideas of individualists have been welcomed here, bringing forward and enhancing ideas for further thought. Their creativity is an abundant source of cultural enrichment. The creative force of continuing cultural evolution does not depend solely on individual geniuses thinking great thoughts in splendid isolation. They also need, at times, the friction deriving from controversial theorists pushing the boundaries of what is considered knowable, thinking previously unthinkable thoughts, and robustly communicating them. Such thoughts may derive from maverick thinkers and innovators working within and outside of established institutions.

Eccentrics are living proof that one does not necessarily have to go through life with a rigid set of rules. Conventions are a conveniently ever-present part of human social life that act as useful guides for positive behaviours. They also create a whole host of taken-for-granted inhibitions that impact adversely on human creativity.

The lives of eccentric people encourage us to take seriously those ways of behaving that conformists are inclined to dismiss. They believe that they have greater awareness and perception; they believe they see things, including social arrangements, in depth. They do not accept mundane everyday objects at face value. They keep the torches of questioning and dissent burning. Because of all this, their lives are richer. They see more, and in so doing, this points to how much positive experience people routinely miss. Their actions pose a serious question, that being whether conventional behaviour is necessarily or ontologically the right existential choice for everyone. For eccentrics, it's about not being conditioned by what life perpetually throws at all of us, but instead adventuring forward, attempting to find a better way of living. Some advise a way of life that needs a degree of bravery, such as that put forward by the noted fashion and portrait photographer, stage and costume designer Cecil Beaton (1904 - 1980): "Be daring, be different, be impractical; be anything that will assert integrity of purpose and imaginative vision against the play-it-safers, the creatures of the commonplace, the slaves of the ordinary." Or as the writer Muriel Spark has one of her writerly characters say in her final novel, "Art is an act of daring."

Like certain religions, classical psychoanalysis has asserted a monopoly on the truth about how people should behave and adapt to their wider society, whilst ignoring the actual conditions under which individuals exist. Sigmund Freud maintained that people had to relinquish a certain amount of their natural inclinations, in order to "find an expedient accommodation in order to live in society." Indeed, the taming of desires to be different may be a social imperative in some repressive cultures. In some societies, mainstream psychiatrists have participated or colluded in this, and have put themselves in a position to be agents of social control. Some people say that this still goes on, though in a more subtle, "caring" way.

The theories of eccentrics may be their Achilles' heels. Their ideas may be denigrated. Their minds are always buzzing furiously with ideas. Some worry about their lack of credibility. Many have said that the respect of the wider community is not that important to them, or that it is something they simply do not care about. It *is* though, even if they say something to the contrary. If someone actively challenges their ideas, they will strive to provide "proof" for them. Whether or not they are able to do so, the eccentrics feel that it is *our* understanding that is wanting, that it is *our* loss, and not wholly their problem.

Their attitude to their different scientific methods and practices would be --- "Why not?" After all, if individuals were not willing to experiment, science would not be where it is today. Eccentrics have a part to play in the forward movement of science, at the risky end of the push towards more knowledge. They believe that currently unknown aspects of nature are not beyond the capacity of the human imagination, and will be discovered sooner or later.

Psychologists have looked at others and seen their own reflections. Eccentrics are anomalous in several ways, and, therefore, they are genuinely puzzling. The examination of such anomalous people could lead to further revelations, and possibly, changes, if not revolutions, in our thinking.

After having met and attempted to empathize with the individuals in this study, I have come to think that we are all perhaps stranger in our thinking than we presume to be. It may be that we try to control that unique strangeness, perhaps because we're frightened of what we may find. Nevertheless, it is the eccentrics' courage to be themselves, and their great resilience, that I find admirable.

The research presented herein shows that certain types of deviant behaviour can be healthy, good and life-enhancing. The eccentrics in the historical sample, which covered the period from 1550 to 1950, lived, on average, to the age of sixty five during times when people were fortunate to live to be thirty-five. Modern-day eccentrics rarely visit their general practitioners --- the eccentrics in our sample averaged only one consultation every eight and a half years, whereas during the period of my study the average person in the general population went to their general practitioner twice a year --- seventeen times more often than the eccentric typically does. How can this difference be explained?

Eccentrics are happier because they generally are doing what they want to be doing. Time and again, the eccentrics in my study, with a few notable exceptions, clearly evinced that shining sense of positivism and buoyant self-confidence that comes from being comfortable in one's own skin. They often showed a certainty about how they were living combined with an inner personal serenity. Because they are much less concerned about conforming, whether that has to do with "keeping up with the neighbours" or worrying about what others think about them, and are happier in themselves, they suffer from fewer of the negative effects of stress. Knowing that they are significantly different themselves, they are more accepting of other people's differences. One of the hallmarks of mental health and emotional maturity is tolerance for those who are different. While not saying that eccentricity is necessarily good for a person, the adoption of some of the eccentrics' perspectives on life and related ways of thinking may well improve one's quality of life.

Much of the above chimes with broader critiques of modern Western society, and its effects on people. However, there are those who are of the opinion that science is a dehumanising activity. I for one do not see it that way, because it can lead to a greater understanding of our selves and of our social and physical environments. That we sometimes act too rashly or unwisely, or act not at all, represents a fault in us, not in our different forms of scientific or humanistic activity.

In my roles as a psychotherapist and public health advocate, it has become patently clear to me that getting people to be more interested in where their thinking is taking them should be a significant component of all of our lives. The goal of that would be so that we can gain, hopefully, a greater freedom of action and thought.

Health should surely be one of our guiding principles, and mental health matters in particular should receive more attention. Whenever, through complacency, we fail to be concerned with the limits and extremes of mental health, we make ourselves guilty of emotional myopia. If the keepers of the gates to our mental health services should err, in either direction, we are all deprived: deprived of the spur of challenge from unorthodox ideas; deprived of human contact with people so intensely humane that they suffer for the rest of us; deprived of the privilege of knowing them, of seeing their unusual and positive perspectives. In our personal uniqueness and unknowability of others' hidden uniqueness, we all have a touch of eccentricity, whether in thought, wish, word or action. If we could promote a little more eccentricity, or allow more variations on the norm, then mental illness too might become a little less intolerable, less painful, and less full of stigma. By upholding greater respect for differentness, and those who are different and were once called "abnormal", it might be possible to consign social stigma to the dustbin of history.

In an era when human beings seem typecast by their culture or genes, eccentrics are a refreshing reminder of everyone's intrinsic uniqueness. The eccentricity of *any* individual is unique and specific. For those who want it, adult subjective individuation is not only possible; as shown by the eccentrics, it is eminently feasible. By veering significantly away from conventional behaviour, or by flouting norms of behaviour that most of us never question, their examples remind us how much of our liberty we forfeit without thought, and how great our ability is, in fact, to forge our own identities and shape our own lives. It is positively empowering to break free from the constant need to conform to other people's expectations. It remains arguable that what has carried humanity forward, and yet restrains the worst parts of our natures, is either our presumed greater connected-up intelligence or our emotional empathy and altruistic concerns for the well-being of others.

References

Chapter 1

1. Marcus, G. E., (1995), "On Eccentricity", in *Rhetorics of Self-Making,* edited by Debbora Battaglia. Berkeley: University of California Press.

Chapter 2

1. Jones, B., (1974), *Follies and Grottoes*. London.

2. Lees-Milne, J., (1976), *William Beckford*. Tisbury, Wiltshire, England.

3. Roscoe, W., (1991), *The Zuni man-woman*. Albuquerque, New Mexico.

4. Roscoe, W., (1998), *Changing Ones: Third and Fourth Genders in native North America*. New York: St. Martin's Press.

Chapter 3.

1. Henderson, D. and Gillespie, R. D., (1962), *Textbook of Psychiatry*. Oxford: Oxford University Press.

2. Crowcroft, A., (1973), *The Psychotic*. Harmondsworth: Penguin.

3. Lewis, N. D. C. and Piotrowski, Z. A., (1954), "Clinical diagnosis of manic-depressive psychosis", in: *Depression* (Editors P. Hock and J. Zubin). New York: Grune and Stratton.

4. Stone, M. H., (1980), *The Borderline Syndromes*. New York: McGraw-Hill.

5. Zilboorg, G., (1941), "Ambulatory Schizophrenia", *Psychiatry*, 4, 149 - 155.

6. Nadzharov, R. A., (1972), "Course Forms", in: *Schizophrenia* (Editor A.V. Snezhnevsky). Moscow, Russia: Metsina, 16 - 76.

7. Reich, W., (1975), "The spectrum concept of schizophrenia: problems for diagnostic practice", *Archives of General Psychiatry*, 32, 489 - 498.

8. Laing, R. D., (1960), *The Divided Self*. London: Tavistock Publications.

9. American Psychiatric Association, (1980), *Diagnostic and Statistical Manual of Mental Disorders*, Third Edition. Washington, D. C.: American Psychiatric Association.

10. Kegan, R., (1982), *The Evolving Self, Problems and Processes in Human Development*. Cambridge, Massachusetts: Harvard University Press.

11. Frosch, J., (1983), *The Psychotic Process*. New York: International Universities Press.

12. Swanson, G. E. and Phillips, S. S., (1984), "Schizotypic and other profiles in college students: some social correlates", Department of Sociology and Institute of Human Development, University of California, Berkeley.

13. Tyrer, P., Casey, P. and Gall, J., (1983), "Relationships between neurosis and personality disorder", *British Journal of Psychiatry*, 142, 404 - 408.

14. Coulter, J., (1973), *Approaches to Insanity*. London: Martin Robertson.

15. Kreitman, N., Sainsbury, P., Morrissey, J., Towers, J. and Scrivener, J., (1961), "The reliability of psychiatric assessment analysis", *Journal of Mental Science*, 107, 887 - 908.

16. Beck, A. T., Ward, C. H., Mendelson, M., Mock, J. and Erbough, J., (1962), "Reliability of psychiatric diagnoses: a study of consistency of clinical judgement and ratings", *American Journal of Psychiatry*, 119, 351 - 357.

17. Schneider, K., (1959), *Clinical Psychopathology* (Translated by M. W. Hamilton). New York: Grune and Stratton.

18. Wing, J. K., Cooper, J. E., and Sartorius, N., (1974), *The Measurement and Classification of Psychiatric Symptoms*. London: Cambridge University Press.

19. Cooper, J. E., Kendell, R. E., Gurland, B. J., Sharpe, L., Copeland, J. R. M. and Simon, R., (1972), *Psychiatric Diagnosis in New York and London*. London: Oxford University Press.

20. World Health Organisation, (1973), *The International Pilot Study of Schizophrenia (IPSS)*, Volume 1. Geneva: WHO.

21. Fish, F., (1976), *Fish's Schizophrenia*. Edited by Max Hamilton, Bristol: John Wright and Sons.

22. Wing, J. K. and Nixon, J., (1975), "Discriminating symptoms in schizophrenia", *Archives of General Psychiatry*, 32, 853 - 859.

23. Tausk, V., (1919), "Über den beeinflussungsapparat in der Schizophrenie", *Int. Z. Psychoanalysis*, 5, 1 - 33.

24. Roazen, P., (1973), *Brother Animal*. Harmondsworth: Penguin.

25. Modell, A., (1963), "Primitive object relationships and the predisposition to schizophrenia", *International Journal of Psychoanalysis*, 44, 282 - 292.

26. Wolff, S., Townshend, R., McGuire, R. J., and Weeks, D. J., (1991), " 'Schizoid' personality in childhood and adult life II.: adult adjustment and the continuity with schizotypal personality disorder", *British Journal of Psychiatry*, 159, 620 – 629.

27. Wolff, S., (1995), *Loners: The Life Path of Unusual Children*. London: Routledge.

28. Kretschmer, E., (1936), *Physique and Character*, 2nd Edition. London: Routledge and Kegan Paul.

29. Tantam, D., (1991), "Asperger's syndrome in adulthood", In Uta Frith (Editor), *Autism and Asperger Syndrome*. Cambridge: Cambridge University Press, 147 - 183.

30. Kendler, K. S., (1985), "Diagnostic approaches to schizotypal personality disorder: A historical perspective", *Schizophrenia Bulletin*, 11(4), 538 - 553.

31. Minkowski, E., (1927), *La schizophrenie*. Paris, France: Payot.

32. Meehl, P. E., (1972), "A critical afterword", in: *Schizophrenia and Genetics* (Editors I. I. Gottesman and J. Shields). New York: Academic Press.

33. Hanssen, M, Bak, M., Bijl, R., Vollebergh, W., and van Os, J., (2005), "The incidence and outcome of subclinical psychotic experience in the general population", *British Journal of Clinical Psychology*, 44 (2), 181 – 191.

34. Scheff, T. J., (1974), *Being Mentally Ill: A Sociological Theory*. Chicago: Aldine.

35. Pasamanick, B., (1961), "A survey of mental disease in an urban population: IV. An approach to total prevalence rates", *Archives of General Psychiatry*, 5, 151 – 155.

36. Ayer, A. J., (1936), *Language, Truth and Logic*. London: Gollancz.

37. Lenz, H., (1983), "Belief and delusion: Their common origin but different course of developments", *Zygon*, 18(2), 117 - 137.

38. Freud, S., (1907), "Obsessive acts and religious practices". *Standard Edition of Complete Psychological Works*, Volume 9, 118.

39. Sarro-Burbano, R., (1981), "The mythic/religious theme in schizo-paraphrenic delusions", *Revista de Psiquiatria y Psicologia Medica de Europa*, 15(3), 127 - 134.

40. Morris, C., (1956), *Varieties of Human Value*. Chicago: University of Chicago Press.

41. Salzman, L., (1960), "Paranoid state, theory and therapy", *Archives of General Psychiatry*, 2, 679 - 693.

42. Vaughn, C. E. and Leff, J. P., (1976), "The influence of family and social factors on the course of psychiatric patients", *British Journal of Psychiatry*, 129, 125 - 137.

43. Greenley, J. R., (1979), "Family symptom tolerance and rehospitalisation experiences of psychiatric patients", in: *Research in Community and Mental Health*. Editor R.G. Simmons, 1, 357 - 386.

44. Kolle, K., (1931), *Die Primäre Verrückheit. Psychopathologische, Klinische und genealogische Untersuchungen*. Leipzig: Thieme.

45. Mayer-Gross, W., (1950), "Psychopathology of delusions", *Congres international de psychiatrie*, Vol. 1, 58 - 87.

46. Anderson, M. and Guerra, A., (1954), "Il Delirio di rapport sensitivo" (contributio clinico), *Rass. studi. psichiatry*, 43, 323 - 338.

47. Done, D. J., Johnstone, E. C., Frith, C. D., Golding, J., and Shepherd, P. M., (1991), "Complications of pregnancy and delivery in relation to psychosis in adult life: data from the British perinatal mortality survey sample", *British Medical Journal*, 302, 1576 - 1580.

48. Kendler, K. S., Gruenberg, A. M. and Tsuang, M. T., (1985), "Psychiatric illness in first-degree relatives of schizophrenic and surgical-control patients: A family study using DSM-III criteria", *Archives of General Psychiatry*, 42(8), 770 - 779.

49. Stanghellini, G. and Ballerini, M., 2007), "Values in persons with schizophrenia", Schizophrenia Bulletin, 33 (1), 131 - 141.

Chapter 4

1. Fortes, M., (1974), "The First Born", *Journal of Child Psychology and Psychiatry*, 15, 81 - 104.

2. Koskinnen, A. A., (1960), *Ariki the First Born*. Helsinki: Academia Scientiarum Fennica.

3. Firth, R., (1967), *Tikopia Ritual and Belief*. London: Athlone Press.

4. Simonton, D. K., (1984), *Genius, Creativity, and Leadership*. Cambridge, Massachusetts: Harvard University Press.

5. Eiduson, B. T., (1962), *Scientists: Their Psychological World*. New York: Basic Books.

6. Donaldson, M., (1978), *Children's Minds*. Glasgow, Scotland: Fontana/Collins.

7. Kaplan, L., (1978), *Oneness and Separateness*. New York: Simon and Schuster.

8. Altus, W. D., (1967), "Birth order and its sequelae", *International Journal of Psychiatry*, 3, 23 - 39.

9. Kagan, J. and Moss, H. A., (1962), *Birth to Maturity: The Fels Study of Psychological Development*. New York: Wiley.

10. Koch, H. L., (1956 a.), "Attitudes of children toward their peers as related to certain characteristics of their siblings", *Psychological Monographs*, 70(426), 1 - 41.

11. Koch, H. L., (1956b.), "Sissiness and tomboyishness in relation to sibling characteristics", *Journal of Genetic Psychology*, 88, 231 - 244.

12. Koch, H. L., (1956c.), "Some emotional attitudes of the young child in relation to sibling characteristics", *Child Development*, 27, 393 - 426.

13. Sulloway, F., (1997) *Born to rebel: Birth order, family dynamics, and creative lives*. New York: Pantheon.

14. Lasko, J. K., (1954), "Parent behaviour towards first and second children", *Genetic Psychology Monographs*, 49 - 137.

15. Buhler, C., (1937), *From Birth to Maturity*. London: Kegan Paul.

16. Berenda, R. W., (1950), *The Influence of the Group on the Judgements of Children*. New York: King's Crown Press.

17. Costanzo, R. R. and Shaw, M. E., (1966), "Conformity as a function of age level", *Child Development*, 37, 967 - 975.

18. McConnell, T. R., (1963), "Suggestibility in children as a function of chronological age", *Journal of Abnormal and Social Psychology*, 67, 286 - 289.

19. Campbell, J. D., (1964), "Peer relations in childhood", in: *Review of Child Developmental Research*, (Editors M.C. Hoffman and L.W. Hoffman). New York: Russell Sage, 289 - 322.

20. Carrigan, W. C. and Julian, J. W., (1966), "Sex and birth-order differences in conformity as a function of need affiliation arousal", *Journal of Personality and Social Psychology*, 3, 479 - 483.

21. Hartrup, W. W., (1970), "Peer interaction and social organisation", in: *Carmichael's Manual of Child Psychology*, Volume 2 (Editor P. H. Mussen). New York: Wiley, 457 - 558.

22. Patel, A. E. and Gordon, J. E., (1960), "Some personal and situational determinants of yielding to influence", *Journal of Abnormal and Social Psychology*, 61, 411 - 418.

23. Desen, M. and Mettel, T., (1984), "Interaction of parents with a firstborn child before and after the birth of a second child in the family: A case study", *Psicologia*, 10(2), 27 - 39.

24. Holman, P., (1968), "Family vicissitudes in relation to personality development", in: *Foundations of Child Psychiatry* (Editor E. Miller). Oxford: Pergamon Press.

25. Sutton-Smith, B. and Rosenberg, B. G., (1970), *The Sibling*. New York: Holt Rinehart.

26. Ziller, R. C., (1964), "Individuation and socialisation: A theory of assimilation in large organisations", *Human Relations*, 17, 344 - 360.

27. Neubauer, P. B., (1982), "Rivalry, envy, and jealousy", *The Psychoanalytic Study of the Child*, 37, 121 – 142.

28. Karniol, R. and Ross, M., (1976), "The development of causal attributions in social perception", *Journal of Personality and Social Psychology*, 34, 455 - 464.

29. Ruble, D. N., Boggiano, A. K., Feldman, N. S. and Loebl, J. H., (1980), "A developmental analysis of the role of social comparison in self-evaluation", *Developmental Psychology*, 16, 105 - 115.

30. Singer, J. L., (1973), *The child's world of make believe*. New York: Academic Press.

31. Miller, A., (1981), *The Drama of the Gifted Child*. New York: Basic Books.

32. Schwarz, J. C. and Getter, H., (1980), "Parental conflict and dominance in late adolescent maladjustment: a triple interaction model", *Journal of Abnormal Psychology*, 89(4), 573 - 580.

33. Brim, O. G., (1959), *Education for Child-Rearing*. New York: Russell Sage.

34. Le Vine, R. A., (1973), *Culture, Behaviour and Personality*. London: Hutchinson.

35. De Man, A. F., (1985), "Parental control in child-rearing and conservatism in young adult women", *Psychological Reports*, 56 (1), 145 - 146.

36. Boe, E. E. and Church, R. M., (1968), *Punishment: Issues and Experiments*. New York: Appleton-Century-Crofts.

37. Belsky, J., Steinberg, L., and Draper, P., (1991), "Childhood experience, interpersonal development, and reproductive strategy: An evolutionary theory of socialization", *Child Development*, 62, 647 – 670.

38. Hobson, R. P., Patrick, M., Crandell, L., Garcia-Perez, R., and Lee, A., (2005), "Personal relatedness and attachment in infants of mothers with borderline personality disorder", *Development and Psychopathology*, 17, 329 – 347.

39. Hobson, R. P., (2002), *The Cradle of Thought: Exploring the origins of thinking*. London: Macmillan.

40. Hobson, R. P., Patrick, M. P. H., Crandell, L. E., Garcia-Perez, R. M., and Lee, A., (2004), "Maternal sensitivity and infant triadic communication", *Journal of Child Psychology and Psychiatry*, 45, 470 – 480.

41. Frender, R., Brown, B. and Lambert, W. E., (1970), "The role of speech characteristics in scholastic success", *Canadian Journal of Behavioural Science*, 2, 299 – 306.

42. Greene, D. and Lepper, M. R., (1974), "Effects of extrinsic rewards on children's subsequent intrinsic interest," *Child Development*, 45, 1141 – 1145.

43. Amabile, T. M., DeJong, W., and Lepper, M. R., (1976), "Effects of externally imposed deadlines on subsequent intrinsic motivation, *Journal of Personality and Social Psychology*, 34, 92 – 95.

44. Ryan, R, M., Mims, V., and Koestner, R., (1983), "The relationship of reward contingency and interpersonal context to intrinsic motivation: A review and test using cognitive evaluation theory," *Journal of Personality and Social Psychology*, 45, 736 – 750.

45. Deci, E. L., (1971), "Effects of externally mediated rewards on intrinsic motivation", *Journal of Personality and Social Psychology*, 18, 105 – 115.

46. Lepper, M. R., Greene, D., and Nisbett, R. E., (1973), "Undermining children's intrinsic interest with extrinsic rewards: A test of the 'over-justification' hypothesis," *Journal of Personality and Social Psychology*, 28, 129 – 137.

47. Deci, E. L., (1975), *Intrinsic Motivation*. New York: Plenum.

48. Anderson, R., Manoogian, S. T., and Reznick, J. S., (1976), "The undermining and enhancing of intrinsic motivation in preschool children," *Journal of Personality and Social Psychology*, 34, 915 – 922.

49. Deci, E. L., Betley, G., Kahle, J., Abrams, L., and Porac, J., (1980), "When trying to win: Competition and intrinsic motivation", *Personality and Social Psychology Bulletin*, 7, 79 – 83.

50. Deci, E. L., Nezlek, J., and Sheinman, I., (1981), "Characteristics of the rewarder and intrinsic motivation of the rewardee," *Journal of Personality and Social Psychology*, 40, 1 – 10.

51. Deci, E. L. and Ryan, R. M., (1985), *Intrinsic motivation and self-determination in human behavior*. New York: Plenum.

52. Cohen, S. and Oden, S., (1974), "An examination of creativity and locus of control in children," *Journal of Genetic Psychology*, 121, 179 – 185.

53. Koestner, R., Ryan, R. M., Bernieri, F., and Holt, K., (1984), "Setting limits on children's behavior: The differential effects of controlling vs. informational styles on intrinsic motivation and creativity", *Journal of Personality*, 52 (3), 233 – 248.

54. Dreistadt, R., (1970), "Reversing, using opposites, negativism, and aggressiveness in creative behaviour in science and philosophy", *Psychology*, 7(2), 38 - 63.

55. Vernon, P. E., Adamson, G., and Vernon, D. F., (1977), *The Psychology and Education of Gifted Children*. London.

56. Dabrowski, K. (with Kawczak, A. and Piechowski, M. M.) (1970), *Mental Growth Through Positive Disintegration*. London: Gryf Publications.

57. Illich, Ivan, (1970), *Deschooling Society*. New York: Harper and Row.

58. Leonard, G. B., (1970), *Education and Ecstasy*. London: John Murray.

59. Minuchin, P., Biber, B., Shapiro, E., and Zimiles, H., (1969), *The Psychological Impact of School Experience*. New York: Basic Books.

60. Nash, R., (1973), *Classrooms Observed*. London: Routledge and Kegan Paul.

61. Silberman, C. E., (1970), *Crisis in the Classroom*. New York: Random House.

62. Stumme, V. S., Gresham, F. M. and Scott, N. A., (1983), "Dimensions of children's classroom behaviour: A factor analysis investigation", *Journal of Behavioural Assessment*, 5(3), 161 - 177.

63. Freud, A., (1958), "Adolescence", In *Research at the Hampstead Child-Therapy Clinic and other papers 1956 – 1965*. London: International Universities.

64. Balswick, J. O. and Macrides, C., (1975), "Parental stimulus for adolescent rebellion", *Adolescence*, 10(38), 253 - 266.

65. Clemens, P. W. and Rust, J. O., (1979), "Factors in adolescent rebellious feelings", *Adolescence*, 14(53), 159 - 173.

66. Holmberg, A. R., (1969), *Nomads of the Long Bow*. New York: The Natural History Press.

67. Elliott, G. C., (1982), "Self-esteem and self-presentation among the young as a function of age and gender", *Journal of Youth and Adolescence*, 11(2), 135 - 153.

68. Mugny, G., Souchet, L., Codaccioni, C., and Quiamzade, A., (2008), "Social Representation and Social Influence", *Psychologie Francais*, 53 (2), 223 - 237.

69. Mugny, G., Souchet, L., Codaccioni, C., and Quiamzade, A., (2009), "Processus d'influence sociale et representations sociales", in P. Rateau & P. Moliner (Editors), *Representations Socials et Processus Sociocognitifs*, 123 – 149. Rennes: PUR.

70. Stone, L. J. and Church, J., (1968), *Childhood and Adolescence: A Psychology of the Growing Person.* New York: Random House.

71. Magnussen, D., Stattin, H. and Allen, V. L., (1985), "Biological maturation and social development: A longitudinal study of some adjustment processes from mid-adolescence to adulthood", *Journal of Youth and Adolescence*, 14(4), 267 - 283.

Chapter 5

1. Berger, P. and Luckmann, T., (1967), *The social construction of reality.* Garden City, New York: Anchor Books.

2. Chaika, E., (1974), "A linguist looks at schizophrenic language", *Brain and Language*, 1(3), 257 - 276.

3. Reilly, F., Harrow, M., Tucker, G., Quinlan, D. and Siegel, A., (1975), "Looseness of associations in acute schizophrenia", *British Journal of Psychiatry*, 127, 240 - 246.

4. Rochester, S. and Martin, J. R., (1979), *Crazy Talk.* New York: Plenum Press.

5. Salzinger, K., Portnoy, S. and Feldman, R. S., (1964), "Experimental manipulation of continuous speech in schizophrenic patients", *Journal of Abnormal and Social Psychology*, 68, 508 - 518.

6. Tucker, G. J. and Rosenberg, S. D., (1975), "Computer content analysis of schizophrenic speech: A preliminary report", *American Journal of Psychiatry*, 132 (6), 611 - 616.

7. Vetter, H. J., (1969), *Language Behaviour and Psychopathology.* Chicago: Rand McNally.

8. Wykes, J. and Leff, J. P., (1982), "Disordered speech: differences between manics and schizophrenics", *Brain and Language*, 15, 117 - 124.

9. Durin, C., (1983), "The implications of general semantics for the diagnosis of 'Mental Illness' ", *Et Cetera*, 40, 67 – 73.

10. Bion, W. R., (1967), "Attacks on linking", *Second Thoughts.* New York: Jason Aronson.

11. Gellner, E., (1973), "The savage and the modern mind", In *Modes of Thought* (Editors R. Horton and R. Finnegan). London: Faber and Faber.

12. Schweder, R. A., (1977), "Likeness and likelihood in everyday thought: magical thinking in judgements about personality", *Current Anthropology*, 18(4), 637 - 658.

13. Buyssens, E., (1954), "Thinking and speaking from the linguistic standpoint", in: *Thinking and Speaking* (Edited by Geza Revesz). Amsterdam: North Holland.

14. Coward, R. and Ellis, J., (1977), *Language and Materialism: Developments in Semiology and the Theory of the Subject.* London: Routledge and Kegan Paul.

15. Clifford, P. and Frosh, S., (1982), "Towards a non-essentialist psychology: A linguistic framework", *Bulletin of the British Psychological Society*, 35, 267 - 270.

16. Johnson O'Connor Research Foundation, (1977), *Personality Worksample 35A Manual.* Chicago: Human Engineering Laboratory.

17. Hunt, W. A. and Walker, R. E., (1966), "Schizophrenics' judgements of schizophrenic test responses", *Journal of Clinical Psychology*, 22, 118 - 120.

18. Tellenbach, H., (1980), "Imagining delusion and madness in Sophocles' Oedipus Tyrannus", *Zeitschrift für Klinische Psychologie und Psychotherapie*, 28 (4), 337 - 349.

19. Outhwaite, W., (1975), *Understanding Social Life.* London: Allen and Unwin.

20. Andreasen, N. C., (1986), "Scale for the assessment of thought, language, and communication", *Schizophrenia Bulletin*, 12(3), 473 - 481.

21. Andreasen, N. C. and Grove, W. M., (1986), "Thought, language, and communication in schizophrenia: diagnosis and prognosis", *Schizophrenia Bulletin*, 12(3), 348 - 359.

22. Armstrong, M. S. and McConaghy, N., (1977), "Allusive thinking, the word halo and verbosity", *Psychological Medicine*, 7, 439 - 445.

23. Tucker, P. K., Rothwell, S. J., Armstrong, M. S., and McConaghy, N., (1982), "Creativity, divergent and allusive thinking in students and visual artists", *Psychological Medicine*, 12, 835 – 841.

24. Hall, J. A., (1984), *Nonverbal Sex Differences.* Baltimore: Johns Hopkins University Press.

25. Ruesch, J., (1958), "The Tangential Response", in: *Psychopathology of Communication*, (Edited by P. H. Hoch and J. Zubin). New York: Grune & Stratton.

26. Andreasen, N. C., (1979), "Thought, language and communication disorders: II. Diagnostic significance", *Archives of General Psychiatry*, 36, 1325 - 1330.

27. Ellsworth, R. B., (1951), "The regression of schizophrenic language", *Journal of Consulting Psychology*, 15, 387 - 391.

28. Heims, S. J., (1981), *John Neumann and Norbert Wiener.* Cambridge, Massachusetts: Harvard University Press.

29. Davidson, D. A., Short, M. A. and Nelson, D. L., (1984), "The measurement of empathic ability in normal and atypical five and six year old boys", *Occupational Therapy in Mental Health*, 4(4), 13 - 24.

30. Wolff, S., (1984), "Schizoid personality", in: *Mental Retardation and Developmental Disabilities*, Vol. 1 (Edited by J. Wortis). New York: Plenum.

31. Wolff, S., Townshend, R., McGuire, R. J., and Weeks, D. J., (1991), " 'Schizoid' personality in childhood and adult life II: adult adjustment and the continuity with schizotypal personality disorder", *British Journal of Psychiatry*, 159, 620 – 29.

32. Wolff, S., (1995), *Loners: The Life Path of Unusual Children*. London: Routledge.

33. Gruen, R. J. and Mendelsohn, G., (1986), "Emotional responses to affective displays in others: The distinction between empathy and sympathy", *Journal of Personality and Social Psychology*, 51(3), 609 - 614.

34. Watson, P. J., Grisham, S. O., Trotter, M. V. and Biderman, M. D., (1984), "Narcissism and empathy: Validity evidence for the Narcissistic Personality Inventory", *Journal of Personality Assessment*, 48 (3), 301 - 305.

35. Chick, J., Waterhouse, L., and Wolff, S., (1979), "Psychological construing in schizoid children grown up", *British Journal of Psychiatry*, 135, 425 - 430.

36. Weeks, D. J., (1985), "Conceptual structure in hypochondriasis, arthritis, and neurosis", *British Journal of Clinical Psychology*, 24, 125 - 126.

Chapter 6

1. Allen, V. L., (1965), "Situational factors in conformity", in: *Advances in Experimental Social Psychology*, Vol. 2 (Edited by L. Berkowitz), New York: Academic Press.

2. Asch, S. E., (1951), "Studies of independence and conformity: a minority of one against a unanimous majority", *Psychological Monographs*, 70 (9), Whole No. 416.

3. Allen, V. L. and Newtson, D., (1972), "Development of conformity and independence", *Journal of Personality and Social Psychology*, 22, 18 - 30.

4. Walker, E. L. and Heyns, R. W., (1962), *Anatomy for conformity*. Englewood Cliffs, N.J.: Prentice-Hall.

5. Jahoda, M., (1959), "Conformity and independence", *Human Relations*, 12, 99 - 120.

6. Krech, D., Crutchfield, R. S. and Ballachey, E. L., (1962), *Individual in society*. New York: McGraw-Hill.

7. Willis, R. H., (1963), "Two dimensions of conformity-nonconformity", *Sociometry*, 26, 499 - 513.

8. Levine, J. M. and Hogg, M. A., (2009), "Anticonformity", in *Encyclopedia of group processes and intergroup relations*.

9. Santee, R. T. and Maslach, C., (1982), "To agree or not to agree: personal dissent amid social pressure to conform", *Journal of Personality and Social Psychology*, 42 (4), 690 - 700.

10. Stricker, L. J., Messick, S. and Jackson, D. N., (1970), "Conformity, anticonformity, and independence: Their dimensionality and generality", *Journal of Personality and Social Psychology*, 16, 494 – 507.

11. Willis, R. H., (1965), "Conformity, independence, and anticonformity", *Human Relations*, 18, 373 – 388.

12. Bond, R. and Smith, P. B., (1996), "Culture and conformity: A meta-analysis of studies using Asch's line judgement task", *Psychological Bulletin*, 119, 111 – 137.

13. Di Vesta, F. and Cox, L., (1960), "Some dispositional correlates of conformity behaviour", *Journal of Social Psychology*, 52, 259 - 268.

14. Martin, J. D., Blair, G. E. and Bottoms, S. H., (1979), "A correlation of Barron's Ego Strength Scale and Smith's Non-Conformity Scale", *Educational and Psychological Measurement*, 39, 959 - 963.

15. Seybert, J. A. and Weiss, W. F., (1974), "The negative reinforcing functions of non-conformity", *Memory and Cognition*, 2 (4), 791 - 795.

16. Eagly, A. H. and Chrvala, C., (1986), "Sex differences in conformity: status and gender role interpretations", *Psychology of Women Quarterly*, 10 (3), 203 – 220.

17. Sistrunk, F. and McDavid, J. W., (1971), "Sex variable in conforming behavior", *Journal of Personality and Social Psychology*, 17(2), 200 – 207.

18. Eagly, A. H., (1978), "Sex differences in influenceability", *Psychological Bulletin*, 85, 86 – 116.

19. Eagly, A. H. and Carli, L. L., (1981), "Sex of researchers and sex-type communications as determinants of sex differences in influenceability: A meta-analysis of social influence studies," *Psychology Bulletin*, 90, 1 – 20.

20. Eagly, A. H., Wood, W., and Fishbaugh, L., (1981), "Sex differences in conformity: Surveillance by the group as a determinant of male nonconformity," *Journal of Personality and Social Psychology*, 40, 384 – 394.

21. Cooper, H. M., (1979), "Statistically combining independent studies: A meta-analysis of sex differences in conformity research", *Journal of Personality and Social Psychology*, 37, 131 – 146.

22. Boyanowsky, E. O., Allen, V. L., Bragg, B. W. E. and Lepinski, J., (1981), "Generalisation of independence created by social support", *Psychological Record*, 31, 475 - 488.

23. Diekman, A. B. and Eagly, A. H., (2000), "Stereotypes as dynamic constructs: Women and men of the past, present, and future," *Personality and Social Psychology Bulletin*, 26, 1171 – 1188.

24. Diekman, A. B. and Goodfriend, W., (2006), "Rolling with changes: A role congruity perspective on gender norms," *Psychology of Women Quarterly*, 30, 369 – 383.

25. Osman, L. M., (2011), "Conformity or compliance? A study of sex differences in pedestrian behaviour", *British Journal of Social Psychology*, 21 (1), 19 – 21.

26. Cialdini, R. B. and Trost, M. R., (1998), "Social influence: Social norms, conformity, and compliance". In D. T. Gilbert and S. T. Fiske (Editors), *The handbook of social psychology, Vol. 2*, 4th Edition. Boston: McGraw-Hill, 151 - 192.

27. Kurosawa, K., (1993), "The effects of self-consciousness and self-esteem in conformity to a majority," *The Japanese Journal of Psychology*, 63(6), 379 – 387.

28. McDavid, J. and Sistrunk, F., (1964), "Personality correlates of two kinds of conforming behaviour", *Journal of Personality*, 32 (3), 420 - 435.

29. Spence, J. T. and Helmreich, R., (1972), "Who likes competent women? Competence, sex-role congruence of interests, and subjects' attitude toward women as determinants of interpersonal attraction", *Journal of Applied Social Psychology*, 2, 197 - 213.

30. Wahrman, R. and Pugh, M. D., (1974), "Sex, nonconformity, and influence", *Sociometry*, 37 (1), 137 - 147.

31. Prager, K. J., (1982), "Identity development and self-esteem in young women", *Journal of Genetic Psychology*, 141 (2), 177 - 182.

32. Endler, N. S., (1961), "Conformity analysed and related to personality", *Journal of Social Psychology*, 53, 271 - 283.

33. McGuire, W. J., (1968), "Personality and susceptibility to social influence", in: *Handbook of personality theory and research* (Edited by E. F. Borgatta and W. W. Lambert). Chicago: Rand McNally.

34. Couch, A. and Keniston, K., (1960), "Yeasayers and naysayers: agreeing response set as a personality variable", *Journal of Abnormal and Social Psychology*, 60, 151 - 174.

35. Mann, R. D., (1959), "A review of the relationships between personality and performance in small groups", *Psychological Bulletin*, 56, 241 - 270.

36. Appley, M. and Moeller, G., (1963), "Conforming behaviour and personality variables in college women", *Journal of Abnormal and Social Psychology*, 66(3), 284 - 290.

37. Allen, V. L. and Levine, J. M., (1968), "Social support, dissent, and conformity", *Sociometry*, 31, 138 - 149.

38. Allen, V. L. and Levine, J. M., (1971), "Social support and conformity: the role of independent assessment of reality", *Journal of Experimental Social Psychology*, 7, 45 - 58.

39. Boyanowsky, E. O. and Allen, V. L., (1973), "In group norms and self-identity as determinants of discriminatory behaviour", *Journal of Personality and Social Psychology*, 25, 408 - 418.

40. Malof, M. and Lott, A. J., (1962), "Ethnocentrism and acceptance of Negro support in a group pressure situation", *Journal of Abnormal and Social Psychology*, 65, 254 -258.

41. Nunnally, J. C., (1961), *Popular conceptions of mental health: their development and change*. New York: Holt, Rinehart and Winston.

42. Erikson, K. T., (1966), *Wayward Puritans: A Study in the Sociology of Deviance*. Needham Heights, Massachusetts: Simon and Schuster.

43. Laing, R. D., (1971), *The Politics of the Family and Other Essays*. Harmondsworth, Middlesex, England: Penguin Books Ltd.

44. Phillips, D. L., (1964), "Rejection of the mentally ill: The influence of behaviour and sex", *American Sociological Review*, 29 (5), 669 - 686.

45. Dohrenwend, B. P. and Chin-Shong, E., (1967), "Social status and attitudes toward psychological disorder: the problem of tolerance of deviance", *American Sociological Review*, 32 (3), 417 - 433.

46. Sarbin, T. R. and Mancuso, J. C., (1970), "Failure of a moral enterprise: Attitude of the public toward mental illness", *Journal of Consulting and Clinical Psychology*, 35 (2), 159 - 173.

47. Bourgeois, M., (1979), "The shunning of incest in human and non-human primates: A preliminary remark", *Annales Medico-Psychologiques*, 137 (6-7), 612 - 620.

48. Salem, G., (1980), "A theoretical review of the bases of the incest taboo", *Annales Medico-Psycologiques*, 138 (4), 431 - 442.

49. Arkin, A. M., (1984), "A hypothesis concerning the incest taboo", *Psychoanalytic Review*, 71 (3), 375 - 381.

50. Frances, V. and Frances, A., (1976), "The incest taboo and family structure", *Family Process*, 15(2), 235 - 244.

51. Parker, S., (1976), "The pre-cultural basis of the incest taboo: Toward a bio-social theory", *American Anthropologist*, 78 (2), 285 - 305.

52. Kitayama, O., (1985), "Pre-oedipal 'taboo' in Japanese folk tragedies", *International Review of Psychoanalysis*, 12(2), 173 - 186.

53. Teoh, J. (1976), "Taboo and Malay tradition", *Australian and New Zealand Journal of Psychiatry*, 10 (1-A), 105 - 110.

54. Paige, K. E., (1977), "Sexual pollution: Reproductive sex taboos in American society", *Journal of Social Issues*, 33 (2), 144 - 165.

55. Aberle, D. F., Cohen, A. K., Davis, A. K., Levy, M. J. and Sutton, F. X., (1950), "The functional prerequisites of a society", *Ethics*, 60, 100 - 111.

56. Firth, R., (1964), "Social organisation and social change", in: *Social Organisation and Values*. London: Athlone Press.

Chapter 7

1. Bonney, M., (1964), "Some correlates of a social definition of normal personality", *Journal of Clinical Psychology*, 20 (4), 415 - 422.

2. Thomas, E. J., (1968), "Role Theory, personality, and the individual", in: *Handbook of Personality Theory and Research* (Editors E. F. Borgatta and W. W. Lambert). Chicago: Rand McNally, 691 - 727.

3. Jones, E. E. and Pittman, T. S., (1982), "Toward a general theory of strategic self-presentation", in: *Psychological Perspectives on the Self*, Vol. 1 (Editor J. Suls). Hillsdale: Lawrence Erlbaum.

4. Cattell, R. B., Eber, H. W., and Tatsuoka, M. M., (1970), *Handbook for the Sixteen Personality Factor Questionnaire (16PF)*. Champaign, Illinois: Institute for Personality and Ability Testing.

5. Karson, S. and O'Dell, J. W., (1976), *Clinical Use of the 16PF*. Champaign, Illinois: Institute for Personality and Ability Testing.

6. Weeks, D. J., (1985), "Conceptual structure in hypochondriasis, arthritis, and neurosis", *British Journal of Clinical Psychology*, 24, 125 - 126.

7. Snyder, M., (1983), "The influence of individuals on situations: Implications for understanding the links between personality and social behaviour", *Journal of Personality*, 51, 497 - 516.

8. McClelland, D. C., (1951), *Personality*. New York: William Sloane.

9. Ivy, A. C., (1944), "What is normal or normality?", *Quarterly Bulletin Northwestern University Medical School*, 18, 22 - 32, Spring.

10. Ryle, J. A., (1961), "The meaning of normal", in: *Concepts of Medicine* (Editor B. Lush). Oxford: Pergamon.

11. Cattell, R. B., (1957), *Personality and Motivation: Structure and Measurement*. New York: World Books.

12. Chesler, P., (1972), *Women and Madness*. New York: Avon Books.

13. Hundleby, J. D., Pawlik, K. and Cattell, R. B., (1965), *Personality factors in objective test devices: A critical integration of a quarter of a century's research*. San Diego: Robert R. Knapp.

14. Philip, A. E., (1972), "Cross-cultural stability of second-order factors in the 16PF", *British Journal of Social and Clinical Psychology*, 11, 276 - 283.

15. Peterson, D. R., (1965), "Scope and generality of verbally defined personality factors", *Psychological Review*, 72, 48 - 59.

16. Wolff, S. and Chick, J., (1980), "Schizoid personality in childhood: a controlled follow-up study", *Psychological Medicine*, 10, 85 - 100.

17. Wolff, S., (1995), *Loners: The Life Path of Unusual Children*. London: Routledge.

18. Zubin, J., (1967), "Classification of the behaviour disorders", *Annual Review of Psychology*, 18, 373 - 406.

19. Walton, H. J. and Presly, A. S., (1973), "Use of a category system in the diagnosis of abnormal personality", British Journal of Psychiatry, 122, 259 - 268.

20. Tyrer, P., Strauss, J. and Cicchetti, D., (1983), "Temporal reliability of personality in psychiatric patients", Psychological Medicine, 13(2), 393 - 398.

21. Merikangas, K. and Weissman, M. M., (1986), "Epidemiology of DSM-III axis II personality disorders", in: American Psychiatric Association Annual Review, Volume 5, (Edited by A. J. Frances and R. E. Hales). Washington, D.C.: American Psychiatric Press.

22. Tyrer, P., Alexander, M. S., Cicchetti, D., Cohen, M. S. and Remington, M., (1979), "Reliability of a schedule for rating personality disorders", British Journal of Psychiatry, 135, 168 - 174.

23. Tyrer, P. and Alexander, J., (1979), "Classification of personality disorder", British Journal of Psychiatry, 135, 163 - 167.

24. Mittal, V. A., Kalus, O., Bernstein, D. P., and Siever, L. J., (2007), "Schizoid personality disorder" in Personality disorders: Toward the DSM-V (Edited by W. O'Donohue and K. A. Fowler. Thousand Oaks, CA.: Sage Publications, Inc., 63 – 79.

25. Tyrer, P., Casey, P. and Gall, J., (1983), "Relationship between neurosis and personality disorder", British Journal of Psychiatry, 142, 404 - 408.

26. Vince, G., (2002), "Eccentric people more extreme as they age", New Scientist, 28 June.

27. Kohut, H., (1975), The Analysis of the Self: A Systematic Approach to the Psychoanalytic Treatment of Narcissistic Personality Disorders. New York: International University Press.

28. Kernberg, O., (1975), Borderline Conditions and Pathological Narcissism. New York: Science House.

29. Masterton, J. F., (1981), The Narcissistic and Borderline Disorders. New York: Brunner Mazel.

30. Berelowitz, M. and Tarnopolsky, A., (1993), "The validity of borderline personality disorder: an updated review of recent research", In P. Tyrer and G. Stein (Editors), Personality Disorder Reviewed. London: Gaskell, Royal College of Psychiatrists.

31. Patrick, M., Hobson, R. P., Castle, D., Howard, R., and Maughan, B., (1994), "Personality disorder and the mental representation of early social experience", Development and Psychopathology, 6, 375 – 388.

32. Gunderson, J. G., (2001), Borderline personality disorder: A clinical guide. Washington, D. C.: American Psychiatric Association publishing.

33. Stein, K. B., (1968), "The TSC scales: The outcome of a cluster analysis of the 550 MMPI items", in Advances in Psychological Assessment, (Edited by P. McReynolds). Palo Alto, California: Science and Behavior Books.

34. Siever, L. J., Keefe, R., Bernstein, D. P., Coccaro, E. F., Klar, H. M., Zemishlany, Z., Peterson, A. E., Davidson, M., Mahon, T., and Mohs, R., (1990), "Eye tracking impairment in

clinically identified patients with schizotypal personality disorders", *American Journal of Psychiatry*, 147, 740 – 745.

35. Siever, L. J., Koenigsberg, H. W., Harvey, P., Mitropolou, V., Laruelle, M., Abi-Dargham, A., Goodman, M., and Buchsbaum, M., (2002), "Cognitive and brain function in schizotypal personality disorder", *Schizophrenia Research*, 54 (1 – 2), 157 – 167.

36. Brown, J. H., Berkal, A., Barakat, S. and McIlwraith, R., (1985), "Personality diagnosis and illness diagnosis", *Canadian Journal of Psychiatry*, 30 (6), 428 - 433.

37. Boyd, J. H., Burke, J. D., Gruenberg, E., Holzer, C. E., Rae, D. S., George, L. K., Karno, M., Stolzman, R., McEvoy, L. and Nestadt, G., (1984), "Exclusion criteria of DSM-III", *Archives of General Psychiatry*, 41, 983 - 989.

38. Plakun, E. M., Burkhardt, P. E. and Muller, J. P., (1985), "Fourteen-year follow-up of borderline and schizotypal personality disorders", *Comprehensive Psychiatry*, 26 (5), 448 - 455.

39. Siever, L._J. and Klar, H., (1986), "A review of DSM-III criteria for the personality disorders", in: *American Psychiatric Association Annual Review*, Vol. 5 (Editors A. J. Frances and R. E. Hales). Washington, D.C.: American Psychiatric Press.

Chapter 8

1. Ribot, T., (1900), "The nature of creative imagination", *International Monthly*, 1, 648 - 675; 2, 1 - 25.

2. Rothe, R., (1930), "Die Quelle, Versinigt Monatsheft für Pedagogische Reform", *Kunst und Schule*, No. 12.

3. Mackinnon, D. W., (1962), "The nature and nurture of creative talent", *American Psychologist*, 17, 484 - 495.

4. Price, B. M. and Bell, B. S., (1965), "The relationship of C.A., N.A., I.Q. and sex to a divergent thinking test", *Journal of Psychological Researches*, 9 (1), 1 - 9.

5. Barron, F., (1968), *Creativity and personal freedom*. Princeton, N.J.: Van Nostrand.

6. Albert, R. S., (1969), "Genius: Present-day study status of the concept and its implications for the study of creativity and giftedness", *American Psychologist*, 24, 743 - 753.

7. Dellas, M. and Gaier, E. L., (1970), "Identification of creativity: The individual", *Psychological Bulletin*, 73, 55 - 73.

8. Komarik, E., (1972), "Creativity and orthogonal factors of personality", *Sharnik Praci Filosoficke Fakulty, Brnenske University*, 20 (17), 115 - 124.

9. Rossman, B. B. and Horn, J. L., (1972), "Cognitive, motivational and temperamental indicants of creativity and intelligence", *Journal of Educational Measurement*, 9 (4), 265 - 286.

10. Vernon, P. E., (1972), "The validity of divergent thinking tests", *Alberta Journal of Educational Research*, 18 (4), 249 - 258.

11. Corder, B. E. and Corder, R. F., (1974), "A study of the relationships of IQ and cognitive and personality rigidity to performance on concept learning tasks", *Education and Psychological Measurement*, 34, 83 - 90.

12. Kubie, L. S., (1958), *Neurotic Distortion of the Creative Process*. Lawrence, Kansas: University of Kansas Press.

13. Kris, E., (1953), "Psychoanalysis and the study of creative imagination", *Bulletin of the N.Y. Academy of Medicine*, 29, 334 - 351.

14. Holt, R. R., (1967), "The development of the primary process: a structural view", *Psychological Issues*, 5 (2 - 3), 344 - 383.

15. Taylor, I. A., (1959), "The nature of the creative process", in: *Creativity* (Edited by P. Smith). New York: Hastings House, 51 - 82.

16. Ghiselin, B., (1952), *The Creative Process*. Berkeley: University of California Press.

17. Wallas, G. (1926), *The Art of Thought*. New York: Harcourt Brace and Company.

18. Kounios, J. and Beeman, M., (2009), "The *Aha!* Moment: The cognitive neuroscience of insight", *Current Directions in Psychological Science*, 18 (4), 210 – 216.

19. Ghiselin, B., (1963), "Ultimate criteria for two levels of creativity", *Scientific creativity: Its recognition and development* (Edited by C.W. Taylor and F. Barron). New York: Wiley.

20. Weisberg, P. S. and Springer, K. J., (1961), "Environmental factors in creative function", *Archives of General Psychiatry*, 5, 554 - 564.

21. McGuire, C., (1958), "Dimensions of creativity", *Proceedings of the Southwest Psychological Association*. Austin, Texas: American Psychological Association.

22. Newell, A., Shaw, J. C. and Simon, H. A., (1958), "The elements of a theory of human problem solving", *Psychological Review*, 65, 151 - 166.

23. Newell, A., Shaw, J. C. and Simon, H. A., (1962), "The processes of creative thinking", in: *Contemporary Approaches to Creative Thinking*, (Editors H. E. Gruber, G. Terrell and M. Wertheimer). New York: Atherton Press.

24. Wallach, M. A. and Kogan, H., (1965), *Modes of thinking in young children*. New York: Holt Rinehart & Winston.

25. White, R. K., (1931), "The versatility of genius", *Journal of Social Psychology*, 2, 460 - 489.

26. Bartlett, F. C., (1958), *Thinking: An experimental and social study*. London: Allen and Unwin.

27. Polanyi, M., (1958), *Personal knowledge*. London: Routledge & Kegan Paul.

28. Izumi, K., (1971), "LSD and architectural design", In: *Psychedelics* (Editors B. Aaronson and H. Osmond). London: Hogarth Press.

29. Gardner, H., (1993), *Creating Minds*. New York: Basic Books.

30. Osgood, C. E., Suci, G. J., and Tannenbaum, P. H., (1957), *The Measurement of Meaning*. Chicago: University of Illinois Press.

31. Taussig, M., (1992), *Mimesis and Alterity*. New York: Routledge.

32. Smith, E. E. and White, H. L., (1965), "Wit, creativity and sarcasm", *Journal of Applied Psychology*, 49 (2), 131 – 134.

33. Treadwell, Y., (1970), "Humor and creativity", *Psychological Reports*, 26, 55 - 58.

34. McGhee, P. E., (1980), "Development of the creative aspects of humor," In P. E. McGhee and A. J. Chapman (Editors), *Children's Humour*, 119 – 139. Chichester, England: Wiley.

35. Murdock, M. C. and Ganim, R. M., (1992), "Creativity and humor: Integration and incongruity," *Journal of Creative Behavior*," 27, 57 – 70.

36. O'Quin, K. and Derks, P., (1997), "Humor and creativity: A review of the empirical literature". In M. Runco (Editor), *Creativity research handbook*, Volume 1, 223 – 252. Cresskill, New Jersey: Hampton Press.

37. Mednick, S., (1962), "The associative basis of the creative process", *Psychological Review*, 69 (3), 222 - 232.

38. Cropley, A. J., (1966), "Creativity and intelligence", *British Journal of Educational Psychology*, 36, 259 - 266.

39. Martindale, C., (1972), "Anxiety, intelligence and access to primitive modes of thought in high and low scores on the Remote Associations Test", *Perceptual and Motor Skills*, 35(2), 375 - 381.

40. Stein, M. I., (1968), "Creativity", in: *Handbook of Personality Theory and Research* (Editors E. F. Borgatta and W. W. Lambert). Chicago: Rand McNally, 900 - 942.

41. Carson, S. H., Peterson, J. B., and Higgins, D. M., (2003), "Decreased latent inhibition is associated with increased creative achievement in high-functioning individuals", *Journal of Personality and Social Psychology*, 85, 499 – 506.

42. Carson, S. H., (2011), "The unleashed mind: why creative people are eccentric", *Scientific American*, May/June edition, 22 – 29.

43. Eisenman, R. and Brownstein, G. M., (1970), "Restriction of emotional release and creativity", *Perceptual and Motor Skills*, 31(2), 647 - 650.

44. O'Haire, T. D. and Marcia, J. E., (1980), "Some personality characteristics associated with Ananda Marga meditations: A pilot study", *Perceptual and Motor Skills*, 51, 447 - 452.

45. Glover, J. A., (1977), "Risky shift and creativity", *Social Behaviour and Personality*, 5 (2), 317 - 320.

46. Andreasen, N. C., (2011), "A Journey into Chaos: Creativity and the Unconscious", *Mens Sana Monograph*, 9 (1), 42 – 53.

47. Martindale, C., Hines, D., Mitchell, L., and Covello, E., (1984), "EEG alpha asymmetry and creativity", *Personality and Individual Differences*, 5 (1), 77 – 86.

48. Molle, M., Marshall, L., Lutzenberger, W., Pietrowsky, R., Fehm, H. L., and Born, J., (1996), "Enhanced dynamic complexity in the human EEG during creative thinking", *Neuroscience Letters*, 208 (1), 61 – 64.

49. Fink, A. and Neubauer, A. C., (2006), "EEG alpha oscillations during the performance of verbal creativity tasks: Differential effects of sex and verbal intelligence", *International Journal of Psychophysiology*, 62 (1), 46 – 63.

50. Arnheim, R., (1969), *Visual Thinking*. Berkeley: University of California Press.

51. Lewin, B. D., (1969), "Remarks on creativity, imagery and the dream", *Journal of Nervous and Mental Diseases*, 149, 115 - 121.

52. Khatena, J., (1976), "Autonomy of imagery and production of original verbal images", *Perceptual and Motor Skills*, 43, 245 - 246.

53. Barrios, M. V. and Singer, J. L., (1981 - 1982), "The treatment of creative blocks: A comparison of waking imagery, hypnotic dream, and rational discussion techniques", *Imagination, Cognition and Personality*, 1 (1), 89 - 109.

54. Shaw, G. A. and Belmore, S. M., (1982-83), "The relationship between imagery and creativity", *Imagination, Cognition and Personality*, 2 (2), 115 - 123.

55. Morris, P. E. and Hampson, P. J., (1983), *Imagery and Consciousness*. London: Academic Press.

56. Shaw, G. A., (1985), "The use of imagery by intelligent and by creative schoolchildren", *Journal of General Psychology*, 112 (3), 153 - 71.

57. Shaw, G. A. and DeMers, S. T., (1986), "The relationship of imagery to originality, flexibility and fluency in creative thinking", *Journal of Mental Imagery*, 10 (1), 65 – 74.

58. Finke, R. A., (1989), *Principles of Mental Imagery*. Cambridge, Massachusetts: M.I.T. Press.

59. Singer, J. L., (1981), *Daydreaming and fantasy*. Oxford: Oxford University Press.

60. Singer, J. L. and Switzer, E. L., (1980), *Mind play: The creative uses of fantasy*. Englewood Cliffs, New Jersey: Prentice-Hall.

61. Durndell, A. J. and Wetherick, N. E., (1976), "The relation of reported imagery tests to cognitive performance", *British Journal of Psychology*, 67, 501 - 506.

62. Ernest, C. H., (1977), "Imagery ability and cognition: a critical review", *Journal of Mental Imagery*, 2, 181 - 216.

63. Okada, H., Matsuoka, K., and Hatakeyama, T., (2000), "Dream recall frequency and waking imagery," *Perceptual and Motor Skills*, 91 (3, 1), 759 – 766.

64. Domhoff, G. W., (1996), *Finding meaning in dreams: A quantitative approach.* New York: Plenum.

65. Singer, J. L., (1999), "Imagination", In *Encyclopedia of Creativity, Volume 2.* (Editors M. A. Runco and S. R. Pritzker), 13 - 25. San Diego and London: Academic Press.

66. Kozmova, M. and Wolman, J. A., (2006), "Self-awareness in dreaming", *Dreaming*, 16 (3), 196 – 214.

67. Fosse, R., Stickgold, R., and Hobson, J. A., (2001), "The mind in REM sleep: reports of emotional experience," *Sleep*, 24, 947 – 955.

68. Hobson, J. A., (1988), *The dreaming brain.* New York: Basic Books.

69. Domhoff, G. W., (2003), *The Scientific Study of Dreams: Neural Networks, Cognitive Development, and Content Analysis.* Austin, Texas: American Psychological Association.

70. Goldstein, L., (1984), "A reconsideration of right hemisphere activity during visual imagery, REM sleep, and depression", *Research Communications in Psychology, Psychiatry and Behavior*, 9 (1), 138 - 148.

71. Berlucchi, F., (1965), "Callosal activity in unrestrained unanaesthetised cats", *Archives Italiennes de Biologie*, 103, 623 - 634.

72. Wagner, U., Gais, S., Haider, H., Verleger, R., and Born, J., (2004), "Sleep inspires insight," *Nature*, 427, 352 - 355.

73. Sperry, R. W., (1968), "Hemisphere deconnection and unity in conscious awareness", *American Psychologist*, 23, 723 - 733.

74. Farah, M. J., (1984), "The neurological basis of mental imagery: A componential analysis", *Cognition*, 18 (1-3), 245 - 272.

75. Schwartz, S. and Maquet, P., (2002), "Sleep imaging and the neuro-psychological assessment of dreams," *Trends in Cognitive Science*, 6, 23 – 30.

76. Hobson, J. A., Stickgold, R., and Pace-Schott, E. F., (1998), "The neuropsychology of REM sleep dreaming," *Neuroreport*, 9, R1 – 14.

77. Wolman, R. N. and Kozmova, M., (2007), "Last night I had the strangest dream: Varieties of rational thought processes in dream reports," *Consciousness and Cognition*, 16, 838 - 849.

78. Hobson, J. A., Pace-Schott, E. F., and Stickgold, R. J., (2000), "Dreaming and the brain: toward a cognitive neuroscience of conscious states", *Behavior and Brain Science*, 23, 793 – 842, and Discussion, 904 – 1121.

79. Csikzentmihalyi, M., (1992), *Flow: The Psychology of Optimal Experience*. New York: Harper & Row.

80. Csikzentmihalyi, M. and Larson, R., (1984), *Being adolescent: Conflict and growth in the teenage years*. New York: Basic Books.

81. Kubey, R. and Csikzentmihalyi, M., (1990), *Television and the quality of life*. Hillsdale, New Jersey: Lawrence Erlbaum.

82. Crawford, H. J., (1982), "Hypnotisability, daydreaming styles, imagery vividness, and absorption: A multidimensional study", *Journal of Personality and Social Psychology*, 42 (5), 915 - 26.

83. Martinetti, R. F., (1985), "Cognitive antecedents of dream recall", *Perceptual and Motor Skills*, 60 (2), 395 - 401.

84. Joesting, J. and Whitehead, G. D., (1976), "Equalitarianism, curiosity and creativity: Partial replication", *Psychological Reports*, 38 (2), 369 - 370.

85. Lazare, S., (1967), "Creativity and curiosity: The overlap", *Child Study*, 29 (2), 22 - 29.

86. Maw, W. H. and Maw, E. W., (1970), "Nature of creativity in high and low-curiosity boys", *Developmental Psychology*, 2 (3), 325 - 329.

87. Vidler, D. C. and Karan, V. E., (1975), "A study of curiosity, divergent thinking and test-anxiety", *Journal of Psychology*, 90 (2), 237 - 243.

88. Weintraub, H., (1968), *Case Studies of Boys Identified as High or Low in Curiosity*. Ph.D. Dissertation: Rutgers University, N.J.

89. Henderson, B. B., Gold, S. R. and McCord, M. T., (1982), "Daydreaming and curiosity in gifted and average children and adolescents", *Developmental Psychology*, 18 (4), 576 - 582.

90. Keri, S., (2009), "Genes for psychosis and creativity: a promoter polymorphism of the neuregulin 1 gene is related to creativity in people with high intellectual achievement", *Psychological Science*, 20 (9), 1070 – 1073.

91. Olson, K. R. and Camp, C. J., (1984), "Factor analysis of curiosity measures in adults", *Psychological Reports*, 54 (2), 491 - 497.

92. Hartmann, T. and Havik, O., (1980), "Exploring curiosity: A curiosity-exhibitionism inventory, and some empirical results", *Scandinavian Journal of Psychology*, 21 (2), 143 - 149.

93. Houston, J. P. and Mednick, S. A., (1963), "Creativity and the need for novelty", *Journal of Abnormal and Social Psychology*, 66, 137 - 141.

94. See www.thecreativeindustries.co.uk

95. Therivel, W. A., (1999), "Why are eccentrics not eminently creative?", *Creativity Research Journal*, 12 (1).

Chapter 9

1. Ziman, J., (1968), *Public Knowledge: The Social Dimension of Science.* London: Cambridge University Press.

2. Bunge, M., (1972), "Technology as applied science", in: *Philosophy and Technology* (Editors C. Mitcham and R. Mackay). New York: New York Free Press.

3. Popper, K. R., (1963), *Conjectures and Refutations.* London: Routledge and Kegan Paul.

4. Weld, C. R., (1848), *History of the Royal Society,* Vol. 1., London.

5. Dobbs, B. J. T., (1975), *Newton and Alchemy.* London: Cambridge University Press.

6. Dunbar, K., (1995), "How scientists really reason: Scientific reasoning in real-world laboratories". In R. J. Sternberg and J. Davidson (Editors), *Mechanisms of insight,* 365 – 395. Cambridge, Massachusetts: MIT Press.

7. Klein, J. T., (1997), *Crossing boundaries.* Charlottesville, Virginia: University Press of Virginia.

8. Feyeraband, P. K., (1975), *Against Method: Outline of an Anarchistic Theory of Knowledge.* London: New Left Books.

9. Schmaus, W., (1983), "Fraud and the norms of science", *Science, Technology and Human Values,* 8 (45), 12 - 21.

10. Kuhn, T. S., (1962), *The Structure of Scientific Revolutions.* Chicago: University of Chicago Press.

11. Bhaskar, R., (1978), *A Realist Theory of Science.* Brighton: Harvester Press.

12. Truzzi, M., (1972), "The occult revival as popular culture: some random observations on the old and nouveau witch", *The Sociological Quarterly,* 13, 16 - 36.

13. Barnes, B. and MacKenzie, D., (1979), "On the role of interests in scientific change", in: *On the Margins of Science: The Social Construction of Rejected Knowledge* (Edited by R. Wallis). Sociological Review Monograph, 27, 49 - 66.

14. McClelland, D. C., (1962), "On the dynamics of creative physical scientists", in *Contemporary Approaches to Creative Thinking,* Edited by H. E. Gruber et al. New York: Atherton.

15. Eiduson, B. T., (1962), *Scientists: Their Psychological World.* New York: Basic Books.

16. Dijksterhuis, E. J., (1961), *The Mechanisation of the World Picture,* translated by C. Dikshoorn. Oxford: Clarendon Press.

17. Popper, K. R., (1959), *The Logic of Scientific Discovery.* London: Hutchinson.

18. Cornelius, A., (1986), "Who wants to buy a brainwave?", *The Guardian,* London, September 15, page 18.

Chapter 10.

1. Seivewright, H., Tyrer, P., and Johnson, T., (2002), "Change in personality status in neurotic disorders", *The Lancet*, 359, Issue 9325, 2253 – 2254.

ACKNOWLEDGEMENTS
It is impossible to accomplish any long-term research project without wanting to thank many people. These friends and colleagues generously provided much good advice, encouragement, practical help or support, inspiration and frank feedback. I would like to express my gratitude to the following people: Dr. Patch Adams, Professor Nancy Andreasen, Dr. Gunter Ammon, Dr. Isaac Asimov, Dr. Simon Backett, Professor Halla Beloff, Ms. Caroline Brook-Thompson, Professor Emeritus Eric Burke, Dr. Jonathan Chick, Dr. Sheldon Cholst, Professor Anthony Clare, Mr. John Clark, The Eccentric Club UK, Mr. Vincent Egan, Dr. Kevin J. Fleming, Dr. David Fontana, Mr. Peter Gabriel, Mr. Samuel Gallu, Ms. Clare Gittings, Mr. David Graham, Ms. Jackie Grant, Dr. Ruth Brill Gross, Mr. Zenya Hamada, Professor Dr. Hartman Hinterhuber, Mr. Drummond Hunter, Dr. Cecilia Hurwich, Mr. Ralph McGuire, Dr. P. J. McKenna, Professor Robert Morris, Ms. Melissa Peterson, the staff of Project Ability Glasgow, Dr. Margaret Reid, Ms. Hilary Roxborough, Professor Rudolf Schaffer, the staff of the Social Statistics Laboratory of the University of Strathclyde, Professor Digby Tantam, Professor Henry L. Tischler, Professor Peter Tyrer, Mrs. Kate Ward, Dr. David Warden, Dr. Sula Wolff, and Dr. Helen Zealley.
I am indebted to the following professionals working in the field of comedy entertainment: Clive Anderson, Jeremy Beadle, Peter Cook, Ivor Cutler, Fred Macauley, Spike Milligan, Emo Phillips, Sir Harry Secombe, Arthur Smith, and David "Screaming Lord" Sutch. They each greatly helped me to understand how they approached their life and work, and/or how a playful attitude toward joke making to live audiences had come about in their lives.
I am also indebted to the following professionals working in broadcasting, documentaries, writing, print journalism, and media production and research staff. The following individuals asked me pertinent questions that helped my thinking by sharing their insights with me. They also enabled me to reach out to many of the people in my research study, invariably treating my endeavours with courtesy and understanding. I express my appreciation and gratitude to Ben Adler, Trish Adudu, Linda Albin, Barbara Altounyan, Andrew Anderson, Richard Baker, John Bald, Anthony Barnes, Nicola Barry, Simon Bates, Colin Bell, Jane Benham, Mark Bourdillon, Janet Boyle, Melvyn Bragg, Tim Cabral, Liz Canon, Penny Chorlton, Marcus Chown, Angela Clark, John Clark, Andrew Clement, Glen Collins, Thomas Congdon, Alison Curran, John Darnton, Ben Davies, John Davis, Rachel Delahaye, Cate Devine, Aileen Docherty, Ian Dovaston, Jeff Dubin, Andrew Duncan, Douglas Eby, Bob Edward, Jordan Elgrably, Dorothy Grace Elder, Harold Evans, Karen Evennett, Ronald Faux, Jean Ferguson, Giusi Ferre, Judy Finnegan, Dymphna Flynn, Louise France, Mae Frances, Samuel Gallu, Cathy Garfield, Danielle Gelsand, Ron Geraci, Bill Gibb, Antoinette Grote Gansey, Joyce Hannah, Brian Hayes, Graham Heathcote, Steven Hedges, Roger Highfield, Amelia Hill, Dietrich von Hoegstratten, Dan Holland, Victoria Hollingworth, Carl Honore, Takako Hoshino, Brenda Houghton, Gloria Hunniford, Matthew Hulme, Gabrielle Jackson, Derek Jamieson, Ann Japenga, Sarah Johnson, Myrion Jones, Andre Kennedy, Phillipa Kennedy, Alex Kirsta, Lisa Koenig, Jack Laurence, Maggy Lennon, Nellie Lide, Magnus Linklater, Ed Lion, Gerald C. Lubenow, Rheiner Luyken, Angus Lyon, Richard Madeley, Melissa Malkovich, Brian

Mathews, Della Matheson, Maxine McDowell, Peter McKay, Victoria McKee, Ron McManus, Geraldine Mellet, York Membery, Russell Michaels, Mike Miller, Joanna Moorehead, Lauris Morgan-Griffiths, Brian Morton, Dr. Peter Munder, Jenni Murray, Carol Mynott, Angela Neustatter, Vivian Nicholl, Pam Nowicka, Christopher Ogden, John O'Rourke, Gilly Orr, Maxine Osto, Gabriele Pantucci, Julian Pettifer, Gail Phillips, Gian Quaglieni, Howard Rifkin, Gary Robertson, Pam Rutherford, Joy Schaverien, Iona Scott, Martin Sharp, Richard Shepherd, Jo Smith, Julie Smythe, Nicki Solloway, John Stapleton, Corinne Streich, Pam Sykes, Roberta Symes, Ann Taylor, John Taylor, Laurie Taylor, Sarah Kate Templeton, Patricia Trautman, Francesca Turbey-Green, Youki Vattier, Diana Waggoner, Johnny Walker, Susan Wallace, Steve Webb, Lowell Weiss, James Whale, Robert Wiering, Gavin Wilson, Monica Wilson, Ruth Wishart, Judith Woods, Nigel Wrench, Agnes Wright, Jimmy Young, and the great documentary film director John Zaritsky.

I reserve especial acknowledgement and warmest gratitude for the research participants, community research volunteers, and independent raters who took part. Throughout my studies they gave of themselves unstintingly, assisting greatly in providing information about themselves and their thoughts, perceptions, attitudes and activities.

CPSIA information can be obtained at www.ICGtesting.com
Printed in the USA
LVOW10s1745180615

442985LV00035B/2078/P

9 781505 546736